Study Guide

for Nairne's

Psychology
The Adaptive Mind

Third Edition

Janet Proctor
Purdue University

Australia • Canada • Mexico • Singapore • Spain • United Kingdom • United States

Printer: Globus Printing

0-534-59950-8

For more information about our products,
contact us at:
Thomson Learning Academic Resource Center
1-800-423-0563

For permission to use material from this text,
contact us by:
Phone: 1-800-730-2214
Fax: 1-800-731-2215
Web: http://www.thomsonrights.com

Asia
Thomson Learning
5 Shenton Way #01-01
UIC Building
Singapore 068808

Australia
Nelson Thomson Learning
102 Dodds Street
South Street
South Melbourne, Victoria 3205
Australia

Canada
Nelson Thomson Learning
1120 Birchmount Road
Toronto, Ontario M1K 5G4
Canada

Europe/Middle East/South Africa
Thomson Learning
High Holborn House
50/51 Bedford Row
London WC1R 4LR
United Kingdom

Latin America
Thomson Learning
Seneca, 53
Colonia Polanco
11560 Mexico D.F.
Mexico

Spain
Paraninfo Thomson Learning
Calle/Magallanes, 25
28015 Madrid, Spain

TABLE OF CONTENTS

INTRODUCTION

Throughout your text you will find an emphasis on the *adaptive mind*, the fact that we use our brains in a purposive and strategic fashion to meet the challenges of a changing environment. Each chapter will address certain conceptual, adaptive or practical problems facing most organisms and will guide you to an understanding of how these adaptive and practical problems are resolved.

As a student in this introductory psychology class, you face certain adaptive and practical problems, also. Stated most broadly, you must learn the material presented in class and in the text, and you must demonstrate your knowledge on tests and other assignments. The purpose of this study guide is to help you solve these adaptive and practical problems.

USING THE STUDY GUIDE

Part of the challenge of introductory psychology is the amount of material to be learned. There is a great deal of new vocabulary, in addition to many concepts and specific facts. The study guide's organization breaks down the material into more manageable units. Studying an entire chapter at one time is overwhelming to many students and can lead to very poor learning. Taking too big a bite of food can lead to choking; trying to tackle too much new material at one time can have a similar effect. Therefore, each chapter in this study guide is divided into smaller units that follow the major sections of the text material.

Exercises designed to help you learn the vocabulary, practice recalling specific facts, and evaluate your basic comprehension of the material are provided for each section of the chapter. You will not need to study the entire chapter before doing these early exercises in the study guide. You can study one topic, work with the material, and evaluate your comprehension before moving on to another topic. Then, at the end of each chapter there are additional exercises that revisit the entire chapter and give you additional opportunity to practice working with the material and to evaluate your readiness for an exam. I hope this will encourage you to study for mastery on a daily basis, rather than trying to learn an entire chapter (or chapters, worse yet) in a single marathon study session a day or two before your exam.

Establishing Learning Goals

Each study guide chapter begins with a set of learning goals. These will provide a quick summary of what the text chapter covers, and what you should be trying to accomplish. Review them before you read the text, and use them to test your comprehension of each section. If your instructor gives essay exams, use these objectives as possible essay questions, and practice formulating a response to them. If your exams will include only multiple choice questions, use the objectives to evaluate your knowledge. If you can recite the relevant information for each objective, you probably have a good understanding of the material.

Mastering the Material

Mastering the Vocabulary. Each section of the chapter has a list of important terms. In most cases these terms are defined and printed in bold in your text. You might develop a set of note cards instead of writing the definitions in the study guide. Many students keep their note cards handy to pull out and review during short breaks. You will be surprised at your progress if you use those occasional spare minutes.

Mastering the Concepts. This fill-in-the-blanks exercise will give you practice recalling the vocabulary and basic conceptual material from a section of the text. When completed, this exercise will provide a reasonably detailed review you can use when doing your final work before an exam. If you have great difficulty with this section, you need to go back and work with the text again. An answer key is provided, but try to complete the exercise on your own first, working with the text if necessary.

Evaluating Your Progress. Each section includes multiple choice questions to help you evaluate whether you have achieved at least a basic level of mastery of the facts and vocabulary. For the most part, these questions will require lower levels of comprehension than the questions in the pretests found at the end of each chapter. Many will emphasize definitions or will address general issues. Errors here indicate you have missed some basic information or do not know the important terms. Go back and fill in those gaps before you begin new material. Note that the answer key includes explanations about why the wrong answers are wrong. Use this feature to understand your mistakes and learn even more.

Making Final Preparations

You should work on this section after you feel you have achieved a basic mastery of the entire chapter. In fact, it is a good idea to wait a day or two before beginning this section. As you will learn in Chapter 8, the most significant forgetting occurs soon after the original learning period. You will overestimate your mastery if you complete these exercises right after studying the chapter.

Short Essay Questions. Each chapter includes several practice essay questions. Answering essay questions requires that you recall the information, rather than just recognize it, so essay questions provide a more difficult test of your knowledge. Answering essay questions is excellent practice regardless of the format of your exams, but it is essential if your exams will include essay questions. Sample answers are provided, but write your own answers before looking at the answers.

Matching. This exercise provides practice with a matching format and requires that you link terms with their definitions or their importance to the chapter. This is also the exercise that tests your recognition of the names of notable people. Some instructors require their students to know the names of major researchers or theorists; others do not. Find out your instructor's policy before your first exam.

Multiple Choice Pretests. Two pretests are provided to give you practice answering multiple-choice questions and to help you evaluate your mastery of the text material prior to your exams. Pretest 1 tends to focus more on specific factual information than Pretest 2. Pretest 2 emphasizes application and prediction. Can you recognize a concept in action? Can you take a theory and make predictions about what will happen in a new situation? Can you see the relationships between concepts? These questions require more complete conceptual understanding.

If you have no trouble with Pretest 1, but make many errors on Pretest 2, you probably know facts but do not really understand them or their significance. You might try discussing the material with a study partner or friend, or go to your instructor and ask for some help in reaching this level of comprehension. Also, be sure to look at the explanations for the incorrect alternatives given in the answer key. Knowing *why* something is wrong is often as informative as knowing that something is right.

Language Development Guide

This material, originally prepared by Mary Beth Foster, will help you understand some of the more difficult vocabulary. This section explains non-technical terms and idioms that might be unfamiliar (especially to non-native English readers), and provides exercises to improve language comprehension.

Core Terms. These words may or may not appear in the chapter, but you are very likely to hear them in lecture. They are words that instructors sometimes use *without ever explaining them.* Understanding them should help you get more out of the lectures and the text. You might want to read this part before the lectures on a given chapter begin.

Idioms. A list of difficult words and "idioms" -- phrases that have a special meaning (e.g., "has its roots," or "coined a term") and their explanations are provided. Because of the large number of idioms in each chapter, these lists include only those most likely to be difficult to interpret without context.

Word Parts. The meaning of many new words often can be understood by breaking the complex word into its component segments, or word parts. Knowing the meaning of these small segments is the key to developing a rich vocabulary. This section will break down words from the chapter into their component parts and provide an exercise for using word parts to define other words.

Pronunciation. New to this edition of the study guide is a section to help you learn how to pronounce some of the more challenging words in the chapter. The words included are those that are important terms or names and are most likely to give non-native English speakers trouble because of unusual letter to sound relationships.

Answers and Explanations

Use this feature to evaluate why you made a mistake and to help you understand difficult material. Each question is page-referenced to direct you to the relevant material in the text, and where appropriate, in *PsykTrek* or *PsychNow!* modules (PT = *PsykTrek*, PN = *PsychNow!*). Even if you answer correctly, review the explanations of incorrect answers and see if your reasoning was similar.

STRATEGIES FOR MASTERING THE MATERIAL

Being a successful student requires more than a text and study guide. The best materials are worthless if the student approaches the course inappropriately or uses poor study strategies. This section discusses some basic behaviors that are important for success in any class, not just introductory psychology.

Go to Class Regularly. This seems pretty obvious, right? Still, many students miss class frequently, especially in large lecture classes in which their absence is unlikely to be noticed. Going to class has many benefits. First, the lectures might be the only source of some of the information you are expected to learn. Second, the focus of the lectures may be a good guide to the topics your instructor feels are important, and exams are likely to reflect this emphasis. Third, your instructor will present the material in a different "voice" or perhaps from a different orientation than your text. Material in the text that you have difficulty understanding might be easier to understand when presented in class. Also, the different style or form of presentation may help create more retrieval cues. The more ways and times information is presented, the more likely you are to remember it. Also, demonstrations, videos, and exercises that are included in class can provide wonderful memory cues for the related material and keep things interesting.

Simply showing up for class is insufficient, however. To get the most benefit from your attendance you need to come prepared and you need to be an active participant. Try to survey the material to be discussed. Look through the chapter, paying attention to section headings, figures, and tables. Familiarize yourself with the topic and some of the vocabulary. If you go to class with a foundation, the lecture will be easier to understand, and you will be able to take notes more effectively.

Pay attention in class. If you are socializing rather than paying attention, you not only miss the information you supposedly came to class to learn, but you also interfere with your neighbors' ability to pay attention. Try to sit in the front of the class, especially in large lecture halls. You will be better able to see and hear, and there will be fewer distracting things between you and the instructor.

Get involved in the lecture. Think about what is being said; do not just listen passively. Active involvement in learning produces better memory for the material. Taking notes is one way to actively process the information, but do not try to write down every word. Be selective, and use your own words except in cases in which exact recall will be necessary. Have an organization to your notes. Indicate major topic headings and the supporting information, and include enough information to make your notes meaningful. Find a time soon after class to review your notes. If something is unclear then, it certainly will be unclear later when you begin studying. Clarify those points as soon as possible.

Use Your Textbook. Failing to read your textbook is similar to cutting class: you are wasting an important source of information, not to mention the money you spent. Why buy a book and then not use it?

Your textbook not only presents the information you will be expected to know, but also includes many features that will help make your studying easier and more effective. The important terms are highlighted and defined right in the chapter. Summary tables for concepts and theories are provided and make great study aids. Use them to quickly review the concepts and compare the different theories. Figures and other illustrations provide a clear visual representation of information. Learning goals and self-tests help you organize your studying and evaluate your progress. Chapter summaries offer a chance to preview the material before you begin your reading and to review the material when you are preparing for an exam.

Ask Questions. Asking questions serves several purposes. Most obviously, if you do not understand something, asking questions can get you the needed information. If you are unable to ask questions during class, talk with your instructor or TA before or after class or during their office hours. Don't be shy about asking for help understanding something. This is also true during exams. If you do not understand a question or a specific word, ask for help interpreting it. If you are generally struggling in class, ask your instructor or TA for help or go to your school's learning center for suggestions.

Asking questions is also a wonderful way to get involved in the material and to process it to a deeper level of understanding. As you study and as you listen in class, ask yourself what the information really means or what the point of the discussion is. The more deeply you process material, the more you will remember.

Make a Plan. Once you have a syllabus for each of your classes, evaluate what each class will require and mark important assignments on your calendar. For most courses you should plan to study about two hours per week for every hour spent in class. Carve out a regular study time for each class and consider those work periods comparable to a job. You do not put off going to work; do not put off studying. Do not waste free time between classes. Use it to study, or make it part of your planned recreational time.

Each time you sit down to study, set objectives about how long you will study and what material you will cover. Be realistic about your objectives. Consider both the study time needed and your attention span. If you have trouble concentrating for more than 30 minutes, do not plan to study 3 hours. Plan shorter but more frequent study sessions, or plan brief breaks within a study session.

Study As You Go. This requires discipline, but it is essential for most students. For classes that cover a large amount of material, waiting until a few days before an exam to begin serious study is deadly and is a mistake that many students make.

As you will learn in Chapter 8, massed practice (cramming) produces poorer memory than distributed (day by day) practice. Study for mastery on a daily (or at least weekly) basis, focusing on a small amount of material as if you will have a test the next day. By the time the actual exam approaches, you will have learned most of what you need to know, and you can spend the final study periods filling in details and expanding your comprehension to deeper levels. You will be less likely to end up with everything in a jumble in your mind than if you try to learn it all at the last minute.

Study Effectively When You Study. A popular study technique is the SQ3R method: *S*urvey, *Q*uestion, *R*ead, *R*ecite, *R*eview. My recommendations do not conform to this plan exactly, but the emphasis is similar: To study effectively requires action and thought on the part of the student.

1. Know where you are headed when you begin to study. Have learning goals. To formulate goals, briefly survey the material and identify the general issues. This is basically the S(urvey) and Q(uestion) steps in the SQ3R study method. Compare your goals to those listed in this study guide.

2. Organize your studying and reading. Focus on a topic to be mastered. Integrate your class notes with the text material. The topic context will help you learn and remember the information. Develop outlines or create tables that summarize and relate material. Make use of the Concept Summary tables in your text. They provide a clear summary and comparison of many of the concepts and theories you will need to know. Expand these tables with information from lectures.

3. Be an *active* reader and learner. Reading passively and hoping that the material will find its way into your memory automatically is not an adaptive strategy. You might understand everything you read, but understanding and remembering are two different things. You need to understand something to maximize the chance you will remember it, but remembering requires more. Simple repetition is better than nothing, but thinking deeply is the best way to ensure you will remember. Look for relationships or critical differences between terms or concepts. Apply the concepts to your own life. Generate your own examples. Tell somebody what you have learned. Get involved.

4. Develop materials for later review. As mentioned before, some students find note cards with a term on one side, and a definition and other important material on the other side to be very useful. You might also develop outlines, or create summary tables similar to your text's Concept Summary tables mentioned above. Your active involvement will help you remember the information, and you will be creating study materials for use during final preparations for exams.

5. Periodically evaluate your progress. Use the learning goals as cues for recall. Recite (the second R in SQ3R) the basic ideas and the important details. Answer the questions in the study guide to quiz yourself. Do not move to new material until you understand and can recall the current material.

Be A Teacher. Teaching a concept to someone else is an excellent way to ensure you will remember that information for a long time. It also is one of the quickest ways to find out that you do not really understand something and that you need to do more work. Teaching a parent or friend will work, but taking turns teaching with a study partner is best. Encourage your "student" to ask questions to test your comprehension. The act of recalling, organizing, and presenting information develops additional retrieval cues and reviews the material at the same time.

Practice, Practice, Practice. Review (the final R in SQ3R) material right after you finish reading and frequently during the following week. Do not consider it learned and then never think about it again. Make part of each study session a quick review of past material. Each time you review material you are strengthening the retrieval cues for that information.

Practice answering questions similar to those you will encounter on the exam. The study guide has questions in different formats. Ask your instructor if any old exams are available for students to use for practice. Sometimes dorms or campus organizations maintain test files. Don't assume that your exam will focus on the same material or be exactly the same difficulty. Use old tests simply to practice using your knowledge, not to figure out what will be on your exam. You might also find a different study guide and use the questions in it for additional practice. Most introductory psychology texts overlap considerably in what they cover, so many of the exercises will be appropriate.

Adapt Your Strategies. Evaluate your study strategies periodically. If you do not perform well on the first exam, try to figure out why. Look over your exam, and ask your instructor or TA for suggestions. Modify your strategies to fit your particular learning style and the demands of your particular course.

STRATEGIES FOR TAKING TESTS

Although how well you comprehend the material is certainly the most critical determinant of test performance, taking tests is somewhat an acquired skill. Poor test-taking behaviors can undo much of the hard work done to prepare for the test. Here are some general suggestions concerning taking tests:

Come Prepared. As stated above, the critical requirement for doing well on an exam is to know the material. Being well prepared has another benefit, though. Feeling confident about your knowledge reduces the anxiety you will experience during the exam. Being a little nervous is a good thing, but in large doses it interferes with the ability to concentrate and think. No matter how well prepared you are, there likely will be a question or two that will require you to stop and think for a minute.

Come Alert and Well-Rested. Being tired increases the chance you will make careless mistakes and degrades your ability to reason through difficult questions. As you will discover in Chapter 6, sleeping several hours after studying can improve memory for the material, too.

Survey the Test Before You Begin. Review the format of the questions, and evaluate how to budget your time. If you are unsure what you are supposed to do on some parts of the exam, ask for assistance.

Budget Your Time. Figure out approximately how long you can work on each question. For essay or other non-objective questions, the point value provides information about how complete an answer should be and how much time you might need for a question. Do not spend 30 minutes on one 5-point question and 5 minutes on a 25-point question. If you encounter a question you cannot answer in your budgeted time, make your best guess (if multiple choice), mark it for reconsideration, and move on. After finishing the rest of the questions, go back and spend any extra time on the ones that need more thought.

Be an Intelligent Test-Taker. Read the entire question before formulating an answer. Do not focus on one or two key terms and then assume you know what the question is asking. Be careful to notice critical words such as "not" or "except." On multiple choice questions, try to figure out the answer before you look at the alternatives. If your answer is listed (make sure it really says what you think it says), it probably is the right choice. However, read all the alternatives to be sure your choice is the best.

If you do not immediately know the answer to a question, do not panic. First, reread the question to make sure you know what it is asking. For multiple choice questions, reread the alternatives. Sometimes the alternatives will alert you to important details to consider. Then ask yourself what you *do* know about the topic. Use this information to reconsider the possibilities and to eliminate any answers that are clearly inappropriate. Finally, if all else fails, guess. For a multiple choice question, you probably will be able to eliminate one or two of the alternatives, increasing your odds of picking the correct answer. Essay questions are a greater challenge, but if you know anything, you have a chance for partial credit.

Don't be afraid to change an answer. Your first impression is not always right. Information you find later in the exam or a miraculous release from your blocked memory might show you an earlier answer needs to be reconsidered. If you can clearly explain why your first choice is wrong, change it.

Be Careful and Check Your Work. If you must record your answers on a scan sheet for computer scoring, be careful to record answers correctly. Periodically check to make sure you are on the same number on your answer sheet as on your exam. Some students prefer to mark their answers on the test first, and then transfer them to the answer sheet. If time is a major factor, this approach may create problems. As you hurry to finish transferring answers, careless mistakes become more likely.

Adapt Your Strategies to the Type of Test. Obviously, an essay exam requires a different strategy than a multiple-choice exam. First, make sure you know what the question is asking. A great answer to the wrong question is worthless. Second, take a minute to plan your answer. Jot down the important points, and think about how to organize those points. An organized answer gives the impression that you know the material and often will receive a higher grade. Also, information is more likely to be overlooked if your answer is a jumble of unorganized facts. Third, be concise. Include adequate details, but do not add irrelevant information. Get to the point, and stay there. Fourth, make sure your answer says what you intend. You know what you mean to say, but sometimes that is not what actually ends up on paper. Finally, write legibly and use reasonable grammar. What cannot be read or understood will earn no points.

A FINAL WORD

I hope this study guide helps you reach your goals in introductory psychology. I welcome any comments that you care to share with me. Let me know what worked well for you, what didn't, and what you think would be valuable to include in future editions.

Janet Proctor, Ph.D.
Department of Psychological Sciences
Purdue University
West Lafayette, Indiana 47907-1364
jproctor@purdue.edu

CHAPTER 1: INTRODUCTION TO PSYCHOLOGY

ESTABLISHING LEARNING GOALS

Use these learning goals as a preview of the chapter, a guide for active reading, and to evaluate your mastery of the material. Review the relevant goals as you begin and end your reading of each major section of the chapter of your text.

I.   Solve the conceptual problem of how to define and describe psychology.
   A. Give the modern definition of psychology.
   B. Discuss the different ways to study the mind scientifically.
   C. Distinguish among clinical, applied, and research psychologists.
       1. Describe the activities and typical workplace of clinical, applied, and research psychologists.
       2. Distinguish between psychologists and psychiatrists.

II. Solve the conceptual problem of tracing the evolution of psychological thought.
   A. Explain what is meant by the mind-body problem.
       1. Describe Descartes' position on this issue.
       2. Describe the modern approach to the mind-body problem.
   B. Discuss differing viewpoints on the origins of knowledge.
       1. Define natural selection and explain how it relates to the debate about the origin of knowledge and behavior.
       2. Discuss the current view of the influence of "nature" and "nurture" on the mind and behavior.
   C. Trace the development of the first scientific schools of psychology.
       1. Describe the guiding focus and methods of structuralism, functionalism, and behaviorism.
       2. Identify the major figures associated with each school, and the early women in psychology.
       3. Explain why these different approaches to the study of psychology developed.
   D. Discuss the early clinical contributions of Freud and the humanists.
       1. Compare the central concepts and techniques of psychoanalysis and humanistic psychology.
       2. Identify the major figures associated with each approach.
   E. Discuss the contributions of women to the development of psychology as a field.

III. Solve the conceptual problem of understanding the focus of modern psychology.
   A. Describe what it means to adopt an eclectic approach.
   B. Discuss the factors that started the cognitive revolution.
   C. Describe recent developments in biology and evolutionary psychology, and discuss how they influence modern psychology.
   D. Discuss why psychologists think cultural factors are important determinants of behavior and mind.

Mastering the Material

Preview & Defining and Describing Psychology (pp. 4-11)

Mastering the Vocabulary. Define or explain each of the following terms. To check your answers, consult the text pages listed.

1. psychology (p. 4)

2. mind (p. 7)

3. behavior (p. 7)

4. clinical psychologists (p. 8)

5. applied psychologists (p. 9)

6. research psychologists (p. 9)

7 psychiatrists (p. 10)

Mastering the Concepts. Fill in the blanks to create a summary of this section. Answers are on page 15.

Psychology is defined as the scientific study of _____ (1) and _____ (2). The _____ (3), the contents and processes of subjective experience, cannot be observed directly, so psychologists observe behavior, noting the conditions accompanying a behavior, and make _____ (4) about the mental processes involved. Behavior includes actions, expressed feelings, and cellular activity.

_____ (5) psychologists treat psychological problems or counsel people about parenting or relationships. _____ (6) are not psychologists; they are medical doctors trained in psychology who treat mental disorders. _____ (7) psychologists, such as human factors or industrial/organizational psychologists, extend principles of psychology to industry. _____ (8) psychologists explore basic principles of psychology by conducting experiments, often in laboratories at universities.

Evaluating Your Progress. Select the best response. Answers are found on page 15. If you make any errors, reread the relevant material before proceeding.

1. Which of the items below would not be considered an example of behavior by most psychologists?
    a. the electrical activity of cells in the brain
    b. marking an answer on a survey
    c. reciting a list of words from memory
    d. your subjective experience of the color red

2. The mind cannot be studied directly because mental processes
    a. are very easily observed.
    b. are subjective.
    c. are too rapid to record.
    d. come from the pineal gland.

3. Which of the following people is most likely to be considered an applied psychologist?
    a. Jack, who advises parents about dealing with drug abuse in teenagers
    b. Pat, who conducts experiments on the basic memory processes of children
    c. Sara, who uses the principles of psychology to design control panels in new airplanes
    d. Miko, who treats patients with serious mental disorders such as schizophrenia

4. Studying how people influence each other and relate to each other is the primary focus of
    a. a social psychologist.
    b. a human factors psychologist.
    c. a developmental psychologist.
    d. a school psychologist.

5. Which of the following types of psychologists is likely to work in an academic setting (e.g., a college)?
    a. applied psychologist
    b. research psychologist
    c. clinical psychologist
    d. all of the above

6. Chris has a medical degree and specializes in treating mental disorders. Chris is
    a. a clinical psychologist.
    b. a counseling psychologist.
    c. an applied psychologist.
    d. a psychiatrist.

Tracking Psychological Thought: A Brief History (pp. 11-19)

Mastering the Vocabulary. Define or explain each of the following terms. To check your answers, consult the text pages listed.

1. empiricism (p. 11)

2. nativism (p. 12)

3. Gestalt psychology (p. 13)

4. structuralism (p. 15)

5. systematic introspection (p. 15)

6. functionalism (p. 16)

7. behaviorism (p. 16)

8. psychoanalysis (p. 18)

9. humanistic psychology (p. 19)

Mastering the Concepts. Fill in the blanks to create a summary of the section. Answers are on page 15.

The roots of psychology are in _____(9) and _____(10) and date back to ancient Greece. Psychology merges these, studying both the mind and the biological processes of mental activity. How the mind relates to the body is known as the _____(11) question. Descartes, a philosopher, said that mind and body are _____(12), but the mind controls the body through the _____(13) gland. Psychologists now view the mind as a product of brain activity and inseparable from the body.

Another question that interests psychologists concerns the origins of knowledge. The empiricist view of Aristotle states knowledge is obtained through _____(14), whereas the _____(15) view of Kant states some knowledge is innate. Darwin's concept of _____(16) predicts adaptive traits are likely to be passed on in the genes, making inherited behavioral tendencies a possibility. The _____(17) psychologists suggested perceptual organization is one of these innate abilities. Most modern psychologists agree both _____(18) (innate factors) and _____(19) (experience) are important.

In 1879 in Leipzig, Germany, _____(20) founded psychology by establishing the first psychology _____(21), and psychology became a distinct scientific discipline. Since then, psychologists have debated the proper focus of psychology. _____(22), such as Wundt and

4

Titchener, sought to study the mind by breaking experiences into basic components using systematic

_____(23). Later, _____(24) emerged in America and emphasized the function and purpose of

mental operations. In the 20th century, the _____(25), including Watson, argued that scientific

psychology should study observable _____(26) rather than the mind. Mary Calkins and Margaret

Washburn are two of the women who contributed to early psychology, in spite of intense discrimination.

Clinical psychology changed in the early 20th century with the development of Freud's theory of

mind and therapy called _____(27). Here, the emphasis was on _____(28) determinants of

behavior, which could only be discovered through the symbolic analysis of such things as dreams, and the

experiences and _____(29) urges of childhood. Disliking Freud's negative view, the

_____(30), such as Rogers and Maslow, proposed that humans possess the potential for positive

growth and self-awareness.

Evaluating Your Progress. Select the best response. Answers are on page 16. If you miss any
questions, reread the relevant material before proceeding.

1. Darwin suggested that certain traits are likely to persist due to natural selection because they are
    a. subjective.
    b. adaptive.
    c. reflexive.
    d. empirical.

2. "Nature" in the nature-nurture issue refers to
    a. innate factors that influence behavior.
    b. the influence of experience.
    c. subjective experiences.
    d. empiricism.

3. Which movement in psychology suggested humans are born with innate, unchangeable rules for
    organizing sensory input?
    a. behaviorism
    b. gestalt psychology
    c. humanistic psychology
    d. psychoanalysis

4. Psychology emerged as a science in _____ when _____ established a psychology laboratory.
    a. 364 BC; Aristotle
    b. 1879; Wilhelm Wundt
    c. 1884; William James
    d. 1913; John Watson

5. Structuralists studied the mind by
   a. using systematic introspection.
   b. analyzing dreams and slips of the tongue.
   c. examining the adaptive function of behavior.
   d. studying the pineal gland.

6. The early functionalist approach was most influenced by the work of
   a. Margaret Floy Washburn.
   b. Sigmund Freud.
   c. Carl Rogers.
   d. Charles Darwin.

7. The view that psychology should study only observable behavior and attempt to relate changes in the environment to changes in behavior is most characteristic of
   a. the humanistic perspective.
   b. psychoanalysis.
   c. structuralism.
   d. behaviorism.

8. Freud's psychoanalytic approach to psychology gave great importance to
   a. the therapist being a friend and supporter of the client.
   b. the role of natural selection in determining behavior.
   c. discovering hidden conflicts and desires in the unconscious mind.
   d. immediate conscious experience.

Setting Directions in Modern Psychology (pp. 20-25)

Mastering the Vocabulary. Define or explain each of the following terms. To check your answers, consult the text pages listed.

1. eclectic approach (p. 20)

2. cognitive revolution (p. 21)

3. evolutionary psychology (p. 23)

4. culture (p. 23)

Mastering the Concepts. Fill in the blanks to create a summary of the section. Answers are on page 15.

Modern psychology is best described as _____(31), not tied to one point of view, but an emphasis of cognitive and biological factors is common. The _____(32) revolution was stimulated by the invention of the _____(33). This renewed interest in mental processes was a shift away from _____(34), and it emphasized an appreciation of how thoughts and perception influence behavior. New technology also promoted the study of biological aspects of behavior. _____(35) psychology studies how evolution influences behavior. Psychologists also consider the role that shared values, customs, and beliefs, or _____ (36), has in behavior.

Evaluating Your Progress. Select the best response. Answers are found on page 16. If you make any errors, reread the relevant material before proceeding.

1. Most modern psychologists use
    a. a strict structuralist approach.
    b. a strict functionalist approach.
    c. a strict behaviorist approach.
    d. a mixture of approaches.

2. In the mid-20th century, psychology moved away from a _____ to a _____ emphasis.
    a. cognitive; behaviorist
    b. behaviorist; cognitive
    c. structuralist; humanistic
    d. humanistic; structuralist

3. The cognitive approach represents a return to
    a. the study of the mind.
    b. the study of only observable behavior.
    c. the study of the brain.
    d. the study of the adaptive function of behaviors.

4. Both the cognitive and biological approaches were influenced by the development of
    a. new technology.
    b. better introspective techniques.
    c. dream analysis.
    d. Darwin's concept of natural selection.

5. The idea that humans have innate mental mechanisms that have been acquired through natural selection, represents
    a. cognitive psychology.
    b. behaviorism.
    c. evolutionary psychology.
    d. human factors psychology

6. If a behavior is influenced by the values or beliefs of the community, the behavior is influenced by
    a. innate factors.
    b. cultural factors.
    c. humanistic factors.
    d. natural selection factors.

MAKING FINAL PREPARATIONS

Complete these sections without consulting your book or notes. For a more accurate estimate of how well you know this material, wait at least a day or two after studying the chapter before working on the questions. Some of the material you "know" immediately after working with the chapter will be quickly forgotten. Immediate tests will overestimate what you know well.

Short Essay Questions. Write a brief answer to each question. Sample answers are on page 17.

1. Explain why scientifically studying the mind is not simple, and describe how it can be studied.

2. Compare the structuralist and behaviorist views about the proper focus and techniques of psychology.

3. Compare Freud's psychoanalytic approach with the humanistic approach of Rogers.

4. Describe the cognitive revolution, and discuss why it occurred.

Matching. Select the correct definition or description for each item. Answers are on page 17.

_____ 1. systematic introspection	**a.** was especially interested in the mind-body problem
_____ 2. tabula rasa	**b.** founded behaviorism
_____ 3. Wundt	**c.** treats less serious disorders or adjustment problems
_____ 4. nature-nurture issue	**d.** view that certain knowledge is innate
_____ 5. Watson	**e.** idea that knowledge comes from experience
_____ 6. Calkins	**f.** the idea that at birth the mind is a "blank slate"
_____ 7. empiricism	**g.** issue of the role of innate & environmental factors
_____ 8. Descartes	**h.** major figure in functionalism
_____ 9. nativism	**i.** favorite technique of structuralists
_____ 10. psychiatrist	**j.** medical doctor who treats mental disorders
_____ 11. evolutionary psychology	**k.** original structuralist
_____ 12. developmental psychologist	**l.** studies how behavior changes through the life span
_____ 13. counseling psychologist	**m.** studies innate behavioral tendencies
_____ 14. mind-body problem	**n.** problem of the relationship between consciousness or the mind and the brain and body
_____ 15. James	**o.** one of the first female psychologists

Multiple Choice Pretest 1. Select the one best response. Answers are on page 18.

1. According to your text, psychology is currently defined as
   a. the scientific study of mind and behavior.
   b. the systematic study of mental processes.
   c. the systematic study of brain activity.
   d. the scientific study of mental illness.

2. The origins of psychology are in
   a. literature and philosophy.
   b. philosophy and physiology.
   c. education and literature.
   d. education and physiology.

3. Which view suggests that personality is determined by one's biological or genetic makeup?
   a. empiricist
   b. nativist
   c. functionalist
   d. behaviorist

4. Who is credited with establishing psychology as a science?
   a. William James
   b. Sigmund Freud
   c. John Watson
   d. Wilhelm Wundt

5. You are scheduled to take part in an experiment examining basic processes in memory and reasoning. The psychologist in charge is most likely
   a. an applied psychologist.
   b. a clinical psychologist.
   c. a research psychologist.
   d. a school psychologist.

6. Gestalt psychologists propose that _____ is (are) innate.
   a. perceptual organization
   b. cross-cultural differences
   c. introspection
   d. empiricism

7. A young man is sitting in a lab giving a detailed account of his subjective experiences concerning the taste of lemonade in hopes of discovering the basic units of the mind and perception. This is most characteristic of the research of
   a. behaviorism.
   b. structuralism.
   c. functionalism.
   d. psychoanalysis.

8. "Yes, there are four basic tastes, but I'm interested in how this has helped us adapt and survive." What kind of psychologist is most likely to make such a statement?
   a. a psychoanalyst
   b. a structuralist
   c. a behaviorist
   d. a functionalist

9. Which statement most likely would be heard in a therapy session with a Freudian psychoanalytic psychologist?
   a. "There is a great person in there if you'll just let her out."
   b. "I don't want to hear about your dream. I'd rather talk about what you think is making you anxious."
   c. "I want you to tell me as completely as possible what you experience as you feel this satin cloth."
   d. "Your fear of dogs is really just a symptom of your real problem – a failure to resolve important sexual conflicts in childhood."

10. Calkins and Washburn are notable for
    a. establishing the first psychology laboratory.
    b. developing humanistic psychology.
    c. first studying cross-cultural differences in behavior.
    d. being among the first female psychologists.

11. Why did behaviorists think the structuralist approach to psychology was not truly scientific?
    a. Structuralists based their theories on a person's report of subjective events.
    b. Structuralists emphasized unconscious conflicts and sexual urges, rather than the person's potential.
    c. Structuralists studied animal behavior instead of human behavior.
    d. Structuralists took a too deterministic view of behavior.

12. The cognitive revolution refers to
    a. the shift away from behaviorism's emphasis on behavior and to a renewed interest in the mind.
    b. the development of computers by using data about the organization and processes of the mind.
    c. the rapid shift in thinking that accompanied each shift in approach to studying psychology.
    d. the furor created by Freud's theory of sexual urges during childhood.

13. Current explanations of behavior tend to refer to the person's memories or interpretation of events. This reflects the popularity of which approach to psychology?
    a. humanistic
    b. cognitive
    c. biological
    d. behaviorist

14. Utilizing a variety of theoretical approaches rather than a single approach is referred to as the
    a. eclectic approach.
    b. humanistic approach.
    c. nativist approach.
    d. behaviorist approach.

15. A steering wheel that must be turned right in order to turn the car to the right was designed to use
    a. an eclectic orientation.
    b. Gestalt principles.
    c. natural mappings.
    d. unnatural mappings.

Multiple Choice Pretest 2. Select the one best response. Answers are found on page 19.

1. Mary is an M.D. who specializes in treating people with mental disorders. Mary is
   a. a clinical psychologist.
   b. a psychiatrist.
   c. an applied psychologist.
   d. a cognitive psychologist.

2. Personality psychologists, developmental psychologists, and social psychologists are categorized as
   a. clinical psychologists.
   b. research psychologists.
   c. applied psychologists.
   d. counseling psychologists.

3. Descartes' answer to the mind-body problem proposes
   a. the mind is the same thing as the body.
   b. the mind is what the brain does.
   c. the mind and body are separate, but they can influence each other.
   d. the mind and body are separate and do not interact.

4. You are in a time machine. If you want to visit the beginning of the science of psychology how should you set the time machine?
   a. Greece, 350 BC
   b. Leipzig, Germany, 1879
   c. Vienna, Austria, 1900
   d. Johns Hopkins University, Baltimore, Maryland, 1929

5. "How can you think that our consciousness is simply the result of activity of our brain cells? Do you really believe that our ability to love, to remember our past, and to plan for the future is just biochemical activity?" your classmate argued. "I know if the brain is damaged there can be changes in consciousness and mental abilities, but surely the mind is something apart from blood and tissue." Your classmate is considering the
   a. mind-body problem.
   b. structuralist-functionalist debate.
   c. nature-nurture problem.
   d. cognitive revolution.

6. Which person-item pair is incorrectly linked?
   a. Carl Rogers---unconscious mind
   b. John Watson---observable behavior
   c. Wilhelm Wundt---systematic introspection
   d. William James---adaptive function

7. You believe that psychology should strive to discover the elements of immediate experience and how they combine to produce meaningful wholes. Your view is most similar to
    a. functionalism.
    b. behaviorism.
    c. structuralism.
    d. psychoanalysis.

8. A pigeon pecks a key and is then given food. A psychologist records each response and notes the environmental conditions that influence pecking. To what "school" does this psychologist belong?
    a. structuralist
    b. functionalist
    c. behaviorist
    d. cognitive

9. A major difference between Watson's behaviorism and Freud's psychoanalysis is that
    a. behaviorism stresses the function of the mind, but psychoanalysis stresses the potential for growth.
    b. behaviorism stresses the potential for growth, but psychoanalysis stresses unconscious urges.
    c. behaviorism stresses biological activity, but psychoanalysis stresses observable behavior.
    d. behaviorism stresses observable behavior, but psychoanalysis stresses unconscious urges.

10. With which of the following are you most likely to agree if you fall on the "nurture" side of an issue?
    a. Preschool programs like Head Start are unlikely to improve school performance because intelligence is a matter of genes, not experience.
    b. Aristotle and the British Empiricists were wrong to believe the mind is a "tabula rasa" at birth.
    c. The personality characteristics of an individual are determined by biological factors prior to birth.
    d. Watching violence on TV is responsible for much of the increase in violent behavior in children.

11. A capacity for self-awareness and personal growth are most associated with
    a. psychoanalysis.
    b. empiricism.
    c. humanistic psychology.
    d. cognitive psychology.

12. Dr. Hart is interested in the differences in dating behavior found in communities with different religious, ethnic, and socioeconomic characteristics. Dr. Hart's research emphasizes
    a. a humanistic view.
    b. a psychoanalytic view.
    c. a cognitive view.
    d. a cultural view.

13. Psychologists studying smoking and nicotine addiction emphasize the examination of the smoker's physiology, their attitudes and perceptions about smoking, and the behaviors and environmental conditions that are associated with smoking and addiction. What best describes this approach?
    a. behaviorism
    b. cognitive
    c. psychoanalytic
    d. eclectic

14. Mary believes that innate mechanisms help us learn language, find a mate, and engage in certain types of social behavior. She believes these innate mechanisms have developed because of natural selection. Mary's beliefs suggest she is
   a. a behaviorist.
   b. a humanist.
   c. an evolutionary psychologist.
   d. a human factors psychologist.

LANGUAGE DEVELOPMENT GUIDE

Core Terms

You might hear the word *discipline* or *school* in a discussion of psychology. Psychology, sociology, anthropology, history, and so on., are all disciplines -- branches of knowledge -- that study behavior, but each has its own unique focus and methods of study. Even within a discipline there may be different *schools* of thought -- different ideas about the best way to study or explain something. Sometimes, as Dr. Nairne puts it, these different ideas can lead to "vigorous arguments."

Psychology is considered a *social science*, which means that it uses the principles of scientific investigation to study individual people and groups. As in sciences like chemistry and biology, psychology has *theories* -- detailed explanations -- that are tested through experiments. *Empirical research*, including experiments, involves the systematic observation of an event or behavior. Similarly, the philosophical view of *empiricism* that is discussed in your text suggests that knowledge comes from a person's own observations (experience).

Idioms

p. 4	method of inquiry	a way of thinking and questioning
p. 4	think critically	to ask questions and actively think about a topic
p. 7	to reflect on	to think about
p. 7	in a sense	in some ways
p. 11	determinants of	things which cause
p. 14	principle vehicle for the transmission and expression of an inherited predisposition	the main way that a trait is passed along and then shown in an organism's offspring
p. 21	to infer	to guess or predict based upon what you already know
p. 17	drawing special attention to	emphasizing

13

p. 18	slip of the tongue	an error in word choice
p. 15	in conjunction with	together; at the same time
p. 20	conceive of	think of in a new way, develop a way of thinking about
p. 24	an integral part	an important, necessary part; essential

Word Parts

Here are some words that are made up of word parts, and that you can find in this chapter. After you've looked at these, you can look for others in the chapter with the same word parts.

WORD	WORD PART IT USES	MEANING
exclusively	ex = out of clud, clus = to shut, close	only, keeping out all others
influential	in = in, into, within flu, flux = to flow	exerting power over others, affecting the direction of events
intact	in = in, into, within tact, tang = touch	whole, not broken
predictors	pre = before dict = speak, say, tell	things which foretell
reconstruction	re = again con = together struct = build	to put back together, rebuild; that which has been rebuilt

Knowing the word parts listed above, you can also create the following words. You can get an idea of their meanings from the word parts they use. You fill in the blanks!

conclusive	con + clus	finally, to come together in a final way
confluence	con + flu	_____
influx	_____ + _____	a flowing in
reflux	re + flux	_____

contact	con + tact	_____
intangible	in + tang	_____

(That last one was tricky! In some cases, "in" can mean "not", as in incorrect or inadequate. How do you know when it means "in" and when it means "not"? You have to figure it out from context, or look it up!)

Pronunciation

p. 4	psychology	sy-col'-o-gee	p. 12	nativism	nay'-ti-viz-um
p. 10	psychiatrists	sy-ky'-a-trist	p. 13	Gestalt	ge-stalt'
p. 11	empiricism	im-peer'-i-siz-um	p. 20	eclectic	ee-klek'-tik

ANSWERS AND EXPLANATIONS

To find relevant material in your textbook, consult the pages cited with each answer. Also, PN and PT citations refer to modules in *PsychNow!* and *Psyk.trek* materials, respectively.

Mastering the Concepts

1. mind (p. 4)
2. behavior (p. 4)
3. mind (p. 7)
4. inferences (p. 8)
5. Clinical (p. 8)
6. Psychiatrists (p. 9)
7. Applied (p. 9)
8. Research (p. 9)
9. philosophy (p. 11)
10. physiology (p. 11)
11. mind-body (p. 12)
12. separate (p. 12)
13. pineal (p. 12)
14. experience (p. 12)
15. nativist/nativism (p.12)
16. natural selection (p.12)
17. Gestalt (p. 13)
18. nature (p. 14)
19. nurture (p. 14)
20. Wundt (p. 14)
21. laboratory (p. 14)
22. Structuralists (p. 15)
23. introspection (p. 15)
24. functionalism (p. 16)
25. behaviorists (p. 17)
26. behavior (p. 17)
27. psychoanalysis (p. 18)
28. unconscious (p. 18)
29. sexual (p. 18)
30. humanists (p. 19)
31. eclectic (p. 20)
32. cognitive (p. 21)
33. computer (p. 21)
34. behaviorism (p. 21)
35. Evolutionary (p. 23)
36. culture (p. 24)

Evaluating Your Progress

Preview & Defining and Describing Psychology

1. **d**	a. Wrong.	Electrical activity can be measured (observed), so it is a behavior.
(p. 7)	b. Wrong.	Marking an answer is an overt action, and therefore, a behavior.
	c. Wrong.	Speaking is an overt action, and therefore, a behavior.

2. **b**	a. Wrong.	Mental processes cannot be observed directly.
(p. 8)	c. Wrong.	The brain activity accompanying mental activity can be recorded.
(PN1B)	d. Wrong.	The pineal gland is not the location of the mind.

3. **c**	a. Wrong.	Jack is a clinical or counseling psychologist.
(p. 9)	b. Wrong.	Pat is a research psychologist studying basic principles of behavior and mind.
	d. Wrong.	Miko is a clinical psychologist or psychiatrist.

4. **a**   b. Wrong.   Human factors psychologists apply psychology to engineering and design.
(p. 11)   c. Wrong.   Developmental psychologists study how and why behavior changes over the life span.
          d. Wrong.   School psychologists apply psychology to school settings to help students adjust.

5. **d**   a, b, & c.   Wrong.   Applied, research, and clinical psychologists all work in academic settings.
(p. 9)

6. **d**   a. Wrong.   Clinical psychologists have a Ph.D., not a medical degree (M.D.).
(p. 9)   b. Wrong.   Counseling psychologists have a Master's degree or a Ph.D., not a medical degree.
          c. Wrong.   An applied psychologist doesn't treat mental disorders and doesn't have a medical degree.

Tracking Psychological Thought: A Brief History

1. **b**   a. Wrong.   Subjective means relative to one's personal mental experience.
(p. 14)   c. Wrong.   A reflex is an automatic response to environmental events.
          d. Wrong.   Empirical refers to observations or learning.

2. **a**   a. Wrong.   Experience is related to nurture, not nature.
(p. 13)   c. Wrong.   Subjective experience is personal experience, not part of the nature-nurture issue.
          d. Wrong.   Empiricism is the view that knowledge develops from experience (nurture).

3. **b**   a. Wrong.   Behaviorism stressed the role of experience, not innate factors.
(p. 13)   c. Wrong.   Humanistic psychology stressed the potential for growth, not perceptual organization.
          d. Wrong.   Psychoanalysis stressed the unconscious mind's importance, not rules of perception.

4. **b**   a. Wrong.   Aristotle wrote about topics related to psychology from a philosopher's approach.
(p. 14)   c. Wrong.   William James was an important figure in functionalism, a later development.
(PT1A)   d. Wrong.   John Watson was an important figure in behaviorism, a later development.

5. **a**   b. Wrong.   Freud used these techniques in psychoanalysis, which is not part of structuralism.
(p. 15)   c. Wrong.   The functionalists were concerned with the adaptive function of behavior.
          d. Wrong.   Structuralists didn't study brain structures. Descartes was interested in the pineal gland.

6. **d**   a. Wrong.   Wasburn, a structuralist, was the first woman to receive a Ph.D. in psychology.
(p. 16)   b. Wrong.   Freud founded the psychoanalytic approach, but did not influence functionalism.
          c. Wrong.   Carl Rogers, a humanistic psychologist, is more contemporary than early functionalism.

7. **d**   a. Wrong.   Humanistic psychologists do not believe only observable behavior is important.
(p. 16)   b. Wrong.   The main focus of psychoanalysis is the unconscious mind, not observable behavior.
          c. Wrong.   Structuralism emphasized subjective experience, not just observable behavior.

8. **c**   a. Wrong.   This is characteristic of client-centered therapy, a humanistic approach, not psychoanalysis.
(p. 18)   b. Wrong.   Natural selection is relevant to functionalism, not Freud's psychoanalytic approach.
          d. Wrong.   This is characteristic of structuralism. Freud emphasized unconscious influences.

Setting Directions In Modern Psychology

1. **d**   a, b, & c.   Wrong.   Most are eclectic, not tied to one approach.
(p. 20)

2. **b**   a. Wrong.   The order is reversed here.
(p. 21)   c. Wrong.   Structuralism was replaced by functionalism, not the humanistic approach, much earlier.
(PN1B)   d. Wrong.   The humanistic view was developed more recently than structuralism.

3. **a**   b. Wrong.   This describes behaviorism.
    (p. 21)   c. Wrong.   This describes the physiological approach.
               d. Wrong.   This describes functionalism.

4. **a**   b. Wrong.   Introspection is not widely used in either approach.
    (pp. 21-22) c. Wrong.   Dream analysis is a psychoanalytic technique.
               d. Wrong.   Natural selection does not directly relate to these approaches.

5. **c**   a. Wrong.   Cognitive psychology stresses the role of thoughts and perception, not natural selection.
    (p. 23)   b. Wrong.   Behaviorism stresses experience, not natural selection and innate tendencies.
               d. Wrong.   Human factors stresses behavioral tendencies of the human user, not natural selection.

6. **b**   a. Wrong   Innate factors are present at birth and are not due to environmental influences.
    (p. 23)   c. Wrong   Humanistic psychology involves environmental influences, but not really those given.
    (PT1A)   d. Wrong   Natural selection is a process by which traits either persist or die out through evolution.

MAKING FINAL PREPARATIONS

Short Essay Questions

1. The mind is the contents and processes of subjective experience, perception, and feelings. Because it is subjective, it cannot be observed directly. Without directly observable activities, it is difficult to study scientifically. Three approaches are possible: (1) a person can report subjective experiences using systematic introspection to provide information about the mind; (2) the structure and function of the brain can be studied; and (3) a person's behavior can be observed under different conditions and regularities and relationships in behavior can be noted. Because of limitations of the first two, modern research utilizes method three. (pp. 7-8)

2. The structuralists focused on immediate conscious experience and attempted to determine the basic elements of the mind and how they combine into meaningful wholes. They sought to understand the structure of the mind. To do so, they employed the research technique of systematic introspection, in which trained observers gave detailed accounts of their subjective experiences. Behaviorists, on the other hand, argued that to be a science, psychology should not attempt to study the mind or consciousness because its subjective nature made direct observation impossible and placed it outside of science. Instead, they proposed studying only overt behavior and how changes in environmental events affect behavior. (pp. 14-17)

3. Freud's psychoanalytic approach emphasized the role of unconscious influences. He felt that people had little insight into these unconscious, animalistic urges, conflicts, and memories. Mental problems would be solved only by insight through an analysis of the symbolic content of dreams, slips of the tongue, etc. His view was a very pessimistic, deterministic view of people. Humanists such as Rogers had a more optimistic view. They proposed that people had great abilities to achieve growth, self-awareness, and self-determination. The therapist's role is to nurture these strengths to allow the person to develop to their potential. (pp. 18-19)

4. The cognitive revolution was a turn away from the behaviorist approach of studying only overt behavior, back to an interest in studying the mind and cognitive processes (perception, memory, reasoning, etc.). The cognitive revolution was possible because: (1) advances in research techniques in which measurements of behavior (reaction time, etc.) could be used to infer the characteristics of mental processes; and (2) computers were developed and provided a convenient model for mental processes (information processing systems). (p. 21)

Matching

1. **i** (p. 15)	4. **g** (p. 12)	7. **e** (p. 11)	10. **j** (p. 9)	13. **c** (p. 8)
2. **f** (p. 11)	5. **b** (p. 16)	8. **a** (p. 12)	11. **m** (p. 23)	14. **n** (p. 12)
3. **k** (p. 14)	6. **o** (p. 17)	9. **d** (p. 12)	12. **l** (p. 11)	15. **h** (p. 16)

Multiple Choice Pretest 1

1. **a**   b. Wrong.   Psychology is a science and it studies more than mental processes.
   (p. 4)   c. Wrong.   Psychology is a science and studies more than just brain activity.
             d. Wrong.   Psychology studies more than just mental illness.

2. **b**   a, c, & d.   Wrong.   Psychology did not originate in literature or education.
   (p. 11)

3. **b**   a. Wrong.   Empiricists stress learning and experience.
   (p. 13)   c. Wrong.   Functionalists stress the function of a behavior or characteristic.
             d. Wrong.   Behaviorists stress experience and environmental influences.

4. **d**   a. Wrong.   James founded functionalism after psychology had become a science.
   (p. 14)   b. Wrong.   Freud is important in the development of clinical, but not scientific, psychology.
   (PN1B)   c. Wrong.   John Watson founded behaviorism after psychology had become a science.

5. **c**   a. Wrong.   Applied psychologists apply psychology to practical settings, not basic research.
   (p. 9)   b. Wrong.   Clinical psychologist research and treat mental disorders or problems with adjustment.
             d. Wrong.   School psychologists counsel students concerning basic adjustment, career choice, etc.

6. **a**   b. Wrong.   Cross-cultural differences are environmental, not innate, in origin.
   (p. 13)   c. Wrong.   Introspection is a self-report technique used by the structuralists, not an innate process.
             d. Wrong.   Empiricism is the idea that knowledge comes from experience, not innate processes.

7. **b**   a. Wrong.   Behaviorism didn't use introspection and studied only observable behavior, not the mind.
   (p. 15)   c. Wrong.   Functionalism was concerned with the function of the mind, not its basic units.
             d. Wrong.   Psychoanalysis, Freud's approach to therapy, did not use systematic introspection.

8. **d**   a. Wrong.   A psychoanalyst is interested in unconscious determinants of behavior, not adaptation.
   (p. 16)   b. Wrong.   A structuralist is interested in the structure of mind, rather than its adaptive value.
             c. Wrong.   A behaviorist is interested in environmental determinants of behavior, not function.

9. **d**   a. Wrong.   Psychoanalysis is more negative.   This is probably from a humanistic therapist.
   (p. 18)   b. Wrong.   A psychoanalyst would analyze dreams. This is probably from a humanistic therapist.
   (PN1B)   c. Wrong.   This describes systematic introspection, not a therapy.

10. **d**   a. Wrong.   Wilhelm Wundt established the first psychology lab.
    (p. 17) b. Wrong.   Carl Rogers developed humanistic psychology.
             c. Wrong.   Wasburn studied consciousness, and Calkins studied learning, not cultural differences.

11. **a**   b. Wrong.   This is the point of disagreement between psychoanalysis and humanism.
    (p. 16) c. Wrong.   This is not true, and behaviorists used animals in much of their research.
             d. Wrong.   This is not true of structuralism, and behaviorists were equally deterministic.

12. **a**   b. Wrong.   Computers provided a model of the mind and promoted the cognitive revolution.
    (p. 21) c. Wrong.   Cognitive revolution only refers to the shift from behaviorism to a cognitive view.
             d. Wrong.   Freud's theory did raise a furor, but not the cognitive revolution.

13. **b**   a. Wrong.   The humanistic approach stresses personal choice and potential.
    (p. 21) c. Wrong.   The biological approach stresses the biochemical and cellular activity of the brain.
             d. Wrong.   The behaviorist approach stresses the influence of experience and the environment.

14. **a**   b. Wrong.   The humanistic approach utilizes a single philosophy, centered on personal growth.
(p. 20)   c. Wrong.   The nativist approach emphasizes the influence of innate tendencies.
          d. Wrong.   The behaviorist approach utilizes a single philosophy, centered on experience.

15. **c**   a. Wrong.   An eclectic orientation is an orientation that uses many different ideas.
(p. 10)   b. Wrong.   Gestalt principles relate to perceptual organization, not functional relations.
          d. Wrong.   Unnatural mappings make use more difficult and are avoided in human factors design.

Multiple Choice Pretest 2

1. **b**   a. Wrong.   A clinical psychologist is a Ph.D., not an M.D. (medical doctor).
(p. 9)   c. Wrong.   Applied psychologists work with practical environmental problems, not mental problems.
          d. Wrong.   Cognitive psychologists study primarily normal thought processes, not mental problems.

2. **b**   a. Wrong.   Clinical psychologists include clinical and counseling psychologists.
(p. 11)   c. Wrong.   Applied psychologists are school, industrial/organizational, and human factors psychologists.
          d. Wrong.   Counseling psychologists fall within the category of clinical psychology.

3. **c**   a. Wrong.   Descartes believed the mind and body should be considered separate.
(p. 12)   b. Wrong.   This is the modern view, not the view of Descartes.
          d. Wrong.   Descartes did not believe in complete separation.

4. **b**   a. Wrong.   The philosophical, not scientific, roots of psychology began in Greece at about this time.
(p. 14)   c. Wrong.   Freud's psychoanalysis originated in Vienna at about this time.
          d. Wrong.   Psychology did not originate in America; this is the origin of early behaviorism.

5. **a**   b.   Wrong.   Your friend's view is fairly similar to the interactionist theory of Descartes.
(p. 12)   c & d.   Wrong.   The nature-nurture problem involves the origin of knowledge, not mind-body issues.

6. **a**   b. Wrong.   Watson, a behaviorist, stressed studying observable behavior.
(p. 19)   c. Wrong.   Wundt, a structuralist, used systematic introspection.
          d. Wrong.   James, a functionalist, was interested in the adaptive function of the mind and behavior.

7. **c**   a. Wrong.   Functionalism stresses discovering the function of an experience, not the contents.
(p. 15)   b. Wrong.   Behaviorism stresses studying only observable behaviors, not consciousness.
(PN1B)   d. Wrong.   Psychoanalysis stresses the discovery of hidden conflicts that affect behavior.

8. **c**   a. Wrong.   Structuralism was more concerned with the mind than stimulus-response relations.
(p. 17)   b. Wrong.   Functionalism was more concerned with the adaptive function of behavior.
          d. Wrong.   Cognitive psychologists are more concerned with mental processes behind behavior.

9. **d**   a. Wrong.   This is functionalism and humanism.
(pp. 16,18)   b. Wrong.   This is humanism and psychoanalysis.
          c. Wrong.   This is the biological approach and behaviorism.

10. **d**   a. Wrong.   This view would put you on the "nature" (genes, biology) side.
(p. 12)   b. Wrong.   *Tabula rasa* emphasizes experience, or the "nurture" factor.
          c. Wrong.   This view would put you on the "nature" (genes, biology) side.

11.	**c**	a.	Wrong.	Psychoanalysis stresses the unconscious and determinism.
	(p. 19)	b.	Wrong.	Empiricism is the idea that knowledge results from experience.
		d.	Wrong.	Cognitive psychology stresses information processing.

12.	**d**	a.	Wrong.	The humanist view stresses the potential for personal growth, not cultural variables.
	(p. 23)	b.	Wrong.	Psychoanalysis emphasizes unconscious influences, not cultural differences.
		c.	Wrong.	Cognitive research involved memory and thinking, not differences in dating behavior.

13.	**d**	a.	Wrong.	Behaviorist aspects are present, but the variety of emphases describes an eclectic approach.
	(p. 20)	b.	Wrong.	Cognitive aspects are present, but the variety of emphases describes and eclectic approach.
		c.	Wrong.	Nothing was said about unconscious components or other aspects of psychoanalytic theory.

14.	**c**	a.	Wrong.	Belief in innate mechanisms is not very characteristic of behaviorists.
	(p. 23)	b.	Wrong.	Humanists emphasize the potential for self-growth, not innate mechanisms of behavior.
		d.	Wrong.	Human factors psychologists believe humans have certain behavioral tendencies, but not necessarily that these are innate or due to natural selection.

CHAPTER 2: THE TACTICS OF PSYCHOLOGICAL RESEARCH

ESTABLISHING LEARNING GOALS

Use these learning goals as a preview of the chapter, a guide for active reading, and to evaluate your mastery of the material. Review the relevant goals as you begin and end your reading of each major section of the chapter.

I. Describe the role of the scientific method in psychology.
    A. Describe the scientific method.
    B. Identify the roles of observation and operational definitions.

II. Solve the practical problem of how best to observe and describe behavior.
    A. Describe the techniques and goals of descriptive research.
    B. Explain how psychologists conduct naturalistic research.
        1. Discuss possible solutions to the practical problem of making truly unobtrusive observations.
        2. Evaluate the strengths and weaknesses of the naturalistic observation procedure.
    C. Discuss the gains and costs of case studies and surveys.
        1. Discuss the problem of external validity in relation to surveys and case studies.
        2. Explain how and why representative samples are obtained.
    D. Describe the major purpose of psychological tests.
    E. Explain how statistics can summarize and help interpret data.
        1. Define central tendency and variability, and discuss why both types of measures are needed.
        2. Compare descriptive and inferential statistics.

III. Solve the practical problem of how to predict behavior.
    A. Define correlation and discuss how correlations can be used to predict behavior.
        1. Compare positive and negative correlations, and give examples of each.
        2. Characterize the relationship between two variables based on the correlation coefficient.
    B. Explain why correlations cannot normally be used to determine the cause of behavior.

IV. Solve the practical problem of determining why a behavior occurs.
    A. Define experimental research and explain why experiments are conducted.
    B. Discuss the differences between independent and dependent variables.
    C. Explain what is meant by experimental control and how it allows for the determination of causality.
        1. Discuss the problem of confounded variables and how they can be avoided.
        2. Describe random assignment, and explain why it is used.
    D. Describe the problems caused by expectancies and biases and how these problems are solved.
    E. Discuss the problems associated with generalizing experimental conclusions.

V. Solve the practical problem of how to ensure research participants are treated ethically.
    A. Explain the principle of informed consent.
    B. Discuss the roles of debriefing and confidentiality in research.
    C. Discuss the ethical issues involved in animal research.

MASTERING THE MATERIAL

Preview & Observing Behavior: Descriptive Research (pp. 32-43)

Mastering the Vocabulary. Define or explain each of the following terms. To check your answers, consult the text pages listed.

1.   scientific method (p. 32)

2.   operational definition (p. 33)

3.   descriptive research (p. 34)

4.   reactivity (p. 34)

5.   external validity (p. 34)

6.   naturalistic observation (p. 34)

7.   participant observation (p. 35)

8.   case study (p. 36)

9.   survey (p. 37)

10. random sampling (p. 38)

11. achievement test (p. 39)

12. aptitude test (p. 39)

13. mean (p. 40)

14. mode (p. 40)

15. median (p. 40)

16. variability (p. 40)

17. range (p. 41)

18. standard deviation (p. 41)

19. descriptive statistics (p. 41)

20. inferential statistics (p. 42)

21. law of large numbers (p. 43)

Mastering the Concepts. Fill in the blanks to create a summary of the section. Answers are on page 38.

Psychology uses the _____(1) method to examine the mind and behavior. This approach involves four steps: _____(2) of a behavior, detection of _____(3) in the data, the generation of a _____(4), and additional observations to check the _____(5) of the hypothesis. To ensure that psychological terms or concepts can be observed, _____ (6) definitions are used.

This chapter examines four conceptual and practical problems: how to observe and describe behavior; how to _____(7) behavior; how to determine what _____(8) a behavior; and how to ensure research participants are treated ethically.

_____(9) research involves observing and describing behavior. One possible problem is that the observer's presence can cause _____(10), a change in behavior caused by being observed. As a result, observations will not _____(11) to other situations and will lack _____(12) validity. This problem can be reduced by using unobtrusive techniques such as _____(13) observation, in which behavior is observed in its natural environment without interference by the experimenter. In a related method, _____(14) observation, the experimenter becomes a participant in the activities of interest. _____(15) observation, examining the aftereffects of a behavior, is also useful for avoiding reactivity.

A _____(16) involves detailed observations of a single person. The detailed information helps develop hypotheses, but because only one person is observed, _____(17) validity may be poor, and verifying the accuracy of the information is difficult. _____(18) relationships cannot be determined.

23

Another approach, using _____(19), gathers less detailed information from many individuals. To get representative data and to avoid bias, _____(20) sampling must be used. Every member of a population must have an equal chance of participation. Limitations of surveys include a lack of in-depth information and poor _____(21) of the information, so surveys often are combined with other techniques.

Psychological testing can be used to measure _____(22) differences. Achievement tests measure current level of knowledge, while _____(23) tests measure potential ability.

_____(24) are used to summarize and interpret the results of observations. Measures of central tendency describe the point at which scores tend to cluster and include the _____(25) (average), the _____(26) (most frequent), and the _____(27) (middle score). Measures of _____(28) describe how far apart scores are spread and include the _____(29) and the standard deviation.

_____(30) statistics are used to decide whether the data are representative and to evaluate the probability that observed differences are due to chance. If the probability of being due to chance is 5% or less, the difference is statistically _____(31).

Without a statistical education, people often draw general conclusions based on only a few observations. This violates the law of _____(32), which states larger samples are more likely than smaller samples to accurately represent the entire population.

Evaluating Your Progress. Select the one best response. Answers are on page 38. If you make any errors, reread the relevant material before proceeding.

1. The scientific method begins and ends with
   a. observation.
   b. operational definitions.
   c. data analysis.
   d. detecting regularities in behavior.

2. An operational definition defines a concept in terms of
   a. the most current hypothesis concerning the concept.
   b. how the concept can be measured.
   c. a tentative hypothesis.
   d. the most general and abstract characteristics of the concept.

3. If you study one person in great detail, you are using
   a. a survey.
   b. inferential statistics.
   c. a case study.
   d. naturalistic observation.

4. People's behavior sometimes changes simply because they are being observed. This effect is known as
    a. external validity.
    b. standard deviation.
    c. reactivity.
    d   experimental control.

5. What technique is used to obtain a representative sample of a population?
    a. naturalistic observation
    b. participant observation
    c. random sampling
    d. voluntary, self-selection by participants

6. What statistic identifies a typical score in your data or the value around which the scores cluster?
    a. the standard deviation statistic
    b. a measure of external validity
    c. a measure of variability
    d. a measure of central tendency

7. Inferential statistics are used to help
    a. increase external validity.
    b. measure the central tendency of the data.
    c. reduce the variability in the data.
    d. interpret the results of research.

8. What is the law of large numbers?
    a. The larger the sample size, the more likely observations will accurately represent the population.
    b. The larger the number of possible outcomes, the more likely the conclusion will be wrong.
    c. The more people surveyed, the less agreement there will be in the responses.
    d. The larger the number of observations, the more chance there will be careless errors.

Predicting Behavior: Correlational Research (pp. 44-47)

Mastering the Vocabulary. Define or explain each of the following terms. To check your answers, consult the text pages listed.

1. correlation (p. 44)

2. positive correlation (p. 45)

3. negative correlation (p. 45)

Mastering the Concepts. Fill in the blanks to create a summary of the section. Answers are on page 38.

Another purpose of research is to predict behavior. _____(33) research looks for relationships between behaviors. A correlation (or correlation coefficient) reflects the way and degree to which two measures of behavior vary systematically together. _____(34) correlations indicate that the measures vary in the same direction; _____(35) correlations indicate that the measures vary in opposite directions. The strength of the correlation, determined by how close the coefficient is to 1.0 (or -1.0), reflects the variability of the relationship. Zero correlations indicate no statistical relationship. Correlations describe relationships, but they do not prove _____(36) and effect, mainly because of the problem of possible _____ (37) variables.

Evaluating Your Progress. Select the one best response. Answers are found on page 39. If you make any errors, reread the relevant material before proceeding.

1. Which is false concerning correlational research?
   a. Measures of two variables are obtained from each person in the group.
   b. Correlational research can be used to predict behavior.
   c. Correlational research can establish the cause of a behavior.
   d. Correlational research determines whether there is a relationship between two variables.

2. Suppose the correlation between behaviors X and Y is +0.90. This means that
   a. as Behavior X increases, Behavior Y would be expected to increase.
   b. as Behavior X increases, Behavior Y would be expected to decrease.
   c. as Behavior X decreases, Behavior Y would be expected to increase.
   d. there is no predictable relationship between Behavior X and Behavior Y.

3. Which of the following correlation coefficients represents the strongest (most reliable) relationship?
   a. +0.50
   b. +0.20
   c. -0.10
   d. -0.60

Explaining Behavior: Experimental Research (pp. 48-55)

Mastering the Vocabulary. Define or explain each of the following terms. To check your answers, consult the text pages listed.

1. experimental research (p. 48)

2. independent variable (p. 49)

3.   dependent variable (p. 49)

4.   confounding variable (p. 51)

5.   internal validity (p. 51)

6.   random assignment (pp. 52)

7.   placebo (p. 53)

8.   single-blind study (p. 53)

9.   double-blind study (p. 54)

Mastering the Concepts. Fill in the blanks to create a summary of the section. Answers are on page 38.

Experiments can evaluate the cause of behavior because _____(38) is possible. Experiments differ from correlational studies because the experimenter directly _____(39) some environmental condition thought to influence the behavior being studied. The condition that is varied is the _____(40) variable. The experimenter observes behavior to see whether it changes when conditions change. The behavior observed and measured is called the _____(41) variable.

To make cause-effect statements, the only systematic changes in the experimental conditions that can occur are those of the independent variable. For this reason, two groups are used: an _____ (42) group, which receives the independent variable manipulation, and a _____(43) group, which does not. If a _____(44) variable, an uncontrolled variable that varies systematically with the independent variable, is present, differences between groups might be due to this variable rather than the independent variable, and the experiment will have poor _____(45) validity. Experimenters control as many variables as possible and use _____(46) assignment to reduce initial differences between groups.

The expectations of the subjects and the experimenter can influence their behavior and the research outcome. This is controlled by using placebos or misleading information to equate people's expectations or by restricting the available information. _____(47) studies keep the experimental condition secret from the subject to avoid subject expectancy effects. _____(48) studies keep group membership secret from subjects and experimenter to avoid both subject and experimenter expectancy effects.

Laboratory research often has good _____ (49) validity and generalizes to natural environments, but the control needed to prove cause-effect may lead to behavior that would not occur in natural environments.

Evaluating Your Progress. Select the one best response. Answers are on page 39. If you make any errors, reread the relevant material before proceeding.

1. In an experiment, the researcher
   a. makes observations of naturally occurring behavior and does not interfere in any way.
   b. changes some aspect of the environment and observes the effect of that change.
   c. takes measurements of two variables for every person in the group being observed.
   d. examines one person in great detail.

2. What is the independent variable in an experiment?
   a. the behavior that is being measured
   b. a characteristic that is not under experimental control
   c. an environmental condition that is manipulated by the experimenter
   d. a group of participants not given the experimental treatment (e.g., gets no drug)

3. A confounding variable in an experiment is an uncontrolled variable that
   a. varies systematically with the independent variable.
   b. increases the internal validity of the experiment.
   c. reduces the problem of expectancy effects.
   d. is produced by random assignment.

4. How would members of the control group be treated in a study on the effect of caffeine on heart rate?
   a. They would drink coffee with caffeine.
   b. They would drink coffee with no caffeine.
   c. They would not have their heart rate measured.
   d. They would be tested at home, not in a laboratory.

5. If random assignment is used, researchers assume differences in group performance are not due to
   a. experimenter expectancies about the experiment.
   b. subject expectancies about the experiment.
   c. differences in the personal characteristics of subjects in each group.
   d. the environmental conditions that are intentionally manipulated in the experiment.

6. A placebo is used in drug studies to
   a. equate subject expectancies.
   b. avoid the need for a control group.
   c. fulfill the requirements for ethical research.
   d. increase the likelihood of confounding variables.

7. To avoid experimenter expectancy effects, researchers use
   a. a control group.
   b. at least two dependent variables.
   c. a single-blind procedure.
   d. a double-blind procedure.

The Ethics of Research: Human and Animal Guidelines (pp. 55-58)

Mastering the Vocabulary. Define or explain each of the following terms. To check your answers, consult the text pages listed.

1. informed consent (p. 56)

2. debriefing (p. 57)

3. confidentiality (p. 57)

Mastering the Concepts. Fill in the blanks to create a summary of this section. Answers are on page 38.

Researchers follow ethical guidelines to protect the rights of research participants. One requirement is _____(50) consent, consent given after information about the risks and procedures of the research have been provided. Deception is allowed if it does not involve potential harm and would not affect the person's willingness to participate. Researchers also _____(51) participants by explaining the research, and must protect their privacy by maintaining the _____(52) of personal information.

Ethical requirements have been established that require animals be treated humanely and given proper care. Animal research is important because of the greater ability to _____(53) the environment, to complete studies rapidly, and to deal with simpler systems. In spite of criticisms that conclusions from animal research are invalid for humans, many findings do generalize.

Evaluating Your Progress. Select the one best response. Answers are on page 40. If you make any errors, reread the relevant material before proceeding.

1. Telling potential research participants the nature and possible risks of the research prior to their participation is part of the ethical requirement of
   a. debriefing.
   b. informed consent.
   c. confidentiality.
   d. compensation.

2. Keeping personal information about research participants private is part of the ethical requirement of
   a. debriefing.
   b. informed consent.
   c. confidentiality.
   d. compensation.

3. Which of the following is not an advantage of using animals in research?
   a. There are no ethical requirements to be followed with animals.
   b. The environment and experiences of the animals can be tightly controlled.
   c. Some animals have simpler systems than humans, which makes research simpler.
   d. Animals often have short life spans, so developmental research may be conducted more quickly.

MAKING FINAL PREPARATIONS

Complete these sections without consulting your book or notes. For a more accurate estimate of how well you know this material, wait at least a day or two after studying the chapter before working on the questions. Some of the material you "know" immediately after working with the chapter will be quickly forgotten. Immediate tests will overestimate what you know well.

Short Essay Questions. Write a brief answer to each question. Sample answers are on page 40.

1. Briefly outline the four steps of the scientific method.

2. Compare measures of central tendency and measures of variability. Why are both needed?

3. Explain what a correlation describes, and give examples of positive and negative correlations.

4. Compare reactivity and expectancy effects, and explain how they can be reduced in research.

5. Why can experiments establish cause-effect relationships but correlational research cannot?

6. What is random assignment, and why is it used in experiments?

7. Identify and briefly explain the three major ethical requirements for research with humans.

Matching. Select the correct definition or description for each item. Answers are on page 41.

_____	1. positive correlation	**a.**	ability of data to generalize to other situations
_____	2. standard deviation	**b.**	a change in behavior because of being observed
_____	3. case study	**c.**	mathematical techniques used to describe data
_____	4. external validity	**d.**	detailed description of a single person
_____	5. reactivity	**e.**	subjects do not know their group assignment
_____	6. inferential statistics	**f.**	observing while taking part in the observed activity
_____	7. dependent variable	**g.**	measure of how much a score differs from the mean
_____	8. median	**h.**	mathematical techniques for evaluating data and estimating whether differences are due to chance
_____	9. negative correlation	**i.**	behavior that is measured in an experiment
_____	10. participant observation	**j.**	two variables related such that a change in one is accompanied by an opposite change in the other
_____	11. internal validity		
_____	12. independent variable	**k.**	condition manipulated by the experimenter
_____	13. descriptive statistics	**l.**	the middle point or score in a set of scores
_____	14. single-blind study	**m.**	two variables related such that a change in one is accompanied by similar changes in the other
		n.	amount of control over confounding variables

Multiple Choice Pretest 1. Select the one best response. Answers are on page 41.

1. Which describes the components of the scientific method in the correct order?
    a. hypothesis formation, observation, evaluation of hypothesis accuracy, observation
    b. hypothesis formation, observation, search for regularities in data, revision of hypothesis if needed
    c. observation, search for regularities in data, hypothesis formation, observation to check hypothesis
    d. observation, hypothesis formation, observation, search for regularities in data

2. Naturalistic observation, case studies, and surveys are all examples of
    a. descriptive research.
    b. experimental research.
    c. double-blind research designs.
    d. single-blind research designs.

3. Survey results will be more likely to accurately represent the opinions of the entire population if
    a. a control group is used.
    b. random sampling is used.
    c. a double-blind design is used.
    d. a single-blind design is used.

4. You obtained the following data (2, 2, 3, 5, 8). The mean, median, and mode of these data are
    a. 2, 3, 6
    b. 3, 3, 2
    c. 4, 3, 2
    d. 3, 3, 3

5. To study age differences in personal space, researchers sat in a mall and watched people walking and sitting together. What research approach did they use?
    a. a case study
    b. an experiment
    c. a survey
    d. naturalistic observation

6. Correlations
    a. identify cause-effect relationships.
    b. are measures of central tendency.
    c. predict behavior.
    d. require the manipulation of some aspect of the environment.

7. Ed's class' average on Exam 1 was 75 and your class' average was 70. What should you use to help interpret the data and determine whether the difference is due to chance or to class differences?
    a. a measure of central tendency
    b. a measure of variability
    c. a descriptive statistic
    d. an inferential statistic

8. Which represents a positive correlation?
    a. Older drivers tend to have fewer accidents than younger drivers.
    b. People with less education tend to have lower salaries than people with more education.
    c. People with few friends have higher rates of depression than people with many friends.
    d. People who exercise a lot have lower cholesterol levels than people who exercise little.

9. You read that there is a statistically significant difference in the rate of depression among men and women. This means that the difference is not likely to be due to
    a. chance.
    b. reactivity.
    c. a confounded variable.
    d. an expectancy effect.

10. When results from laboratory research fail to predict behavior in the real world, the research lacks
    a. external validity.
    b. internal validity.
    c. an independent variable.
    d. a dependent variable.

11. To examine whether sleep deprivation reduces problem solving ability, researchers woke groups of 10 subjects after 2, 4, 6, or 8 hours of sleep and had them try to solve 5 difficult math problems. They found that subjects allowed 2 or 4 hours of sleep answered fewer problems correctly than subjects who had had 6 or 8 hours of sleep. The dependent variable in this experiment is
    a. the amount of sleep allowed.
    b. the number of math problems answered correctly.
    c. the number of subjects in each group (10).
    d. the personal backgrounds of the students who participated.

12. To determine the cause of a behavior researchers use
    a. a descriptive research method.
    b. a correlational research method.
    c. an experimental research method.
    d. all of the above

13. A potential problem of correlational research that limits the types of conclusions possible is
    a. negative correlations.
    b. participant observations.
    c. standard deviation.
    d. third variables.

14. Neither the subjects nor the experimenter recording the data knows which subject belongs to a particular group. This is an example of
    a. a confounding variable.
    b. random assignment.
    c. a single-blind experiment.
    d. a double-blind experiment.

15. After Chris finished the experiment, she was given a sheet explaining the purpose of the research and the name of a person to contact for any further information. This was part of the ethical requirement of
    a. humane treatment.
    b. informed consent.
    c. debriefing.
    d. confidentiality.

16. The law of large numbers suggests conclusions should not be based on limited observations because
    a. behavior is variable.
    b. negative correlations are possible.
    c. reactivity is possible.
    d. expectancy effects are possible.

Multiple Choice Pretest 2. Select the one best response. Answers are on page 42.

1. A good operational definition of aggression might be
    a. "the number of times someone hits, kicks, or yells at a person or object within a 1 hour period."
    b. "behavior intended to harm someone or something."
    c. "a violent response most often accompanying frustration or anger directed toward someone."
    d. "a personality characteristic in which the individual tends to solve problems with violence."

2. An advice columnist asked her readers to write and tell her whether they prefer being cuddled or having sex. Most responses were in favor of cuddling. Why should we hesitate to accept these data?
    a. There is too much opportunity for reactivity to influence the data.
    b. Random selection of participants was not used in the survey.
    c. A placebo was not used in the survey.
    d. Surveys can't determine cause-effect relationships.

3. Production at the factory was poor, so management had a team of observers film the workers on the job. The films showed everyone working at top speed, and production was the highest in a year. A likely explanation for the change in the workers' behavior is
   a. external validity.
   b. placebo effect.
   c. reactivity.
   d. random assignment.

4. Channel 6 News heard reports that a bar was serving watered down liquor. They had a reporter get a job as a bartender so he could find out how the liquor was handled. This technique is
   a. a case study.
   b. introspection.
   c. participant observation.
   d. naturalistic observation.

5. To determine a person's potential for success in a particular occupation, rather than the person's current level of knowledge, researcher would use
   a. an aptitude test.
   b. an achievement test.
   c. measures of central tendency.
   d. correlation coefficients.

6. Range and standard deviation represent
   a. correlations.
   b. the average score.
   c. central tendency.
   d. variability.

7. The primary advantage of experimental research over correlational research is that experiments
   a. are easier to conduct than correlational studies.
   b. use descriptive statistics rather than inferential statistics.
   c. involve more natural behavior than correlational studies.
   d. can determine cause-effect relationships.

8. Sam, an autistic boy, took part in Dr. John's new therapy program. Dr. John's reported Sam's behavior in great detail to argue his new program works. The research technique used here was
   a. an experiment.
   b. naturalistic observation.
   c. a case study.
   d. a single-blind procedure.

9. Seat location and course grades are correlated. The closer to the front students sit, the higher their grades. Motivation might actually cause both good grades and a preference for sitting near the front. In other words, there might be the problem of
   a. reactivity.
   b. a third variable.
   c. an unrepresentative sample.
   d. an expectancy effect.

10. Researchers found a moderate correlation between the length of a customer's driveway and the size of the tips the customer gave pizza delivery people. The longer the driveway, the smaller the tip the delivery person received. Which correlation coefficient most likely represents this relationship?
   a. +0.90
   b. +0.45
   c. -0.45
   d. -0.90

11. To discover whether highlighting terms in texts help students learn, researchers had one group of students read a biology chapter with highlighted terms and had another group read the same chapter with the terms in normal type. Both groups then took the same 10-item test over the material, and their test scores were recorded. The independent variable in this experiment was
   a. the format of the chapter (highlighted terms or no highlighting).
   b. the students' test performance (the test score).
   c. the content of the chapter (the factual material).
   d. the personal backgrounds of the students who participated (intelligence, age).

12. A researcher noticed that all 50 of the subjects given the "good mood" manipulation happened to be tested at 8:00 p.m., whereas all 50 of the subjects given the "bad mood" manipulation happened to be tested at 8:00 a.m. She found a statistically significant difference in the memory scores for the two groups. She is not sure she should conclude that mood affects memory. What is the likely cause of her uncertainty?
   a. Her research is not an experiment.
   b. The memory scores for the two conditions were significantly different.
   c. The time the subjects were tested is a confounding variable.
   d. She had the same number of subjects (50) in both groups.

13. Before beginning each experiment session, Kit reads aloud a description of what participants will be asked to do. Kit is fulfilling the ethical requirement of
   a. humane treatment.
   b. informed consent.
   c. debriefing.
   d. confidentiality.

14. Teachers in a small town are protesting because their pay raises are based on teaching evaluations of one class period each year. They claim that such limited sampling of their teaching is likely to produce inaccurate evaluations, and they want at least five observations. What concept supports their argument?
   a. operational definition
   b. random assignment
   c. placebo effect
   d. law of large numbers

15. All of the following are used to reduce the problem of expectancy effects or bias in research EXCEPT
   a. control groups.
   b. double-blind experiments.
   c. placebos.
   d. deception.

LANGUAGE DEVELOPMENT GUIDE

Core Terms

When you signed up for this course, you probably thought that a certain amount of what you would study would be "common sense." But it's the job of psychologists to question common sense, and to want to test it. Instead of "common sense," psychologists would use the term *intuitive* -- that is, coming from your intuition. You can't build a science on intuition or common sense; a science requires that before a fact is accepted as a fact it must be tested empirically. That means that psychologists have to set up some experiments to check whether things really work the way they seem to work.

Your instructor might use the term *classic* study or *seminal* study when describing an experiment. This is research that is very important because it proved some major fact to be true or because it changed the way people viewed a topic. *Seminal experiments* usually lead to a new theory and inspire many new experiments. When discussing a classic study, your professor might say something like, "This study clearly establishes *causality* between a lack of dopamine and Parkinson's disease." That means that the experiment is important because it showed that one thing (the amount of dopamine) causes another thing (Parkinson's disease). Remember, though, that some "classic" studies are discussed because of their impact in the past, not their current value. For example, because of problems with confirming it's accuracy, Freud's theory of personality is not the most popular theory, but it is discussed because of its past and current influence on psychology.

You might also hear other unfamiliar terms. The first is *methodology*, the specific procedures used in research. Your instructor might describe a study as having *rigorous* methodology, which means that the procedures used were very good and very carefully planned. In many cases, this will mean proper *controls* were used. The term *control* has several uses. The experimenter *controls* (has the power to determine or influence) the conditions in an experiment, such as controlling whether a room is cool or hot. The experimenter *controls for* (takes steps to avoid) differences in conditions that are not intended. A *control group* is an "untreated" group in an experiment, a neutral condition. Also, when your professor says an experiment must be *replicated*, the experiment must be repeated to show that the same results can be obtained again.

Idioms

p. 33	meet this criterion	to have the necessary characteristics; to meet one necessary requirement. (A criterion is one requirement; criteria are several.)
p. 36	a poor vehicle for determining causality	not a good way to tell whether one thing causes another
p. 36	phenomenon	an event; something that happens (plural is phenomena)
p. 38	establish the generality of	to show that something is common; to show that it is usually what happens
p. 36	place all their (theoretical) eggs in one basket	to unwisely depend upon just one thing to support you; for example, to build a whole theory on one example

p. 39	to characterize a person's tendencies to act in consistent ways	to describe the ways that a person usually acts
p. 43	attributed to chance	"blamed on" random factors; caused by chance
p. 46	a social outcry for the monitoring of televised violence	lots of people saying that they want violence on TV to be monitored by the government
p. 51	interpretation of the results will be hopelessly compromised	making sense of the results will be impossible
p. 54	a devastating critique	criticism that will make something useless
p. 57	justify the invasive procedures	have good reasons for using methods that invade (and might permanently hurt)
p. 57	advocated the complete elimination	spoke out for completely stopping
p. 58	can result in censure or termination of membership by the governing body of the association	can mean you are formally criticized by the organization, or that you are no longer allowed to belong to it

Word Parts

Here are some words that are made up of word parts, and that you can find in this chapter. After you've looked at these, you can look for others in the chapter that use the same word parts.

WORD	WORD PART IT USES	MEANING
advocated	ad = to, toward voc = voice, speak	to speak for
dependent	de = away, from, down pend = to hang	to hang upon, to require
incredibly	in = not cred = to believe	not believably
perspective	per = around spect = to look	a different view, a viewing angle
produce	pro = forward duc = to lead	to create, to make

Knowing the word parts listed above, you can also create the following words. You can get an idea of their meanings from the word parts they use. You fill in the blanks!

independent	in + de + pend	_____
conduct	_____ + _____	to lead together, bring together
reduce	re + duc	_____
inspect	_____ + _____	to look into, to look at closely
impending	_____ + _____	to hang in the balance; about to happen
deduce	de + duc	_____

Pronunciation

p. 53   placebo   pla-see'-bo   p. 57   debriefing   dee-breef'-ing

ANSWERS AND EXPLANATIONS

To find relevant material in your textbook, consult the pages cited with each answer. Also, PN and PT citations refer to modules in *PsychNow!* and *Psyk.trek* materials, respectively.

Mastering the Concepts

1. scientific (p. 32)
2. observation (p. 32)
3. regularities (p. 33)
4. hypothesis (p. 33)
5. accuracy (p. 33)
6. operational (p. 33)
7. predict (p. 33)
8. causes (p. 33)
9. Descriptive (p. 34)
10. reactivity (p. 34)
11. generalize (p. 34)
12. external (p. 34)
13. naturalistic (p. 34)
14. participant (p. 35)
15. Indirect (p. 35)
16. case study (p. 36)
17. external (p. 37)
18. Cause-effect (p. 37)
19. surveys (p. 37)
20. random (p. 38)
21. accuracy (p. 39)
22. individual (p. 39)
23. aptitude (p. 39)
24. Statistics (p. 40)
25. mean (p. 40)
26. mode (p. 40)
27. median (p. 40)
28. variability (p. 40)
29. range (p. 41)
30. Inferential (p. 41)
31. significant (p. 42)
32. large numbers (p. 43)
33. Correlational (p. 44)
34. Positive (p. 45)
35. negative (p. 45)
36. cause (p. 46)
37. third (p. 47)
38. control (p. 48)
39. manipulates (p. 48)
40. independent (p. 49)
41. dependent (p. 49)
42. experimental (p. 50)
43. control (p. 50)
44. confounding (p. 51)
45. internal (p. 51)
46. random (p. 52)
47. Single-blind (p. 53)
48. Double-blind (p. 54)
49. external (p. 54)
50. informed (p. 56)
51. debrief (p. 56)
52. confidentiality (p. 56)
53. control (p. 57)

Evaluating Your Progress

Preview & Observing Behavior

1.   **a**   b. Wrong.   Operational definitions are used early in the process, but not at the end.
  (p. 33)   c. Wrong.   Data analysis is done late in the process, but not at the beginning.
            d. Wrong.   Detecting regularities in the data is done after observation.

2. **b**　　a. Wrong. Measurement, not hypotheses, are the basis of operational definitions.
　(p. 33)　　c. Wrong. How the concept can be measured, not a hypothesis, is important.
　(PN1C)　　d. Wrong. Operational definitions are based on specific, objective measurements of the concept.

3. **c**　　a. Wrong. Surveys involve many people, not just one.
　(p. 36)　　b. Wrong. Inferential statistics are not standard with single participant research.
　　　　　　d. Wrong. Although naturalistic observation can involve a single person, this term would not be used to describe single participant studies in general.

4. **c**　　a. Wrong. External validity is the generalizablity of observations or conclusions to other situations.
　(p. 34)　　b. Wrong. Standard deviation is a descriptive statistic reflecting the variability of the data.
　　　　　　d. Wrong. Experimental control involves controlling or equating variables in an experiment.

5. **c**　　a & b.　Wrong. These are observation techniques, not ways to select research participants.
　(p. 38)　　d.　　　Wrong. Self-selection causes bias. Some people are more likely to volunteer than others.

6. **d**　　a. Wrong. Standard deviation is a measure of variability (spread) of the scores, not central tendency.
　(p. 40)　　b. Wrong. External validity refers to the extent to which data will generalize to other situations.
　(PT1C)　　c. Wrong. The question implies central tendency, not variability (spread).

7. **d**　　a. Wrong. The ability to generalize the results is not influenced by the statistic used.
　(p. 41)　　b. Wrong. Measures of central tendency and variability are descriptive, not inferential statistics.
　　　　　　c. Wrong. Statistics do not influence variability; they sometimes measure it.

8. **a**　　b, c, & d.　Wrong. The law of large numbers emphasizes the benefits of repeated observations.
　(p. 43)

Predicting Behavior: Correlational Research Methods

1. **c**　　a, b, & d.　Wrong. These statements are all true, but correlations can't prove cause-effect.
　(p. 46)
　(PN1D)

2. **a**　　b. Wrong. +0.90 is a positive correlation, so increases in X must be linked to increases in Y.
　(p. 45)　　c. Wrong. +0.90 is a positive correlation, so decreases in X must be linked to decreases in Y.
　(PT1D)　　d. Wrong. +0.90 is a strong correlation. A 0.00 correlation indicates no predictable relationship.

3. **d**　　a, b, & c.　Wrong. The sign (+) indicates the type, not strength, of a relationship. Strength is
　(p. 45)　　　　　　　　　　indicated by the absolute value of the coefficient. That is, ignore the + or - .

Explaining Behavior: Experimental Research Methods

1. **b**　　a. Wrong. This describes naturalistic observation, not an experiment.
　(p. 5148　　c. Wrong. This describes the correlational research method, not an experiment.
　　　　　　d. Wrong. This describes the case study method, not an experiment.

2. **c**　　a. Wrong. This describes the dependent variable.
　(p. 49)　　b. Wrong. This is similar to a confounding variable.
　(PT1D)　　d. Wrong. This describes a control group.

3. **a**　　b. Wrong. Confounding variables *reduce* internal validity.
　(p. 51)　　c. Wrong. Expectancy effects may be a confounding variable.
　　　　　　d. Wrong. Random assignment helps *reduce* the chance of confounding variables.

4. **b**   a. Wrong.   The experimental group would drink the caffeinated coffee.
(p. 50)   c. Wrong.   Control groups do not get the environmental manipulation, but they are tested.
(PN1C)   d. Wrong.   The testing location would be the same for both experimental and control groups.

5. **c**   a. Wrong.   Experimenter expectancy effects are not eliminated by random assignment.
(p. 52)   b. Wrong.   Subject expectancy effects are not eliminated by random assignment.
            d. Wrong.   Differences are *more* likely to be due to the experimental manipulation.

6. **a**   b. Wrong.   Placebos are usually given to the control group.
(p. 53)   c. Wrong.   Placebos are not required by ethical rules.
            d. Wrong.   Confounding variables (expectancy differences) are less likely with placebos.

7. **d**   a. Wrong.   A control group does not reduce experimenter expectancy effects.
(p. 54)   b. Wrong.   Expectancy is not related to the number of dependent variables.
            c. Wrong.   Single-blind procedures reduce *subject* expectancy effects

The Ethics of Research: Human and Animal Guidelines

1. **b**   a. Wrong.   Debriefing is disclosing the purpose of the research at its conclusion.
(p. 57)   c. Wrong.   Confidentiality involves keeping personal information private.
            d. Wrong.   There is no requirement that participants be compensated, but some are.

2. **c**   a. Wrong.   Debriefing is discussing the purpose of the research after someone participates.
(p. 57)   b. Wrong.   Informed consent involves getting the person's consent to participate after providing
                          information about the risks and nature of the research.
            d. Wrong.   There is no requirement that participants be compensated, but some are.

3. **a**   b, c, & d.   Wrong.   These are major advantages of using animals, but there are ethical requirements
(p. 57)   for animal research.

MAKING FINAL PREPARATIONS

Short Essay Questions

1. The four steps of the scientific method are: (1) Observations of a behavior are made. (2) The data are examined for systematic regularities. (3) An hypothesis is formulated. (4) More observations are made to evaluate the accuracy of the hypothesis. (pp. 32-33)

2. Measures of central tendency describe the point around which most data cluster. They describe a typical score. Measures of variability describe how the distribution of scores is spread out. To have the full description of the score distribution necessary to accurately interpret the data requires both types of measures. (pp. 40-41)

3. A correlation describes a relationship between two variables. In a positive correlation, both variables change in the same direction (e.g., height and shoe size: Taller people tend to have bigger feet than shorter people). In a negative correlation the variables change in opposite directions (e.g., class absences and grades: Students with many absences tend to have lower grades than those with few absences). (pp. 44-45)

4. Reactivity and expectancy effects are biases that can occur. Reactivity, a change in a subject's behavior caused by being observed, can lead to inaccurate conclusions. Expectancy effects, changes in a subject's (or experimenter's) behavior caused by their expectations about the research, also lead to errors. A solution is to restrict the subject's knowledge about the research. Naturalistic observation or other unobtrusive observation techniques can reduce reactivity. "Blind" designs, in which group assignments are not known, reduce expectancy effects. Deception also can be used. (pp. 34; 53-54)

5. Correlational research lacks the experimental control that is possible in experiments. By controlling for the influence of other variables, behavior changes can be attributed to the variables under study. (pp. 48)

6. In random assignment, participants have an equal chance to be assigned to any group in the experiment. This reduces group differences in uncontrolled variables and equates the characteristics of the groups. (pp. 51-52)

7. (1) Informed consent: Participants must be informed of the nature of the research and any possible effects of their participation and must give their consent prior to participating. (2) Debriefing: Participant must be informed about the purpose of the experiment and any deception after their participation. (3) Confidentiality: Personal information about participants must not be disclosed to other people. (pp. 56-57)

Matching

1. **m** (p. 45)	4. **a** (p. 34)	7. **i** (p. 49)	10. **f** (p. 35)	13. **c** (p. 41)
2. **g** (p. 41)	5. **b** (p. 34)	8. **l** (p. 40)	11. **n** (p. 51)	14. **e** (p. 53)
3. **d** (p. 36)	6. **h** (p. 31)	9. **j** (p. 45)	12. **k** (p. 49)	

Multiple Choice Pretest 1

1. **c**   a & b. Wrong. Observation comes first and is the basis of later hypothesis formation.
(pp. 32-33) d.   Wrong. Regularities in data are the basis for hypothesis formation and precede it.

2. **a**   b.   Wrong. Experiments involve manipulation of conditions; case studies, etc., don't.
(pp. 34-37) c & d. Wrong. "Blind" designs restrict information about group assignment, not relevant to surveys.

3. **b**   a. Wrong. Surveys can't include control groups; there is no variable being manipulated.
(p. 37)   c. Wrong. Double-blind designs can't be used in surveys; subjects aren't assigned to groups.
            d. Wrong. Single-blind designs can't be used in surveys; subjects aren't assigned to groups.

4. **c**   a, b, & d. Wrong. The mean (average) = (sum of scores / number of scores) = 20/5 = 4. The
(p. 40)   median is the middle score (3). The mode is the most common score (2).
(PT1C)

5. **d**   a. Wrong. A case study is a detailed study of one person; here, many people were observed.
(p. 34)   b. Wrong. They didn't manipulate any condition, so it wasn't an experiment.
            c. Wrong. Surveys are interviews or paper-and-pencil questionnaires.

6. **c**   a. Wrong. Correlations can't establish cause-effect relationships.
(p. 44)   b. Wrong. Measures of central tendency include mean, median, and mode, not correlations.
            d. Wrong. Experiments involve manipulations; correlations involve only observations.

7. **d**   a & b. Wrong. Inferential statistics indicate statistical significance, not descriptive statistics.
(p. 42)   c.   Wrong. You need an inferential statistic to test statistical significance.

8. **b**   a, c, & d. Wrong. Opposite changes equal negative correlation.
(p. 45)

9. **a**   b, c, & d. Wrong. Statistical significance only indicates a result is unlikely to be due to chance. It
(p. 42)   does not address whether or not the data are accurate or unbiased.

10. **a**   b. Wrong. Internal validity relates to having the proper controls, not generalizing to other settings.
(p. 54)   c. Wrong. Poor generalization can occur in experiments with independent variables.
            d. Wrong. If there are results from an experiment, there is a dependent variable.

11. **b**
(p. 49)
(PN1C)

a. Wrong. The amount of sleep is the independent variable.
c & d. Wrong. The dependent variable is the behavior that is measured.

12. **c**
(p. 48)

a, b, & d. Wrong. Only experiments determine cause-effect relationships.

13. **d**
(p. 47)

a. Wrong. Negative correlations are a specific type of relationship, not a limitation on conclusions.
b. Wrong. Participant observation is an observation technique, not a limitation on conclusions.
c. Wrong. Standard deviation is a measure of variability, not a limitation on conclusions.

14. **d**
(p. 54)

a. Wrong. Confounding variables are uncontrolled variables that vary systematically with the independent variable.
b. Wrong. Random assignment doesn't involve keeping group membership secret.
c. Wrong. A single-blind design keeps group membership secret from only the subject.

15. **c**
(p. 56)

a. Wrong. Humane treatment is proper care (usually referring to animals).
b. Wrong. Informed consent is obtained before a person participates.
d. Wrong. Confidentiality is the right to have personal information kept private.

16. **a**
(p. 43)

b. Wrong. Negative correlations aren't a problem, and don't relate to the law of large numbers.
c. Wrong. Reactivity is not eliminated by multiple observations.
d. Wrong. Expectancy effects are not found only when limited sampling is done.

Multiple Choice Pretest 2

1. **a**
(p. 33)
(PN1C)

b, c, & d. Wrong. These aren't based on how the concept of aggression can be measured directly.

2. **b**
(p. 38)

a. Wrong. Nobody was observed, so reactivity doesn't directly apply.
c. Wrong. A placebo is an inert substance used to prevent expectancy effects in drug studies.
d. Wrong. Surveys don't give cause-effect, but this question deals with description, not cause-effect.

3. **c**
(p. 34)

a. Wrong. External validity refers to the extent to which data will generalize to other situations.
b. Wrong. There's no reason here for an expectancy effect. Being observed was the key factor.
d. Wrong. Workers were not assigned to groups, so random assignment is not relevant.

4. **c**
(p. 35)

a. Wrong. A case study is a detailed description of an individual.
b. Wrong. The observations would involve external events, not personal, subjective experiences.
d. Wrong. In naturalistic observation the observer doesn't participate in the activities being studied.

5. **a**
(p. 39)

b. Wrong. Achievement tests evaluate a person's current state of knowledge or competence.
c. Wrong. Measures of central tendency are statistics that describe data, not tests potential success.
d. Wrong. Correlation coefficients are the mathematical representation of a correlation, not tests of potential success.

6. **d**
(p. 40)

a. Wrong. Range and standard deviation represent variability.
b. Wrong. The average (mean) represents central tendency; range and standard deviation represent variability.
c. Wrong. Mean, median, and mode represent central tendency.

7. **d** a. Wrong. Experiments are often more complicated than correlational studies.
(p. 48) b. Wrong. The data from experiments are analyzed using inferential statistics.
  c. Wrong. Experiments are sometimes criticized for their artificial behaviors and settings.

8. **c** a. Wrong. An experiment requires more than one person and systematic manipulation of a variable.
(p. 36) b. Wrong. Dr. Johnson did not merely observe Sam in his natural environment.
  d. Wrong. Single-blind procedures require an experiment; this is not an experiment.

9. **b** a. Wrong. The additional variable (motivation) is important here, not changes due to being observed.
(p. 47) c. Wrong. The additional variable (motivation) is important here, not how participants were selected.
  d. Wrong. The additional variable (motivation) is important here, not bias.

10. **c** a. Wrong. +0.90 is a strong positive correlation, not a moderate negative correlation.
(p. 45) b. Wrong. +0.45 is a positive correlation, not a negative correlation.
  d. Wrong. -0.90 is a strong negative correlation, not a moderate one.

11. **a** b. Wrong. Test performance is the dependent variable.
(p. 49) c. Wrong. Content was held constant; independent variables are manipulated by the experimenter.
(PT1B) d. Wrong. Personal background was not manipulated, so it isn't the independent variable.

12. **c** a. Wrong. This is an experiment, so cause-effect conclusions are possible.
(p. 51) b. Wrong. Significant differences are necessary for concluding mood affects memory.
  d. Wrong. Equal size groups is an example of experimental control and is necessary and good.

13. **b** a. Wrong. Humane treatment involves the experimental manipulation or living conditions, not
(p. 56)   knowing what the experiment is about.
  c. Wrong. Debriefing is telling the person about the purpose of the experiment after it is over.
  d. Wrong. Confidentiality involves keeping information about *participants* private.

14. **d** a. Wrong. There's no argument over defining good teaching, just the accuracy of single samples.
(p. 43) b. Wrong. Randomly assigning subjects to groups is not involved here.
  c. Wrong. A placebo effect, subject expectancies influencing behavior, is not an issue here.

15. **a** b. Wrong. Double-blind designs reduce expectancy effects by keeping group identity secret.
(p. 53) c. Wrong. Placebos are inactive substances that keep secret whether a subject is getting a drug.
  d. Wrong. Deception to keep secret the true purpose of the study reduces expectancy effects.

CHAPTER 3: BIOLOGICAL PROCESSES

ESTABLISHING LEARNING GOALS

Use these learning goals as a preview of the chapter, a guide for active reading, and to evaluate your mastery of the material. Review the relevant goals as you begin and end your reading of each major section of the chapter.

I. Solve the adaptive problem of how the nervous system communicates internally, linking world and brain.
    A. Describe the structure and function of neurons.
        1. Identify three types of neurons, and explain their functions.
        2. Describe how a reflex operates, and explain why reflexes are important.
        3. Identify the component parts of a neuron, and explain their functions.
    B. Explain how neurons transmit information.
        1. Define resting potential, and explain its adaptive role in neural transmission.
        2. Explain how action potentials are generated and travel down the axon.
        3. Explain the role of neurotransmitters in neural transmission.
        4. Identify three common neurotransmitters and the behaviors with which they are associated.
        5. Explain how drugs effect the nervous system to alter behavior.
    C. Explain how neurons work together to communicate.
        1. Explain how information is represented and communicated by neurons.
        2. Describe how computerized "neural" networks can simulate brain activities.

II. Solve the adaptive problem of how the nervous system initiates and coordinates behavior efficiently.
    A. Describe the basic organization of the nervous system.
    B. Describe the techniques researchers use to study the brain.
    C. Describe the major structures of the brain and the functions associated with each structure.
        1. Identify the structures of the hindbrain, midbrain, and forebrain and their major functions.
        2. Describe the organizational structure of the cortex, and identify the higher mental functions associated with each area.
    D. Explain how the two hemispheres divide and coordinate brain functions.
        1. Describe what happens when the two hemispheres are surgically "split."
        2. Summarize the current view concerning lateralization of hemispheric functions.

III. Solve the adaptive problem of how to regulate growth and internal functions.
    A. Explain how the endocrine system controls long-term and widespread communication needs.
    B. Discuss the role that hormones play in establishing sexual identity and gender-specific behaviors.

IV. Solve the adaptive problem of how to store and transmit the genetic code.
    A. Review natural selection and adaptation.
    B. Describe the basic principles of the genetic transmission.
    C. Explain how psychologists study genetic influences on behavior.

MASTERING THE MATERIAL

Preview & Communicating Internally: *Connecting World and Brain*   (pp. 64-75)

Mastering the Vocabulary. Define or explain each of the following terms. To check your answers, consult the text pages listed.

1.   neuroscience (p. 64)

2.   central nervous system (p. 64)

3.   peripheral nervous system (p. 64)

4.   neuron (p. 66)

5.   sensory neuron (p. 66)

6.   interneuron (p. 66)

7.   motor neuron (p. 66)

8.   glial cell (p. 66)

9.   myelin sheath (p. 66)

10. reflexes (p. 67)

11. dendrites (p. 68)

12. soma (p. 68)

13. axon (p. 68)

14. terminal buttons (p. 68)

15. synapse (p. 68)

16. resting potential (p. 68)

17. action potential (p. 69)

18. depolarization (p. 69)

19. hyperpolarization (p. 69)

20. neurotransmitters (p. 70)

21. acetylcholine (p. 71)

22. dopamine (p. 71)

23. serotonin (p. 72)

24. GABA (p. 72)

25. endorphins (p. 72)

26. refractory period (p. 73)

Mastering the Concepts. Fill in the blanks to create a summary of the section. Answers are on page 64.

All behavior originates in the _____(1). Brain cells interact to form a communication network and to control behavior. The _____(2) and _____(3) make up the central nervous system. The _____(4) nervous system, the remaining nerves, links the central nervous system and the body.

This chapter addresses four adaptive problems: How does internal communication occur to allow adaptation to the environment? How does the brain initiate and _____(5) behavior? How are _____(6) and internal functions regulated? How is the _____(7) code stored and transmitted?

_____(8) are cells of the nervous system and come in three major types. _____(9) neurons contact the environment and carry messages to the spinal cord and brain. _____(10) serve as links between neurons. _____(11) neurons carry information from the brain and spinal cord to muscles and glands. The nervous system also contains _____(12) cells that perform "housekeeping" functions and form the _____(13) sheath, a kind of insulation on some neurons. Not all behavior is controlled by the brain. The spinal _____(14), in which responses originate in the spinal cord, allows a speedier response than one initiated in the brain.

Neurons are composed of four major parts. _____(15) are branches that receive and transfer input to the _____(16), the main body of the cell. The _____(17) transmits input (in the form of an action potential) to another cell. In the end of the axon's branches are _____(18) that contain chemicals that communicate with the next cell. Neurons are separated by a space, the _____(19).

If inactive, neurons have a _____(20), or imbalance of ions inside and outside the cell. Stimulation causes ion movement and either _____(21) or _____(22), depending on whether the stimulation is excitatory or inhibitory. If depolarization occurs, an _____(23) is generated. Action potentials are _____(24); they either occur or not. They have a constant speed and intensity, but axon size affects the speed. Nodes of Ranvier are _____ (25) in the myelin that increase transmission speed.

Neurotransmitters flow into the synapse and contact the next cell, stimulating or inhibiting initiation of another action potential. Neurotransmitters include acetylcholine, serotonin, GABA and _____(26). Imbalances cause physical and mental disorders. Some drugs act as _____(27) and mimic neurotransmitters, or as _____(28) and block neurotransmitter action. _____(29), natural painkillers in the body, are neuromodulators that influence neurotransmitter levels.

Information is represented by the _____(30) of activation across many neurons and by changes in the neuron's _____(31). A _____(32) period when neurons cannot fire again limits firing rate. Computer programs simulate neural _____(33) and behave in brain-like ways. Input is represented by the _____(34) activity of many units.

Evaluating Your Progress. Select the one best response. Answers are on page 64. If you make any errors, reread the relevant material before proceeding.

1. The type of neuron that is a communication link between the world and the spinal cord or brain is the
    a. motor neuron.
    b. sensory neuron.
    c. glial neuron.
    d. interneuron.

2. The neuron's branching fibers that receive input from a sensory organ or another neuron are called
   a. cell bodies.
   b. axons.
   c. terminal buttons.
   d. dendrites.

3. The pathway information travels in a spinal reflex is
   a. sensory neuron, interneuron, motor neuron.
   b. motor neuron, interneuron, sensory neuron.
   c. sensory neuron, brain, motor neuron.
   d. motor neuron, brain, sensory neuron.

4. The resting potential is caused by
   a. an uneven distribution of charged ions inside and outside the neuron.
   b. neurotransmitters being released by the terminal buttons of the neuron.
   c. a change in the axon cell membrane that allows depolarization of the neuron.
   d. strong input from another neuron stimulating the dendrites of the cell.

5. Action potentials
   a. are larger if the stimulus is intense rather than weak.
   b. travel faster if the stimulus is intense rather than weak.
   c. are generated along the axon.
   d. all of the above

6. The fluid-filled space between neurons is
   a. the interneuron.
   b. the soma.
   c. the synapse.
   d. the node of Ranvier.

7. The neural impulse is transferred to the next neuron via
   a. interneurons in the synapse.
   b. the myelin sheath.
   c. the sodium-potassium pump.
   d. neurotransmitters.

8. Parkinson's disease and schizophrenia both involve imbalances of the neurotransmitter
   a. acetylcholine.
   b. endorphin.
   c. dopamine.
   d. serotonin.

9. Stimulus characteristics are represented in the nervous system by the pattern of activation and the
   a. specific neurotransmitter involved in neural transmission.
   b. firing rates of the neurons.
   c. refractory period of the neurons.
   d. speed of neural transmission.

Initiating Behavior: A Division of Labor (pp. 75-90)

Mastering the Vocabulary. Define or explain each of the following terms. To check your answers, consult the text pages listed.

1. nerves (p. 76)

2. somatic system (p. 77)

3. autonomic system (p. 77)

4. electroencephalograph (EEG) (p. 79)

5. computerized tomography scan (CT scan) (p. 79)

6. positron emission tomography (PET) (p. 79)

7. magnetic resonance imaging (MRI) (p. 80)

8. hindbrain (p. 81)

9. medulla (p. 81)

10. pons (p. 81)

11. reticular formation (p. 82)

12. cerebellum (p. 82)

13. midbrain (p. 82)

14. forebrain (p. 83)

15. cerebral cortex (p. 83)

16. thalamus (p. 83)

17. hypothalamus (p. 83)

18. limbic system (p. 84)

19. amygdala (p. 84)

20. hippocampus (p. 84)

21. frontal lobe (p. 85)

22. parietal lobe (p. 86)

23. temporal lobe (p. 86)

24. occipital lobe (p. 87)

25. corpus callosum (p. 88)

Mastering the Concepts. Fill in the blanks to create a summary of this section. Answers are on page 64.

The two divisions of the nervous system are the _____(35) and the _____(36) nervous systems. Messages are sent to the brain via _____(37) (sensory) pathways and out from the brain via _____(38) (motor) pathways. The peripheral nervous system contains the _____(39) nervous system, which serves the sensory and motor systems, and the _____(40) nervous system, which controls basic bodily functions and adjusts the body to meet emergency situations.

Brain function is studied by recording brain activity, stimulating the brain, and examining the effects of _____(41). Changes in behavior associated with stimulation or destruction help link a function to an area of the brain. EEG, PET, and functional MRI record brain activity; MRI and CT reveal structures.

The brain is organized into three major regions: the _____(42), midbrain, and _____(43). The hindbrain contains the _____(44) and pons, which control life-support systems, the reticular formation, which controls arousal, and the _____(45), which is important for smooth, coordinated movements. The midbrain contains the tectum, which includes areas used to relay sensory input, and the

substantia nigra, which produces dopamine. Damage to the substantia nigra reduces dopamine and causes

_____(46) disease. The forebrain includes the _____(47) and subcortical structures, including

the thalamus, hypothalamus, and limbic system. The thalamus processes and relays _____(48) input.

The _____(49) is involved in eating, drinking, body temperature, sexual behavior and the control of

the pituitary. The _____(50) includes the amygdala, which is involved in emotion and motivation,

and the hippocampus, which is important for _____(51), and several other structures.

The cerebral hemisphere has four lobes. The _____(52) lobes contain the motor cortex, and

areas important for planning and thought. The _____(53) lobes contain the somatosensory area for

touch. The motor and somatosensory cortex are arranged topographically (areas close on the body are

handled by areas close in the brain) and the size of a body part's brain area is related to the sensitivity or

level of control of the body part. Auditory and language comprehenshion centers are in the _____(54)

lobe, with language usually processed by the left hemisphere. The occipital lobe processes visual input.

Processing also is lateralized, with each hemisphere handling certain tasks. The right hemisphere

receives input from and controls the _____(55) side of the body and the left visual field; the left

hemisphere receives input from and controls the right. Input is available to both hemispheres due to eye

movements and because a bridge of tissue, the _____(56), allows information from one side to

transfer to the other. Split-brain patients with no corpus callosum behave normally except in situations

that restrict both how information is received and how responses are made.

The hemispheres are specialized for certain tasks. The right hemisphere is important for

_____(57) tasks; the left hemisphere is important for verbal tasks. However, the hemispheres usually

work together, and ideas about "right-brained" or "left-brained" general styles have little scientific support.

Evaluating Your Progress. Select the one best response. Answers are on page 65. If you make any
errors, reread the relevant material before proceeding.

1. The central nervous system is composed of
    a. the parasympathetic and sympathetic divisions.
    b. the autonomic and somatic divisions.
    c. the brain and spinal cord.
    d. all the nerves outside the brain and spinal cord.

2. The nerves that transmit information to the muscles are part of the
    a. autonomic nervous system.
    b. somatic nervous system.
    c. parasympathetic nervous system.
    d. sympathetic nervous system.

3. To identify the function of an area of the brain you might use all of the following techniques except
   a. damaging the area of interest.
   b. stimulating the area of interest.
   c. doing positron emission tomography (PET).
   d. doing standard magnetic resonance imaging (MRI).

4. Basic life-support systems are controlled by the
   a. forebrain.
   b. midbrain.
   c. hindbrain.
   d. cerebral cortex.

5. The cerebral cortex, limbic system, and hypothalamus are part of the
   a. hindbrain.
   b. midbrain.
   c. forebrain.
   d. tectum.

6. Parkinson's disease patients lack an adequate amount of dopamine due to malfunction of the
   a. substantia nigra of the midbrain.
   b. medulla and pons of the hindbrain.
   c. hypothalamus of the forebrain.
   d. cerebral cortex of the forebrain.

7. Aggression and other motivational and emotional behaviors are controlled by the
   a. thalamus.
   b. reticular formation.
   c. cerebellum.
   d. limbic system.

8. Based on the case of Phineas Gage and other cases of brain damage, we might reasonably conclude that the sense of self or personality is associated with activity in the
   a. frontal lobe.
   b. occipital lobe.
   c. parietal lobe.
   d. temporal lobe.

9. If a picture of a dog is flashed on the far right and a picture of a cat is flashed on the far left, a person whose corpus callosum has been destroyed will
   a. say a cat was presented if asked to respond verbally.
   b. indicate a dog was presented if asked to point to a matching picture with the right hand.
   c. report that a half-dog, half-cat creature was presented if asked to draw the figure with either hand.
   d. be unable to remember what was presented, regardless of the type of response.

10. Which statement is true concerning the motor cortex and somatosensory cortex?
    a. The size of a brain area reflects the relative size of the body part controlled by that brain area.
    b. Areas that are near each other on the body are associated with brain areas that are near each other.
    c. The motor cortex is in the parietal lobe, and the somatosensory cortex is in the frontal lobe.
    d. The body's left side is associated with the motor and somatosensory cortex in the left hemisphere.

11. Most psychologists would agree that
    a. the idea of localization or lateralization of brain function has little scientific support.
    b. localization occurs for functions handled by subcortical structures, but not for cortical functions.
    c. almost all functions are highly localized or lateralized; each area works almost independently.
    d. even highly localized or lateralized tasks involve much cooperation between different brain areas.

Regulating Growth and Internal Functions: Extended Communication (pp. 91-94)

Mastering the Vocabulary. Define or explain each of the following terms. To check your answers, consult the text pages listed.

1. endocrine system (p. 91)

2. hormones (p. 91)

3. pituitary gland (p. 92)

Mastering the Concepts. Fill in the blanks to create a summary of the section. Answers are on page 64.

The _____ (58) system uses hormones to regulate growth and biological systems. Its activity is more widespread and of _____ (59) duration than neural activity. The brain, mostly the hypothalamus, controls the "master" endocrine gland, the _____ (60), which controls other endocrine glands, including those important for sexual and "fight or flight" behavior. Prenatal sex hormones may affect the brain and later gender behavior. Adult hormone levels may produce gender differences in mental tasks.

Evaluating Your Progress. Select the one best response. Answers are found on page 66. If you make any errors, reread the relevant material before proceeding.

1. The "master gland" of the body is the
    a. pituitary gland.
    b. adrenal gland.
    c. ovary or testes.
    d. pineal gland.

2. The nervous system controls the endocrine system, because the "master gland" is controlled by
    a. the cerebellum.
    b. the hippocampus.
    c. the hypothalamus.
    d. the medulla.

3. The communication system provided by the endocrine system complements that of the nervous system because the actions of the endocrine system are
   a. more localized and more short-term.
   b. more localized and more long-term.
   c. more widespread and more short-term.
   d. more widespread and more long-term.

4. Research on gender differences in behavior has found that high verbal ability is correlated with
   a. high levels of testosterone at the time of testing.
   b. high levels of estrogen at the time of testing.
   c. high levels of epinephrine during the prenatal period of development.
   d. high levels of norepinephrine during the prenatal period of development.

5. In the flight-or-fight response, which adapts the body in threatening situations, epinephrine is released by
   a. the pituitary gland.
   b. the hypothalamus.
   c. the adrenal glands.
   d. ovaries or testes.

Adapting and Transmitting the Genetic Code (pp. 94-97)

Mastering the Vocabulary. Define or explain each of the following terms. To check your answers, consult the text pages listed.

1. adaptation (p. 95)

2. genes (p. 96)

3. genotype (p. 96)

4. phenotype (p. 96)

5. mutation (p. 96)

6. family studies (p. 97)

7. twin studies (p. 97)

Mastering the Concepts. Fill in the blanks to create a summary of the section. Answers are on page 64.

The genetic code has two adaptive functions: providing a flexible blueprint for development, and providing for specific, often adaptive, traits to be transmitted to future generations. Humans have 23 pairs of chromosomes which contain the _____ (61) that determine personal traits. _____ (62) genes cause the expression of a trait even if the two genes for the trait differ. A matching pair of genes is needed for the expression of a _____ (63) trait. Most physical traits and behaviors are influenced by a complex interaction of many genes and environmental conditions. _____ (64) studies look for similarities in behavior among blood relatives. Comparisons of traits in identical and fraternal twins raised in same or different environments provide even better data about the genetic component of a trait.

Evaluating Your Progress. Select the one best response. Answers are on page 66. If you make any errors, reread the relevant material before proceeding.

1. A chromosome segment that contains instructions for the development of a hereditary trait is called
    a. a phenotype.
    b. an efferent.
    c. an afferent.
    d. a gene.

2. To differentiate the genetic and environmental components of schizophrenia, researchers might use
    a. twin studies.
    b. CT scan studies.
    c. MRI studies.
    d. EEG studies.

3. A person's phenotype concerning a genetic trait describes
    a. how many gene pairs determine the trait.
    b. whether the trait is dominant or recessive.
    c. the person's observable characteristics regarding a trait.
    d. the person's specific genetic pattern (AA, Aa, aa) regarding a trait.

4. If a trait is expressed even if the person has only one gene for that trait, the gene must be
    a. dominant.
    b. recessive.
    c. a mutation.
    d. adaptive.

5. To be an adaptation, a trait must be adaptive, economical, and
    a. dominant.
    b. recessive.
    c. physical.
    d. universal.

MAKING FINAL PREPARATIONS

Complete these sections without consulting your book or notes. For a more accurate estimate of how well you know this material, wait at least a day or two after studying the chapter before working on the questions. Some of the material you "know" immediately after working with the chapter will be quickly forgotten. Immediate tests will overestimate what you know well.

Short Essay Questions. Write a brief answer to each question. Sample answers are on page 67.

1. Explain how drugs work in the nervous system to cause changes in behavior.

2. Movement can be initiated either by the usual neural pathway or by a spinal reflex. Compare these pathways for removing your hand from a sharp object. Explain a spinal reflex's adaptive value.

3. Describe three techniques to determine structure-function relationships for the brain.

4. Imagine your left hemisphere has been removed. Describe and explain at least two effects.

5. Explain the adaptive nature of the genetic code.

Matching. Select the correct function for each structure. Answers are on page 67.

_____ 1. cerebellum	**a.** allows transfer of information between hemispheres
_____ 2. amygdala	**b.** releases neurotransmitters
_____ 3. hippocampus	**c.** processes touch and temperature input
_____ 4. glial cell	**d.** aids formation of memories
_____ 5. medulla	**e.** regulates basic functions (heart rate, respiration)
_____ 6. axon	**f.** coordinates smooth movements
_____ 7. substantia nigra	**g.** relays sensory information to the cortex
_____ 8. terminal button	**h.** controls cellular metabolism of neuron
_____ 9. reticular formation	**i.** controls other endocrine glands
_____ 10. soma	**j.** receives neural input from a sense organ or neuron
_____ 11. corpus callosum	**k.** controls eating, drinking and sexual behaviors
_____ 12. hypothalamus	**l.** generates and transmits the action potential
_____ 13. thalamus	**m.** produces dopamine
_____ 14. dendrite	**n.** insulates and assists in function of neuron
_____ 15. somatosensory cortex	**o.** controls aggression and motivational behaviors
_____ 16. pituitary	**p.** controls general arousal and consciousness

Multiple Choice Pretest 1. Select the one best response. Answers are on page 67.

1. You just moved your finger. The command to activate the finger's muscles involved came via
    a. motor neurons.
    b. sensory neurons.
    c. glial cells.
    d. hormones.

2. The correct sequence describing the pathway neural information travels is
    a. axon, soma, dendrite, terminal button.
    b. terminal button, axon, soma, dendrite.
    c. dendrite, soma, axon, terminal button.
    d. soma, dendrite, axon, terminal button.

3. Researchers are recording the gross electrical activity of a man's brain. This procedure probably is
    a. a PET scan.
    b. an MRI.
    c. an EEG.
    d. a CT scan.

4. The adaptive value of the spinal reflex is due to its
    a. speed of response.
    b. use of no neurotransmitters.
    c. long-lasting communication capabilities.
    d. use of hormones to communicate.

5. The term most closely related to "depolarization" is
    a. inhibition.
    b. refractory period.
    c. resting potential.
    d. action potential.

6. The function of the terminal buttons is
    a. to receive incoming stimulation from another neuron.
    b. to store and release neurotransmitters.
    c. to insulate the neuron to assist transmission.
    d. to physically attach one neuron to another.

7. If an inhibitory message is passed to a neuron, the neuron will
    a. be hyperpolarized.
    b. be depolarized.
    c. release its neurotransmitters.
    d. begin saltatory conduction.

8. Neurotransmitters affect receptor molecules in
    a. the axon.
    b. the synapse.
    c. the myelin sheath.
    d. the postsynaptic membrane.

9. Uncle Joe has Alzheimer's disease. The type of neurotransmitter involved in this disease is
   a. acetylcholine.
   b. serotonin.
   c. dopamine.
   d. an endorphin.

10. The medulla, pons, and cerebellum are part of the
   a. hindbrain.
   b. midbrain
   c. forebrain.
   d. cerebral cortex.

11. Cleo has a disorder of the autonomic nervous system. She is likely to have problems with
   a. controlling movements such as walking.
   b. one or more sensory systems such as vision.
   c. regulating heart rate, digestion, or other internal functions.
   d. thinking or problem solving.

12. Grandpa had a stroke and now has difficulty seeing. His stroke probably damaged the
   a. limbic system.
   b. reticular activating system.
   c. frontal lobe.
   d. occipital lobe.

13. Damage to the hypothalamus, a limbic system structure, is least likely to affect
   a. sexual behavior.
   b. changes in learning or memory.
   c. eating behavior.
   d. hormonal changes.

14. In a "split-brain" operation, the surgeon destroys the
   a. midbrain.
   b. corpus callosum.
   c. cerebral cortex.
   d. reticular formation.

15. A split-brain patient is allowed to examine a key with her left hand, but not to see it. The patient will
   a. be able to name the object and to point to a picture of it with either hand.
   b. be able to name the object and to point to a picture of it with the left hand only.
   c. be unable to name the object but will be able to point to a picture of it with either hand.
   d. be unable to name the object but will be able to point to a picture of it with the left hand only.

16. Behaviors, thought, and feelings are represented in the nervous system by
   a. the length of the refractory period.
   b. the pattern of activation of groups of neurons.
   c. the particular neurotransmitter that has been released.
   d. the particular node of Ranvier stimulated.

17. The somatosensory cortex is important for
    a. regulating heart rate.
    b. language production.
    c. controlling eating and drinking
    d. processing touch sensations.

18. On the battlefield, the soldiers hearts were racing, and their muscles were tense. This was due to
    a. estrogen.
    b. testosterone.
    c. endorphins.
    d. epinephrine.

19. The trait of red hair is recessive. If you have red hair, you can conclude that you must have
    a. no red hair genes.
    b. only one red hair gene.
    c. at least one (maybe two, but not necessarily) red hair genes.
    d. two red hair genes.

Multiple Choice Pretest 2. Select the one best response. Answers are on page 69.

1. Myelin is associated with
    a. inhibitory neurotransmitters.
    b. excitatory neurotransmitters.
    c. rapid neural transmission.
    d. the dendrites.

2. When sodium ions flow into the neuron
    a. hyperpolarization occurs.
    b. depolarization occurs.
    c. a resting potential is established.
    d. the refractory period ends.

3. The adaptive value of the resting potential is that it
    a. allows quick response to stimulation.
    b. protects the cell from over-stimulation.
    c. slows neurotransmitter loss.
    d. inhibits nearby neurons.

4. Drugs that mimic the action of neurotransmitters are called
    a. agonists.
    b. antagonists.
    c. afferents.
    d. efferents.

5. The midbrain and thalamus are both important for
   a. regulating basic body functions such as heart rate.
   b. relaying and processing sensory input.
   c. controlling sexual behavior.
   d. controlling hormone production in the pituitary.

6. Depression often is treated with drugs that influence the activity of
   a. acetylcholine.
   b. dopamine.
   c. epinephrine.
   d. serotonin.

7. Alzheimer's disease involves serious memory disorders. This suggests Alzheimer's disease affects
   a. the medulla and pons.
   b. the tectum.
   c. the hippocampus.
   d. the cerebellum.

8. Tia's smooth, coordinated gymnastic movements are primarily the result of her well-functioning
   a. temporal lobe.
   b. cerebellum.
   c. limbic system.
   d. tectum.

9. Aunt Bess no longer can plan activities or make decisions sensibly. She has also become very uninhibited, undressing in public. Her doctor probably suspects Aunt Bess has damage to
   a. the pons.
   b. the substantia nigra.
   c. the frontal lobe.
   d. the occipital lob.

10. To reduce the aggressive behavior of a wolverine, which limbic system structure should be lesioned?
    a. the hippocampus.
    b. the superior colliculus.
    c. the tectum.
    d. the amygdala.

11. Damage to the reticular formation will most directly affect
    a. eating behavior.
    b. speech and language.
    c. thought and reason.
    d. consciousness and arousal.

12. Grandma's stroke damaged Wernicke's area of the left temporal lobe. She is most likely to experience
    a. problems moving the left half of her body.
    b. major personality changes.
    c. a reduced sense of touch.
    d. difficulty understanding spoken language.

13. Dr. Sperry stimulated the patient's brain and the patient's mouth moved. Based on the topographic organization of the brain, if the patient's brain is stimulated slightly to one side of the first spot, we should expect the patient to
    a. say something.
    b. report seeing a spot of light.
    c. twitch her cheek.
    d. report tasting something.

14. When Dr. Sperry caused the patient's mouth to move, he probably was stimulating cells in the
    a. temporal lobe.
    b. occipital lobe.
    c. parietal lobe.
    d. frontal lobe.

15. When the parasympathetic nervous system is activated
    a. sensory neurons increase their firing rate.
    b. most activity occurs in the form of spinal reflexes.
    c. heart rate and blood pressure are reduced.
    d. the body is readying itself for action.

16. Some data links "tomboy" behavior (rough and tumble play) in girls to
    a. prenatal exposure to testosterone.
    b. prenatal exposure to estrogen.
    c. early childhood (age 6) exposure to epinephrine.
    d. early childhood (age 6) exposure to pituitary growth hormone.

17. Suppose curly hair is a dominant trait controlled by a single gene pair. If Tom has curly hair, we know
    a. both of Tom's parents must have curly hair.
    b. at least one of Tom's parents has curly hair.
    c. it is possible that neither of Tom's parents has curly hair.
    d. None of the above. No conclusions are possible based on the information given.

18. If identical twins differ greatly in some trait, researchers would conclude the trait is determined by
    a. the environment.
    b. a dominant gene.
    c. a recessive gene.
    d. more than one pair of genes.

19. If an adaptive trait is economical,
    a. it is found in all members of the species.
    b. it is not costly to the survival of the organism.
    c. it solves specific adaptive problems the organism faces.
    d. the genes involved have undergone a spontaneous, sudden change.

LANGUAGE DEVELOPMENT GUIDE

Core Terms

In the lectures on this chapter, there are a few terms you are almost certain to hear. The first is *physiology*, the study of how a part of the body works. There are two ways to study body parts: you can look at their *structure* (their cells or how they are put together) or their *function* (what the parts do). Your instructor will probably cover both structure and function for each of the *anatomical features* (brain parts) discussed. The discussion will range all the way from the *grossest* structures (meaning the largest) to the *finest* (smallest), from whole sections of the brain to the inner workings of individual brain cells.

The nervous system is a *hierarchy*, a strictly organized system with definite divisions and subdivisions, but organizing its functions is not simple. The discussion of the functions of each *hemisphere* (half) of the brain will probably include the terms *lateralized* (found in only one of the halves) and *localized* (found in one specific area). Some functions seem to be controlled by a specific brain region. At the same time, other functions may be described as *diffuse* (spread among several locations). You also need to keep in mind the *malleability* and *plasticity* of the brain. Both of these terms mean that the brain is somewhat flexible in how it works, and can change some aspects of its functioning if necessary.

Idioms

p. 64	"designer" drugs	illegal drugs that differ slightly from other "street drugs"
p. 71	maintain posture	stand upright steadily
p. 72	a mimicking of	behaving just like; seeming just like
p. 72	modulating	controlling the effects of; keeping an effect from being too extreme
p. 73	tapped briefly into	gotten a quick look into
p. 76	via	by way of
p. 78	capitalizing on	making use of
p. 79	gross electrical activity	a general picture of the electrical activity of the brain
p. 79	global	overall, throughout the whole thing
p. 79	pictorial blueprint	a picture that maps out the parts in great detail
p. 86	fine motor control	ability to move very small muscles in precise ways
p. 89	anecdotal	from stories of personal experiences told by individuals
p. 90	holistic rather than analytic	as a whole, rather than analyzing individual parts

Word Parts

Here are some words that are made up of word parts, and that you can find in this chapter. After you've looked at these, you can look for others that use the same word parts.

WORD	WORD PART IT USES	MEANING
transmission	trans = across mit, mis = to send	sending something across
peripheral	peri = around	around the edges
hemispheric	hemi, demi, semi = half sphere = ball-shaped	having to do with half of a spherical object
receptor	re = again cept, cieve = to take	that which receives or takes back
ingest	in = in, into, within gest = to take in, to hold inside	to eat or otherwise take in
degenerate	de = down, from, away gen = birth, race, kind	to become worse than when it began
depolarize	de = down, from, away polar = opposite ends	to reduce the differences between opposite ends

Knowing the word parts listed above, you can also create the following words. You can get an idea of their meanings from the word parts they use.

hyperpolarize	_____ + _____	to increase the differences between two opposites (hyper means over or more)
remit	re + mit	_____
gestate	_____	to incubate, to grow inside something
repolarize	re + polar	_____

Pronunciation

p. 64	neuroscience	nur'-o-sy-ince	p. 66	myelin	my'-e-lin
p. 66	glial	glee'-ul	p. 68	soma	so'-muh

p. 68	synapse	sin'-aps	p. 82	substantia nigra	sub-stan'-shia ny'-gra
p. 71	acetylcholine	a-see'-tull-koh-leen	p. 84	amygdala	a-mig'-duh-luh
p. 71	dopamine	doh'-pa-meen	p. 86	parietal	puh-ry'-i-tull
p. 72	serotonin	se-re-toh'-nin	p. 91	endocrine	in'-doh-krin
p. 79	tomography	toh-mog'-ra-fee	p. 92	pituitary	pi-too'-i-tair-ee

ANSWERS AND EXPLANATIONS

To find relevant material in your textbook, consult the pages cited with each answer. Also, PN and PT citations refer to modules in *PsychNow!* and *Psyk.trek* materials, respectively.

Mastering the Concepts

1. brain (p. 64)
2. brain (p. 64)
3. spinal cord (p. 64)
4. peripheral (p. 64)
5. coordinate (p. 65)
6. growth (p. 65)
7. genetic (p. 65)
8. Neurons (p. 66)
9. Sensory (p. 66)
10. Interneurons (p. 66)
11. Motor (p. 66)
12. glial cells (p. 66)
13. myelin (p. 66)
14. reflex (p. 67)
15. Dendrites (p. 68)
16. soma (p. 68)

17. axon (p. 68)
18. terminal buttons (p. 68)
19. synapse (p. 68)
20. resting potential (p. 68)
21. depolarization (p. 69)
22. hyperpolarization (p. 69)
23. action potential (p. 69)
24. all or none (p. 69)
25. gaps (p. 70)
26. dopamine (p. 71)
27. agonists (p. 72)
28. antagonists (p. 72)
29. Endorphins (p. 72)
30. pattern (p. 73)
31. firing rate (p. 73)
32. refractory (p. 73)

33. networks (p. 73)
34. distributed (p. 75)
35. central (p. 76)
36. peripheral (p. 76)
37. afferent (p. 76)
38. efferent (p. 76)
39. somatic (p. 77)
40. autonomic (p. 77)
41. brain damage (p. 77)
42. hindbrain (p. 81)
43. forebrain (p. 83)
44. medulla (p. 81)
45. cerebellum (p. 82)
46. Parkinson's (p. 83)
47. cerebral cortex (p. 83)
48. sensory (p. 83)

49. hypothalamus (p. 83)
50. limbic system (p. 84)
51. memories (p. 84)
52. frontal (p. 85)
53. parietal (p. 86)
54. temporal (p. 86)
55. left (p. 88)
56. corpus callosum (p. 88)
57. spatial (p. 90)
58. endocrine (p. 91)
59. longer (p. 92)
60. pituitary (p. 92)
61. genes (p. 96)
62. Dominant (p. 96)
63. recessive (p. 96)
64. Family (p. 97)

Evaluating Your Progress

Preview & Communicating Internally: Connecting World and Brain

1. **b**   a. Wrong.   Motor neurons link the brain or spinal cord with the muscles and glands.
   (p. 66) c. Wrong.   Glial cells (aren't neurons!) fill space and perform "housekeeping" duties for neurons.
            d. Wrong.   Interneurons link other neurons only and have no contact with the world.

2. **d**   a. Wrong.   The cell body receives input from the dendrites and contains the cell's nucleus.
   (p. 68) b. Wrong.   Axons transmit the impulse from the cell body to the next neuron or body organ.
   (PN2A)   c. Wrong.   Terminal buttons are located at the end of the axons and contain neurotransmitters.

3. **a**   b. Wrong.   This is the opposite order. Sensory neurons receive input from the environment.
   (p. 66)   c. Wrong.   The brain is not involved in a spinal reflex.
             d. Wrong.   Motor neurons are last, and the brain is not involved in a spinal reflex.

4. **a**   b. Wrong.   Neurotransmitters are released when the cell is active, not resting.
   (p. 68)   c. Wrong.   Depolarization creates the action potential, not the resting potential.
             d. Wrong.   The resting potential is present when the neuron is inactive and not being stimulated.

5. **c**   a. Wrong.   For a given neuron, the action potential is the same magnitude for all stimuli.
   (p. 69)   b. Wrong.   For a given neuron, the action potential has the same speed for all stimuli.
             d. Wrong.   Only one is correct.

6. **c**   a. Wrong.   Interneurons are cells, not spaces.
   (p. 68)   b. Wrong.   The soma is the part of the neuron that contains the cell nucleus.
             d. Wrong.   Nodes of Ranvier are gaps in myelin, not spaces between neurons..

7. **d**   a. Wrong.   Interneurons are a type of neuron, not a structure in the synapse.
   (p. 70)   b. Wrong.   The myelin sheath is an insulating wrap on the axon.
   (PT2B)   c. Wrong.   The sodium-potassium pump maintains the ion distribution in the neuron.

8. **c**   a. Wrong.   A shortage of acetylcholine is associated with memory loss in Alzheimer's disease.
   (p. 72)   b. Wrong.   Endorphins are substances produced by the brain that mimic the action of morphine.
             d. Wrong.   Serotonin is associated with sleep, depression, and other mental disorders.

9. **b**   a. Wrong.   Neurotransmitters are specific to a neuron, not to a stimulus characteristic.
   (p. 73)   c. Wrong.   A refractory period is a time in which neurons can't fire, not a code for a stimulus.
             d. Wrong.   Neural transmission speed is determined by the neuron, not the stimulus.

Initiating and Coordinating Behavior: A Division of Labor

1. **c**   a. Wrong.   The parasympathetic and sympathetic systems are in the peripheral nervous system.
   (p. 76)   b. Wrong.   The autonomic and somatic systems are in the peripheral nervous system.
             d. Wrong.   The peripheral nervous system contains the nerves outside the brain and spinal cord.

2. **b**   a. Wrong.   The autonomic nervous system controls basic bodily functions, not movements.
   (p. 77)   c. Wrong.   The parasympathetic nervous system returns the body to normal after emergencies.
             d. Wrong.   The sympathetic nervous system activates the body to deal with emergencies.

3. **d**   a. Wrong.   Looking for changes in behavior after brain damage is used to identify an area's function.
   (p. 80)   b. Wrong.   Observing behavior during brain stimulation is used to identify an area's function.
             c. Wrong.   PET indicates brain activity and is used to identify an area's function.

4. **c**   a. Wrong.   The forebrain controls movement, motivation, emotion, and aspects of thought.
   (p. 81)   b. Wrong.   The midbrain contains neural relay stations, particularly for sensory information.
   (PN2A)   d. Wrong.   The cerebral cortex is part of the forebrain and controls higher mental processes.

5. **c**   a. Wrong.   The hindbrain contains the medulla, pons, and cerebellum.
   (p. 83)   b. Wrong.   The midbrain contains the tectum structures and substantia nigra.
             d. Wrong.   The tectum is part of the midbrain and contains sensory structures.

6. **a**   b. Wrong.   The medulla and pons control breathing, respiration, and other life support systems.
   (p. 82)   c. Wrong.   The hypothalamus is involved in eating, drinking, temperature, and sexual behavior.
             d. Wrong.   The cerebral cortex in involved in higher mental processes.

7. **d**   a. Wrong. The thalamus is a major sensory center.
   (p. 84)   b. Wrong. The reticular formation controls general arousal and consciousness.
   (PT2E)   c. Wrong. The cerebellum is responsible for smooth, coordinated movements.

8. **a**   b. Wrong. The occipital lobe is responsible for visual processing.
   (p. 85)   c. Wrong. The parietal lobe is responsible for the skin senses and higher visual processes.
                d. Wrong. The temporal lobe is responsible for auditory processing and aspects of language.

9. **b**   a. Wrong. Items on the left go to the right hemisphere, which cannot respond verbally.
   (pp. 88-89) c. Wrong. Depending on the hand used, a dog or a cat would be drawn; information doesn't merge.
   (PT2G)   d. Wrong. Memory is not damaged by cutting the corpus callosum.

10. **b**   a. Wrong. A body part's sensitivity or control, not its size, predicts the size of the related brain area.
   (p. 86)   c. Wrong. The motor cortex is in the frontal lobe, and the somatosensory cortex is in the parietal lobe.
                d. Wrong. The body's left side is associated with the cortex in the right hemisphere.

11. **d**   a. Wrong. Data support some amount of localization / lateralization of function.
   (p. 90)   b. Wrong. Cortical functions are at least as lateralized or localized as sub-cortical functions.
                c. Wrong. Data support cooperative processes in addition to some localization of function.

Regulating Growth and Internal Functions: Extended Communication

1. **a**   b. Wrong. Adrenal hormones energize the body for action, but don't control other glands.
   (p. 92)   c. Wrong. The ovaries and testes produce sex hormones, but don't control other glands.
                d. Wrong. The pineal gland in involved with biological cycles, but doesn't control other glands.

2. **c**   a. Wrong. The cerebellum is involved in coordination of movement, not endocrine control.
   (p. 92)   b. Wrong. The hippocampus is responsible for memory functions, not endocrine control.
                d. Wrong. The medulla controls life-support functions like heart rate, not the endocrine system.

3. **d**   a. Wrong. Endocrine system effects are more widespread and longer-term.
   (p. 92)   b. Wrong. Endocrine system effects are more widespread, not localized.
                c. Wrong. Endocrine system effects are longer-term,

4. **b**   a. Wrong. Testosterone (male hormone) has been linked to spatial skill, in which men excel.
   (p. 93)   c. Wrong. Prenatal sex hormones, not epinephrine, may be linked to behavioral gender effects.
                d. Wrong. Prenatal sex hormones, not norepinephrine, may be linked to gender effects.

5. **c**   a. Wrong. The pituitary doesn't secrete epinephrine; it stimulates the adrenal glands to do so.
   (p. 92)   b. Wrong. The hypothalamus doesn't secrete epinephrine; it stimulates the pituitary, which stimulates
   (PT8E)   the adrenal glands to do so.
                d. Wrong. The ovaries and testes secrete sex hormones (estrogen, testosterone), not epinephrine.

Storing and Transmitting the Genetic Code: Genetic Influences on Behavior

1. **d**   a. Wrong. A phenotype is a person's observable characteristic, such as eye color.
   (p. 96)   b. Wrong. Efferent refers to a neural pathway carrying information away from the brain.
                c. Wrong. Afferent refers to a neural pathway carrying information to the brain.

2. **a**   b. Wrong. CT scans would examine brain structure, not genetic or environmental determinants.
   (p. 92)   c. Wrong. MRIs provide an image of brain structure or function (functional MRI).
   (PT7D)   d. Wrong. EEGs represent brain activity, but cannot differentiate genetic and environmental factors.

3. **c**
(p. 96)
a.	Wrong.	Phenotypes describe the observable characteristics of a trait, not the number of genes.
b.	Wrong.	Phenotypes describe the observable characteristics of a trait, not dominant/recessive.
d.	Wrong.	The specific genetic pattern is described by the genotype.

4. **a**
(p. 96)
b.	Wrong.	There must be two recessive genes for the trait to appear in the phenotype.
c.	Wrong.	Mutations do not necessarily allow a trait to be expressed with only one gene of that type.
d.	Wrong.	Whether a trait is adaptive has no impact on whether it is expressed or the genetic pattern.

5. **d**
(p. 95)
a.	Wrong.	Adaptations can involve recessive traits, too.
b.	Wrong.	Adaptations can involve dominant traits, too.
c.	Wrong.	Behavioral traits, not just physical ones, can be adaptations.

MAKING FINAL PREPARATIONS

Short Essay Questions

1. Drugs act like natural neurotransmitters (agonists), by increasing the effectiveness of natural neurotransmitters (neuromodulators), or by blocking neurotransmitter activity (antagonists). The behavioral effects will depend on the specific combinations of inhibition and excitation of the nervous system. (pp. 71-72)

2. In the usual pathway, sensory input about the object is carried via sensory neurons to the spinal cord and then to the brain. The brain initiates commands to move which are carried via motor neurons to the spinal cord and the muscles. In a spinal reflex the sensory input is carried by sensory neurons to the spinal cord. Commands to move are initiated in the spinal cord (without involving the brain) and carried to the muscles by motor neurons. The spinal reflex allows more rapid responses because input does not have to travel all the way to and from the brain. This is advantageous in dangerous situations. (pp. 66-67)

3. Brain functions are studied by damaging, recording, or stimulating the brain. The function of a brain area is inferred based on changes in behavior after brain damage, or based on changes in that area's level of activity during a particular behavior, or when a change in behavior occurs when that area is stimulated. (pp. 77-80)

4. Because the left hemisphere controls language in most people, I would lose the ability to use and comprehend speech. Sensory input from the right side of the body and right visual field is handled in the left hemisphere, so I would lose sight, touch, temperature, and pain information from the right. The left hemisphere controls movement on the right side of the body, so I'd be paralyzed in my right arm and leg. (pp. 87-88)

5. The genetic code is adaptive because it provides a way to transmit traits to future generations. Traits that increase the likelihood of survival tend to remain in the genetic code due to natural selection, so future generations accumulate adaptive traits. Also, random selection of genes during of egg and sperm formation produces diversity and ensures some members of the species will have traits necessary for survival. (p. 95-96)

Matching

1. f (p. 82)	4. n (p. 66)	7. m (p. 82)	10. h (p. 68)	13. g (p. 83)	16. i (p. 92)
2. o (p. 84)	5. e (p. 81)	8. b (p. 68)	11. a (p. 88)	14. j (p. 68)	
3. d (p. 84)	6. l (p. 68)	9. p (p. 82)	12. k (p. 83)	15. c (p. 86)	

Multiple Choice Pretest 1

1. **a**
(p. 66)
b.	Wrong.	Sensory neurons carry input from the sensory organs to the brain.
c.	Wrong.	Glial cells do not transmit impulses. They provide support services to neurons.
d.	Wrong.	Hormones do not transmit movement commands to the muscles.

2. **c**
    (p. 68)
    a. Wrong.   The axon is not the first structure. Dendrite--soma--axon--terminal button.
    b. Wrong.   The terminal button is the last structure. Dendrite--soma--axon--terminal button.
    d. Wrong.   The soma is not the first structure. Dendrite--soma--axon--terminal button.

3. **c**
    (p. 79)
    (PT2C)
    a. Wrong.   PET involves imaging metabolic activity in specific locations, not gross electrical activity.
    b. Wrong.   MRI provides an image of brain structure.
    d. Wrong.   CT scans provide an image of brain structure.

4. **a**
    (p. 67)
    b. Wrong.   Neurotransmitters are used in all neural transmission.
    c. Wrong.   Hormones, not the spinal reflex, provide long-lasting communication.
    d. Wrong.   The spinal reflex is neural, not hormonal, activity.

5. **d**
    (p. 69)
    a. Wrong.   Inhibition would be related to hyperpolarization.
    b. Wrong.   The refractory period is the time after a neural impulse when the cell can't fire again.
    c. Wrong.   The resting potential is the charge present in the neuron when at rest, not when firing.

6. **b**
    (p. 68)
    (PN2A)
    a. Wrong.   The dendrites receive incoming stimulation, not the terminal buttons.
    c. Wrong.   The myelin insulates some neurons.
    d. Wrong.   Neurons are not attached. They are separated by a fluid-filled space, the synapse.

7. **a**
    (p. 70)
    b. Wrong.   Excitatory activity causes depolarization.
    c. Wrong.   Hyperpolarization prevents neural firing, so no neurotransmitters are released.
    d. Wrong.   Saltatory conduction only occurs with excitatory input (an action potential).

8. **d**
    (p. 70)
    a. Wrong.   Neurotransmitters generally contact the dendrites, not the axon.
    b. Wrong.   The synapse is a fluid-filled space. Receptor molecules are structures.
    c. Wrong.   The myelin sheath insulates the axon and is not influenced by neurotransmitters.

9. **a**
    (p. 72)
    b. Wrong.   Serotonin is important in sleep and some psychological disorders, but not Alzheimer's.
    c. Wrong.   Dopamine is associated with schizophrenia and Parkinson's disease, not Alzheimer's.
    d. Wrong.   Endorphins are morphine-like substances, not a factor in Alzheimer's.

10. **a**
     (p. 81)
    b. Wrong.   The midbrain contains the structures of the tectum and the substantia nigra.
    c. Wrong.   The forebrain contains the cerebral cortex, hypothalamus and limbic system.
    d. Wrong.   The cerebral cortex is part of the forebrain.

11. **c**
     (p. 77)
    a. Wrong.   Movement is controlled by the somatic and central nervous systems.
    b. Wrong.   Sensation is controlled by the somatic and central nervous systems.
    d. Wrong.   Thinking or problem solving is controlled by the central nervous system.

12. **d**
     (p. 87)
     (PN2B)
    a. Wrong.   The limbic system is involved with motivational and emotional behaviors.
    b. Wrong.   The reticular activating system controls arousal and consciousness.
    c. Wrong.   Frontal lobe damage would involve personality, movement, or thinking, more likely.

13. **b**
     (p. 84)
    a. Wrong.   The hypothalamus is important for sexual behavior.
    c. Wrong.   The hypothalamus is important for eating and hunger.
    d. Wrong.   The hypothalamus controls the pituitary, the "master gland."

14. **b**
     (p. 88)
    a. Wrong.   The midbrain doesn't connect the hemispheres, the corpus callosum does.
    c. Wrong.   The two hemispheres of the cerebral cortex are separated, not destroyed.
    d. Wrong.   The reticular formation doesn't connect the hemispheres, the corpus callosum does.

15. **d**
     (p. 89)
     (PT2G)
    a. Wrong.   Input will go to the right hemisphere, with no speech or control of right hand.
    b. Wrong.   Input will go to the right hemisphere, with no speech.
    c. Wrong.   Input will go to the right hemisphere, which doesn't control the right hand.

16. **b**   a. Wrong.   The refractory period is a characteristic of a neuron, not a neural code.
(p. 73)   c. Wrong.   Neural activity, not specific neurotransmitters represent the information.
              d. Wrong.   Nodes of Ranvier are gaps in the myelin and do not represent information.

17. **d**   a. Wrong.   The medulla and other hindbrain areas control heart rate.
(p. 86)   b. Wrong.   The motor cortex of the frontal lobes is important for controlling movement.
              c. Wrong.   The hypothalamus is important for controlling eating and drinking.

18. **d**   a. Wrong.   Estrogen is a female sex hormone, not a fight-or-flight adrenal hormone.
(p. 92)   b. Wrong.   Testosterone is a male sex hormone, not a fight-or-flight adrenal hormone.
              c. Wrong.   Endorphins cause reduced pain, not a fight-or-flight response.

19. **d**   a. Wrong.   Two dominant (non-red hair) genes produce the dominant trait (non-red hair).
(p. 96)   b. Wrong.   Recessive traits appear only if both genes are the recessive (red hair) type.
              c. Wrong.   One recessive (red hair) gene will not produce the recessive trait. It takes two.

Multiple Choice Pretest 2

1. **c**   a, b, & d.   Wrong.   Myelin is an insulating substance on the axon that helps speed neural
(p. 66)   transmission.
(PN2A)

2. **b**   a. Wrong.   Hyperpolarization occurs if more sodium is pushed out or chloride comes in.
(p. 69)   c. Wrong.   The resting potential occurs when the neuron is inactive and sodium is not flowing in.
              d. Wrong.   The refractory period ends when the resting potential is reestablished.

3. **a**   b. Wrong.   The resting potential is the charge of the neuron at rest, and unrelated to protection.
(p. 69)   c. Wrong.   The resting potential is the charge of the neuron at rest, not a neurotransmitter issue.
              d. Wrong.   Activity inhibits other neurons, not the charge of the neuron at rest (resting potential).

4. **a**   b. Wrong.   Antagonists block the action of neurotransmitters.
(p. 72)   c. Wrong.   Afferents are sensory pathways.
              d. Wrong.   Efferents are motor pathways.

5. **b**   a. Wrong.   The medulla and pons control basic functions like heart rate.
(pp. 82-83)   c Wrong.   The hypothalamus or other limbic system structures control sexual behavior.
(PT2E)   d. Wrong.   The hypothalamus control the pituitary.

6. **d**   a. Wrong.   Acetylcholine is influential in Alzheimer's disease memory disorders.
(p. 72)   b. Wrong.   Dopamine is associated with Parkinson's disease.
              c. Wrong   Norepinephrine may influence depression, but not epinephrine.

7. **c**   a. Wrong.   The medulla and pons control basic functions like breathing and blood pressure.
(p. 84)   b. Wrong.   The tectum of the midbrain has important sensory pathways.
              d. Wrong.   The cerebellum controls coordination of movements.

8. **b**   a. Wrong.   The temporal lobe is important for auditory functions. Coordination is cerebellar.
(p. 82)   c. Wrong.   The limbic system is involved with motivation and emotion, not coordination.
              d. Wrong.   The tectum contains sensory centers important for responding to sensory events.

9. **c**   a. Wrong.   The pons regulates basic bodily functions, not higher cognitive processes.
(p. 85)   b. Wrong.   The substantia nigra produces dopamine and is involved in Parkinson's disease.
              d. Wrong.   The occipital lobe is important for vision, not thinking.

10. **d**   a. Wrong.   The hippocampus is involved with memory, not aggression.
(p. 84)   b. Wrong.   The superior colliculus is a sensory area in the midbrain.
          c. Wrong.   The tectum is the midbrain area with sensory functions.

11. **d**   a. Wrong.   The reticular formation controls general arousal; the hypothalamus is linked to eating.
(p. 82)   b. Wrong.   The reticular formation controls general arousal; the cortex controls language.
(PN2B) c. Wrong.   The reticular formation controls general arousal; the cortex controls thought.

12. **d**   a. Wrong.   The frontal lobe controls movement, and the left hemisphere controls the *right* side.
(p. 86)   b. Wrong.   Personality changes are associated with frontal lobe damage.
          c. Wrong.   Touch sensations are processed in the somatosensory cortex of the parietal lobe.

13. **c**   a. Wrong.   Speech and movement aren't as closely linked in the brain as movements of nearby areas.
(p. 86)   b. Wrong.   Visual functions are not near motor functions in the brain.
          d. Wrong.   Body part and related functions are not necessarily nearby in the brain.

14. **d**   a, b, & c.   Wrong.   Movement is controlled by the motor cortex of the frontal lobe.
(p. 85)

15. **c**   a. Wrong.   Sensory neurons are not part of, nor affected by, the parasympathetic system.
(p. 77)   b. Wrong.   Spinal reflexes are "hardwired" and are unaffected by the autonomic nervous system.
          d. Wrong.   Activation of the *sympathetic* nervous system produces the "fight or flight" reaction.

16. **a**   b. Wrong.   Estrogen is a female hormone and would facilitate normal "female" development.
(p. 93)   c. Wrong.   Epinephrine is an adrenal hormone with general activation, not sexual, effects.
          d. Wrong.   Pituitary growth hormone controls bone growth and is normally present in childhood.

17. **b**   a. Wrong.   With a dominant trait, only one dominant gene (from one parent) is needed.
(p. 96)   c. Wrong.   If neither have curly hair, neither have a curly hair gene to pass on to Tom.
          d. Wrong.   Dominant traits appear any time the dominant gene is present, so we know at least one parent has the gene and curly hair because Tom has curly hair, and thus, the gene.

18. **a**   b, c, & d.   Wrong.   Identical twins have the same genes, so if traits differ, they are not caused by genes.
(p. 97)

19. **b**   a. Wrong.   Being common to all members makes the trait universal.
(p. 95)   c. Wrong.   Solving problems makes the trait adaptive.
          d. Wrong.   A spontaneous change in genes describes mutation.

CHAPTER 4: HUMAN DEVELOPMENT

ESTABLISHING LEARNING GOALS

Use these learning goals as a preview of the chapter, a guide for active reading, and to evaluate your mastery of the material. Review the relevant goals as you begin and end your reading of each major section of the chapter.

I. Solve the adaptive problem of how the individual develops physically through the life span.
    A. Describe the physical changes that occur prenatally.
        1. Describe the three periods of prenatal development and the major events of each.
        2. Discuss the factors that influence or disrupt prenatal development.
    B   Discuss how we grow from infancy through adolescence.
        1. Discuss the influence of "nature" and "nurture" on the development of motor skills.
        2. Describe physical growth from infancy through adolescence.
    C. Discuss adulthood and the aging body and brain.
        1. Describe the physical and mental changes associated with menopause.
        2. Describe the neural changes in the brain and how they relate to behavioral changes.

II. Solve the adaptive problem of how individuals develop the intellectual skills needed to deal effectively with the constantly changing circumstances encountered throughout life.
    A. Discuss the research tools that are used to study infant perception and memory.
    B. Describe the perceptual capabilities of an infant.
    C. Describe the characteristics of memory loss in the elderly.
    D. Discuss and evaluate Piaget's theory of cognitive development.
        1. Discuss the characteristics of the stages of cognitive development and how changes occur.
        2. Discuss the criticism of Piaget's theory of cognitive development.
    E. Discuss and evaluate Kohlberg's theory of moral development.
        1. Describe moral reasoning in the preconventional, conventional, and postconventional stages.
        2. Evaluate Kohlberg's theory in terms of its general approach and its applicability to all cultures.

III. Solve the adaptive problem of how individuals form the social relationships and a personal identity.
    A. Discuss the short- and long-term consequences of early attachments.
        1. Describe the artificial mother research and how it relates to humans.
        2. Identify four types of attachment.
        3. Discuss the role of friendships in development.
        4. Discuss the impact of child care on social and intellectual development.
    B. Explain Erik Erikson's stage theory of personal identity development.
        1. Describe the personal crises characteristic of each stage, and explain their importance.
        2. Evaluate Erikson's theory.
    C. Describe the issues that affect gender role development.
    D. Discuss the psychological issues associated with death and dying.
        1. Discuss ageism.
        2. Describe Kubler-Ross' stages of confronting death.

MASTERING THE MATERIAL

Preview & Developing Physically (pp. 104-114)

Mastering the Vocabulary. Define or explain each of the following terms. To check your answers, consult the text pages listed.

1. development (p. 104)

2. zygote (p. 106)

3. germinal period (p. 106)

4. embryonic period (p. 107)

5. fetal period (p. 107)

6. teratogens (p. 108)

7. puberty (p. 112)

8. menopause (p. 113)

9. dementia (p. 113)

Mastering the Concepts. Fill in the blanks to create a summary of the section. Answers are on page 91.

_____(1) is the age-related change in behavior and physical features that occurs over time. Developmental psychologists consider development to be due to the _____(2) of biological and environmental factors. Development is adaptive; it solves practical problems and allows for the _____(3) necessary to deal with a changing environment. This chapter involves three adaptive problems: How does the individual adapt _____(4), _____(5), and socially or personally?

Physical development begins with the formation of the single-celled _____(6) at conception. Not all survive the two-week _____(7) period and implant in the uterus. During the six-week

_____(8) period the cells develop into a more recognizable structure and sexual differentiation occurs. From the eighth week until birth, the _____(9) period, development continues. Development can be disrupted if the mother exposes the developing child to _____(10), environmental agents that harm development. Alcohol use can lead to _____(11) syndrome. Structures have critical periods of susceptibility to teratogens, but exposure at any time can be dangerous.

Although the brain is only 25% of its adult weight at birth, its growth involves development of branches and interconnections, not increased numbers of neurons. Plasticity allows the brain to respond to _____(12) influences. Development of the nervous system occurs in a _____(13) fashion and produces a predictable sequence of motor development, although the timing may be modified by the environment. Growth slows during early childhood, and increases again at _____(14) when the release of estrogen or androgen initiates a growth spurt accompanied by _____(15) development. Age at puberty varies with sex and environment.

After age 20, a gradual _____(16) in physical condition begins. Women reach _____(17) at about age 50, and men may lose some reproductive capacity. The brain loses cells, and by age 80 Alzheimer's disease or other types of _____(18) may appear. However, cell loss might be offset by adaptation of other cells to compensate and maintain function.

Evaluating Your Progress. Select the one best response. Answers are on page 92. If you make any errors, reread the relevant material before proceeding.

1. The fertilized egg is called the
    a. embryo.
    b. fetus.
    c. zygote.
    d. teratogen.

2. Sexual differentiation, the development of the sexual reproductive system, occurs during the
    a. early germinal period.
    b. middle of the germinal period.
    c. late embryonic period.
    d. late fetal period.

3. The structures that are most likely to be affected by a teratogen are those that
    a. develop first (nervous system and heart).
    b. are undergoing initial development when the teratogen is present.
    c. have just completed their initial development when the teratogen is present.
    d. would be affected by the teratogen in adulthood (alcohol--liver).

4. The brain grows dramatically in size from birth to age 2 due to
    a. a rapid increase in the number of neurons present.
    b. a rapid growth of blood vessels within the brain.
    c. the development of the ventricles, fluid filled spaces found in the normal adult brain.
    d. the increase in the number of glial cells and the complexity of the neurons.

5. Prenatal development sets down basic neural circuitry, but environmental factors influence final circuitry. This describes the principle of
    a. schemata.
    b. habituation.
    c. critical periods.
    d. plasticity.

6. Neural development and thus, motor development, progresses
    a. in a top-down sequence.
    b. in a bottom-up sequence.
    c. in an outside-in sequence.
    d. in no predictable direction.

7. The developmental period during which individuals mature sexually is called
    a. menarche.
    b. puberty.
    c. the climacteric.
    d. menopause.

8. The age of the onset of puberty has decreased 3-4 years in the last century, probably due to
    a. changes in the genetic makeup of people today.
    b. poor diets that are high in junk foods.
    c. the emphasis on strenuous daily exercise and sports.
    d. improved medical care and living conditions.

9. Which of the following is FALSE?
    a. Most physical functions decline during adulthood.
    b. Most women do not experience depression or other serious mood problems during menopause.
    c. Poorer sensory abilities, slowed reaction time, and changes in memory are common after age 50.
    d. Most people in their 80's develop Alzheimer's disease or other serious mental deterioration.

10. The physically based loss in mental functioning is called
    a. dementia.
    b. the climacteric.
    c. teratogenesis.
    d. ageism.

Developing Intellectually (pp. 114-130)

Mastering the Vocabulary. Define or explain each of the following terms. To check your answers, consult the text pages listed.

1. preference technique (p. 115)

2. habituation (p. 115)

3. longitudinal design (p. 118)

4. cross sectional design (p. 118)

5. schemata (p. 120)

6. assimilation (p. 121)

7. accommodation (p. 121)

8. sensorimotor period (p. 121)

9. object permanence (p. 122)

10. preoperational period (p. 122)

11. principle of conservation (p.122)

12. egocentrism (p. 123)

13. concrete operational period (p. 123)

14. formal operational period (p. 124)

15. morality (p. 127)

16. preconventional level (p. 128)

17. conventional level (p. 128)

20. postconventional level (p. 128)

Mastering the Concepts. Fill in the blanks to create a summary of the section. Answers are on page 91.

Infants' limited ability to respond makes infant perception research difficult, but three characteristics of infants are useful: they show _____(19); they notice _____(20); and they can learn to make a _____(21). In the _____(22) technique, looking at one stimulus longer than another suggests that the infant can tell the two stimuli are different. Another method for testing an infant's ability to remember or discriminate stimuli is to use the _____(23) technique, repeating a stimulus until the infant quits responding, then changing to a new stimulus and noting any response. Also, rewarding a simple action such as sucking or kicking produces responses that can be used to study infant abilities.

The infant's perceptual system is immature, but it functions well. All senses are operational. Adaptive capabilities, such as recognizing the mother by _____(24), are particularly sophisticated. Their acuity is poor, but "visual cliff" experiments show infants perceive _____(25). In general, their perceptual systems need to be fine-tuned by maturation and experience.

Memory skills improve during childhood, mostly due to improved _____ (26). Loss of memory skill is common in older adults, but the way memory is tested is very important. _____(27) is most likely to be affected by aging.

Piaget proposed people develop _____(28), mental models of the world, that influence their interpretation of their experiences. Piaget suggested development proceeds in _____(29) characterized by different schemata. The _____(30) of development is variable, but the _____(31) is the same for all children. Cognitive development involves both assimilation and accommodation. _____(32) occurs when the child fits new experiences into existing schemata. In _____(33), schemata are modified to fit the new experiences.

Behavior in Piaget's first stage, the _____(34) period, includes survival reflexes such as the _____(35) and the sucking reflex. Children move from reflexive to deliberate interaction with the world. They develop object _____(36), the ability to symbolically represent objects not in view. From age 2 to 7, children are in the _____(37) period, and they lack an understanding of _____(38). Due to _____(39), or focusing on one dimension, and difficulty with reversibility, children think that changing shape causes a change in amount. Preoperational children also have difficulty seeing the world from others' perspectives, a trait called _____ (40). Children between 7 and 11 are in the _____ (41) operations period, and the ability to think abstractly is greatly limited. Abstract thought and systematic problem solving is characteristic of the _____ (42) operations period.

Piaget's theory has been criticized for underestimating what children know, for proposing sudden shifts from stage to stage, and for failing to explain the processes of change and the role of _____ (43) context, the key to cognitive development according to Vygotsky. Postformal thinking might be needed to explain differences in adolescent and adult thought. Adults tend to use more _____ (44) thinking and systems of ideas.

Kohlberg proposed morality develops in 3 stages: the _____ (45), conventional, and _____ (46) stages. He assessed moral development by examining the _____ (47) given for deciding right or wrong. Preconventional reasoning is based on the external results of an action (e.g., punishment). Conventional reasoning is based on how an action affects the _____ (48). Postconventional reasoning is based on _____ (49) principles that may conflict with accepted norms.

Research supports the sequence of development and the link to cognitive skills. Criticisms of Kohlberg's theory include that it does not generalize across sexes or _____ (50), and that analyzing reasoning is not adequate.

Evaluating Your Progress. Select the one best response. Answers are on page 92. If you make any errors, reread the relevant material before proceeding.

1. Two stimuli are presented simultaneously, and the time spent looking at each one is monitored in
    a. the habituation method.
    b. the reward method.
    c. the preference method.
    d. the cross-sectional method.

2. Research has shown that infants just a few days old can do all of the following except
    a. recognize their mother's voice.
    b. recognize their mother's smell.
    c. see clearly.
    d. taste sour, sweet, and salty substances.

3. Research that follows a group of people of the same age over an extended period of time, retesting them periodically and comparing their performance at different ages uses a
    a. cross-sectional design.
    b. longitudinal design.
    c. time-linked design.
    d. continuous design.

4. The process of fitting new information into existing schemata is called
   a. generalization.
   b. centration.
   c. accommodation.
   d. assimilation.

5. Piaget's stages, in order from first to last, are
   a. preoperational, sensorimotor, concrete operational, formal operational.
   b. concrete operational, formal operational, sensorimotor, preoperational.
   c. sensorimotor, preoperational, concrete operational, formal operational.
   d. preoperational, formal operational, concrete operational, sensorimotor.

6. The stage characterized initially by reflexive behavior that eventually broadens to voluntary behavior is
   a. the sensorimotor period.
   b. the formal operational period.
   c. the preoperational period.
   d. the concrete operational period.

7. Object permanence is the knowledge that
   a. the basic properties of an object don't change if superficial changes are made.
   b. if one operation causes a change, another operation can reverse that change.
   c. an object can still exist even if it is not currently in view or other sensory contact.
   d. changes in one dimension can be offset by changes in another dimension.

8. The rooting reflex is the tendency to
   a. consider only one dimension of an object or situation.
   b. consider an action in relation to others.
   c. suck on anything that comes in contact with the mouth.
   d. turn the head toward the side of the cheek that was touched.

9. The conservation concept develops by the end of Piaget's
   a. preoperational period.
   b. formal operational period.
   c. sensorimotor period.
   d. concrete operational period.

10. Systematically solving problems and working with abstract concepts are characteristic of Piaget's
    a. preoperational period.
    b. concrete operational period.
    c. formal operational period.
    d. sensorimotor period.

11. Children in the concrete operational period are usually
    a. 3-6 years old.
    b. 7-11 years old.
    c. 12-17 years old.
    d. 18 years old or older.

12. All of the following are criticisms of Piaget's theory of cognitive development EXCEPT:
    a. Research shows that children's schemata are not the same as adults'.
    b. Children know more, and sooner, than Piaget proposed.
    c. Piaget doesn't address the role social context plays in cognitive development.
    d. Children do not make sudden transitions from one stage to another as Piaget proposes.

13. Kohlberg's theory of moral reasoning proposes that
    a. moral reasoning develops differently in different countries.
    b. children's moral reasoning is developed fully by the time they are 6.
    c. development proceeds through a series of orderly stages.
    d. the "yes" or "no" decision about a moral dilemma determines the level of moral reasoning.

14. Postconventional moral reasoning is based on
    a. whether the action disrupts or maintains the social order.
    b. the personal consequences of the action.
    c. abstract moral principles.
    d. the standards of morality defined by an authority figure.

15. Research on Kohlberg's theory of moral development has found that
    a. moral reasoning in India is quite different from moral reasoning in Western cultures.
    b. the moral reasoning of men and women differs greatly in most circumstances.
    c. the orderly progression of moral reasoning is found only in Western cultures, not elsewhere.
    d. the analysis of reasoning judgements accurately predicts moral values.

Developing Socially and Personally (pp. 130-144)

Mastering the Vocabulary. Define or explain each of the following terms. To check your answers, consult the text pages listed.

1. attachments (p. 131)

2. temperament (p. 131)

3. strange-situation test (p. 133)

4. personal identity (p. 137)

5. gender roles (p. 140)

6. ageism (p. 141)

Mastering the Concepts. Fill in the blanks to create a summary of this section. Answers are on page 91.

Attachment, the _____(51) ties to another individual, may be controlled by biological predispositions in both parent and child. Harlow's research with monkeys suggests contact _____(52), pleasant physical contact, is more important for attachment than being a food source. Parental responsiveness is also important and is influenced by the child's _____(53), which can be easy or difficult, uninhibited or inhibited. Attachment is evaluated using the _____(54) situation test. Most children have _____(55) attachment, 20% have avoidant attachment, and a smaller percentage have resistant or disorganized/disoriented attachment. Secure attachment is associated with social and intellectual benefits. Assessments are not always stable, attachment can vary across parents, the data is correlational, and later experiences are important. Friendships are also beneficial. Research on the effects of day care indicates it has little effect on attachment and may benefit social and _____(56) development, depending on the quality of care and other factors.

Erikson states that personal _____(57) is shaped by a series of psychosocial crises confronted in life. They extend from the trust vs. mistrust crisis of infancy to the integrity vs. despair crisis of _____(58). The ideas of life-long development and the importance of _____(59) and cultural interactions are valid contributions. Criticisms of the theory include the problem of distinct stages, the lack of an explanation as to how progress occurs, and its testability.

Basic gender identity seems to be present by age _____(60). By school age, gender identity is seen as permanent, and behavior reflects gender _____(61), behavior fitting society's concept of male or female behavior. In _____(62) theory, gender roles develop because certain behaviors are rewarded. Gender roles lead to gender schemas, beliefs about men and women, that guide behavior.

Many beliefs about the elderly are myths, but the elderly do face physical concerns, difficult end-of-life decisions, and _____(63), prejudice against the elderly. Kubler-Ross proposed a theory of dying: denial, anger, bargaining, depression, and _____(64). Her theory has been criticized for its stage format. Dying trajectories provide an alternative without implying a "right" way to die.

Evaluating Your Progress. Select the one best response. Answers are on page 94. If you make any errors, reread the relevant material before proceeding.

1. The strong emotional bond between individuals is known as
   a. personal identity.
   b. contact comfort.
   c. dependency.
   d. attachment.

2. Harlow's research found that most monkeys raised with artificial mothers formed attachments if
   a. the "mother" had a warm, fuzzy cover.
   b. the "mother" provided the infant monkey's food.
   c. the "mother" was made out of wire mesh with no cover.
   d. all of the above conditions led to attachment in most monkeys.

3. Attachment is sometimes evaluated by placing a child in a new and stressful situation and observing how the child interacts with the mother. This is called the
   a. contact comfort test.
   b. stress reaction test.
   c. strange situation test.
   d. social stressor test.

4. Which of the following is not a classification of attachment?
   a. resistant attachment
   b. avoidant attachment
   c. antagonistic attachment
   d. secure attachment

5. Tina is described as an "easy" child who is fairly uninhibited. This is a description of
   a. temperament.
   b. moral development.
   c. attachment.
   d. cognitive development.

6. Recent studies of day care suggest that
   a. essentially all day care harms the development of attachment.
   b. even quality day care is associated with poor social development.
   c. quality day care is associated with improved cognitive skills for almost all children.
   d. general conclusions are difficult because of the many factors that interact.

7. Erikson's stage theory of personal identity development proposes
   a. contact comfort is more important than supplying food.
   b. development begins at puberty.
   c. identity is determined by several psychosocial crises.
   d. friends are the primary determinants of personal identity.

8. At what point in life do people try to resolve the crisis of integrity vs. despair?
   a. adolescence
   b. early adulthood
   c. middle adulthood
   d. late adulthood

9. The social learning theory of gender role development states that gender roles develop because
   a. children are rewarded for certain "masculine" or "feminine" behavior.
   b. children have few models for gender-appropriate behavior.
   c. children quickly determine that their genitals are different from others'.
   d. children are innately programmed to behave in stereotypically "masculine" or "feminine" ways.

10. Kubler-Ross' stages of death and dying are, in order,
    a. denial, depression, anger, bargaining, acceptance.
    b. denial, anger, bargaining, depression, acceptance.
    c. denial, bargaining, depression, anger, acceptance.
    d. denial, bargaining, anger, depression, acceptance.

MAKING FINAL PREPARATIONS

Complete these sections without consulting your book or notes. For a more accurate estimate of how well you know this material, wait at least a day or two after studying the chapter before working on the questions. Some of the material you "know" immediately after working with the chapter will be quickly forgotten. Immediate tests will overestimate what you know well.

Short Essay Questions. Write a brief answer to each question. Sample answers are on page 94.

1. Discuss why exposure to a teratogen during the first three months produces different effects than exposure during the last three months of pregnancy.

2. Describe a newborn infant's perceptual capabilities and how and why they change with time.

3. Describe the preference technique and explain what it tells us about an infant's perceptual capabilities.

4. Give an example of preconventional, conventional, and postconventional moral reasoning for the druggist moral dilemma and explain why each exemplifies the relevant level.

5. Identify three types of attachment and describe how each is reflected in the strange situation test.

6. Explain the identity vs. role confusion crisis and how it is resolved.

7. Compare the gender identities of a 3-year-old and a 7-year-old.

Matching. Select the correct definition or description for each item. Answers are on page 95.

_____	1. schemata	**a.**	first two weeks of prenatal period
_____	2. Harlow	**b.**	set of beliefs about men and women
_____	3. fetal period	**c.**	loss of mental function due to physical causes
_____	4. Erikson	**d.**	morality based on external consequences of action
_____	5. concrete operational period	**e.**	time of final development of physical systems
_____	6. menopause	**f.**	proposed theory of personal identity development
_____	7. sensorimotor period	**g.**	time of initial development of physical systems
_____	8. gender schema	**h.**	proposed theory of moral development
_____	9. embryonic period	**i.**	found importance of contact comfort in attachment
_____	10. Piaget	**j.**	mental models of the world
_____	11. preconventional level	**k.**	proposed classification system for attachment
_____	12. germinal period	**l.**	proposed theory of cognitive development
_____	13. conventional level	**m.**	morality based on maintaining social order
_____	14. dementia	**n.**	period when woman's menstrual cycles cease
_____	15. Kohlberg	**o.**	reflexive behavior and no object permanence
_____	16. habituation	**p.**	can't deal with abstract or hypothetical situations
_____	17. Ainsworth	**q.**	emotional ties formed to other people
_____	18. attachment	**r.**	decline in responsiveness to a repeated stimulus

Multiple Choice Pretest 1. Select the one best response. Answers are found on page 95.

1. During the third through eighth weeks of development, the organism is called a(n)
    a. fetus.
    b. embryo.
    c. zygote.
    d. menarche.

2. The disease rubella produces heart defects if contracted during the first 6 weeks of pregnancy, but it is unlikely to produce heart defects if contracted later. This is most consistent with the concept of
    a. plasticity.
    b. habituation.
    c. critical periods.
    d. assimilation.

3. The sequential development of motor skills is most dependent on
    a. the sequential development of muscle strength.
    b. the sequential development of bone strength.
    c. the sequential development of neural connections.
    d. the sequence of behaviors to which parents pay most attention.

4. Lou, age 70, and Sara, age 20, participated in a memory experiment. What were the likely results?
    a. Lou did better on all tests of memory skills due to his extensive life experiences.
    b. Lou did worse than Sara on recall tests, but did as well as Sara on recognition tests.
    c. Lou did as well as Sara on all tests of memory skills.
    d. Lou did worse than Sara on all tests of memory skills.

5. To study moral development, researchers tested a group of fifty 3-year-olds at yearly intervals over the next 20 years. This procedure is an example of
   a. a cross-sectional design.
   b. a trajectory technique.
   c. longitudinal design.
   d. centration technique.

6. Which is false?
   a. Infants perceive depth at least by the time they are 6 months old.
   b. Infants have at least basic color vision at birth.
   c. Infants prefer pictures of normal faces more than "scrambled" faces.
   d. A newborn's visual acuity is about 20/20.

7. An across the board decline from peak physical functioning typically begins between the ages of
   a. 20-30.
   b. 40-50.
   c. 50-60.
   d. 60-70.

8. The process of changing existing schemata to fit new information is called
   a. accommodation.
   b. conservation.
   c. assimilation.
   d. relativistic thinking.

9. Not being able to understand conservation is partly due to centration. Centration is
   a. the inability to symbolically represent information.
   b. the tendency to consider only one dimension at a time.
   c. the inability to systematically explore problem solutions.
   d. thinking in terms of systems rather than isolated cases.

10. Kiri acts as if her toy doesn't exist when it rolls under the sofa. Kiri is probably in Piaget's
    a. formal operational period.
    b. concrete operational period.
    c. preoperational period.
    d. sensorimotor period.

11. Dee understands conservation, but she can't handle questions that deal with the abstract. She is in
    a. the sensorimotor period.
    b. the formal operational period.
    c. the preoperational period.
    d. the concrete operational period.

12. Object permanence research suggests that
    a. even 1-4 month-olds show surprise when an object does not reappear when a screen is removed.
    b. Piaget's estimate of good object permanence by about age 1 is reasonably accurate.
    c. children do not develop object permanence until they are close to age 3, rather than by age 1.
    d. children have object permanence for living things at birth, but not for nonliving things.

13. Some researchers argue for the addition of a post-formal stage of cognitive development emphasizing
    a. centration.
    b. autonomy.
    c. seriation.
    d. relativistic thinking.

14. Fred said that stealing the drug would be wrong because if caught, the man would go to jail. This is an example of Kohlberg's
    a. preconventional reasoning.
    b. postconventional reasoning.
    c. conventional reasoning.
    d. concrete operational reasoning.

15. Attachment is strongly influenced by all of the following EXCEPT
    a. a biological predisposition for attachment behavior in the infant.
    b. a biological predisposition for attachment behavior in the parent.
    c. contact comfort.
    d. providing a source of food.

16. Tom always acts nervous in mildly strange situations and won't leave his mother's side. He cries if she leaves, but displays affection when she returns. Tom would most likely be classified as having
    a. secure attachment.
    b. resistant attachment.
    c. disorganized/disoriented attachment.
    d. avoidant attachment.

17. Patterns of behavior consistent with society's definition of how males and females should act are
    a. gender schemas.
    b. gender roles.
    c. gender identities.
    d. gender trajectories.

18. If Mike is struggling to achieve generativity rather than stagnation, Mike is probably
    a. an adolescent.
    b. a young adult.
    c. middle-aged.
    d. elderly.

19. Ed is no longer angry he is dying of lung cancer. If Kubler-Ross is correct, Ed will now experience
    a. acceptance.
    b. denial.
    c. bargaining.
    d. depression.

20. Which best represents the conclusions of research on the effects of day care on most children?
    a. Day care seriously damages normal social development.
    b. Day care seriously damages normal cognitive development.
    c. Day care seriously damages both social and cognitive development.
    d. Day care has no serious long-term effects on social or cognitive development.

Multiple Choice Pretest 2. Select the one best response. Answers are found on page 97.

1. The critical factor that causes a female reproductive system to develop is
   a. testosterone release in the 7th-8th week of development.
   b. estrogen release in the 7th-8th week of development.
   c. having no testosterone released in the 7th-8th week of development.
   d. having a Y sex chromosome.

2. Although avoiding drugs, alcohol, smoking, and other toxins throughout pregnancy is best, generally the most important time to avoid them in order to prevent abnormalities is
   a. the first 2 weeks of the prenatal period.
   b. the first three months of the prenatal period.
   c. the middle three months of the prenatal period.
   d. the last three months of the prenatal period.

3. The adaptive value of the plasticity of the brain is
   a. the stability provided by having neural circuits firmly established and operating in a set way.
   b. the capability of adjusting to a particular environment and compensating for cell loss.
   c. the ability to prevent teratogens from entering the brain.
   d. the advantage of being able to grow new neurons to replace those lost through damage or aging.

4. Tom was given little opportunity to move around during the first 9 months of life. He probably will
   a. show life-long problems in motor development, especially walking.
   b. begin to walk at least 1 year later than children given free movement.
   c. begin to walk at least 6 months later than children given free movement.
   d. begin to walk at about the same time as children given free movement.

5. To study changes in processing speed with age, Ted is currently testing a group of 20-year-olds, a group of 30-year-olds and a group of 40-year-olds and comparing their speeds. This is an example of
   a. a horizontal design.
   b. a vertical design.
   c. a cross-sectional design.
   d. a longitudinal design.

6. Meg knows cats are small furry animals. When she saw a mink at the zoo, she kept calling it a cat, even after being told it was a mink. Meg's behavior represents
   a. conservation.
   b. object permanence.
   c. accommodation.
   d. assimilation.

7. To stop Rudy's fussing for an attractive (but dangerous) object, Rudy's mother put it in her pocket. "Out of sight, out of mind," she said, and it worked. Rudy's mother made use of his lack of
   a. conservation.
   b. object permanence.
   c. rooting reflex.
   d. assimilation.

8. Although she saw both pieces taken out of their cans, Amy now thinks that she has less clay than her brother because his has been squashed flat into a big circle. This behavior is characteristic of Piaget's
    a. preoperational period.
    b. formal operational period.
    c. postformal period.
    d. concrete operational period.

9. Lee doesn't understand why his friend doesn't like the same things he does. Lee's inability to consider the perspective of another person represents
    a. accommodation.
    b. reversibility.
    c. habituation.
    d. egocentrism.

10. Kim decided that stealing a drug would be wrong because it is against the law, and because laws are needed to maintain social order. Kim is reasoning at Kohlberg's
    a. postconventional level.
    b. conventional level.
    c. preconventional level.
    d. preoperational level.

11. Clarence is struggling to develop a sense of autonomy. Clarence is probably
    a. a toddler.
    b. between 6 and 12 years old.
    c. an adolescent.
    d. a young adult.

12. Who is most likely to have reached puberty?
    a. Jack, age 12, an avid computer hacker from Los Angeles.
    b. Tom, age 12, who lives in a war-torn, primitive environment.
    c. Yolanda, age 12, whose hobby is horseback riding.
    d. Maria, age 12, whose diet is seriously deficient.

13. The same tone was presented repeatedly until the infant quit responding, then a new, slightly higher pitch tone was presented, and the infant responded again. This is an example of the
    a. longitudinal technique.
    b. habituation technique.
    c. preference technique.
    d. use of reward.

14. In general, the role of experience in perceptual development is
    a. to establish all the basic neural circuits used in perception.
    b. to establish the basic neural circuits used for taste and touch, but not for the other senses.
    c. to make adjustments to the basic neural circuits already established at birth.
    d. very minimal; the neural circuits present at birth allow perception like that in adulthood.

15. Perhaps the most valid criticism of Kohlberg's theory of moral development is that
    a. men and women reason very differently about morality.
    b. people do not seem to go through orderly stages of moral reasoning.
    c. moral development has no relationship to cognitive development.
    d. cross-cultural differences in moral reasoning are not handled well by his theory.

16. Based on Harlow's artificial mother research, hospitals might best promote parent-child attachment if
    a. parents are encouraged to cuddle their newborn often.
    b. parents are encouraged to give their baby its bottle right from the start.
    c. parents are encouraged to wait a few minutes before seeing to the baby's needs.
    d. parents are encouraged to change the baby's diaper right from the start.

17. Evaluations of attachment indicate that about 70% of children have
    a. resistant attachment.
    b. disorganized/disoriented attachment.
    c. secure attachment.
    d. avoidant attachment.

18. Frank, age 70, can't find a part-time job because many employers mistakenly believe all the elderly are sickly, unable to think clearly, and cranky. Frank is experiencing the effects of
    a. ageism.
    b. stagnation.
    c. assimilation.
    d. dementia.

19. A strength of Erikson's psychosocial theory of the development of personal identity is
    a. its proposal that personal identity development is a lifelong process.
    b. its clear and precise description of the psychological mechanisms that resolve the crises.
    c. its scientific rigor (ability to be tested scientifically).
    d. its emphasis on genetic determinants.

20. To avoid the problems of a stage approach, psychologists discuss death in terms of
    a. death trajectories.
    b. death watches.
    c. death schemata.
    d. death cascades.

LANGUAGE DEVELOPMENT GUIDE

Core Terms

In this chapter, you can expect the terms *quantitative* and *qualitative* to be used. Your instructor may say something like, "the differences between children's cognitive development are not merely quantitative, but qualitative." What they are saying is that children don't think LESS than adults do, but DIFFERENTLY than adults do. The form, or quality, of their thinking is different.

Another pair of terms you might hear are *abstract* and *concrete*. Something that is concrete can be touched, seen, and so on. Something that is abstract cannot. For example, a math problem using real beads or coins is concrete; a math problem using just numbers is abstract.

Some other terms have to do with the models of development. Most of these models present development as a *continuum* or *spectrum*, straight lines with different points along the way. You might imagine a number-line or time-line as a continuum, and the colors of a rainbow as a spectrum. Your instructor may talk about someone moving *sequentially* -- that is, step by step in one direction -- through the stages of development. But another pattern of movement is *recursive* -- that is, moving forward a bit, and then stepping back, and then moving forward.

Idioms

p. 105	milestones	important points along a path
p. 108	susceptibility	vulnerability, openness to disease or damage
p. 109	Russian Roulette	a game of chance in which, if you lose, you die
p. 112	teen, teenage	ages 13-18
p. 115	devise a way to infer perceptual capabilities	figure out a way to determine what someone can perceive with their senses
p. 115	immobile, essentially uncommunicative infants	babies who can't move around or say much
p. 115	switching their relative positions from trial to trial	switching them around each time before showing them to the subject
p. 116	operating at peak efficiency	working at the best possible level
p. 116	their biological equipment	their senses, brains and bodies
p. 118	attend selectively to pertinent information	pay attention only to things that are important right now
p. 118	help us interpret ambiguous stimuli	help us perceive things that aren't straightforward or clear
p. 121	attaining adequate nourishment	getting enough food
p. 122	initial stirrings	first signs of; first movements
p. 124	hypothetical outcomes	thinking through an imaginary situation to see what would happen next in it
p. 127	the hallmark of	a main feature of; a good way of recognizing

p. 128	the resident authority figures	the people in charge
p. 128	society's dictum	society's rule
p. 135	well-adjusted	mentally happy and healthy
p. 135	detrimental effects	damaging effects
p. 136	multifaceted concept	an idea with many different possible perspective
p. 140	rudimentary foundations	basic building-blocks
p. 141	at an economic disadvantage	be poor
p. 142	sensitized legions of surgeons	made a great many surgeons aware of
p. 142	dismissed out of hand	ignored or put aside without careful consideration

Word Parts

Here are some words that are made up of word parts, and that you can find in this chapter. After you've looked at these, you can look for others in the chapter that use the same word parts (they are there, but YOU have to find them!)

WORD	WORD PART IT USES	MEANING
prenatal	pre = before natal = birth	before birth
germinal	germ = seed	from the earliest stage of development
conception	con = together cept = to receive	a beginning, a coming together
deform	de = down, from, away form = shape	to be or cause something to be misshapen
quadruple	quad = four	to multiply by four
reproduce	re = again pro = forward duce = to carry	to make another copy
supervise	super = over vise = to look	to watch over, to direct behavior

Knowing the word parts listed above, you can also create the following words. You can get an idea of their meanings from the word parts they use. You fill in the blanks!

misconception   mis (bad) + _____   a bad idea; an idea that was mistaken from the beginning

     + _____

deception   _____ + _____   to lead someone away from the true idea

native   natal   _____

Pronunciation

p. 106	embryonic	im-bree-on′-ick	p. 120	schemata	skee-ma′-ta
p. 107	fetal	fee′-tul	p. 123	egocentrism	ee-go-sin′-tris-um
p. 112	puberty	pew′-ber-tee	p. 140	gender	jin′-der

ANSWERS AND EXPLANATIONS

To find relevant material in your textbook, consult the pages cited with each answer. Also, PN and PT citations refer to modules in *PsychNow!* and *Psyk.trek* materials, respectively.

Mastering the Concepts

1. Development (p. 104)
2. interaction (p. 104)
3. plasticity (p. 105)
4. physically (p. 105)
5. intellectually (p. 105)
6. zygote (p. 106)
7. germinal (p. 106)
8. embryonic (p. 106)
9. fetal (p. 107)
10. teratogens (p. 108)
11. fetal alcohol (p. 109)
12. environmental (p. 109)
13. down and out (p. 110)
14. puberty (p. 112)
15. sexual (p. 112)
16. decline (p. 112)
17. menopause (p. 113)
18. dementia (p. 113)
19. preferences (p. 115)
20. novelty (p. 116)
21. response (p. 115)
22. preference (p. 115)
23. habituation (p. 115)
24. smell (p. 116)
25. depth (p. 117)
26. strategies (p. 118)
27. Recall (p. 118)
28. schemata (p. 120)
29. stages (p. 121)
30. timing (p. 121)
31. order (p. 121)
32. Assimilation (p. 121)
33. accommodation (p. 121)
34. sensorimotor (p. 121)
35. rooting (p. 121)
36. permanence (p. 122)
37. preoperational (p. 122)
38. conservation (p. 122)
39. centration (p. 122)
40. egocentrism (p. 123)
41. concrete (p. 123)
42. formal (p. 124)
43. social (p. 126)
44. relativistic (p. 127)
45. preconventional (p. 128)
46. postconventional (p. 128)
47. reasons (p. 128)
48. social order (p. 128)
49. abstract (p. 128)
50. cultures (p. 129)
51. emotional (p. 131)
52. comfort (p. 132)
53. temperament (p. 132)
54. strange (p. 133)
55. secure (p. 133)
56. cognitive (p. 135)
57. identity (p. 137)
58. old age (p. 138)
59. social (p. 139)
60. two or three (p. 140)
61. roles (p. 140)
62. social learning (p. 140)
63. ageism (p. 141)
64. acceptance (p. 142)

Evaluating Your Progress

Preview & Developing Physically

1. **c**
    (p. 106)
    (PT9A)
    - a. Wrong. The fertilized egg develops into an embryo after two weeks.
    - b. Wrong. The developing child isn't called a fetus after the eighth week of development.
    - d. Wrong. A teratogen is an environmental agent that causes prenatal damage.

2. **c**
    (p. 107)
    - a. Wrong. Differentiation occurs at 7-8 weeks. The germinal period is the first 2 weeks.
    - b. Wrong. Differentiation occurs at 7-8 weeks, not at 1-2 weeks.
    - d. Wrong. Differentiation occurs at 7-8 weeks, not during the 8th or 9th month.

3. **b**
    (p. 108)
    - a. Wrong. Order is not important; whatever is in early stages of development is affected most.
    - c. Wrong. Once initial development is over, the threat is greatly reduced.
    - d. Wrong. The adult effect is not relevant; the structure in its early development is at most risk.

4. **d**
    (p. 109)
    - a. Wrong. Neurons do not significantly increase in number after birth.
    - b. Wrong. Blood vessel growth is minimal compared to that of neural branches and glial cells.
    - c. Wrong. Ventricle enlargement is minimal compared to that of neuron size and complexity.

5. **d**
    (p. 109)
    - a. Wrong. Schemata refers to mental models of the world, not the adaptability of neural circuitry.
    - b. Wrong. Habituation is the reduction in responsiveness to repeated stimuli.
    - c. Wrong. Critical periods are times that are particularly important to aspects of development.

6. **a**
    (p. 110)
    - b, c, & d. Wrong. Development is generally top-down.

7. **b**
    (p. 112)
    - a. Wrong. Menarche is the onset of menstruation, not a developmental period.
    - c. Wrong. The climacteric is the loss of reproductive ability in older men.
    - d. Wrong. Menopause is the cessation of menstruation in older women.

8. **d**
    (p. 112)
    - a. Wrong. Age of puberty seems linked to environmental factors, not genetics.
    - b. Wrong. Unhealthy lifestyles are associated with later, not earlier, puberty onset.
    - c. Wrong. Too much strenuous exercise tends to delay, not speed up, puberty.

9. **d**
    (p. 113)
    (PN6D)
    - a. Wrong. The physical decline tends to be across the board, not limited to one physical dimension.
    - b. Wrong. The idea that menopause is traumatic for most women is a myth.
    - c. Wrong. These are all common changes after age 50.

10. **a**
    (p. 113)
    - b. Wrong. The climacteric is the loss of male reproductive capacity.
    - c. Wrong. Teratogens disrupt prenatal development. Teratogenesis is a fabricated term.
    - d. Wrong. Ageism is discrimination or prejudice based on physical age.

Developing Intellectually

1. **c**
    (p. 115)
    - a. Wrong. The habituation method looks for a renewed response if a new stimulus is presented.
    - b. Wrong. The reward method teaches the infant to make a simple response in order to get a reward.
    - d. Wrong. The cross-sectional method looks at groups of different ages to study changes in behavior.

2. **c**
    (p. 116)
    - a, b, & d. Wrong. These are all possible, but the infant has poor visual acuity.

3. **b**   a. Wrong.   A cross-sectional design would test groups of people of different ages all at once.
  (p. 118)   c. Wrong.   There is no such thing as a time-linked design.
               d. Wrong.   There is no such thing as a continuous design.

4. **d**   a. Wrong.   Generalization is the application of a concept or response to new, similar situations.
  (p. 121)   b. Wrong.   Centration is the tendency to take into account only one dimension.
               c. Wrong.   Accommodation involves changing schemata to accommodate new information.

5. **c**   a, b, & d.   Wrong.   These are all out of order. The sensorimotor period is first.
  (p. 121)
  (PT9C)

6. **a**   b. Wrong.   The formal operational period is characterized by adult-like thought, not reflexes.
  (p. 121)   c. Wrong.   The preoperational period involves primarily voluntary behavior, but thought is limited.
               d. Wrong.   The concrete operational period involves mental operations mostly limited to the concrete.

7. **c**   a. Wrong.   This describes conservation.
  (p. 121)   b. Wrong.   This describes reversibility.
  (PN6B)   d. Wrong.   This describes the ability to avoid centration.

8. **d**   a. Wrong.   This describes centration.
  (p. 121)   b. Wrong.   This describes relativistic thinking.
               c. Wrong.   This describes the sucking reflex.

9. **a**   b, c, & d.   Wrong.   Conservation develops during the preoperational period.
  (p. 122)

10. **c**   a, b, & d.   Wrong.   Systematic and abstract thought are not characteristic of these periods.
  (p. 124)

11. **b**   a. Wrong.   This is the age range for preoperational children.
  (p. 123)   c. Wrong.   This is the lower portion of the age range for the formal operational period.
               d. Wrong.   This is the likely age range for the proposed postformal period.

12. **a**   b. Wrong.   Research shows earlier object permanence, for example, than Piaget proposed.
  (p. 125)   c. Wrong.   Vygotsky suggests that social context is a critical factor in cognitive development.
               d. Wrong.   Different conservation skills are acquired at different times, producing a gradual transition.

13. **c**   a. Wrong.   His theory is supposedly applicable world-wide (but critics say it isn't).
  (p. 128)   b. Wrong.   He proposes development continues into adulthood.
               d. Wrong.   He examines the justification for the "yes" or "no," not the "yes" or "no" itself.

14. **c**   a. Wrong.   This is conventional reasoning.
  (p. 128)   b. Wrong.   This is preconventional reasoning.
               d. Wrong.   This is conventional reasoning.

15. **a**   b. Wrong.   Research finds minimal sex differences in moral reasoning.
  (p. 129)   c. Wrong.   Cross-cultural research confirms an orderly progression of reasoning.
               d. Wrong.   Research suggests Kohlberg's technique is not adequate.

1. **d**   a. Wrong.   Personal identity is one's sense of self.
    (p. 131)   b. Wrong.   Contact comfort is important for forming attachments, but is not attachment.
                c. Wrong.   Dependency is a reliance on, or need for, another person or thing.

2. **a**   b. Wrong.   Attachment was not based on being provided food.
    (p. 131)   c. Wrong.   Monkeys did not become attached to wire mothers.
                d. Wrong.   b & c did not produce attachment.

3. **c**   a, b, & d.   Wrong.   The strange situation test is used to evaluate attachment.
    (p. 133)

4. **c**   a, b, & d.   Wrong.   These are all types of attachment.
    (p. 133)

5. **a**   b, c , & d.   Wrong.   Easy vs. difficult, and uninhibited vs. inhibited are dimensions of temperament.
    (p. 132)

6. **d**   a. Wrong.   Early studies showed this, but recent ones show little, if any, negative effect.
    (p. 135)   b. Wrong.   Quality care is associated with improved social development.
                c. Wrong.   Cognitive benefits are found only if the child's home environment is deficient.

7. **c**   a   Wrong.   Contact comfort is Harlow's idea and relates to attachment, not identity.
    (p. 137)   b. Wrong.   Erikson proposed personal identity development begins during early infancy.
    (PT 9B)   d. Wrong.   Friendship is not a major component in Erikson's theory.

8. **d**   a. Wrong.   The crisis of adolescence is identity vs. role confusion.
    (p. 138)   b. Wrong.   The crisis of early adulthood is intimacy vs. isolation.
    (PN6D)   c. Wrong.   The crisis of middle adulthood is generativity vs. stagnation.

9. **a**   b. Wrong.   Many models are available through other people, television, etc.
    (p. 140)   c. Wrong.   Genitals influence gender identity but don't relate to social learning theory.
                d. Wrong.   The learning in social learning refers to the impact of experience, not innate factors.

10. **b**   a. Wrong.   Depression is out of place.
    (p. 142)   c. Wrong.   Anger is out of place.
                d. Wrong.   Bargaining is out of place.

MAKING FINAL PREPARATIONS

Short Essay Questions

1. Teratogens usually affect whatever is undergoing initial development. Most organs undergo most of their development in the first three months of pregnancy, so teratogens during that period are likely to cause damage. The specific damage depends on the exact timing of the teratogen. Teratogens during the last three months are less likely to have an effect, because most development is complete except for the central nervous system. Thus, the nervous system is the likely site of damage from late teratogens. (p. 108)

2. All of the newborn's senses are operational, but they do not have the capabilities of an older child. In general, the senses lack the precision and perhaps the sensitivity of more mature systems. Changes occur due to maturation of the nervous system, and to some extent, experience. (pp. 116-118)

3. In the preference technique, two stimuli are presented and the amount of time spent looking at each is recorded. If the infant looks at one more than the other (controlling for position, etc.) the infant must be able to discriminate one from the other. Thus, this technique can evaluate color vision, pattern perception, pattern recognition variables, etc. (p. 115)

4. Preconventional (focus on external consequences): He shouldn't steal the drug because he will get caught and sent to jail. Conventional (focus on maintaining social order): He shouldn't steal the drug because stealing is against the law. If everyone stole what they needed, it would be chaos. Postconventional (focus on abstract principles): He shouldn't steal the drug because it is not right to take someone else's property. (p. 128)

5. Secure attachment: The child is upset by the mother's absence or a stranger but is calmed by the mother's return. Resistant attachment: The child is upset by the mother's absence or stranger but is not calmed by the mother's return. Avoidant attachment: The child is not upset by the mother's absence or a stranger. The mother's return receives little attention. (pp. 133-134)

6. This crisis is typical of adolescence. Teenagers are faced with determining who they are and integrating their various attributes into a unified sense of self. Some develop their identity by using information from others (e.g., basing their identity on their parents' attitudes), others perform a personal evaluation, and others just don't define themselves at all. (p. 138)

7. A basic gender identity (I'm a girl) is present at age 3, but it is not stable. The 3-year-old will likely say that a boy can change into a girl if he grows his hair long or wears a dress. By age 7, the gender identity is stable (dresses don't make a boy a girl), and the child will be operating within well-developed gender roles (behavior consistent with society's view of appropriate male or female behavior). (p. 140)

Matching

1. **j** (p. 120)	4. **f** (p. 137)	7. **o** (p. 121)	10. **l** (p. 120)	13. **m** (p. 128)	16. **r** (p. 113)
2. **i** (p. 131)	5. **p** (p. 123)	8. **b** (p. 141)	11. **d** (p. 128)	14. **c** (p. 113)	17. **k** (p. 133)
3. **e** (p. 107)	6. **n** (p. 113)	9. **g** (p. 106)	12. **a** (p. 106)	15. **h** (p. 128)	18. **q** (p. 133)

Multiple Choice Pretest 1

1. **b**
    (p. 106)
    - a. Wrong. The term fetus is used after the 8th week.
    - c. Wrong. The term zygote is used in the 1st-2nd week.
    - d. Wrong. The term menarche refers to the onset of menstruation in females.

2. **c**
    (p. 108)
    - a. Wrong. Plasticity is the ability to change or adapt. It is not related to teratogens.
    - b. Wrong. Habituation is a decrease in the response to repeated stimuli.
    - d. Wrong. Assimilation is a concept in relating to cognitive development, not physical development.

3. **c**
    (p. 110)
    - a. Wrong. Without neural development, muscle strength is a minor factor.
    - b. Wrong. Without neural development, bone strength is a minor factor.
    - d. Wrong. The expectations of parents are not important in determining the sequence.

4. **b**
    (p. 118)
    - a & c. Wrong. Memory deficits are common in the elderly.
    - d.   Wrong. No differences are found for recognition memory.

5. **c**
    (p. 118)
    - a. Wrong. A cross-sectional design would test people of different ages at one point in time.
    - b. Wrong. Trajectory is not a research technique.
    - d. Wrong. Centration is not a research technique. It is a limitation of early thought.

6. **d**   a, b, & c.   Wrong.   Infants do all these things, but their acuity is about 20/600.
(p. 118)

7. **a**   b, c, & d.   Wrong.   The decline begins earlier.
(p. 112)

8. **a**   b. Wrong.   Conservation is the idea that superficial changes don't change the basic properties.
(p. 121)   c. Wrong.   Assimilation involves fitting new information into old schemata.
                d. Wrong.   Relativistic thinking involves considering the relative nature of things.

9. **b**   a. Wrong.   This describes a component of the lack of object permanence.
(p. 122)   c. Wrong.   This describes a component of concrete operational thought.
                d. Wrong.   This describes postformal thought.

10. **d**   a. Wrong.   A lack of object permanence is not typical of the formal operational period.
(p. 122)   b. Wrong.   A lack of object permanence is not typical of the concrete operational period.
                c. Wrong.   A lack of object permanence is not typical of the preoperational period.

11. **d**   a. Wrong.   Neither conservation nor the abstract are understood during the sensorimotor period.
(p. 123)   b. Wrong.   Both conservation and the abstract are understood during the formal operational period.
(PN6B)   c. Wrong.   Neither conservation nor the abstract are understood during the preoperational period.

12. **a**   b & c.   Wrong.   Research shows object permanence develops earlier than Piaget's estimate.
(p. 122)   d.   Wrong.   A living-nonliving distinction has not been made, especially as an innate ability.

13. **d**   a. Wrong.   Centration is characteristic of early childhood.
(p. 127)   b. Wrong.   Autonomy is one of Erikson's personal identity crises.
                c. Wrong.   Seriation is an ordering skill that develops in early childhood.

14. **a**   b. Wrong.   Postconventional reasoning is based on abstract principles, not personal consequences.
(p. 128)   c. Wrong.   Conventional reasoning is based on maintaining social order, not personal consequences
(PT9D)   d. Wrong.   This is not one of Kohlberg's levels of moral reasoning.

15. **d**   a & b.   Wrong.   Both infant and child seem to be predisposed to attachments.
(p. 131)   c.   Wrong.   Contact comfort is an important influence, probably for both monkeys and humans.

16. **b**   a. Wrong.   A securely attached child explores a situation and shows affection when its mother returns.
(p. 133)   c. Wrong.   Disorganized/disoriented attachment involves behavior that is inconsistent, sometimes
                             appearing secure and very disordered at other times.
                d. Wrong.   In avoidant attachment, the child shows no concern about the mother's absence.

17. **b**   a. Wrong.   Gender schemas are organized sets of beliefs held about men and women.
(p. 140)   c. Wrong.   Gender identities are the genders people assign themselves.
                d. Wrong.   Gender theories is a fabricated term.

18. **c**   a. Wrong.   Adolescents struggle with identity vs. role confusion.
(p. 138)   b. Wrong.   Young adults struggle with intimacy vs. isolation.
                d. Wrong.   The elderly struggle with integrity vs. despair.

19. **c**   a. Wrong.   Acceptance is the fifth stage. Ed is just entering the third.
(p. 142)   c. Wrong.   Denial is the first stage. Ed is just entering the third.
                d. Wrong.   Depression is the fourth stage. Ed is just entering the third.

20. **d**   a, b, & c.   Wrong.   Day care does not produce serious problems in social or cognitive development.
(p. 135)

Multiple Choice Pretest 2.

1. **c**   a. Wrong.   Testosterone produces a male system; the lack of testosterone produces a female system.
(p. 106)   b. Wrong.   The lack of testosterone, not the presence of estrogen, produces a female system.
               d. Wrong.   A Y would cause testosterone release, which would cause male genitals to develop.

2. **b**   a.   Wrong.   Little differentiation occurs during the first two weeks, so susceptibility is limited.
(p. 108)   c & d. Wrong.   Susceptibility is greatest when systems are undergoing initial development. Initial
                                     development occurs between the 3rd and 12th weeks (first 3 months).

3. **b**   a. Wrong.   Plasticity involve changeable circuits, not set ones.
(p. 109)   c. Wrong.   Plasticity is the ability to change. It does not block teratogens.
               d. Wrong.   Plasticity is not this great; lost neurons cannot be replaced with new ones.

4. **d**   a, b, & c.   Wrong.   Children learn to walk at about the same time as long as some opportunity to
(p. 111)   move around is available prior to the normal age of walking (12 months).

5. **c**   a & b. Wrong.   These are not actual designs.
(p. 118)   d.   Wrong.   A longitudinal design repeatedly tests groups of same-age people over time.

6. **d**   a. Wrong.   Conservation is the idea that superficial changes don't change the amount of an substance.
(p. 121)   b. Wrong.   Object permanence is the ability to know an object still exists even if it is out of sight.
               c. Wrong.   Accommodation is changing schemata to fit new experiences. Here, no change occurred.

7. **b**   a. Wrong.   Conservation is knowledge that objects' basic properties don't change with surface changes.
(p. 122)   c. Wrong.   The rooting reflex is turning the head to the side toward the cheek that was touched.
               d. Wrong.   Assimilation is the fitting of new experiences into existing schemata.

8. **a**   b. Wrong.   Amy lacks conservation, which is not characteristic of the formal operational period.
(p. 122)   c. Wrong.   Amy lacks conservation, which is not characteristic of the postformal period.
(PN6B)   d. Wrong.   Amy lacks conservation, which is not characteristic of the concrete operational period.

9. **d**   a. Wrong.   Accommodation occurs when schemata are changed to fit new information.
(p. 123)   b. Wrong.   Reversibility is the ability to understand that actions can be reversed.
               c. Wrong.   Habituation is the reduction of a response to repeated stimulation.

10. **b**   a. Wrong.   Postconventional reasoning uses abstract principles, not protecting the social order.
(p. 128)   c. Wrong.   Preconventional reasoning is based on the personal consequences of an action.
(PT9D)   d. Wrong.   The preoperational level is one of Piaget's levels, not Kohlberg's.

11. **a**   b. Wrong.   At ages 6-12, the crisis is industry vs. inferiority.
(p. 137)   c. Wrong.   In adolescence, the struggle is for identity.
               d. Wrong.   In early adulthood, the crisis is intimacy vs. isolation.

12. **c**   a. Wrong.   Average onset of puberty for boys is age 13-14, but for girls it is age 12-13.
(p. 112)   b. Wrong.   Boys enter puberty at age 13-14, girls at 12-13, and stressful, poor conditions delays onset.
               d. Wrong.   Maria's poor diet is likely to delay onset of puberty.

13. **b**   a. Wrong.   The longitudinal technique tests people at different times to examine development.
(p. 115)   c. Wrong.   The preference technique measures gaze time to stimuli presented simultaneously.
          d. Wrong.   Reward is used to teach an infant a response.

14. **c**   a. Wrong.   Infants have relatively good perception at birth; the basic neural circuits are in place.
(p. 109)   b. Wrong.   The basic circuitry for taste and touch is present at birth, along with that for other senses.
          d. Wrong.   Experience influences perceptual development significantly.

15. **d**   a. Wrong.   Research indicates that sex differences are minimal.
(p. 129)   b. Wrong.   Research supports an orderly progression in moral reasoning.
          c. Wrong.   The link between cognitive development and moral reasoning is well accepted.

16. **a**   b. Wrong.   Being the food supplier, especially in a bottle, is not a major factor in attachment.
(p. 131)   c. Wrong.   Attachment is more likely if parents react promptly to the infant's needs.
          d. Wrong.   Providing basic physical needs is not the most important factor in attachment.

17. **c**   a. Wrong.   About 10% have resistant attachment.
(p. 133)   b. Wrong.   Less than 10% have disorganized/disoriented attachment.
          d. Wrong.   About 20% have avoidant attachment.

18. **a**   b. Wrong.   Stagnation is a feeling of meaninglessness in middle age.
(p. 141)   c. Wrong.   Assimilation is a concept in cognitive development, not prejudice against the elderly.
          d. Wrong.   Dementia is a cognitive problem, not prejudice against the elderly.

19. **a**   b. Wrong.   It does not clearly describe the psychological mechanisms of crisis resolution.
(p. 139)   c. Wrong.   It is not scientifically rigorous; its concepts are vague and difficult to test.
          d. Wrong.   Erikson's theory does not propose genetic determinants.

20. **a**   b. Wrong   A death watch involves waiting with a person who is near death.
(p. 143)   c. Wrong.   Death schemata are personal versions of a concept of death.
          d. Wrong.   This is not a valid term.

CHAPTER 5: SENSATION AND PERCEPTION

ESTABLISHING LEARNING GOALS

Use these learning goals as a preview of the chapter, a guide for active reading, and to evaluate your mastery of the material. Review the relevant goals as you begin and end your reading of each major section of the chapter.

I.   Describe the adaptive problem of creating an internal representation of the external world.
    A. Distinguish between sensation and perception.

II. Solve the adaptive problem of creating an effective perception of visual information.
    A. Explain how light gets translated into the electrochemical language of the brain.
       1. Describe the path light travels through the eye, and explain the function of each eye structure.
       2. Describe the process of dark adaptation.
    B. Describe how essential features of the visual message, such as color, are extracted by the brain.
       1. Trace the neural pathway from eye to brain, and describe the processing done at each level.
       2. Explain how color information is extracted and different colors perceived.
    C. Explain how a stable interpretation of visual information is created, and why the interpretation process sometimes produces visual illusions.
       1. Compare bottom-up and top-down processing.
       2. Discuss how information is organized into groups or forms and then recognized.
       3. List and describe types of information used to create a perception of depth.
       4. Discuss perceptual constancy, and explain its relationship to depth perception and illusions.

III. Solve the adaptive problem of creating an effective perception of auditory information.
    A. Explain how sound, the physical message, is translated into the electrochemical language of the brain.
       1. Describe the sound stimulus.
       2. Describe the path sound travels through the ear, and explain the function of each structure.
    B. Discuss how pitch information is pulled out of the auditory message.
    C. Explain how the auditory message is interpreted and how sound is localized.

IV. Solve the adaptive problem of creating an effective perception of information from the skin and body.
    A. Explain how sensory messages delivered to the skin (touch and temperature) are translated and interpreted by the brain.
    B. Describe how we perceive and interpret pain.
    C. Discuss the operation and function of the body senses: movement and balance.

V.   Solve the adaptive problem of creating an effective perception of information from the chemical senses.
    A. Describe how chemical stimuli produce neural activity that is interpreted as different odors and tastes.

VI. Solve the practical problem of quantifying the relationship of the physical and psychological event.
    A. Explain stimulus detection, including techniques designed to measure it.
    B. Define difference threshold, and explain Weber's Law.
    C. Discuss stimulus adaptation and its adaptive value.

MASTERING THE MATERIAL

Preview & Vision: Building a World of Color and Form (pp. 150-174)

Mastering the Vocabulary. Define or explain each of the following terms. To check your answers, consult the text pages listed.

1. sensations (p. 150)

2. perception (p. 150)

3. transduction (p. 151)

4. light (p. 152)

5. hue (p. 152)

6. brightness (p. 153)

7. cornea (p. 153)

8. lens (p. 153)

9. pupil (p. 153)

10. iris (p. 153)

11. accommodation (p. 153)

12. retina (p. 154)

13. rods (p. 154)

14. cones (p. 154)

15. fovea (p. 155)

16. visual acuity (p. 155)

17. receptive field (p. 155)

18. blind spot (p. 156)

19. dark adaptation (p. 157)

20. feature detectors (p. 158)

21. trichromatic theory (p. 162)

22. opponent-process theory (p. 163)

23. bottom-up processing (p. 165)

24. top-down processing (p. 165)

25. Gestalt principles of organization (p. 165)

26. recognition by components (p. 167)

27. monocular depth cues (p. 168)

28. binocular depth cues (p. 168)

29. retinal disparity (p. 168)

30. convergence (p. 168)

31. phi phenomenon (p. 169)

32. perceptual constancy (p. 167)

33. perceptual illusions (p. 171)

Mastering the Concepts. Fill in the blanks to create a summary of the section. Answers are on page 120.

This chapter explores the adaptive problems of translating the external message into neural activity, extracting the message components for analysis, and producing stable interpretations of changing stimulation. The basic components of experience, _____(1), are processed to produce an interpretation or _____(2) of the stimulus. Light coming directly from a source or reflected by an object enters the eye, is transduced into _____(3) energy, and is processed in the brain to create a perception of form and color. The cornea and lens of the eye _____(4) light on the retina, where it stimulates cones and _____(5), the visual receptors. Rods work in low light, whereas cones work in normal light and provide color vision and good _____(6), the ability to see detail. _____(7) adaptation is needed for top efficiency.

Receptor activity causes a neural response in the bipolar and ganglion cells. Most signals are carried by the optic nerve to the _____(8) and then to the primary visual cortex. _____(9) detectors, single cells that respond to specific stimuli (e.g., 45˚ lines), are found in the visual cortex in a very organized arrangement. Other cortical areas are involved in more complex, visual processing.

Color vision is made possible by three types of cones, each responsive to either short, medium, or long _____(10) of light. _____(11) theory states color is perceived based on the relative activity in three cone types. Color _____(12) occurs when one of type of cone is missing. _____(13) process theory proposes colors are paired, and each member produces opposite neural responses. Data suggest trichromatic processes apply in the retina, and opponent processes apply at higher levels.

Form perception involves both bottom-up (sensory) analysis and top-down analysis using context or _____(14). The _____(15) psychologists proposed principles of perceptual organization, including proximity, similarity, closure, good continuation, and common fate. Recognition by components theory states complex forms are recognized from _____(16), their simpler components.

Cues for depth, such as linear perspective, shading, convergence and _____(17) disparity, allow a 3-dimensional perception. Motion perception provides information about object shape, location, and figure-ground relationships. Retinal image movement is an inadequate cue for motion, and the _____(18) phenomenon proves that no real movement is required to perceive motion. Although sensory input is variable, we are able to maintain an unchanging perception, or perceptual _____(19).

Depth cues serve as cues for constancy, but if misapplied, _____(20) occur.

Evaluating Your Progress. Select the one best response. Answers are found on page 120. If you make any errors, reread the relevant material before proceeding.

1. The wavelength of a light generally corresponds to its perceived
   a. hue.
   b. acuity.
   c. brightness.
   d. accommodation.

2. Without her glasses, Leah sees everything out of focus. She probably has a defective
   a. retina.
   b. pupil.
   c. iris.
   d. lens.

3. Which is not a characteristic of the rods?
   a. located in the periphery (sides)
   b. provide color vision
   c. work well in low light conditions
   d. long and thin in shape

4. Sensitivity to light increases during dark adaptation because
   a. photopigments are replenished.
   b. the receptive fields get larger.
   c. the brain "fills in" missing information.
   d. the vitreous humor becomes thinner.

5. Several receptor cells send input to a single ganglion cell. These receptors define the ganglion cell's
   a. blind spot.
   b. optic chiasm.
   c. receptive field.
   d. fovea.

6. Single cells in the cortex that respond best to lines at a specific angle are called
   a. akinetopsias.
   b. photoreceptors.
   c. feature detectors.
   d. bipolar cells.

7. The relative activity levels of three types of cones are used to perceive color according to the
   a. opponent process theory.
   b. recognition by components theory.
   c. place theory.
   d. trichromatic theory.

8. Each eye receives a slightly different image than the other. This is the cue for depth known as
   a. linear perspective.
   b. convergence.
   c. retinal disparity.
   d. shading.

9. The role knowledge and context have in perception relates to
   a. top-down processing.
   b. bottom-up processing.
   c. opponent processing.
   d. feature processing.

10. All of the following contribute to our perception of motion EXCEPT
    a. changes in the position of our eyes.
    b. changes in the size of the pupil.
    c. changes in the relative positions of objects in a scene.
    d. changes in the characteristics or location of an object's image on the retina.

11. A distant car casts a smaller image than a nearby car, but we perceive them to be the same size due to
    a. bottom-up processing.
    b. feature detectors.
    c. good acuity.
    d. perceptual constancy.

Hearing: Identifying and Localizing Sounds (pp. 175-179)

Mastering the Vocabulary. Define or explain each of the following terms. To check your answers, consult the text pages listed.

1. sound (p. 175)

2. pitch (p. 175)

3. pinna (p. 176)

4. tympanic membrane (p. 176)

5. middle ear (p. 176)

6. cochlea (p. 176)

7. basilar membrane (p. 176)

8. place theory (p. 177)

9. frequency theory (p. 178)

Mastering the Concepts. Fill in the blanks to create a summary of the section. Answers are on page 120.

Sound is mechanical energy from the movement of molecules within a physical medium such as air. The rate of these vibrations, measured in hertz (Hz), produces the _____(21) of the sound, and their amplitude (energy) produces the _____(22), which is measured in units called decibels (dB).

Sound is captured by the _____(23), and travels down the auditory canal to the tympanic membrane, which vibrates. Three tiny _____(24) in the middle ear transfer the vibration to the oval window of the _____(25) in the inner ear. This vibration creates motion in the cochlear fluid, causing the _____(26) membrane to move. The movement bends _____(27) cells, the auditory receptors, generating a neural impulse that travels via the auditory nerve to the brain. Input from each ear is processed primarily by the _____(28) hemisphere. Neurons respond most to specific frequencies and less to others. Auditory cortex cells respond selectively to particular sequences of tones.

Different sound frequencies produce different patterns of movement of basilar membrane, and thus, stimulate different hair cells. Low frequencies cause movement near the _____(29) end of the coiled basilar membrane; high frequencies peak near the _____(30). This location information is used to discriminate pitch, according to the _____(31) theory. The brain interprets activity in neurons from a specific location as reflecting a particular pitch (frequency). This is compatible with patterns of deafness, but it is limited by a lack of independence in hair cell activity. The _____(32) principle of pitch suggests the rate (frequency) of neural firing signals pitch. That is, high frequency impulses reflect a high frequency (high pitch). The firing rate across groups of neurons, or _____(33), extends frequency information. Simple and complex auditory feature detectors are found in the cortex.

Ambiguity in auditory input limits identification based on physical characteristics. Auditory figure-ground is organized on the basis of _____(34), timing, and top-down factors such as knowledge and _____(35). Location is determined by input intensity and timing differences at the two ears.

Evaluating Your Progress. Select the one best response. Answers are found on page 121. If you make any errors, reread the relevant material before proceeding.

1. The frequency of a sound stimulus corresponds to its
    a. intensity.
    b. pitch.
    c. location.
    d. purity.

2. The structure that contains the hair cells, the auditory receptors, is the
    a. semicircular canal.
    b. tympanic membrane.
    c. cochlea.
    d. pinna.

3. A neural impulse is generated by the hair cells when
    a. neurotransmitters are released by the tympanic membrane.
    b. the malleus, incus, and stapes push against them.
    c. they are bent during movement of the basilar membrane.
    d. a chemical change occurs in the fluid of the cochlea.

4. The malleus, incus and stapes are
    a. bones in the middle ear.
    b. membranes in the cochlea.
    c. types of hair cells.
    d. specific characteristics of the auditory waveform.

5. The place theory states that pitch is perceived based on
    a. the frequency of the neural impulses generated in the cochlea.
    b. the strength of the neural impulses generated in the cochlea.
    c. the number of neurons activated by the sound.
    d. which specific neurons are firing the most during a sound.

6. A tone is presented to your left ear a fraction of a second before an identical tone is presented to your right ear. You are most likely to perceive
    a. two tones, with the one in your left ear slightly higher frequency than the one in your right.
    b. two tones, with the one in your left ear slightly louder than the one in your right.
    c. a single tone located to the right of center.
    d. a single tone located to the left of center.

7. The primary factor that allows good auditory localization is
    a. having two ears.
    b. having good pitch discrimination.
    c. knowing the content of the message.
    d. having good frequency detectors in the auditory cortex.

The Skin and Body Senses: *From Movement to Touch* (pp. 180-183)

Mastering the Vocabulary. Define or explain each of the following terms. To check your answers, consult the text pages listed.

1. somatosensory cortex (p. 181)

2. cold fibers (p. 181)

3. warm fibers (p. 181)

4. pain (p. 182)

5. gate control theory (p. 182)

6. kinesthesia (p. 183)

7. semicircular canals (p. 183)

8. vestibular sacs (p. 183)

Mastering the Concepts. Fill in the blanks to create a summary of the section. Answers are on page 120.

The skin senses are touch, _____(36), and pain. Different types of pressure-sensitive receptor cells respond to different aspects of touch stimuli. Touch input goes to the _____(37) cortex. Cold fibers and warm fibers react to _____(38) in skin temperature.

The response to injury-causing stimuli, _____(39), involves stimulus and psychological factors. The _____(40) theory states pain signals can be blocked by closing a "gate" in the _____(41). Physical and cognitive factors close the gate. Pain can be reduced by release of _____(42) in the brain. Kinesthesia is the ability to sense the _____(43) and position of body parts. Receptors are in the skin, tendons, muscles, and _____(44). Input goes to the somatosensory cortex. The _____(45) sense responds to movement, acceleration, and posture changes. Receptors in the _____(46) canals and vestibular sacs send input to the somatosensory cortex. Disturbances of the vestibular system cause dizziness or nausea.

Evaluating Your Progress. Select the one best response. Answers are found on page 121. If you make any errors, reread the relevant material before proceeding.

1. The skin senses include all of the following except
   a. temperature.
   b. touch.
   c. kinesthesia.
   d. pain.

2. Neural responses for touch are generated when touch receptors in the skin are stimulated by
   a. mechanical energy.
   b. electromagnetic energy.
   c. changes in air pressure.
   d. chemical energy.

3. The gate control theory suggests cognitive factors influence pain by opening or closing a "gate" in
   a. the free nerve endings.
   b. the tympanic membrane.
   c. the spinal cord.
   d. the somatosensory cortex.

4. Receptors for the kinesthetic sense are located in the
   a. cortex.
   b. muscles, joints, tendons, and skin.
   c. semicircular canals of the inner ear.
   d. cochlea.

5. If you have a lot of activity coming from the semicircular canals, you probably
   a. are moving.
   b. are touching something.
   c. are listening to something.
   d. are smelling something.

6. The semicircular canals are in the
   a. spine.
   b. muscles of the eyes, neck, and head.
   c. sinuses.
   d. inner ear.

The Chemical Senses: Smell and Taste (pp. 184-186)

Mastering the Vocabulary. Define or explain each of the following terms. To check your answers, consult the text pages listed.

1. chemoreceptors (p. 184)

2. olfaction (p. 184)

3. gustation (p. 185)

4. flavor (p. 186)

5. taste buds (p. 186)

Mastering the Concepts. Fill in the blanks to create a summary of the section. Answers are on page 120.

The receptors for smell and taste are called _____(47). Olfactory receptors found in the roof of the nasal cavity bind with odorant molecules, and a neural impulse is generated and transmitted to the _____(48) and the limbic system. Some odors, pheromones, are related to _____(49) behavior.

Taste, or gustation, relies on receptors found in _____(50) in the papillae of the tongue. Input is sent to the somatosensory cortex. Although there are four basic tastes, receptors are not finely tuned to only one. The pattern across many receptors is critical. Some tastes are dependent on olfaction.

Evaluating Your Progress. Select the one best response. Answers are found on page 122. If you make any errors, reread the relevant material before proceeding

1. The receptors for smell and taste are called
    a. vestibular sacs.
    b. free nerve endings.
    c. chemoreceptors.
    d. mechanoreceptors.

2. Some animals produce chemicals that produce very predictable, specific responses (often sexual) by other members of the species. These chemicals are known as
    a. perfumes.
    b. pheromones.
    c. papillae.
    d. endorphins.

3. There are _____ basic tastes.
    a. 4
    b. 6
    c. 12
    d. over 1000.

From the Physical to the Psychophysical (pp. 187-190)

Mastering the Vocabulary. Define or explain each of the following terms. To check your answers, consult the text pages listed.

1. psychophysics (p. 187)

2. absolute threshold (p. 187)

3. signal detection (p. 188)

4. difference threshold (p. 189)

5. Weber's law (p. 189)

6. sensory adaptation (p. 190)

Mastering the Concepts. Fill in the blanks to create a summary of the section. Answers are on page 120.

Psychophysics studies the relationship between the physical stimulus and the psychological event. The _____(51) threshold is the intensity at which a stimulus is detected 50% of the time. Responses are influenced by both sensitivity and bias. The _____(52) technique is used to find the impact of bias by comparing rates of hits and _____(53). Difference thresholds are the smallest detectable change, the just noticeable difference. Weber's Law states that the difference threshold is a constant _____(54) of the standard stimulus. With continuous stimulation, sensory _____(55) occurs, reducing sensitivity.

Evaluating Your Progress. Select the one best response. Answers are found on page 122. If you make any errors, reread the relevant material before proceeding.

1. The field of psychophysics studies
    a. the relationship between the physical stimulus and the psychological experience.
    b. the way in which the stimulus stimulates the receptor organs.
    c. the neural pathway sensory information travels to the brain.
    d. the stability of perception in spite of changing stimulation.

2. The absolute threshold is
   a. the minimum stimulus energy that can be detected 50% of the time.
   b. the minimum amount of change in stimulus energy that can be detected 50% of the time.
   c. the maximum stimulus energy that does not produce pain sensations.
   d. the stimulus energy at which increases in intensity do not produce changes in perception.

3. To determine whether a person's detection ability is due to true sensory sensitivity or due to strategy or bias, researchers are most likely to use
   a. Weber's Law.
   b. sensory adaptation.
   c. the signal detection technique.
   d. transduction.

4. We don't notice the smell of our own perfume after a period of time. This is best explained by
   a. Weber's Law.
   b. signal detection theory.
   c. perceptual constancy.
   d. sensory adaptation.

MAKING FINAL PREPARATIONS

Complete these sections without consulting your book or notes. For a more accurate estimate of how well you know this material, wait at least a day or two after studying the chapter before working on the questions. Some of the material you "know" immediately after working with the chapter will be quickly forgotten. Immediate tests will overestimate what you know well.

Short Essay Questions. Write a brief answer to each question. Sample answers are on page 123.

1. Describe and explain the time course of dark adaptation.

2. Compare the characteristics and functions of the rods and cones.

3. Explain why expectancy is important and how it influences perception.

4. Define perceptual constancy and explain why it is adaptive.

5. Explain the relationship between depth perception and size perception.

6. Describe the place theory and frequency principle of pitch perception, and explain why both are needed to account for pitch discrimination.

7. Explain why you will have difficulty telling the direction from which an emergency vehicle is approaching if you drive with only your left windows open.

8. Explain why rubbing an injury often reduces the pain.

Matching. Select the correct definition or description for each item. Answers are on page 123.

_____	1. sensation	**a.**	visual center of the retina, containing only cones
_____	2. optic chiasm	**b.**	point in the retina where the optic nerve exits
_____	3. pheromones	**c.**	layer of tissue containing photoreceptors
_____	4. lateral geniculate nucleus	**d.**	brain structure that receives olfactory input
_____	5. Weber's Law	**e.**	the basic components of an experience
_____	6. top-down processing	**f.**	correctly detecting the presence of a stimulus
_____	7. fovea	**g.**	area of the thalamus that receives visual input
_____	8. acuity	**h.**	neurons that are activated by cooling of the skin
_____	9. cold fibers	**i.**	inner ear structures that signal motion and posture
_____	10. olfactory bulb	**j.**	crossover point for visual system neurons
_____	11. feature detectors	**k.**	the ability to perceive fine detail
_____	12. vestibular sacs	**l.**	uses knowledge and expectancy to identify stimuli
_____	13. blind spot	**m.**	neurons that respond to specific stimulus attributes
_____	14. iris	**n.**	scents that produce a specific response
_____	15. hit	**o.**	colored tissue surrounding the pupil
_____	16. retina	**p.**	predicts difference thresholds

Multiple Choice Pretest 1. Select the one best response. Answers are found on page 123.

1. The first structure light encounters when it reaches the eye is the
    a. retina.
    b. lens.
    c. iris.
    d. cornea.

2. Most people need reading glasses when they get older because they lose accommodation power due to
    a. the shrinkage of the eyeball.
    b. a reduction in the amount of photopigment.
    c. reduced flexibility of the lens.
    d. an increase in the pressure in the eyeball.

3. All of the following are characteristics of the cones EXCEPT:
    a. A cone contains any of three photopigments.
    b. Cones work best in bright light.
    c. Cones are concentrated in the periphery (sides) of the retina.
    d. Cones give color vision.

4. To be fully dark-adapted, you must remain in the dark about
   a. 5 minutes.
   b. 10 minutes.
   c. 15 minutes.
   d. 20 minutes.

5. Cells have been found in the lateral geniculate nucleus that increase their firing rate to red and decrease their firing rate to green. This data best supports
   a. opponent process theory.
   b. trichromatic theory.
   c. frequency theory.
   d. top-down processing theory.

6. Biederman's recognition by components theory states that objects are recognized on the basis of
   a. the activity in single-cell feature detectors.
   b. top-down processing more than bottom-up processing.
   c. simple component forms called geons.
   d. binocular disparity information.

7. Small differences in the placement of images on the left and right retinas help create 3-dimensional perception. This depth cue is
   a. convergence.
   b. retinal disparity.
   c. linear perspective.
   d. accomodation.

8. Size perception is inaccurate in the Ames room and the Ponzo illusion because
   a. figure-ground relationships are not clear.
   b. stimulus distance is misjudged.
   c. binocular disparity is reversed.
   d. top-down processing is not possible.

9. Sequentially flashing lights make a wheel in a neon sign appear to turn. This is an example of
   a. convergence.
   b. sensory adaptation.
   c. the volley principle.
   d. the phi phenomenon.

10. Proximity, common fate, and closure are
    a. principles used to organize figure and ground.
    b. examples of top-down processing.
    c. determinants of pitch perception.
    d. determinants of visual acuity.

11. The traveling wave concept is very important for understanding
    a. gate control theory.
    b. place theory.
    c. trichromatic theory.
    d. frequency theory.

12. A cochlear neuron is firing very rapidly. According to the frequency principle, the sound is probably
    a. loud.
    b. located very close by.
    c. high pitch.
    d. composed of several frequencies.

13. We perceive cold only when
    a. the temperature of our skin is reduced.
    b. cold fibers fire at a specific rate.
    c. the stimulus is below 50 degrees.
    d. a papilla is stimulated intensely.

14. Awareness of where your arms and legs are located is the product of the
    a. olfactory sense.
    b. vestibular sense.
    c. gustatory sense.
    d. kinesthetic sense.

15. Sensing movement and balance is the function of
    a. the semicircular canals and vestibular sacs.
    b. the cochlea and basilar membrane.
    c. the tympanic membrane and pinna.
    d. the lateral geniculate nucleus and superior colliculus.

16. If endorphins are released, we should expect the organism to
    a. feel less pain.
    b. be attracted to the source of the endorphins.
    c. experience dizziness or nausea.
    d. see color.

17. Which is false?
    a. Loss of the olfactory system would affect the flavor of food.
    b. The receptors for gustation are located in the taste buds.
    c. Olfactory signals are transmitted from receptor neurons to the olfactory bulb.
    d. There are four specific types of olfactory receptors, corresponding to 4 basic smells.

18. Papillae are
    a. hair-like structures in the taste bud.
    b. bumps on the tongue that contain the taste buds.
    c. the actual receptor cells for taste.
    d. neurons that are linked with the taste receptors.

19. The dark adaptation curve is really a plot of _____ for vision as a function of time in the dark.
    a. Weber's Law
    b. false alarms
    c. absolute threshold
    d. difference threshold

20. In the signal detection technique a hit is recorded when the observer reports
    a. feeling a touch when he was touched.
    b. feeling a touch when he was not touched.
    c. feeling no touch when he was touched.
    d. feeling no touch when he was not touched.

Multiple Choice Pretest 2. Select the one best response. Answers are found on page 125.

1. Hubel and Wiesel found that if they moved the electrode just to the side of a cell that responded only to lines at a 30-degree angle they usually found cells that responded to
    a. lines at a 20 degree angle.
    b. depth.
    c. movement.
    d. faces.

2. A moving object high in the sky was seen as an enemy aircraft by the soldier on guard, but as a bird by the birdwatcher doing a bird count. This is explained best by
    a. recognition by components theory.
    b. top-down processing.
    c. Gestalt principles of perceptual organization.
    d. transduction.

3. The adaptive value of accommodation is that it
    a. allows the lens to focus light from objects located at different distances.
    b. allows the rods to regenerate their photopigment in order to provide better vision in the dark.
    c. allows the organization of the stimulus input into different objects.
    d. allows the brain to "fill in" the blind spot.

4. While drifting with the debris in the river current, the fugitive went undetected. However, as soon as he started swimming across the current, he was spotted. This is an example of the Gestalt law of
    a. closure.
    b. good continuation.
    c. common fate.
    d. proximity.

5. Dana sees no glowing embers when she looks directly at the fireplace, but when she looks a little to the side, she can see a dimly glowing spot. What is the best explanation for this?
    a. Dark adaptation occurs faster outside the fovea.
    b. Rods produce more retinal disparity.
    c. Cones provide better acuity.
    d. Cones are less sensitive than rods.

6. Dick cannot see red or green. His common form of color blindness is due to
    a. having only one kind of rod.
    b. an optic nerve disorder.
    c. lacking one type of cone photopigment.
    d. having no cones.

7. The current view of the trichromatic theory and opponent-process theory of color is that
   a. trichromatic theory applies in the retina, and the opponent process theory applies at higher levels.
   b. opponent process theory applies in the retina, and the trichromatic theory applies at higher levels.
   c. trichromatic theory applies to primary colors, and opponent process theory applies to others.
   d. opponent process theory applies to primary colors, and trichromatic theory applies to others.

8. Ed lost one eye in an accident. His depth perception is still fairly good because he can use
   a. convergence.
   b. common fate.
   c. linear perspective.
   d. retinal disparity.

9. Marika is hearing-impaired because her auditory hair cells and the structure along which they are located were damaged by a strange virus. The virus must have infected
   a. the pinna.
   b. the basilar membrane.
   c. the semicircular canals.
   d. the tympanic membrane.

10. Although both squares are at the same distance, depth cues make one square look farther away than another identical square. The "distant" square will be perceived as _____ than the other.
    a. more square
    b. less square
    c. larger
    d. smaller

11. The firing rate of neurons is limited by their refractory period to a maximum of about 500 impulses per second. This creates a problem for
    a. the frequency theory.
    b. the place theory.
    c. the opponent process theory.
    d. the gate control theory.

12. You're trying to hear an important news bulletin on the radio, but everyone around you is talking excitedly. You will be able to separate the bulletin from the other sounds most easily if
    a. you are male and the bulletin announcer is male, rather than female.
    b. the people talking around you are male and the bulletin announcer is male, rather than female.
    c. everyone is clustered around the radio.
    d. you know something about the expected content of the bulletin.

13. Varying a sound's arrival time at each ear will change
    a. the perceived location of the sound.
    b. the pitch of the sound.
    c. the intensity of the sound.
    d. the comprehension (meaning) of the sound.

14. Which of the following is FALSE concerning the skin senses?
    a. The amount of cortex that processes input from the skin is proportional to the size of the body part.
    b. People are very good at identifying common articles by touch.
    c. "Warm" or "cold" is determined by changes in skin temperature, not an object's actual temperature.
    d. Different types of pressure-sensitive receptors respond to different types of touch stimulation.

15. During a battle for his life, the soldier did not notice the cuts he received from the rocks, but when you fell while rollerblading and received similar injuries, you felt significant pain. This is best explained by
    a. gate control theory.
    b. bottom-up processing.
    c. frequency theory.
    d. assuming you produced more endorphins.

16. The apparent role of olfaction in sexual behavior, feeding, and emotion is not surprising given that the olfactory neural path includes links to
    a. the olfactory bulb.
    b. the amygdala, hippocampus, and hypothalamus.
    c. the somatosensory cortex.
    d. the thalamus.

17. To increase profits, the cereal company wants to reduce the amount of raisins in each cup of cereal, but they don't want consumers to notice the change. To know how many raisins they can remove, they first need to obtain an estimate of the
    a. absolute threshold for raisins in a cup of cereal.
    b. difference threshold for raisins in a cup of cereal.
    c. signal detection threshold for raisins in a cup of cereal.
    d. hit rate for raisin detection in a cup of cereal.

18. The neural code for a specific taste is probably based on
    a. whether or not a specific receptor cell is active.
    b. how many papillae are stimulated.
    c. the relative amount of activity in 4 areas of the tongue.
    d. the pattern of activity across large groups of taste fibers.

19. Tom, 140 lb., Dick, 190 lb., and Harry, 240 lb., are beginning a weight-loss diet. According to Weber's Law (and assuming they all lose the same number of pounds per week) we should expect that
    a. Tom's weight loss will be noticeable first.
    b. Dick's weight loss will be noticeable first.
    c. Harry's weight loss will be noticeable first.
    d. a noticeable reduction in weight will occur at the same time for the three men.

20. What is the major advantage of using signal detection theory for studying sensory abilities?
    a. It measures absolute threshold and difference threshold simultaneously.
    b. It can be used with all senses, rather than just hearing and vision.
    c. It measures sensitivity and bias separately.
    d. It determines the brain areas that are most active in a sensory task.

Language Development Guide

Core Terms

In the discussion of this chapter you are very likely to hear two expressions quite frequently: **to distinguish between, to differentiate** and **to discriminate**. The last one is likely to be confusing the first time you hear it, because it has such a particular meaning in most people's minds (something close to 'prejudice'). Actually, the terms all mean very nearly the same thing -- to tell the difference between. And of course, the ability to tell the difference between things is important when we are discussing the senses.

Also, you will need to be comfortable with several Latin- and Greek-based words relating to the senses:

vis or *vid*, to see, becomes vision or video

aud and *acous*, to hear, becomes auditory or acoustic (The word part *son* means sound)

tact or *tang*, to touch, becomes tactile or tangible

kinet, to move, becomes kinesthetic

olfac, to smell, becomes olfactory

gust, to taste, becomes gustatory

Vestibular, as it turns out, is an exception to the rule. A 'vestibule' is a small entrance area like a lobby or, in anatomical terms, a chamber or channel that leads into another chamber or channel. To figure out why this sense is named as it is, you'll need to know where its sensory organ is located.

Idioms

p. 150	bolt upright	to suddenly sit up straight
p. 150	beckon your interpretation	invite you to figure them out
p. 151	cut across all	work in all cases; be relevant in all
p. 152	tackle the topic	address the subject; talk about
p. 160	upper- or lowercase	capital or small letters
p. 167	three-dimensional	having height, length and depth
p. 167	plastered on	laid onto
p. 181	perceptual enigma	confusing experience of the senses
p. 183	locus of such effects	the location, focus, or origin of the effects
p. 183	analgesic	pain-relieving
p. 183	acupuncture	a medical procedure from Asia that involves the insertion of special needles into body parts
p. 189	strategic bias	a desire or way to achieve a certain goal

Word Parts

Here are some words that are made up of word parts, and that you can find in this chapter. After you've looked at these, you can look for others in the chapter.

WORD	WORD PART IT USES	MEANING
recognize	re = again gno = to think, understand, know	to know again, to find familiar
ambiguous	ambi = both	having multiple interpretations; unclear
extract	ex = out of tract = to pull	to pull out of
translate	trans = across lat = line	to cross over, to change to another
receptive	re = again cept = to get, take	to be willing to take back again
regenerate	re = again gen = birth, race, kind	to start over again
transduce	trans = across duc = to carry	to carry across
dichromats	di = two chrom = color	those who can only see two colors

Knowing the word parts listed above, you can also create the following words. You can get an idea of their meanings from the word parts they use. You fill in the blanks!

except	ex + cept	_____
intractable	in (not) + tract	_____
retract	_____ + _____	to pull back

Pronunciation

p. 153	pupil	pew′-pul	p. 176	tympanic	tim- pan′-ick
p. 155	acuity	a-kew′-i-tee	p. 176	cochlea	cock′-lee-a ; coke′-lee-a
p. 165	Gestalt	ge-stalt′	p. 189	Weber	vay′-ber

119

ANSWERS AND EXPLANATIONS

To find relevant material in your textbook, consult the pages cited with each answer. Also, PN and PT citations refer to modules in *PsychNow!* and *Psyk.trek* materials, respectively.

Mastering the Concepts

1. sensations (p. 150)	15. Gestalt (p. 165)	29. far (p. 177)	43. movement (p. 183)
2. perception (p. 150)	16. geons (p. 166)	30. oval window (p. 177)	44. joints (p. 183)
3. neural (p. 153)	17. retinal (p. 168)	31. place (p. 177)	45. vestibular (p. 183)
4. focuses (p. 153)	18. phi (p. 169)	32. frequency (p. 178)	46. semicircular (p. 183)
5. rods (p. 154)	19. constancy (p. 169)	33. volleys (p. 178)	47. chemoreceptors (p. 184)
6. acuity (p. 155)	20. illusions (p. 171)	34. similarity (p. 179)	48. olfactory bulb (p. 185)
7. Dark (p. 157)	21. pitch (p. 175)	35. expectations (p. 179)	49. sexual (p. 185)
8. thalamus (p. 158)	22. loudness (p. 175)	36. temperature (p. 180)	50. taste buds (p. 186)
9. Feature (p. 158)	23. pinna (p. 176)	37. somatosensory (p. 181)	51. absolute (p. 187)
10. wavelengths (p. 160)	24. bones (p. 176)	38. changes (p. 181)	52. signal detection (p. 188)
11. Trichromatic (p. 162)	25. cochlea (p. 176)	39. pain (p. 182)	53. false alarms (p. 188)
12. blindness (p. 162)	26. basilar (p. 176)	40. gate control (p. 182)	54. proportion (p. 189)
13. Opponent (p. 163)	27. hair (p. 176)	41. spinal cord (p. 182)	55. adaptation (p. 190)
14. knowledge (p. 165)	28. opposite (p. 177)	42. endorphins (p. 183)	

Evaluating Your Progress

Preview & Vision: Building a World of Color and Form

1. **a**
(p. 152)
(PT3A)
  b. Wrong. Acuity is the ability to resolve fine details of a visual stimulus.
  c. Wrong. Brightness is associated with the intensity of a visual stimulus.
  d. Wrong. Accommodation is the adjustment of the lens to properly focus light on the retina.

2. **d**
(p. 153)
(PN 3A)
  a. Wrong. The retina contains the receptor cells. It does not focus the light.
  b. Wrong. The pupil is the opening for the light.
  c. Wrong. The iris is the colored part of the eye and does not focus light.

3. **b**
(p. 155)
  a. Wrong. Unlike the cones, rods are not found in the fovea.
  c. Wrong. The rod photopigment allows operation in low light.
  d. Wrong. Their long slender shape gives them their name.

4. **a**
(p. 157)
  b. Wrong. Receptive field size is a function of neural connections, not light level.
  c. Wrong. The brain fills in information in the blind spot, but this doesn't relate to adaptation.
  d. Wrong. The vitreous humor is the "filler" in the eyeball and does not influence dark adaptation.

5. **c**
(p. 155)
  a. Wrong. The blind spot is the place where the optic nerve exits the retina and there are no receptors.
  b. Wrong. The optic chiasm is the crossover point in the visual pathway to the brain.
  d. Wrong. The fovea, the center of vision, is not determined by receptor-ganglion linkage.

6. **c**
(p. 158)
  a. Wrong. This is not a cell. It's a rare disorder in which only unmoving objects can be seen.
  b. Wrong. The photoreceptors are not in the cortex, and they are selective only for wavelength.
  d. Wrong. Bipolar cells are in the retina and are not selective to specific stimuli.

7. **d**   a. Wrong.   Opponent process theory states pairs of colors are linked to produce opposite responses.
    (p. 162) b. Wrong.   Recognition by components theory is an object recognition, not color, theory.
              c. Wrong.   Place theory is a theory of pitch perception.

8. **c**   a. Wrong.   Linear perspective involves converging lines as a cue for depth.
    (p. 168) b. Wrong.   Convergence is the degree to which the eyes turn inward to focus on near vs. far objects.
              d. Wrong.   Shading does not rely on image differences in each eye.

9. **a**   b. Wrong.   Bottom-up relates to image features, not context or knowledge.
    (p. 165) c. Wrong.   Opponent processing refers to the opposite neural responses generated by certain colors.
              d. Wrong.   Feature- or bottom-up processing relates to the image's features, not context or knowledge.

10. **b**   a, c, & d.   Wrong.   These are all cues for motion. Changes in pupil size are not related to motion.
    (p. 169)

11. **d**   a. Wrong.   Bottom-up processing analyzes image features. Changing features changes perceptions.
    (p. 169) b. Wrong.   Feature detectors alone would respond differently, producing a change in perception.
              c. Wrong.   Key here is the unchanging perception. Acuity does not contribute to that stability.

Hearing: Identifying and Localizing Sounds

1. **b**   a. Wrong.   Intensity relates to amplitude.
    (p. 175) c. Wrong.   Location is signaled by inter-ear differences in the input.
    (PT3H)   d. Wrong.   A sound's purity is reflected in its waveform, not its frequency.

2. **c**   a. Wrong.   The semicircular canals contain vestibular receptors, not auditory receptors.
    (p. 176) b. Wrong.   The tympanic membrane is the eardrum. It transmits sound but has no receptors.
    (PN3A)   d. Wrong.   The pinna is the external ear "flap." It captures sound, but contains no receptors.

3. **c**   a. Wrong.   The impulse is generated in the cochlea, not the eardrum (which has no neurotransmitters).
    (p. 176) b. Wrong.   These are in the middle ear. The hair cells are in the inner ear.
              d. Wrong.   The fluid movement, not its chemistry, is involved in generating the impulse.

4. **a**   b. Wrong.   The membrane in the cochlea that is discussed in your text is the basilar membrane.
    (p. 176) c. Wrong.   There are inner and outer hair cells, but not malleus hair cells, incus hair cells, etc.
              d. Wrong.   The malleus, incus, and stapes are physical structures in the ear.

5. **d**   a. Wrong.   This corresponds to the frequency theory of pitch perception.
    (p. 177) b. Wrong.   Impulses are all or none, remember? They vary in number, but not strength.
              c. Wrong.   Number might relate to intensity, but not to pitch and the place theory.

6. **d**   a. Wrong.   Inter-ear timing differences produce perceptions of spatial location, not pitch changes.
    (p. 179) b. Wrong.   Inter-ear timing differences produce perceptions of spatial location, not intensity
                          differences.
              c. Wrong.   A tone to the right would arrive at the right ear first, not the left.

7. **a**   b & d.   Wrong.   Pitch (frequency) helps in auditory organization, but not in localization.
    (p. 179) c.   Wrong.   Top-down processing is not a factor in auditory localization.

The Skin and Body Senses: From Touch to Movement

1. **c**   a, b, & d.   Wrong.   These are all skin senses. Kinesthesia is a body sense, not a skin sense.
    (p. 180)

2. **a**
(p. 180)

b. Wrong. Electromagnetic energy is the stimulus for vision.
c. Wrong. Change in air pressure is the stimulus for audition (hearing).
d. Wrong. Chemical changes are the stimuli for the chemical senses of taste and smell.

3. **c**
(p. 182)

a. Wrong. The free nerve endings often carry pain input, but they are not the location of the gate.
b. Wrong. The tympanic membrane is part of the auditory system, not the pain system.
d. Wrong. Pain input is processed in the somatosensory cortex, but it is not the gate's location.

4. **b**
(p. 183)
(PN3B)

a. Wrong. No receptors are located in the cortex. The cortex does not contact the environment.
c. Wrong. The semicircular canals have the receptors for the vestibular, not kinesthetic, system.
d. Wrong. The cochlea contains the receptors for audition, not kinesthesia.

5. **a**
(p. 183)

b. Wrong. The semicircular canals are not touch receptors.
c. Wrong. The cochlea would be active with auditory stimulation.
d. Wrong. The olfactory neurons in olfactory epithelium would be very active if smelling something.

6. **d**
(p. 183)

a, b, & c. Wrong. The semicircular canals are in the inner ear and very near the cochlea.

The Chemical Senses: Smell and Taste

1. **c**
(p. 184)

a. Wrong. Vestibular sacs are part of the vestibular system for motion and posture sensation.
b. Wrong. Free nerve endings are usually associated with pain perception.
d. Wrong. Mechanoreceptors respond to the mechanical stimuli for touch.

2. **b**
(p. 185)

a. Wrong. Perfumes do not necessarily have a predictable, specific effect on an organism.
c. Wrong. Papillae are the bumps on the tongue that contain the taste buds.
d. Wrong. Endorphins are brain chemicals that function as natural pain killers.

3. **a**
(p. 185)
(PN3B)

b, c, & d. Wrong. There are 4 basic tastes: sweet, salty, sour, and bitter.

From the Physical to the Psychophysical

1. **a**
(p. 187)

b. Wrong. Psychophysics focuses on stimulus energy and the perceptual result, not receptor activity.
c. Wrong. Psychophysics focuses on stimulus energy and the perceptual result, not neural pathways.
d. Wrong. This describes perceptual constancy, not psychophysics.

2. **a**
(p. 187)

b. Wrong. This is a definition of the difference threshold.
c. Wrong. This is the pain threshold and involves a very intense stimulus.
d. Wrong. Absolute threshold does not represent the upper range of perception.

3. **c**
(p. 188)

a. Wrong. Weber's Law predicts just noticeable differences, not sensitivity vs. bias.
b. Wrong. Adaptation is reduced sensitivity due to constant stimulation. This does not address bias.
d. Wrong. Transduction deals with production of neural activity, not psychophysical measurement.

4. **d**
(p. 190)

a. Wrong. Weber's Law involves difference thresholds, not changes in perceived intensity over time.
b. Wrong. Signal detection theory considers sensitivity and bias in detection responses. It would not predict loss of sensitivity over time.
c. Wrong. Perceptual constancy produces a constant perception, not a reduction.

Making Final Preparations

Short Essay Questions

1. Full dark adaptation requires approximately 20-25 minutes and involves regeneration of photopigments in the rods and cones. Cones adapt quickly, reaching their potential within 3-4 minutes. Adaptation does not increase further until eight minutes into the period when the sensitivity of rods equals and surpasses that of cones. This creates the "break" in the adaptation curve. Rods continue to adapt until 20-25 minutes into the adaptation period. (p. 157)

2. Rods are long, slender visual receptors that are located outside the fovea. They are very sensitive to light but provide poor acuity and no color vision. Cones are short, thick, and pointed and are located in the fovea, and with less density in the periphery. They allow good acuity and color perception, but require a relatively high level of light to operate. (pp. 154-155)

3. Expectancy influences interpretation of the stimulus, especially in cases of incomplete or ambiguous sensory information. It provides a guide for organizing ambiguous input, as in the case of many auditory stimuli, or for identification of other ambiguous stimuli. (pp. 163; 178-179)

4. Perceptual constancy is the unchanging perception of a stimulus even though the physical characteristics of the stimulus change. As an object moves away, its image shrinks. Instead of perceiving the object as shrinking, it is seen as a constant size due to the utilization of other information concerning size and distance. Constancy is adaptive. It prevents a constantly shifting world composed of unstable objects and relationships. (p. 169)

5. The perception of size depends in part on depth perception. Image size, one cue to object size, changes depending on the distance of the object. Thus, in perceiving size, the image is evaluated in relation to the object's depth. If depth is misjudged, size perception is often inaccurate. (p. 170)

6. Place theory states that different pitches stimulate neurons at different places along the basilar membrane. The frequency principle states that a high pitch causes neurons to fire very rapidly, whereas a low pitch produces a lower firing rate. Both are used because place information is not as specific as necessary, and the frequency principle is limited by the refractory period, creating problems for high frequency perception. (pp. 177-178)

7. Auditory localization relies on inter-ear differences in stimulus intensity and arrival time. If only the left windows are open the sound will reach the left ear first and at greater intensity than the right because the sound will come in primarily through the left window, even if the source is to the right. This will result in localization of the sound source to the left in most cases. (p. 179)

8. According to the gate control theory of pain, a gate in the spinal cord controls the transmission of pain signals to the brain. Rubbing an injury simulates the "large" fibers in the body senses' neural path, which closes the gate and reduces the flow of pain signals to the brain. (p. 183)

Matching

1. e (p. 150)	4. g (p. 158)	7. a (p. 155)	10. d (p. 185)	13. b (p. 156)	16. c (p. 154)
2. j (p. 157)	5. p (p. 189)	8. k (p. 155)	11. m (p. 158)	14. o (p. 153)	
3. n (p. 185)	6. l (p. 165)	9. h (p. 181)	12. i (p. 183)	15. f (p. 188)	

Multiple Choice Pretest 1

1. **d** a. Wrong. The retina is at the very back of the eye. It's the last structure encountered.
   (p. 153) b. Wrong. The lens is an internal structure, not the first to be reached.
   c. Wrong. The iris is the second structure to be encountered.

2. **c**   a. Wrong.   This is not a common problem and would not significantly affect accommodation.
    (p. 154)   b. Wrong.   The photopigment only affects the likelihood of neural response, not focusing ability.
                d. Wrong.   Increased pressure will damage the retina but will not affect accommodation.

3. **c**   a, b, & d. Wrong.   These are all attributes of cones.
    (p. 155)
    (PT3B)

4. **d**   a, b, & c. Wrong.   Dark adaptation continues for 20-25 minutes.
    (p. 157)

5. **a**   b. Wrong.   Trichromatic theory uses the relative activity in three cone types, not opposite responses.
    (p.164)   c. Wrong.   Frequency theory is a pitch perception theory, not a color vision theory.
                d. Wrong.   Top-down processing refers to the use of knowledge or context for interpretation.

6. **c**   a. Wrong.   Biederman's theory is based on simple component structures, not feature detectors.
    (p. 167)   b. Wrong.   Biederman's theory is based on simple component structures, not context or knowledge.
                d. Wrong.   Biederman's theory is based on simple component structures, not depth cues.

7. **b**   a. Wrong.   Convergence is the angle of the two eyes, not a difference in image location.
    (p. 168)   c. Wrong.   Linear perspective is a monocular cue, not a binocular cue like the one described.
                d. Wrong.   Accomodation is a change in lens' shape that produces a focused image.

8. **b**   a. Wrong.   These illusions reflect depth perception errors, not figure-ground ambiguity.
    (p. 172)   c. Wrong.   Binocular disparity is either unavailable (peephole view) or normal, not reversed.
    (PT3G)   d. Wrong.   Top-down processing contributes to the illusions (e.g., expect rectangular room).

9. **d**   a. Wrong.   Convergence is the angle of the eyes. Key here is motion from stationary flashing lights.
    (p. 169)   b. Wrong.   Sensory adaptation is reduced sensitivity to repeated stimulation, not a cue for motion.
    (PT3E)   c. Wrong.   The volley principle is related to pitch perception, not motion perception.

10. **a**   b. Wrong.   These are Gestalt principles and are not dependent on knowledge or expectancy.
    (p. 166)   c. Wrong.   These are Gestalt principles of visual perception.
                d. Wrong.   Visual acuity is determined by the nature of the stimulus, receptors, and neural pathway.

11. **b**   a. Wrong.   Gate control is a theory of pain. The traveling wave relates to pitch perception.
    (p. 177)   c. Wrong.   Trichromatic theory is a color perception theory. Traveling wave relates to pitch.
                d. Wrong.   Traveling waves explain how different pitched sounds stimulate certain neurons more than
                            others, not how neural firing rate corresponds to pitch.

12. **c**   a. Wrong.   In the frequency principle, neural firing rate relates to the stimulus' pitch, not its amplitude.
    (p. 178)   b. Wrong.   In the frequency principle for pitch, neural firing rate corresponds to pitch, not its location.
                d. Wrong.   Frequency principle refers to pitch. A complex sound doesn't require a higher firing rate.

13. **a**   b. Wrong.   There is no specific firing rate for cold.
    (p. 181)   c. Wrong.   The key is changing skin temperature, not stimulus temperature.
                d. Wrong.   Papillae are part of the taste system.

14. **d**   a. Wrong.   The olfactory sense is the sense of smell.
    (p. 183)   b. Wrong.   The vestibular sense is the sense of movement and balance.
                c. Wrong.   The gustatory sense is the sense of taste.

15. **a**   b & c. Wrong. These are auditory structures.
(p. 183)   d.   Wrong. These are visual system brain areas.
(PN3B)

16. **a**   b. Wrong. Pheromones produce a set response, such as approaching the source of the pheromone.
(p. 183)   c. Wrong. Abnormal stimulation of the vestibular system produces dizziness or nausea.
             d. Wrong. Endorphins are important in the body senses, not in vision.

17. **d**   a, b, & c.   Wrong.   These are true, but there are over 1000 kinds of olfactory receptors, not 4.
(p. 185)

18. **b**   a. Wrong. Papillae contain taste buds, but papillae are not cilia, hair-like structures.
(p. 186)   c. Wrong. Papillae are not receptors. They are structures that contain the taste buds and receptors.
             d. Wrong. Papillae are not neurons. They are bumps on the tongue that contain the taste buds.

19. **c**   a. Wrong. Weber's Law predicts difference thresholds based on original stimulus intensity.
(p. 157,   b. Wrong. False alarms in signal detection theory represent cases in which a stimulus is
   187)   "detected" even though no stimulus was presented.
             d. Wrong. The difference threshold is the minimum change in energy that can be detected.

20. **a**   b. Wrong. This is a false alarm.
(p. 188)   c. Wrong. This is a miss.
             d. Wrong. This is a correct rejection.

Multiple Choice Pretest 2

1. **a**   b, c, & d.   Wrong.   Although there are feature detectors for these characteristics, they are not side by
(p. 159)   side with the line detectors. Line detectors vary by preferred orientation.

2. **b**   a. Wrong. The key is the different expectations. Recognition by components doesn't address that.
(p. 165)   c. Wrong. The key is the different expectations, which is not part of the Gestalt principles.
             d. Wrong. The key is the different expectations, not the translation of the stimulus to neural energy.

3. **a**   b. Wrong. Accommodation is a change in lens thickness. This answer describes dark adaptation.
(p. 153)   c. Wrong. Accommodation is a change in lens thickness. This answer describes Gestalt laws.
             d. Wrong. Accommodation is a change in lens thickness. It has nothing to do with the blind spot.

4. **c**   a. Wrong. Closure involves filling in gaps. Key here was the man moving differently than the river.
(p. 166)   b. Wrong. Good continuation involves keeping intersected objects intact. Key here was the man
                        moving differently than the river.
             d. Wrong. Proximity involves grouping objects that are close to each other. Key here was the man
                        moving differently than the river.

5. **d**   a. Wrong. Adaptation is slower for rods, which are all outside the fovea.
(p. 155)   b. Wrong. Retinal disparity is a depth cue and does not relate to sensitivity.
             c. Wrong. Acuity is better in the cone-dense fovea, but acuity is not relevant here.

6. **c**   a. Wrong. Having one type of rod is normal, and rods don't provide color vision anyway.
(p. 162)   b. Wrong. Color blindness of this sort is a receptor problem, not a neural one, in essentially all cases.
             d. Wrong. Having no cones at all would eliminate all color vision, not just red and green vision.

7. **a**   b.   Wrong. This is the opposite relationship.
(p. 164)   c & d. Wrong. Primary colors and other colors are processed and perceived in the same way.

8. **c**   a. & d. Wrong. Binocular cues like these would be lost.
(p. 167) b.   Wrong. Common fate is not a depth cue.

9. **b**   a. Wrong. The pinna is in the outer ear. Hair cells are in the cochlea.
(p. 176) c. Wrong. Hair cells are auditory receptors, not vestibular receptors.
(PN3A) d. Wrong. The tympanic membrane is the eardrum, whereas hair cells are in the inner ear.

10. **c**   a & b. Wrong. Shape constancy is not involved (both are square). This involves size constancy.
(p. 172) d.   Wrong. A distant object must be larger than a near object in order to cast the same size image.

11. **a**   b. Wrong. Place theory is based on neuron location, not firing rate, so this is not a problem.
(p. 178) c. Wrong. Opponent process theory doesn't require high firing rates, so this is not a problem.
  d. Wrong. Gate control is a pain theory and is not based on firing rate, so this isn't a problem.

12. **d**   a. Wrong. The listener's sex provides nothing to help separate the bulletin from the rest of the noise.
(p. 179) b. Wrong. Good grouping requires the announcer and crowd to have different sex (frequency) voices.
  c. Wrong. If everyone is around the radio, spatial location would not be a cue to help perceptual organization of the news bulletin.

13. **a**   b. Wrong. Pitch is a function of frequency, not inter-ear timing differences.
(p. 179) c. Wrong. Intensity is a function of the sound wave's amplitude, not of inter-ear timing differences.
  d. Wrong. Meaning is influenced by the sound's physical characteristics and several top-down factors, but not by inter-ear timing differences.

14. **a**   b, c, & d. Wrong. These are all true. However, the size of the cortical area that processes input from the skin is proportional to the sensitivity of the body part, not its size.
(p. 181)

15. **a**   b. Wrong. Bottom-up processing emphasizes stimulus characteristics, so his pain should equal yours.
(p. 182) c. Wrong. Frequency theory is a theory of pitch perception, not pain perception.
  d. Wrong. More endorphins would reduce pain more. The key here is cognitive or context factors.

16. **b**   a. Wrong. The olfactory bulb processes olfactory input, but does not control emotion or motivation.
(p. 185) c. Wrong. The somatosensory cortex is not involved in these motivational or emotional behaviors.
  d. Wrong. Olfaction is the only sense that does not include the thalamus in its neural path.

17. **b**   a. Wrong. The absolute threshold would indicate the number of raisins detectable in cereal, not whether a change is detectable.
(p. 189) c. Wrong. Signal detection theory does not use thresholds.
  d. Wrong. This relates to the detection of raisins, not the detection of differences in raisin number.

18. **d**   a. Wrong. The neural code is not this simple.
(p. 186) b. Wrong. Papillae are not receptors. They contain the receptors.
  c. Wrong. Areas of the tongue differ in sensitivity to certain tastes, but this is not the neural code.

19. **a**   b, c, & d. Wrong. Weber's law states that the just noticeable difference is a constant proportion of the magnitude of the original (standard) stimulus. That is, the greater the stimulus, the larger the absolute change required for detection. Tom weighs least, so he can lose fewer pounds than the others and the change will be noticed.
(p. 189)

20. **c**   a. Wrong. Signal detection theory does not measure absolute threshold or difference threshold.
(p. 188) b. Wrong. Both signal detection and threshold procedures can be used in all senses.
  d. Wrong. Neither signal detection theory nor threshold methods involve finding active brain areas.

CHAPTER 6: CONSCIOUSNESS

ESTABLISHING LEARNING GOALS

Use these learning goals as a preview of the chapter, a guide for active reading, and to evaluate your mastery of the material. Review the relevant goals as you begin and end your reading of each major section of the chapter.

I.   Solve the adaptive problem of how to establish priorities for mental functioning.
    A. Define attention and discuss its adaptive value.
    B. Explain how experiments on dichotic listening can be used to study attention.
    C. Describe automaticity and its effects on awareness.
        1. Explain how automaticity is identified.
        2. Define subliminal, and discuss whether subliminal messages affect behavior.
    D. Describe such disorders as visual neglect and attention deficit/hyperactivity disorder.

II. Understand the characteristics of sleep and sleep's adaptive function.
    A. Define biological rhythms, and discuss how they are controlled.
    B. Describe the various stages and characteristics of sleep.
    C. Discuss the function and adaptive significance of sleep.
        1. Differentiate the restorative and survival views of sleep.
        2. Describe the consequences of sleep deprivation.
    D. Discuss the function of REM sleep and theories of dreaming.
        1. Describe Freud's wish fulfillment theory of dreams.
        2. Describe the activation-synthesis hypothesis of dreams.
    E. Describe the various sleep disorders.
        1. Describe the dyssomnias, and provide examples.
        2. Describe the parasomnias, and provide examples.

III. Solve the adaptive problem of how consciousness can be altered biochemically.
    A. Compare neurotransmitters with psychoactive drugs.
    B. Discuss the different categories of psychoactive drugs, with examples of each.
        1. Describe the effects of each category of drug.
        2. Identify the method of action of each category of drug.
    C. Discuss the psychological factors that influence the effects of psychoactive drugs.

IV. Solve the adaptive problem of how consciousness can be altered without drugs.
    A. Describe the physiological and behavioral effects of hypnosis.
    B. Discuss whether hypnosis can be used effectively to enhance memory.
    C. Describe the dissociation and role-playing accounts of hypnosis.
    D. Discuss the physical, behavioral, and psychological effects of meditation.

MASTERING THE MATERIAL

Preview & Setting Priorities for Mental Functioning: Attention (pp. 196-205)

Mastering the Vocabulary. Define or explain each of the following terms. To check your answers, consult the text pages listed.

1. consciousness (p. 196)

2. attention (p. 198)

3. dichotic listening (p. 199)

4. cocktail party effect (p. 199)

5. automaticity (p. 201)

6. visual neglect (p. 203)

7. attention deficit/hyperactivity disorder (p. 204)

Mastering the Concepts. Fill in the blanks to create a summary of this section. Answers are on page 145.

The subjective awareness of internal and external events, _____(1), was central to 19th century psychology but lost favor due to the limitations of _____(2). Interest in consciousness is increasing. This chapter considers four adaptive problems: How are priorities set for mental functioning? What are the characteristics and roles of sleep and dreams? How do psychoactive drugs alter awareness? What happens under hypnosis and meditation?

By directing _____(3) to only some things, the organism sets priorities for mental function, protects mental resources and improves functioning. However, as the _____(4) effect and _____(5) listening experiments show, the unattended message is monitored, and important input does affect behavior. One's name is recognized, and attention unconsciously follows a message continued in the unattended ear. Divided attention tasks show that _____(6) can develop for some highly practiced tasks, limiting conscious awareness of that task. Stimuli that do not reach conscious awareness can influence behavior, but it is not clear whether the _____(7), below threshold, messages supposedly imbedded in advertising and self-help tapes even exist or are effective. In some cases, there is no evidence embedded messages are present. Also, controlled studies found no influence of subliminal messages on behavior beyond that accounted for by a _____(8) effect.

Right (and sometimes left) parietal lobe damage can cause _____(9), a disorder in which there is no conscious awareness of the left visual field, although input is processed. The inability to maintain or control attention, _____(10) disorder, affects many children. The cause is unknown, but the drug Ritalin often helps reduce the worst symptoms of the disorder.

Evaluating Your Progress. Select the one best response. Answers are found on page 145. If you make any errors, reread the relevant material before proceeding.

1. Subjects shadow (repeat) the message in one ear while ignoring the message in the other ear in the
    a. visual neglect technique.
    b. dichotic listening technique.
    c. spotlight technique.
    d. subliminal technique.

2. The ability to selectively attend to one message while ignoring others (except for the occurrence of one's name) is known as
    a. visual neglect.
    b. consciousness.
    c. automaticity.
    d. the cocktail party effect.

3. The cocktail party effect and Treisman's "ear-switching" experiment demonstrate that
    a. right parietal lobe brain damage disrupts basic attentional mechanisms.
    b. highly practiced tasks require less attention than less well-practiced tasks.
    c. when more than one message is presented, neither message is understood well.
    d. an unattended message is monitored for important content.

4. A task that can be performed rapidly, effortlessly and without focused attention is considered a(n)
    a. automatic process.
    b. controlled process.
    c. split brain process.
    d. dissociated process.

5. A loss of awareness of the contents of one half of the visual field is known as
    a. visual neglect.
    b. attention deficit/hyperactivity disorder.
    c. hypnotic dissociation.
    d. split world disorder.

6. A subliminal message is a message that
   a. motivates you to behave in a certain way.
   b. is extremely appealing and pleasant.
   c. is below the detection threshold.
   d. reduces your attention to the main message.

Sleeping and Dreaming (pp. 205-216)

Mastering the Vocabulary. Define or explain each of the following terms. To check your answers, consult the text pages listed.

1. circadian rhythms (p. 206)

2. biological clocks (p. 206)

3. alpha waves (p. 208)

4. theta waves (p. 209)

5. delta activity (p.209)

6. REM (p. 213)

7. REM rebound (p. 213)

8. manifest content (p. 213)

9. latent content (p. 213)

10. activation-synthesis hypothesis (p. 213)

11. dyssomnias (p. 215)

12. parasomnias (p. 216)

13. insomnia (p. 215)

14. hypersomnia (p. 215)

15. narcolepsy (p. 215)

16. nightmares (p. 216)

17. night terrors (p. 216)

18. sleepwalking (p. 216)

Mastering the Concepts. Fill in the blanks to create a summary of the section. Answers are on page 145.

Sleep, an altered state of consciousness, is an example of a biological rhythm. Because sleep-waking has a 24-hour cycle, it is a _____(11) rhythm. The suprachiasmatic nucleus of the _____(12) may be the _____(13) clock for the sleep cycle, with light playing a key role in pacing the clock.

Brain EEG patterns vary in _____(14), _____(15), and regularity during sleep. Alpha waves are found during relaxation. Stage 1 sleep has mostly _____(16) waves. Irregular EEG patterns called sleep _____(17) and K-complexes occur in Stage 2 sleep. The deeper sleep of Stages 3 and 4 has slower, synchronous waves called _____(18) activity. The EEG of REM sleep has an irregular pattern similar to a waking state, but the person is deeply asleep. Thus, REM sleep is called _____(19) sleep. If awakened in REM sleep, people usually report they were _____(20). Complete sleep cycles last about _____(21) and are repeated. The length of REM increases with each cycle. The function of sleep is unclear, but it may be restorative or a protective, adaptive response to light-dark cycles and past predators. Sleep deprivation leads to poor functioning.

The function of REM sleep is unclear. REM deprivation has only small psychological effects, but it does lead to REM _____(22), increased REM sleep the next night, and it may impair learning. Freud proposed the dreams of REM sleep are a means for _____(23) fulfillment and reflect the contents of the unconsious mind. A dream's manifest content is the actual images of the dream, but the _____(24) content is its hidden meaning. According to the _____(25)-synthesis hypothesis, dreams are the brain's interpretation of random activity. Current concerns, rather than deep-seated problems, might influence these interpretations. REM sleep occurs in many species and in the prenatal period.

Sleep disorders are classified as dyssomnias or parasomnias. Dyssomnias, troubles in timing, quality, or quantity of sleep, include _____(26), a problem getting to sleep or staying asleep, and hypersomnia, excessive sleepiness. In the rare disorder of _____(27), there is a sudden onset of sleep and immediate entry into REM sleep. Parasomnias, abnormal events during sleep, include nightmares, _____(28), and sleepwalking. Nightmares are REM dreams, but night terrors and sleepwalking occur in non-REM sleep.

Evaluating Your Progress. Select the one best response. Answers are found on page 146. If you make any errors, reread the relevant material before proceeding.

1. The biological clock that controls circadian rhythms seems to be in the suprachiasmatic nucleus of the
   a. optic nerve.
   b. pituitary gland.
   c. hypothalamus.
   d. reticular activating system.

2. A person whose EEG shows primarily synchronous, high amplitude, very slow-wave delta activity is
   a. awake and concentrating on a task.
   b. awake and very relaxed.
   c. in Stage 4 sleep.
   d. in REM sleep.

3. REM sleep is called paradoxical sleep because
   a. it is the shortest stage of sleep, but it is the most necessary.
   b. dreams with complex plots are likely, but they are usually colorless.
   c. dreams are very likely to occur, but the brain waves are the slowest, highest amplitude type.
   d. the brain waves are similar to those of a waking state, but the person is very deeply asleep.

4. Which is true?
   a. Most people cycle through REM sleep about twice each night.
   b. Heart rate is very slow and regular during REM sleep.
   c. More time is spent in REM sleep near morning than in the first hours of sleep.
   d. REM stands for "restore energy mode."

5. The survival theory of why we sleep suggests that
   a. because we rely on vision, sleeping at night had the adaptive value of keeping us safe.
   b. without sleep our neurotransmitters would be depleted and we couldn't function.
   c. sleep is needed to restore psychological balance through dreaming.
   d. sleep is needed to resynchronize the various biological clocks so they do not drift.

6. Sleepwalking and night terrors usually
   a. occur during REM sleep.
   b. cease when the person gets older.
   c. are symptoms of a psychological problem.
   d. are accompanied by sleep apnea.

7. Freud proposed that we dream
   a. for wish fulfillment and to deal with highly disturbing desires.
   b. because we try to interpret the random brain activity generated during sleep.
   c. because we need to restore the supply of brain neurotransmitters.
   d. in order to solve the problems that arose during the day.

8. The inability to get to sleep or to stay asleep is
   a. hypersomnia.
   b. insomnia.
   c. parasomnia.
   d. narcolepsy.

Altering Awareness: Psychoactive Drugs (pp. 217-222)

Mastering the Vocabulary. Define or explain each of the following terms. To check your answers, consult the text pages listed.

1. psychoactive drugs (p. 217)

2. tolerance (p. 218)

3. drug dependency (p. 218)

4. withdrawal (p. 218)

5. depressants (p. 218)

6. stimulants (p. 219)

7. opiates (p. 220)

8. hallucinogens (p. 220)

Mastering the Concepts. Fill in the blanks to create a summary of this section. Answers are on page 145.

Mood and consciousness is controlled by neurotransmitters. _____(29) drugs affect mental processes, consciousness, and behavior. Drugs mimic, block, or increase neurotransmitter activity. Use can cause drug dependency, but the underlying cause is unclear. Drug _____(30) can develop, requiring higher doses for an effect, and if drug use ends, withdrawal occurs.

There are four categories of psychoactive drugs. _____(31) slow nervous system activity, and include alcohol, barbiturates, and tranquilizers. They increase GABA activity (also dopamine for alcohol), which reduces anxiety, but they can lead to dependency. _____(32), like caffeine, nicotine, amphetamines, cocaine, and MDMA (Ecstasy), increase neural activity and improve alertness and mood temporarily. The effects of amphetamines and cocaine are due to increased norepinephrine and dopamine activity, with dopamine key to producing positive feelings. _____(33), including morphine, opium, and heroin, elevate mood by depressing nervous system activity, and are likely to cause dependence. _____(34), or psychedelics, include LSD, mescaline, psilocybin, and _____(35) and are likely to produce alteration of sensation and perception. LSD seems to mimic serotonin. Side effects include "bad" trips, and impaired concentration and coordination. Drug effects depend on the user's environment, _____(36), physical condition, and familiarity with the drug.

Evaluating Your Progress. Select the one best response. Answers are found on page 146. If you make any errors, reread the relevant material before proceeding.

1. Repeated use of psychoactive drugs often leads to
   a. increased sensitivity.
   b. tolerance.
   c. withdrawal.
   d. synesthesia.

2. A physical or psychological need for a drug is known as
   a. tolerance.
   b. withdrawal.
   c. synesthesia.
   d. dependency.

3. Which drug is incorrectly assigned to a drug category?
   a. heroin---opiate
   b. diazepam (Valium)---depressant
   c. marijuana---hallucinogen
   d. alcohol---stimulant

4. All of the following drugs are classified as hallucinogens except
   a. mescaline.
   b. LSD.
   c. psilocybin.
   d. cocaine.

5. The effects of alcohol are produced by increased secretion or effectiveness of
   a. GABA.
   b. norepinephrine.
   c. dopamine.
   d. serotonin.

Altering Awareness: Induced States (pp. 222-226)

Mastering the Vocabulary. Define or explain each of the following terms. To check your answers, consult the text pages listed.

1. hypnosis (p. 222)

2. hypnotic hypermnesia (p. 224)

3. hypnotic dissociation (p. 224)

4. meditation (p. 226)

Mastering the Concepts. Fill in the blanks to create a summary of the section. Answers are on page 145.

Hypnosis is a social interaction resulting in a heightened state of _____(37). A technique is to suggest the person is getting very relaxed and _____(38) as the person fixates on an object. Hypnosis has assisted in ending unwanted habits and reducing _____(39) during medical procedures. Evidence that hypnosis can improve memory is poor. Controlled studies find no memory enhancement, and the _____(40) of "recovered" memories and age regression is difficult to verify.

Hilgard suggests that hypnosis involves hypnotic _____(41), a splitting of consciousness into separate parts: a part that acts on the hypnotist's suggestions, and a _____(42) observer with normal awareness. An alternative is that hypnosis involves social _____(43) playing; the subject simply tries to please the hypnotist and acts the hypnotized role. Simulated subjects research and the influence of the subject's _____(44) about hypnosis support this view.

_____(45), a way to self-induce shifts in awareness, is sometimes described as "pure thought" and often involves _____(46) paired with focused concentration on breathing or a mantra to help clear the mind. Research shows meditation reduces arousal and increases _____(47) brain waves, both common to relaxation, and it may help reduce anxiety.

Evaluating Your Progress. Select the one best response. Answers are found on page 147. If you miss any questions, reread the relevant material before proceeding.

1. The individual credited with performing a form of hypnosis in 1783 was
   a. Ernest Hilgard.
   b. Anton Mesmer.
   c. Timothy Leary.
   d. Sigmund Freud.

2. Your text defines hypnosis as
   a. "a form of social interaction that produces a heightened state of suggestibility in willing participants."
   b. "an altered state of consciousness that reduces pain, improves memory, and eliminates bad habits."
   c. "a dissociation of consciousness into multiple parts, each with its own level of awareness."
   d. "a technique to self-induce a state of altered awareness, relaxation, and spiritual reflection."

3. Physiological measurements during hypnosis
   a. are most similar to those of a state of relaxation.
   b. are most similar to those of a deep sleep.
   c. show brain wave patterns unique to hypnosis.
   d. show neurotransmitter activity patterns unique to hypnosis.

4. Hilgard's "hidden observer" experiments are used to provide evidence for
   a. age regression.
   b. social role playing.
   c. hypnotic hypermnesia.
   d. hypnotic dissociation.

5. The most positive benefit of meditation is its ability to
   a. enhance memory for long-forgotten events.
   b. produce a state of relaxation.
   c. increase physiological arousal.
   d. increase theta waves.

MAKING FINAL PREPARATIONS

Complete these sections without consulting your book or notes. For a more accurate estimate of how well you know this material, wait at least a day or two after studying the chapter before working on the questions. Some of the material you "know" immediately after working with the chapter will be quickly forgotten. Immediate tests will overestimate what you know well.

Short Essay Questions. Write a brief answer to each question. Sample answers are on page 147.

1. Discuss why the development of automaticity is adaptive.

2. Cite the data that show that unattended information is not completely ignored.

3. Discuss the possible adaptive value of sleep.

4. Explain why the effects of psychoactive drugs can vary from person to person or from time to time.

5. Cite the evidence supporting the social role playing view of hypnosis.

6. Discuss the idea that stimuli that do not reach conscious awareness can influence behavior.

Matching. Select the correct definition or description for each item. Answers are on page 148.

_____	1. sleep apnea	**a.**	blending of sensory experiences
_____	2. dependency	**b.**	actual images and events in a dream
_____	3. attention	**c.**	physical symptom caused by cessation of drug use
_____	4. parasomnia	**d.**	brain mechanism that controls bodily function cycles
_____	5. manifest content	**e.**	brain waves found in Stage 2
_____	6. alpha waves	**f.**	temporally stopping breathing during sleep
_____	7. biological clock	**g.**	spending more time in REM after REM deprivation
_____	8. withdrawal	**h.**	particular sound or words used during meditation
_____	9. dichotic listening task	**i.**	selective attention task
_____	10. consciousness	**j.**	internal process that sets mental function priorities
_____	11. hypnotic hypermnesia	**k.**	problems of timing or duration of sleep
_____	12. K-complexes	**l.**	subjective awareness of internal and external events
_____	13. REM rebound	**m.**	abnormal disturbances during sleep
_____	14. mantra	**n.**	brain waves associated with relaxed state
_____	15. synesthesia	**o.**	a physical or psychological need, often for a drug
_____	16. dyssomnias	**p.**	memory enhancement with hypnosis

Multiple Choice Pretest 1. Select the one best response. Answers are found on page 148.

1. Automaticity is evaluated by comparing single task performance with a two-task situation known as a

    a. divided attention task.
    b. ear-switching task.
    c. dichotic listening task.
    d. hidden observer task.

2. Liz was told to repeat the message in her right ear and to ignore the message in her left ear. The right ear message was, "Mary had a little lamb, and heard the shattering glass." The left ear message was, "David saw the cars collide, it's fleece was white as snow." Based on the most interesting findings of Treisman's research, Liz probably said
   a. "Mary had a little lamb, and heard the shattering glass."
   b. "Mary had a little lamb, its fleece was white as snow."
   c. alternate words from each message ("Mary saw a cars lamb...").
   d. randomly selected words from each message.

3. Visual neglect most commonly occurs with damage to
   a. the cerebellum.
   b. the occipital lobes.
   c. the hindbrain.
   d. the right hemisphere.

4. How long do most people sleep before entering REM sleep for the first time?
   a. 30 minutes
   b. 90 minutes
   c. 2 hours
   d. 4 hours

5. Which stage of sleep increases in length and frequency as the night progresses?
   a. REM
   b. Stage 2
   c. Stage 3
   d. Stage 4

6. Vokey & Read (1985) presented vacation slides in which the word "sex" was visible, but not highly obvious in some of the pictures. How did the embedded "sex" affect recognition memory?
   a. Recognition was improved.
   b. Recognition was improved, but only if the pictures included people.
   c. Recognition was reduced.
   d. Recognition did not differ.

7. A single-blind study of the effectiveness of subliminal message weight loss tapes found that everyone lost weight, even those given tapes without any subliminal messages. This result is best explained as
   a. a placebo effect.
   b. a statistically significant difference.
   c. a difference in motivation between groups.
   d. good evidence that subliminal messages work.

8. REM sleep is associated with all of the following EXCEPT
   a. rapid eye movements.
   b. alpha wave activity.
   c. dreaming.
   d. extremely relaxed muscle tone.

9. K-complexes and sleep spindles are characteristic of
   a. Stage 1 sleep.
   b. Stage 2 sleep.
   c. Stage 4 sleep.
   d. REM sleep.

10. Ty has sudden periods of extreme sleepiness when he will collapse and enter REM. This describes
    a. sleep apnea.
    b. insomnia.
    c. narcolepsy
    d. hypermnesia

11. Which of the following is an accurate summary of research on hypnosis and memory?
    a. All types of memory are improved by hypnosis, and this cannot be explained by other factors.
    b. Memory for recent events is improved by hypnosis, but memory for older events is not.
    c. Memory for very old events is improved by hypnosis, but memory for more recent events is not.
    d. There is little evidence from controlled research that indicates memory is enhanced by hypnosis.

12. Nils is a wimp about dental work, but gas makes him sick, and he's allergic to most painkilling drugs. If he is facing painful dental work, another effective pain reduction technique he could try is
    a. meditation.
    b. hypnosis.
    c. REM deprivation therapy.
    d. alpha wave therapy.

13. Rao is practicing a technique involving the self-induced manipulation of awareness for the purpose of self-reflection and relaxation. Rao is involved in
    a. meditation.
    b. hypnosis.
    c. psychoactive drug use.
    d. sleep.

14. Freud felt that dreams about guns signified sexual concerns and desires. This represents
    a. the dream's manifest content.
    b. the dream's latent content.
    c. the activation-synthesis hypothesis.
    d. the dissociation hypothesis.

15. Sally has taken a drug that is causing her to hear colors and see music. The drug most likely is
    a. heroin.
    b. a barbiturate.
    c. LSD.
    d. alcohol.

16. Phil broke his leg in a motorcycle accident. To relieve the pain, his doctor is likely to prescribe
    a. an opiate.
    b. hallucinogens.
    c. amphetamines.
    d. cocaine.

17. A rat will press a response bar hundreds of times if barpressing results in the administration of cocaine. Apparently the pleasurable and reinforcing aspects of the drug are due to cocaine's effect on
    a. endorphins.
    b. serotonin.
    c. dopamine.
    d. GABA.

18. Sid, a heroin addict, has not used heroin for over 24 hours. He is sweating, vomiting, and trembling. Sid's symptoms represent
    a. drug tolerance.
    b. drug dependency.
    c. withdrawal.
    d. synesthesia.

Multiple Choice Pretest 2. Select the one best response. Answers are found on page 149.

1. Lars is having difficulty concentrating on his schoolwork, is easily distracted, and never seems to be able to finish a task. This is most likely an example of
   a. visual neglect.
   b. delta activity.
   c. the cocktail party effect.
   d. attention deficit/hyperactivity disorder.

2. Keno was doing great in his driver's license road test until the officer started asking him questions. While replying, he scraped the curb and almost lost control. What conclusion is most likely?
   a. Keno probably has visual neglect.
   b. Keno's driving is not yet automatic.
   c. Keno probably has attention deficit disorder.
   d. The cocktail party effect may occur while driving.

3. Which of the following is adaptive primarily because it establishes processing priorities?
   a. subliminal perception.
   b. visual neglect.
   c. attention.
   d. activation-synthesis.

4. Tim sat entranced by his favorite TV show. His mother began talking to him, but he showed no awareness that she was even there until she said his name. This is most similar to
   a. attentional neglect.
   b. attention deficit/hyperactivity disorder.
   c. the cocktail party effect.
   d. hypnotic hypermnesia.

5. Which of the following statements is not an accurate summary of the subliminal perception research?
   a. Stimuli that do not reach conscious awareness cannot have any influence on behavior.
   b. The cause of the apparent success of subliminal self-help tapes is likely a placebo effect.
   c. Embedded words or images related to sex produce no improvements in memory or preferences.
   d. Some subliminal self-help tapes do not appear to have subliminal messages embedded in them.

6. Jorge quits breathing many times each night and awakens gasping for breath. Jorge's problem is
   a. sleep apnea.
   b. narcolepsy.
   c. night terrors.
   d. insomnia.

7. The sleep spindles and K-complexes present in Lee's EEG a few minutes ago have been replaced by an increasing amount of delta activity. Lee has shifted from
   a. REM sleep to Stage 2 sleep.
   b. Stage 2 sleep to Stage 3 or Stage 4 sleep.
   c. non-REM sleep to REM sleep.
   d. deep sleep to a near-waking state.

8. Your 6-year-old son has started sitting up in bed in the middle of the night, screaming and in a state of extreme panic. He usually doesn't respond when you talk to him. Assuming he is in Stage 4 sleep when this occurs, he probably is experiencing
   a. hypersomnia.
   b. sleep apnea.
   c. a night terror.
   d. a nightmare.

9. A rat's superchiasmic nucleus in the hypothlamus has been destroyed. What is a likely effect?
   a. attention deficit/hyperactivity disorder
   b. visual neglect
   c. problem with circadian rhythms
   d. hypermnesia

10. You dreamed about riding a train into a tunnel. According to the activation-synthesis view, your dream
    a. is really about your need to fulfill an unacceptable sexual desire.
    b. is an attempt by your mind to solve a problem that arose during the last few days.
    c. is your brain's interpretation of the random neural activity generated during sleep.
    d. is an indication of a serious psychological disorder that should be treated.

11. Narcolepsy is an example of
    a. a circadian rhythm.
    b. parasomnia.
    c. dyssomnia.
    d. dissociation.

12. As part of their religious ceremony, the elders of the tribe ate a particular mushroom known to cause "visions" and other intense perceptual effects. The active drug in this mushroom is
    a. mescaline.
    b. marijuana.
    c. psilocybin.
    d. cocaine.

13. Which of the following drugs is in the same general category as alcohol?
    a. barbiturates.
    b. nicotine.
    c. MDMA.
    d. morphine.

14. Glenda is using a drug that increases the effectiveness of GABA and dopamine. The drug is probably
    a. cocaine.
    b. alcohol.
    c. heroin.
    d. LSD.

15. Sam has been drinking alcohol for many years. He can drink much more now than he could when he first started drinking. This change is an example of
    a. dependency.
    b. REM rebound.
    c. withdrawal.
    d. tolerance.

16. Ben feels his eyelids start to sag and he feels very relaxed as he stares at a coin on the table. He is willing to obey commands and might report reduced pain perception. Ben's highly suggestible state is due to
    a. hallucinogenic drugs.
    b. meditation.
    c. sleep deprivation.
    d. hypnosis.

17. If people are told prior to hypnosis that hypnosis causes rigidity of the arms, they are likely to show rigidity while hypnotized, even if rigidity is not part of any hypnotic suggestion. This supports the view that hypnosis is
    a. a dissociation of consciousness.
    b. due to an increase in alpha wave activity.
    c. a kind of social role playing.
    d. an acetylcholine (ACh) imbalance.

18. A hypnotized subject has submerged her hand in ice after being given the suggestion that she will feel little pain. Her "hidden observer" has been told to ring a bell to indicate what she (the hidden observer) feels. Based on Hilgard's research, if the person verbally reports a pain level of 4, the hidden observer will report a pain level of
    a. 0 -- hidden observers have no contact with the environment.
    b. 2 -- hidden observers react more strongly to hypnotic suggestions.
    c. 4 -- hidden observers perceive the same things the hypnotized person does.
    d. 8 -- hidden observers perceive what a non-hypnotized person perceives.

LANGUAGE DEVELOPMENT GUIDE

Core Terms

In the lectures on this chapter you may learn about *illicit* drugs -- that is, illegal drugs (the psychoactive drugs that are used to treat mental illnesses are discussed in chapter 15). You may learn about the *deleterious* (harmful) effects of these drugs on the brain, and about the effects of these drugs on a child *in utero* (in the uterus, before birth). You instructor might also share with you the *prevalence* of their use -- that is, how many people are thought to use them.

Idioms

p. 196	biological seat of consciousness	specific, physical place from which we can find 'consciousness' originating
p. 198	heightened state of suggestibility	a state in which you are likely to do what you are told
p. 198	smorgasbord	a great feast or banquet; a wide and wonderful variety
p. 199	her latest escapade	her latest wild adventure or risky behavior
p. 199	a case in point	an example
p. 200	naive	not sophisticated, not worldly or experienced
p. 200	in the realm of	within the world of; in the same area
p. 201	without a hitch	quite easily and without mistakes
p. 204	can manifest itself	can make itself known; can be seen as
p. 207	stay put	stay where they are
p. 207	play havoc with	make a mess of; badly confuse
p. 207	shrug off	not be affected by; take no notice of
p. 208	eavesdrop	to listen in secretly
p. 208	bears a striking similarity	seems very much like
p. 211	a number of plausible hypotheses	several believable theories about how something works
p. 211	venturing forth	going out
p. 213	in the eye of the beholder	is subjective; depends upon a person's viewpoint

p. 213	spontaneously activate	to start up completely on their own; suddenly
p. 219	euphoric	very happy and excited

Word Parts

Here are some words that are made up of word parts, and that you can find in this chapter. After you've looked at these, you can look for others in the chapter that use the same word parts.

WORD	WORD PART IT USES	MEANING
synchrony	sys, syl, syn, sym = together, along with chron = time	two things happening at the same time; matched in time
dyssomnia	dys = bad, ill som = sleep	poor sleeping
dissociation	dis = take away, not soc = contact; togetherness	to break two things apart; to prevent contact
paradoxical	para = beside, position dox = belief, opinion	two (conflicting) opinions that one believes at the same time
hypersomnia	hyper = overly, too much som = sleep	sleeping too much

Knowing the word parts listed above, you can also create the following words. You can get an idea of their meanings from the word parts they use.

synonymous	syn + nym (name)	_____
parasomnia	_____ + _____	(activities) along with/at the same time as sleep
somnambulism	som + ambul (to walk)	_____
hyperactive	_____	overly active

Pronunciation

p. 199	dichotic	dy-kot′-ic	p. 214	dyssomnia	dis-som′-nee-a
p. 206	circadian	sir-kay′-dee-in	p. 222	hypnosis	hip-no′-sis

ANSWERS AND EXPLANATIONS

To find relevant material in your textbook, consult the pages cited with each answer. Also, PN and PT citations refer to modules in *PsychNow!* and *Psyk.trek* materials, respectively.

Mastering the Concepts

1. consciousness (p. 196)
2. introspection (p. 196)
3. attention (p. 198)
4. cocktail party (p. 199)
5. dichotic (p. 199)
6. automaticity (p. 201)
7. subliminal (p. 202)
8. placebo (p. 203)
9. visual neglect (p. 203)
10. attention deficit (p. 204)
11. circadian (p. 206)
12. hypothalamus (p. 206)
13. biological (p. 206)
14. height (p. 208)
15. frequency (p. 208)
16. theta (p. 208)
17. spindles (p. 208)
18. delta (p. 209)
19. paradoxical (p. 210)
20. dreaming (p. 210)
21. 90 minutes (p. 210)
22. rebound (p. 213)
23. wish (p. 213)
24. latent (p. 213)
25. activation (p. 213)
26. insomnia (p. 215)
27. narcolepsy (p. 215)
28. night terrors (p. 216)
29. Psychoactive (p. 217)
30. tolerance (p. 218)
31. Depressants (p. 218)
32. Stimulants (p. 219)
33. Opiates (p. 220)
34. Hallucinogens (p. 220)
35. marijuana (p. 221)
36. expectations (p. 221)
37. suggestibility (p. 222)
38. sleepy (p. 223)
39. pain (p. 223)
40. accuracy (p. 224)
41. dissociations (p. 224)
42. hidden (p. 225)
43. role playing (p. 225)
44. expectations (p. 225)
45. Meditation (p. 226)
46. relaxation (p. 226)
47. alpha (p. 226)

Evaluating Your Progress

Preview & Setting Priorities for Mental Functioning: Attention

1. **b**
(p. 199)
   - a. Wrong. Visual neglect is a neuropsychological disorder caused by parietal lobe damage.
   - c. Wrong. Attention is often described as a spotlight, but there is no spotlight technique in research.
   - d. Wrong. Subliminal refers to "below threshold." Input is not subliminal in the case described.

2. **d**
(p. 199)
   - a. Wrong. Visual neglect is a disorder in which half of the visual field does not reach awareness.
   - b. Wrong. Consciousness is the subjective awareness of internal and external events.
   - c. Wrong. Automaticity is fast effortless processing requiring little or no controlled attention.

3. **d**
(p. 200)
   - a. Wrong. The cocktail party and ear switching research deals with normal attention, not disorders.
   - b. Wrong. This is true, but it does not relate to the selective attention experiments cited.
   - c. Wrong. An attended message is well-processed, and the unattended message is at least monitored.

4. **a**
(p. 201)
   - b. Wrong. A controlled process requires controlled, conscious attention.
   - c. Wrong. Automaticity does not imply a single, isolated hemisphere is used for processing.
   - d. Wrong. Dissociation is a splitting into parts. This is not required for automaticity.

5. **a**
(p. 203)
   - b. Wrong. Attention deficit disorder involves an inability to sustain or control attention.
   - c. Wrong. Hypnotic dissociation is a splitting of consciousness with multiple forms of awareness.
   - d. Wrong. Split world disorder is not an actual condition.

6. **c**
(p. 202)
   - a. Wrong. Subliminal does not relate to motivation, and such messages are not effective.
   - b. Wrong. Subliminal does not relate to appeal. It relates to detection..
   - d. Wrong. Subliminal does not relate to divided attention, and it does not reduce attention to a task.

Sleeping and Dreaming

1. **c**   a. Wrong.   Light is important for setting biological clocks, but the clock is not in the optic nerve.
(p. 206)   b. Wrong.   Hormones fluctuate in cycles, but the pituitary is not the site of the biological clock.
          d. Wrong.   The biological clock influences the RAS, but that is not the clock's location.

2. **c**   a. Wrong.   While awake and working on a task, the EEG is asynchronous and high frequency.
(p. 209)   b. Wrong.   While awake but relaxed, the EEG is primarily alpha waves.
(PN2C)   d. Wrong.   The EEG for REM is similar to waking (asynchronous, high frequency waves).

3. **d**   a. Wrong.   REM is not the shortest stage of sleep.
(p. 210)   b. Wrong.   Dreams are likely, but the paradox of REM does not concern this or the vividness of dreams.
          c. Wrong.   Delta waves are found in Stage 4 non-REM sleep, but the EEG pattern is important.

4. **c**   a. Wrong.   Most people cycle through four or five times.
(p. 210)   b. Wrong.   Heart rate is very irregular and rapid during REM.
(PT4B)   d. Wrong.   REM stands for rapid eye movements.

5. **a**   b, c, & d.   Wrong.   These describe sleep as restorative or allowing repair of the system.
(p. 211)

6. **b**   a. Wrong.   These parasomnias are associated with non-REM sleep, usually Stage 4 sleep.
(p. 216)   c. Wrong.   These parasomnias usually don't indicate psychological problems, but nightmares might.
          d. Wrong.   Sleep apnea is a separate problem and unrelated to these parasomnias.

7. **a**   b. Wrong.   This is Hobson & McCarley's activation-synthesis theory.
(p. 213)   c. Wrong.   This is a restorative theory of sleep and dreams.
          d. Wrong.   This is Cartwright's problem solving theory of dreams.

8. **b**   a. Wrong.   Hypersomnia is excessive sleepiness, not difficulty sleeping.
(p. 215)   c. Wrong.   Parasomnias are sleep disorders featuring abnormal events during sleep.
          d. Wrong.   Narcolepsy is a sleep disorder in which sleep (REM sleep) onsets suddenly and at inappropriate times.

Altering Awareness: Psychoactive Drugs

1. **b**   a. Wrong.   Continued drug use leads to tolerance, not sensitivity.
(p. 218)   c. Wrong.   Withdrawal occurs when drug use is halted.
          d. Wrong.   Synesthesia is a blended sensory experience found with hallucinogen use.

2. **d**   a. Wrong.   Tolerance is the need to take a higher dose to obtain the same level effect.
(p. 218)   b. Wrong.   Withdrawal occurs when a drug dependency is present and the user quits taking the drug.
          c. Wrong.   Synesthesia is a blending of sensory experiences most common with hallucinogenic drugs.

3. **d**   a, b, & c.   Wrong.   These are all correct. Alcohol is a depressant, not a stimulant.
(p. 218)

4. **d**   a, b, & c.   Wrong.   Mescaline, LSD, and psilocybin are hallucinogens. Cocaine is a stimulant.
(p. 219)

5. **a**   a. Wrong.   Norepinephrine activity is influenced by stimulants such as amphetamine.
(p. 218)   b. Wrong.   Dopamine activity is influenced by stimulants such as amphetamine.
          c. Wrong.   Serotonin is influenced by some hallucinogens.

1. **b**   a. Wrong.   Hilgard, a contemporary psychologist, proposed the dissociation view of hypnosis.
    (p. 222)   c. Wrong.   Timothy Leary was a modern advocate of using LSD to expand consciousness.
                d. Wrong.   Sigmund Freud, the 20th century psychoanalyst, did not originate hypnosis.

2. **a**   b. Wrong.   These are common claims for the uses of hypnosis, but not an accepted definition.
    (p. 222)   c. Wrong.   This is the dissociation theory of hypnosis, but not the accepted definition.
                d. Wrong.   This is a possible definition of meditation, not hypnosis.

3. **a**   b. Wrong.   Brain waves during hypnosis are mostly alpha, not the delta activity of deep sleep.
    (p. 223)   c. Wrong.   Brain waves during hypnosis are mostly alpha, just like the brain waves during relaxation.
                d. Wrong.   Neurotransmitter activity has not been assessed.

4. **d**   a. Wrong.   Hidden observer research usually deals with perceptual alterations, not age regression.
    (p. 225)   b. Wrong.   The expectancy effect experiments support the social role playing view.
                c. Wrong.   Hidden observer research involves dissociation and pain perception, not memory.

5. **b**   a. Wrong.   Meditation does not enhance memory.
    (p. 226)   c. Wrong.   Physiological arousal is decreased with meditation, not increased.
                d. Wrong.   Meditation is associated with increased alpha, not theta, activity.

MAKING FINAL PREPARATIONS

Short Essay Questions

1. Automaticity involves rapid, effortless processing that requires little or no directed attention. Once a task is automatic, it is not a drain on the limited mental resources. Other tasks can be performed at the same time without suffering a reduction in performance. (p. 202)

2. Dichotic listening experiments show that the unattended message does not reach awareness, but is processed. People respond to important information, such as their name, in an unattended message. Also, when the meaningful content of a message is switched to the unattended ear, shadowing switches to follow the meaning, rather than continuing with the "attended" ear. (pp. 199-200)

3. Sleep might serve a restorative function, possibly influencing metabolic activity. Sleep might have developed to keep early man out of trouble during the time we cannot rely on vision to avoid danger. Also, Freud suggested the dreams of sleep were the means for fulfilling wishes that are too unacceptable to be allowed into consciousness. (pp. 211-212)

4. Several factors other than the chemical composition of a drug determine its effect. The physical condition of the user (e.g., tolerance) can modify drug effects. Also important are the mental set or expectations of the user and the environment in which the drug is taken. Expectancy can shape the reaction to a drug's effect or even create an effect where there is no drug. Likewise, the environment provides a context that interacts with the drug's actual effects. (pp. 221-222)

5. First, people's behavior while hypnotized is influenced by their expectations or beliefs about hypnosis. They conform their behavior to fit their expectations, including the expectation that people who are hypnotized obey commands. Also, the suggestions made during hypnosis end when the subject believes they are no longer hypnotized, even if no modification of instructions are made by the hypnotist. Finally, most of the phenomena of hypnosis can be achieved by people "simulating" hypnosis (told to act hypnotized). (p. 225)

6. The cocktail party effect and "ear-switching" effect in dichotic listening research both show that unattended (but detectable) information is processed and can influence behavior, even though the "unattended" message usually doesn't reach conscious awareness. The research on subliminal (below threshold) stimuli, however, indicates that it has no effect on behavior other than possible placebo effects. Controlled studies of subliminal advertising and products have not obtained behavior that differed from that of the control group. (pp. 199-203)

Matching

1. **f** (p. 215)	4. **m** (p. 216)	7. **d** (p. 206)	10. **l** (p. 196)	13. **g** (p. 213)	16. **k** (p. 215)
2. **o** (p. 218)	5. **b** (p. 213)	8. **c** (p. 218)	11. **p** (p .224)	14. **h** (p. 226)	
3. **j** (p. 198)	6. **n** (p. 208)	9. **i** (p. 199)	12. **e** (p. 208)	15. **a** (p. 221)	

Multiple Choice Pretest 1

1. **a**
    (p. 201)
    b. Wrong.   The ear-switching task examines selective attention, not automaticity.
    c. Wrong.   A dichotic listening task examines selective attention, not automaticity.
    d. Wrong.   The hidden observer task is a test of the dissociation view of hypnosis.

2. **b**
    (p. 200)
    a.   Wrong.   The "split ear" research found people followed a meaningful message across ears.
    c & d. Wrong.   Mixing messages occurs only when it retains meaning, not isolated words.

3. **d**
    (p. 203)
    a. Wrong.   Attention is a higher cognitive process and involves the cerebral cortex, not the cerebellum.
    b. Wrong.   Damage to the occipital lobe produces visual, not attention problems.
    c. Wrong.   The hindbrain is responsible mostly for lower-level processes, not attention.

4. **b**
    (p. 210)
    a. Wrong.   Too short.
    c. Wrong.   Too long.
    d. Wrong.   Much too long.

5. **a**
    (p. 210)
    b, c, & d.   Wrong.   These stages tend to become less frequent and briefer.

6. **d**
    (p. 202)
    a, b, & c.   Wrong.   There was no effect of having the word "sex" in the pictures.

7. **a**
    (p. 203)
    b. Wrong.   There was no difference.
    c. Wrong.   Different motivation would be expected to produce a difference in weight loss.
    d. Wrong.   The weight loss didn't differ between groups, so the weight loss can't be due to the tapes.

8. **b**
    (p. 210)
    a. Wrong.   REM stands for rapid eye movements.
    c. Wrong.   Dreams are most commonly reported in REM.
    d. Wrong.   REM is accompanied by very relaxed muscles.

9. **b**
    (p. 208)
    a. Wrong.   The EEG for Stage 1 sleep shows primarily theta waves.
    c. Wrong.   Stage 4 produces delta activity, not sleep spindles or K-complexes.
    d. Wrong.   REM sleep has high frequency, asynchronous waves, but no sleep spindles or K-complexes.

10. **c**
    (p. 215)
    a. Wrong.   Sleep apnea is a disorder in which people quit breathing periodically while asleep.
    b. Wrong.   Insomnia is a difficulty getting to sleep or staying asleep.
    d. Wrong.   Hypermnesia is enhanced memory, not a sleep disorder.

11. **d**   a. Wrong.   Apparent memory enhancement can be accounted for by factors other than hypnosis.
(p. 224) b. Wrong.   Recent events are not recalled more accurately with hypnosis.
          c. Wrong.   Old events are difficult to verify, so memory has not been shown to be better.

12. **b**   a. Wrong.   Meditation causes relaxation, but not pain reduction.
(p. 223) c. Wrong.   REM deprivation does not reduce pain perception.
          d. Wrong.   Alpha waves are associated with relaxation, but not pain reduction.

13. **a**   b. Wrong.   Hypnosis is not generally self-induced nor commonly used for self-reflection.
(p. 226) c. Wrong.   Drugs might manipulate awareness and allow relaxation and self-reflection, but this would
                          not be considered self-induced because it involves an outside agent, drugs.
          d. Wrong.   Sleep is self-induced and relaxing, and alters awareness. It doesn't involve self-reflection.

14. **b**   a. Wrong.   The manifest content is the actual content and images in the dream, not their interpretation.
(p. 213) c. Wrong.   Activation-synthesis is an alternative to Freud's theory.
          d. Wrong.   The dissociation hypothesis proposes that consciousness splits during hypnosis.

15. **c**   a, b & d.   Wrong.   These can produce pleasurable feelings, but synesthesia is most likely with LSD.
(p. 221)

16. **a**   b. Wrong.   Hallucinogens affect perception, but they do not reduce pain sensitivity.
(p. 220) c. Wrong.   Amphetamines increase arousal, not pain tolerance.
(PN2D) d. Wrong.   Cocaine elevates mood, but does not reduce pain sensitivity.

17. **c**   a. Wrong.   Endorphins are affected by opiates. Dopamine is the key to cocaine's reinforcing effects.
(p. 219) b. Wrong.   Serotonin is affected by hallucinogens. Dopamine is the key to cocaine's effects.
(PT4D) d. Wrong.   Depressants affect GABA. Dopamine is the key to cocaine's effects.

18. **c**   a. Wrong.   Tolerance is the need for larger doses with continued drug use.
(p. 218) b. Wrong.   Dependency may lead to these symptoms, but it is not the symptoms themselves.
          d. Wrong.   Synesthesia is a cross-sensory experience (e.g., "seeing" sounds).

Multiple Choice Pretest 2

1. **d**   a. Wrong.   Visual neglect involves being unaware of half of the visual field.
(p. 204) b. Wrong.   Delta activity is a type of brain wave characteristic of deep sleep.
          c. Wrong.   The cocktail party effect is the awareness of important input in an unattended message.

2. **b**   a. Wrong.   He'd never drive well if he lacked awareness of half of the visual field (visual neglect).
(p. 201) c. Wrong.   Key here is the addition of a second task, not a general inability to pay attention.
          d. Wrong.   The cocktail party effect shows unattended input is processed. That is not the case here.

3. **c**   a. Wrong.   Subliminal perception involves stimuli that are below threshold, not setting priorities.
(p. 198) b. Wrong.   Visual neglect is not adaptive. It is an inability to attend to one half of the visual field.
          d. Wrong.   Activation-synthesis is a theory of dreaming.

4. **c**   a. Wrong.   In visual neglect, one side of the visual field does not reach consciousness.
(p. 199) b. Wrong.   In attention deficit/hyperactivity disorder the individual cannot sustain attention.
          d. Wrong.   Hypermnesia is improved memory.

5. **a**   b, c, & d.   Wrong.   These statements are accurate, but events below awareness can have an effect.
(p. 202)

6. **a**   b. Wrong.   Narcolepsy is a tendency to fall asleep at inappropriate times.
(p. 215)   c. Wrong.   Night terrors are feelings of extreme fear, not a tendency to quit breathing.
                d. Wrong.   Insomnia is a difficulty getting to sleep or staying asleep.

7. **b**   a. Wrong.   Sleep spindles are found in Stage 2, not REM sleep.
(p. 209)   c. Wrong.   Delta waves are not found in REM sleep.
                d. Wrong.   Delta waves are associated with deep sleep, not being close to awakening.

8. **c**   a. Wrong.   Hypersomnia is a tendency to be sleepy much more often than normal.
(p. 216)   b. Wrong.   In sleep apnea the person stops breathing periodically while asleep.
                d. Wrong.   Nightmares are REM dreams, and they usually do not cause panic and nonresponsiveness.

9. **c**   a. Wrong.   ADD is not due to superchiasmic nucleus damage. Frontal lobes are more likely involved.
(p. 206)   b. Wrong.   Visual neglect is associated with right parietal lobe damage.
                d. Wrong.   Hypermensia is improved recall. This nucleus doesn't involve memory skills.

10. **c**   a. Wrong.   This would be a Freudian wish-fulfillment view, not the activation-synthesis approach.
(p. 213)   b. Wrong.   This would be a problem solving approach, not the activation-synthesis approach.
                d. Wrong.   The activation-synthesis view doesn't assign dreams any diagnostic value.

11. **c**   a. Wrong.   Circadian rhythms are 24-hour biological cycles. Narcolepsy is a sleep disorder.
(p. 215)   b. Wrong.   Narcolepsy is a sleep disorder, but not a parasomnia.
                d. Wrong.   Narcolepsy is a sleep disorder, not a splitting of consciousness.

12. **c**   a. Wrong.   The hallucinogen mescaline comes from a cactus, not mushrooms.
(p. 220)   b. Wrong.   The hallucinogen marijuana comes from a leafy plant, cannabis sativa, not mushrooms.
                d. Wrong.   The stimulant cocaine comes from the leaf of the coca plant, not mushrooms.

13. **a**   b. Wrong.   Nicotine is a stimulant; alcohol is a depressant.
(p. 218)   c. Wrong.   MDMA is a hallucinogen; alcohol is a depressant.
(PN2D)   d. Wrong.   Morphine is an opiate; alcohol is a depressant.

14. **b**   a. Wrong.   Cocaine increases the activity of norepinephrine and dopamine.
(p. 218)   c. Wrong.   Heroin mimics the activity of endorphins.
(PT4D)   d. Wrong.   LSD mimics serotonin.

15. **d**   a. Wrong.   Dependency is a need for continued drug use.
(p. 218)   b. Wrong.   REM rebound is the tendency to spend a greater than normal time in REM sleep if deprived
                           of REM on previous nights.
                c. Wrong.   Withdrawal is the physical reaction to discontinuing drug use.

16. **d**   a. Wrong.   Hallucinogens do not increase suggestibility or reduce pain perception.
(p. 222)   b. Wrong.   Meditation induces relaxation, but not heightened suggestibility.
                c. Wrong.   Sleep deprivation causes sagging eyelids, but not pain reduction or suggestibility.

17. **c**   a. Wrong.   Hidden observer, not expectancy effect, experiments support the dissociation view.
(p. 225)   b. Wrong.   The key aspect of the research is the subject's expectation, not brain waves.
                d. Wrong.   This is not a view of hypnosis, and ACh has no relation to expectancy effects in hypnosis.

18. **d**   a, b, & c.   Wrong.   A hidden observer perceives reality and is not influenced by hypnotic suggestion.
(p. 225)

CHAPTER 7: LEARNING FROM EXPERIENCE

ESTABLISHING LEARNING GOALS

Use these learning goals as a preview of the chapter, a guide for active reading, and to evaluate your mastery of the material. Review the relevant goals as you begin and end your reading of each major section of the chapter.

I.   Define learning, and explain how learning is studied.

II. Solve the adaptive problem of recognizing and reacting appropriately to significant events.
   A. Describe and compare habituation and sensitization.

III. Solve the adaptive problem of recognizing relationships between events and responding to them.
   A. Describe the basic elements of classical conditioning.
      1. Define conditioned stimulus, unconditioned stimulus, conditioned response and unconditioned response.
      2. Describe Pavlov's experiment, and identify the components of conditioning in that context.
   B. Discuss why and how conditioned responding develops.
      1. Discuss the evidence that suggests that conditioning is more than stimulus substitution.
      2. Discuss how taste aversions develop and explain how they are adaptive but troublesome.
   C. Differentiate among second-order conditioning, stimulus generalization and stimulus discrimination.
   D. Discuss extinction and conditioned inhibition.
      1. Describe the process of extinction and what spontaneous recovery indicates about extinction.
      2. Discuss the adaptive value of conditioned inhibition.

IV. Solve the adaptive problem of recognizing the consequences of a behavior and responding to them.
   A. Define operant conditioning, and discuss the law of effect.
   B. Explain what we mean by discriminative stimulus.
   C. Define reinforcement, and distinguish between positive and negative forms.
      1. Explain the response deprivation theory of reinforcement.
      2. Describe conditioned reinforcers.
   D. Define punishment, and distinguish between its positive and negative forms.
      1. Provide examples of positive and negative punishment.
      2. Discuss the limitations of punishment as a technique for eliminating a behavior.
   E. Discuss different schedules of reinforcement, and compare their effects on behavior.
   F. Explain how complex behaviors can be acquired through shaping.
   G. Discuss how biological factors might limit the responses that can be learned.

V.   Solve the adaptive problem of learning without being a direct participant.
   A. Describe observational learning and the conditions that lead to effective modeling.
   B. Explain why observational learning is adaptive, and discuss its practical effects.

MASTERING THE MATERIAL

Preview & Learning About Events: Noticing and Ignoring (pp. 232-235)

Mastering the Vocabulary. Define or explain each of the following terms. To check your answers, consult the text pages listed.

1. learning (p. 232)

2. orienting response (p. 234)

3. habituation (p. 234)

4. sensitization (p. 235)

Mastering the Concepts. Fill in the blanks to create a summary of the section. Answers are on page 170.

Learning is a relatively _____(1) change in _____(2), or potential to respond, that results from _____(3).   Learning research often uses animals as subjects because of the greater control possible and their simpler learning processes. This chapter examines four adaptive learning problems: How do people notice events? How do they learn about signaling properties of events? How do they learn about the consequences of behavior? How do they learn from others?

Novel stimuli cause _____(4) responses, a shift in attention toward the stimulus. _____(5), a reduction in responsiveness, occurs with repeated stimulation if the stimulus is without serious consequences. Habituation produces selective responding. For intense stimuli, sometimes _____(6) occurs, an increase, rather than a decrease, in responsiveness.

Evaluating Your Progress. Select the one best response. Answers are found of page 170. If you make any errors, reread the relevant material before proceeding.

1. "A relatively permanent change in behavior, or potential to respond, that results from experience" defines
   a. the orienting response.
   b. performance.
   c. learning.
   d. knowledge.

2. When a novel stimulus appears, attention is automatically shifted to it. This describes
   a. modeling.
   b. an orienting response.
   c. spontaneous recovery.
   d. sensitization.

3. Orienting responses sometimes become more selective and decrease when significant consequences do not follow the stimulus. This decrease in the orienting response is called
   a. habituation.
   b. sensitization.
   c. stimulus generalization.
   d. negative reinforcement.

Learning What Events Signal: Classical Conditioning (pp. 236-246)

Mastering the Vocabulary. Define or explain each of the following terms. To check your answers, consult the text pages listed.

1. classical conditioning (p. 234)

2. unconditioned stimulus (US) (p. 237)

3. unconditioned response (UR) (p. 237)

4. conditioned stimulus (CS) (p. 237)

5. conditioned response (CR) (p. 237)

6. second-order conditioning (p. 241)

7. stimulus generalization (p. 242)

8. stimulus discrimination (p. 243)

9. extinction (p. 243)

10. spontaneous recovery (p. 244)

11. conditioned inhibition (p. 245)

Mastering the Concepts. Fill in the blanks to create a summary of the section. Answers are on page 170.

Organisms learn what events _____(7) through the process of _____(8) conditioning. A Russian physiologist, _____(9), identified the process of classical conditioning after noticing that dogs in his digestion research began salivating before food was presented. Certain stimuli, _____(10) stimuli (USs), automatically lead to responses known as _____(11) responses (URs). No learning is required. Stimuli that signal the US can acquire an ability to cause a _____(12) response (CR). These stimuli are called _____(13) stimuli (CSs). In Pavlov's experiments food is a US for the UR of salivation. Footsteps, or a bell rung before food presentation, became CSs and elicited a salivation CR.

To become a CS, a stimulus must provide reliable information about the US. CSs usually must come _____(14) the US (signal the upcoming US) for conditioning to occur. The US usually must follow the CS closely in time; too much delay makes the CS a poor signal. The CS must provide _____(15) information about the US. Other stimuli that accompany the CS will not become CSs if they provide no new information; _____(16) will occur.

The current signaling approach emphasizes that conditioning is not _____(17). The organism actively seeks information about relationships, although conscious intent is not required. This approach does not see the CS as a _____(18) for the US, eliciting a CR very similar to the UR.

Conditioned stimuli can be used to condition other stimuli, a process called _____(20) conditioning. In stimulus _____(21) new stimuli similar to the CS will elicit a CR. "Little Albert" was conditioned to cry when a rat was presented, but other furry items also elicited crying. In contrast, in stimulus _____(22) a new stimulus results in a different response, often after experience shows the new stimulus does not signal the US. If the CS is never again paired with the US, the CS loses its signaling characteristics and _____(23), the loss of the CR, occurs. This is similar to _____(24) but involves a conditioned relationship, not an inborn one. When previously extinguished CRs reappear, spontaneous _____(25) has occurred. In conditioned _____(26), the CS signals the absence of a US and leads to a reduction of responding.

Learning to predict events using signaling stimuli is very adaptive. Conditioned taste _____(26), helps prevent consumption of dangerous foods. Organisms that become ill after eating a food, especially an unusual one, develop an aversion to that food and are unwilling to eat it again. In some cases, such as chemotherapy, conditioned taste aversions are not desirable, but can be prevented by giving a distinctive food as a "decoy" or by presenting bland foods unlikely to cause conditioned taste aversion.

Evaluating Your Progress. Select the one best response. Answers are on page 171. If you make any errors, reread the relevant material before proceeding.

1. Organisms learn relationships between stimuli that are outside of their control through a process called
   a. instrumental conditioning.
   b. sensitization.
   c. classical conditioning.
   d. habituation.

2. A stimulus that automatically produces an observable response prior to any training is called a(n)
   a. conditioned stimulus.
   b. unconditioned stimulus.
   c. discriminative stimulus.
   d. associate stimulus.

3. In Watson's experiment with Albert, Albert cried when a loud noise was suddenly presented. After presenting a rat just before the noise several times, Watson found that Albert cried when the rat was presented, even if the noise wasn't. In this experiment, the rat was the
   a. unconditioned stimulus.
   b. unconditioned response.
   c. conditioned stimulus.
   d. conditioned response.

4. Stimulus discrimination occurs when
   a. only the unconditioned stimulus elicits the conditioned response.
   b. stimuli that are similar to the conditioned stimulus also elicit the conditioned response.
   c. stimuli other than the conditioned stimulus do not elicit the conditioned response.
   d. an established conditioned stimulus is used to condition a second neutral stimulus.

5. Even though a conditioned response has undergone extinction, it sometimes reappears later without any further training. This reappearance is known as
   a. spontaneous recovery.
   b. second-order conditioning.
   c. sensitization.
   d. generalization.

6. Blocking occurs because the new stimulus
   a. signals the occasions when the unconditioned stimulus won't occur.
   b. is separated from the unconditioned stimulus by too much time.
   c. adds no new information about the unconditioned stimulus.
   d. doesn't provide reliable information about the unconditioned stimulus.

7. Chemotherapy patients find foods eaten prior to therapy are not appealing afterward. This illustrates
   a. second-order conditioning.
   b. conditioned inhibition.
   c. stimulus discrimination.
   d. conditioned taste aversion.

8. If the unconditioned stimulus is never again presented with the conditioned stimulus,
   a. extinction occurs.
   b. blocking occurs.
   c. discrimination occurs.
   d. generalization occurs.

Learning About the Consequences of Behavior: Operant Conditioning (pp. 247-259)

Mastering the Vocabulary. Define or explain each of the following terms. To check your answers, consult the text pages listed.

1. operant conditioning (instrumental conditioning) (p. 248)

2. law of effect (p. 248)

3. discriminative stimulus (p. 249)

4. reinforcement (p. 249)

5. positive reinforcement (p. 249)

6. negative reinforcement (p. 250)

7. escape conditioning (p. 251)

8. avoidance conditioning (p. 251)

9. conditioned reinforcer (p. 252)

10. punishment (p. 252)

11. positive punishment (p. 252)

12. negative punishment (p. 252)

13. schedule of reinforcement (p. 254)

14. partial reinforcement schedule (p. 254)

15. fixed-ratio schedule (p. 254)

16. variable-ratio schedule (p. 254)

17. fixed-interval schedule (p. 255)

18. variable-interval schedule (p. 256)

19. shaping (p. 257)

Mastering the Concepts. Fill in the blanks to create a summary of the section. Answers are on page 170.

In classical conditioning, events signal outcomes, but in _____(27) or _____(28) conditioning the organism's own actions produce outcomes. In the late 1800's, Thorndike proposed the law of _____(29): Responses followed by a satisfying or pleasant consequence will be _____(30); responses followed by an unsatisfying or unpleasant consequence will be _____(31).

In the 20th century, Skinner proposed that _____(32) stimuli signal when a response will be rewarded, like the CS signaling the US. Stimulus _____(33) occurs when a response is made to stimuli that are similar to the original, and stimulus _____(34) occurs when responding occurs only to one stimulus.

The formal term for the situation in which a "pleasant" consequence "strengthens" a response is _____(35), which is defined as response consequences that increase the likelihood of the response.

_____(36) reinforcement is an event, that when presented after a response, increases the likelihood of that response. Response _____(37) theory states an event will be reinforcing if it moves the organism closer to its bliss point, or baseline level, for that event. For _____(38) reinforcement, removal of an event after a response increases the likelihood of the response occurring again. Negative reinforcement can involve _____(39) conditioning, in which a response ends an unpleasant event, and _____(40) conditioning, in which a response prevents the occurrence of an unpleasant event. Note that "negative" refers to removing an event, not decreasing the response. All reinforcement increases response likelihood.

Reinforcers can be classified as primary and secondary, or _____(41) reinforcers. Primary reinforcers have intrinsic value (food, water), but secondary reinforcers (money, stars) have acquired (learned) value. Accidental reinforcement is possible and may contribute to some superstitious behavior.

Consequences that decrease the likelihood of a response are called punishment. In _____(42) punishment, an aversive event is presented after a response. In _____(43) punishment a positive event is removed after a response. Problems with punishment include judging its strength, the fact that good behavior is not taught, and possibly the chance of resentment, aggression, and attempted escape.

The rules or _____(44) of reinforcement produce individual patterns of response. A _____(45) schedule of reinforcement reinforces every target response. A _____(46) reinforcement schedule reinforces only some responses. A _____(47) schedule requires a certain number of responses for reinforcement and produces steady responding, but a postreinforcement pause can occur with large ratios. If the number of required responses varies around an average, a _____(48) schedule is in effect, and the response rate will be high and steady. _____(49) schedules require a certain amount of time to pass before another response will be reinforced and produces low rates of responding with a scalloped appearance. If the time interval varies, the schedule is a variable interval schedule and produces steady responding.

When reinforcement is ended, _____(50) begins, and the organism eventually quits responding. The schedule of reinforcement influences how long responding will continue. Continuous schedules produce faster extinction than partial schedules, and fixed schedules result in _____(51) extinction than variable schedules, apparently due to differences in the _____(52) of reinforcement.

The method of successive approximations, or _____(53), is used to train an organism to make a desired response. Responses that approximate the desired response are reinforced, and the standards for reinforcement are increased gradually until the final form of the response is required. Accidental or adventitious reinforcement can also modify behavior. This is one cause of superstitious behavior. Biological constraints also influence learning. Some responses are not easily learned.

Evaluating Your Progress. Select the one best answer. Answers are on page 171. If you make any errors, reread the relevant material before proceeding.

1. Responses followed by pleasant consequences are strengthened; responses followed by unpleasant consequences are weakened. This represents
   a. extinction.
   b. the law of effect.
   c. shaping.
   d. observational learning.

2. A child learned that if she says "please," Dad usually gives her what she wants. This illustrates
   a. classical conditioning.
   b. operant conditioning.
   c. extinction.
   d. sensitization.

3. "Response consequences that increase the likelihood of the response occurring again" describes
   a. shaping.
   b. punishment.
   c. reinforcement.
   d. discrimination.

4. A pigeon was trained to peck a blue key, but it will also peck the key if it is green. This illustrates
   a. generalization.
   b. shaping.
   c. extinction.
   d. spontaneous recovery.

5. The "positive" and "negative" in positive and negative reinforcement refer to whether
   a. the reinforced response increases or decreases in frequency.
   b. the reinforcer is presented before or after the response.
   c. a stimulus or event is presented or removed when a response is made.
   d. the reinforcer has intrinsic value or acquired value.

6. A consequence that decreases a response is
   a. reinforcement.
   b. punishment.
   c. shaping.
   d. generalization.

7. A conditioned reinforcer is a stimulus that
   a. is presented only some of the times a response is made.
   b. identifies the occasions that a response will be followed by a reinforcer.
   c. has acquired, rather than natural, reinforcing characteristics.
   d. produces a very high, continuous rate of responding.

8. The situation in which reinforcement is no longer given following a trained response is called
   a. extinction.
   b. conditioned inhibition.
   c. a postreinforcement pause.
   d. shaping.

9. The Brelands tried to teach a raccoon to put a coin in a bank. They found that
   a. raccoons are not responsive to positive reinforcement; they require negative reinforcement.
   b. teaching a raccoon to put a coin in a bank is as easy as teaching a pigeon to peck a key.
   c. the raccoon's natural behavioral tendencies made teaching it the trick very difficult.
   d. classical conditioning doesn't work with raccoons, although operant conditioning does.

10. June is teaching her dog to roll over. At first she gives him a dog treat any time he makes a slight rolling movement, then only for larger rolling movements, and finally, only if he rolls over. She is using
    a. secondary reinforcement.
    b. partial reinforcement.
    c. extinction.
    d. shaping.

11. A reinforcement schedule that reinforces every sixth response is known as a
    a. fixed ratio schedule.
    b. variable ratio schedule.
    c. fixed interval schedule.
    d. variable interval schedule.

12. The schedule of reinforcement that produces high response rates and high resistance to extinction is
    a. continuous reinforcement.
    b. fixed ratio schedule.
    c. fixed interval schedule.
    d. variable ratio schedule.

Learning From Others: Observational Learning (pp. 260-262)

Mastering the Vocabulary. Define or explain each of the following terms. To check your answers, consult the text pages listed.

1. observational learning (p. 260)

2. modeling (p. 261)

Mastering the Concepts. Fill in the blanks to create a summary of the section. Answers are on page 170.

Organisms do not have to be directly involved in behavior to learn about its consequences. Much is learned through _____(54), or social, learning. Here, the organism observes the behavior of others and imitates, or _____(55) it. Observing others being reinforced or punished for a behavior can result in modification of the observer's behavior due to _____(56) reinforcement or punishment. Bandura has shown that children who watched an adult hitting a doll were more likely to hit the doll than children watching an adult play nonviolently. This research raises questions about the impact of TV violence.

160

Evaluating Your Progress. Select the one best response. Answers are on page 172. If you make any errors, reread the relevant material before you proceed.

1. Another name for observational learning is
   a. instrumental learning.
   b. social learning.
   c. indirect learning.
   d. higher-order learning.

2. The natural tendency to imitate the behavior of significant others in one's surrounding is
   a. shaping.
   b. discrimination.
   c. modeling.
   d. generalization.

3. Which is FALSE?
   a. Observational learning is found only in humans.
   b. An attractive or likeable model increases the likelihood of observational learning.
   c. An observer's self-efficacy influences observational learning.
   d. The consequences of the model's behavior is important.

4. Modeling is more likely if the person being observed is reinforced for his or her behavior. Watching someone be reinforced is called
   a. accidental reinforcement.
   b. vicarious reinforcement.
   c. partial reinforcement.
   d. secondary reinforcement.

MAKING FINAL PREPARATIONS

Complete these sections without consulting your book or notes. For a more accurate estimate of how well you know this material, wait at least a day or two after studying the chapter before working on the questions. Some of the material you "know" immediately after working with the chapter will be quickly forgotten. Immediate tests will overestimate what you know well.

Short Essay Questions. Write a brief answer to each question. Sample answers begin on page 173.

1. Compare habituation and classical conditioning extinction.

2. Explain why stimulus generalization might be adaptive, and give an example.

3. Explain why conditioned taste aversions develop. Identify the US, CS, UR, and CR.

4. Explain why variable schedules of reinforcement produce greater resistance to extinction than fixed and continuous schedules.

5. Explain the development of superstitious behavior using conditioning concepts.

6. Discuss the limitations of punishment as a means of behavior modification.

7. Explain the adaptive value of observational learning.

8. Describe fixed interval and variable interval schedules of reinforcement. Compare their effects.

Matching. Select the correct definition or description for each item. Answers are on page 173.

_____ 1. conditioned inhibition
_____ 2. bliss point
_____ 3. sensitization
_____ 4. postreinforcement pause
_____ 5. Thorndike
_____ 6. Watson & Raynor
_____ 7. spontaneous recovery
_____ 8. modeling
_____ 9. Pavlov
_____ 10. Bandura
_____ 11. second-order conditioning
_____ 12. response deprivation theory
_____ 13. shaping
_____ 14. escape conditioning
_____ 15. orienting response
_____ 16. instrumental conditioning

a. did a famous experiment on observational learning
b. imitation of observed behavior
c. developed principles of classical conditioning
d. proposed the law of effect
e. procedure in which reinforcement is given for successive approximation to a response
f. baseline tendency to respond to events
g. automatic shift of attention to a novel stimulus
h. an established CS conditions a new CS
i. increased responsiveness to a repeated event
j. response delay that occurs in a fixed ratio schedule
k. a negative reinforcement situation
l. did "little Albert" study of conditioned fear
m. reappearance of formerly extinguished CR
n. idea that an event will be reinforcing if it moves an organism toward its bliss point
o. learn an event signals the absence of the US
p. operant conditioning

Multiple Choice Pretest 1. Select the one best response. Answers are found on page 173.

1. Sensitization is most likely to occur when the orienting stimulus is
    a. rare.
    b. visual.
    c. weak.
    d. intense.

2. Classical conditioning is a process by which organisms learn
    a. by observing the actions of others.
    b. the consequences of their voluntary actions.
    c. the signaling properties of events.
    d. to direct attention to a novel stimulus.

3. In Pavlov's experiments, the food was the
    a. unconditioned stimulus.
    b. unconditioned response.
    c. conditioned stimulus.
    d. conditioned response.

4. After the rat was paired with the noise several times in Watson's Little Albert experiment, Albert cried when the rat was presented alone. Crying when the rat was presented without the noise was the
    a. unconditioned stimulus.
    b. unconditioned response.
    c. conditioned stimulus.
    d. conditioned response.

5. In which situation will the tone be most likely to become a conditioned stimulus for salivation?
    a. Food is presented just before the tone is sounded.
    b. After pairing a light with food, a tone is added to the light: (tone + light)--food
    c. The tone is presented several minutes before the food.
    d. The tone is presented before an established conditioned stimulus, a light.

6. A shock is given shortly after a buzzer sounds, but not if the light is also flashing. A rat will act normally if the light and buzzer are presented, but it will freeze if only the buzzer is presented. This is an example of
    a. the law of effect.
    b. conditioned inhibition.
    c. escape conditioning.
    d. avoidance conditioning.

7. One approach to treating alcoholism is to give the person a drug that makes them throw up after they drink alcohol in hopes that alcohol will lose its appeal. This is based on the concept of
    a. conditioned taste aversion.
    b. the blocking procedure.
    c. spontaneous recovery.
    d. second-order conditioning.

8. After months of work, Phil's conditioned fear of flying finally disappeared. However, his fear suddenly reappeared. His renewed fear probably represents
   a. conditioned inhibition.
   b. second-order conditioning.
   c. spontaneous recovery.
   d. extinction.

9. Operant conditioning differs from classical conditioning because in operant conditioning
   a. an organism's behavior produces outcomes, but in classical conditioning events signal outcomes.
   b. an organism is learning something, but in classical conditioning no learning occurs.
   c. the principles apply only to animals, but in classical conditioning the principles apply to humans.
   d. discrimination and generalization do not occur, but in classical conditioning they do.

10. A stimulus or event that, when removed following a response, increases the likelihood the response will be made again is a
    a. positive reinforcer.
    b. negative reinforcer.
    c. positive punishment.
    d. negative punishment.

11. Randy had to write an essay and discuss it with his teacher because he said an obscene word in class. His teacher was frustrated when Randy's use of obscenity became more frequent in spite of being made to write an essay and talk to the teacher each time. In this example, writing the essay and talking to the teacher must be
    a. positive reinforcement.
    b. negative reinforcement.
    c. positive punishment.
    d. negative punishment.

12. Escape and avoidance conditioning involve the use of
    a. positive reinforcement.
    b. negative reinforcement.
    c. positive punishment.
    d. negative punishment.

13. Sam's mother spanked him whenever he ran into the street, so he quit running into the street. His mother used
    a. positive reinforcement.
    b. negative reinforcement.
    c. positive punishment.
    d. negative punishment.

14. When they behave properly, children at a preschool receive tickets that can later be used to get a grab bag or admission to a party. The tickets are an example of a
    a. variable reinforcer
    b. primary reinforcer.
    c. negative reinforcer.
    d. conditioned reinforcer.

15. Slot machines are set to pay off after some average number of plays (let's guess 150), but a machine might pay off after 30 plays one time and after 270 plays another time. This is an example of a
    a. fixed ratio schedule of reinforcement.
    b. fixed interval schedule of reinforcement.
    c. variable ratio schedule of reinforcement.
    d. variable interval schedule of reinforcement.

16. The key peck record from the pigeon shows long periods of few responses followed by brief periods of very rapid responses, creating a scalloped effect. This bird probably was reinforced for on a
    a. fixed ratio schedule.
    b. variable ratio schedule.
    c. fixed interval schedule.
    d. variable interval schedule.

17. A response can be taught by reinforcing successive approximations of the response, this is known as the technique of
    a. shaping.
    b. partial reinforcement.
    c. discrimination.
    d. sensitization.

18. When asked how they taught their children to be so polite, Dee and Sam replied, "We make sure we are polite to everyone when the children are around. Dee and Sam are using
    a. positive reinforcement to teach politeness.
    b. classical conditioning to teach politeness.
    c. second-order conditioning to teach politeness.
    d. observational learning to teach politeness.

19. The Brelands' animal training experiences show that
    a. biological behavioral tendencies limit what behaviors can be conditioned.
    b. reinforcement is a better way to modify behavior than punishment.
    c. behaviors sometimes develop because of accidental reinforcement.
    d. the principles of conditioning work better with animals than with humans.

Multiple Choice Pretest 2. Select the one best response. Answers are found on page 175.

1. Katrina's new apartment is next to the elevator. The day she moved in she found she couldn't study effectively because the elevator bell captured her attention each time it rang. Her behavior in known as
   a. sensitization.
   b. learning.
   c. an orienting response.
   d. habituation.

2. Kim lives near the hospital. At first, the ambulance sirens woke her several times each night, but after a few weeks, she hardly noticed them anymore. This change can be explained as
    a. habituation.
    b. sensitization.
    c. observational learning.
    d. spontaneous recovery.

3. Pat was bitten by a dog, and for months he felt afraid whenever a dog appeared. Eventually, after seeing many dogs without being bitten again, Pat felt no fear when dogs appeared. Pat was "cured" by
    a. spontaneous recovery.
    b. observational learning.
    c. extinction.
    d. conditioned inhibition.

4. Seeing blood always has made Sela feel sick. The movie she saw last week presented a drill-like noise just before the madman butchered each victim. Sela has noticed that she now feels queasy each time she hears the drills at the construction site next door. Sela's problem developed as a result of
    a. operant conditioning.
    b. classical conditioning.
    c. observational learning.
    d. extinction.

5. A conditioned taste aversion is unlikely to develop if
    a. the food and the US for nausea are paired only once.
    b. the true cause of the nausea is known.
    c. the flavor is very common or bland.
    d. there is no adaptive value for the taste aversion.

6. Little Albert was conditioned to fear a white rat. He also acted afraid of rabbits or other small animals, even though they never were paired with the loud noise. This is best explained by
    a. spontaneous recovery.
    b. discrimination.
    c. second-order conditioning.
    d. generalization.

7. Dan cried when the nurse gave him a shot. The sight of the syringe itself became a conditioned stimulus for crying. After a few shots, the appearance of the nurse would cause him to cry. This response to the nurse is best explained by
    a. second-order conditioning.
    b. stimulus generalization.
    c. discrimination.
    d. the bliss point.

8. Thorndike's law of effect is most similar to what B.F. Skinner would describe as
    a. stimulus discrimination and stimulus generalization.
    b. operant conditioning and classical conditioning.
    c. reinforcement and punishment.
    d. habituation and sensitization.

9. A few seconds before your new clock radio sounds its alarm, it makes a tiny click. You've recently noticed that you wake up right after the click and before the alarm even though you previously never woke up to anything but the alarm itself. The click is acting as a(n)
   a. unconditioned stimulus.
   b. conditioned stimulus.
   c. positive reinforcer.
   d. blocking stimulus.

10. Xavier has learned that his requests for money are never granted if he asks when his father is frowning, but that his requests are granted if his father is smiling. His father's facial expressions are examples of
    a. shaping stimuli.
    b. negative reinforcers.
    c. discriminative stimuli.
    d. a fixed-interval schedule.

11. Fred complained loudly and unpleasantly to his teacher about his test grade until his teacher changed the grade. If Fred complains about test grades more often now, Fred's behavior was influenced by
    a. positive reinforcement.
    b. negative reinforcement.
    c. positive punishment.
    d. negative punishment.

12. At first, Tom's father cheered every time Tom swung the bat. He gradually required Tom to make good swings before cheering, and eventually only a hit got a cheer. Tom's father used
    a. social learning.
    b. shaping.
    c. a fixed ratio schedule.
    d. modeling.

13. The idea that an event will be reinforcing if it moves the organism closer to its bliss point is central to
    a. the method of successive approximations.
    b. the partial reinforcement effect.
    c. response deprivation theory.
    d. social learning theory.

14. Cal's mother will answer the question, "How long till we get there?" only after 10 minutes have elapsed since the last time she answered Cal's question. This represents a
    a. fixed ratio schedule of reinforcement.
    b. fixed interval schedule of reinforcement.
    c. variable ratio schedule of reinforcement.
    d. variable interval schedule of reinforcement.

15. Sara's cold water in her shower almost disappears if the toilet is flushed. When Sara hears the toilet flush, she quickly jumps out of the water so she doesn't get burned. This situation represents
    a. avoidance conditioning.
    b. a conditioned reinforcer.
    c. observational learning.
    d. conditioned inhibition.

16. Who will continue to respond the longest after extinction begins?
    a. Alice, who was previously on a continuous reinforcement schedule.
    b. Bill, who was previously on a variable ratio schedule of reinforcement.
    c. Carl, who was previously on a fixed ratio schedule of reinforcement.
    d. Diedre, who was previously on a fixed interval schedule of reinforcement.

17. Dave loses his dessert when he hits his sister. Dave never hits his sister anymore. This illustrates
    a. positive reinforcement.
    b. negative reinforcement.
    c. positive punishment.
    d. negative punishment.

18. The salesman is paid $50.00 for every ten magazine subscriptions he sells. We might think of this as
    a. a variable interval schedule.
    b. a variable ratio schedule.
    c. a fixed interval schedule.
    d. a fixed ratio schedule.

19. Much of the concern about the effects that violence on TV may have on children's behavior is based on Bandura's research on
    a. adventitious (accidental) reinforcement.
    b. orienting responses.
    c. primary vs. secondary reinforcement.
    d. social learning.

20. Seth watched the two shoplifters taken out of the store by the police. He put the CD he had planned to steal back on the shelf and never again tried to take anything without paying. This illustrates
    a. vicarious punishment.
    b. extinction.
    c. conditioned inhibition.
    d. accidental reinforcement.

LANGUAGE DEVELOPMENT GUIDE

Core Terms

There are a few terms your instructor is likely to use without necessarily defining them first. The first is *elicit*, which means "to call forth." If I *elicit* a response from you, I am doing something that causes you to respond. Next, your instructor may use the term *contingent upon*. This means "dependent upon"; you might receive a job offer *contingent upon* graduation from college by a certain date. Finally, you might hear the term *temporal*, as in, "The temporal relationship of the stimulus and the response is important." That means their relation in time -- which comes first, and how close together they happen -- is important.

Idioms

p. 232	lie at the heart of	be central to; be a core idea
p. 233	whose fate has already been sealed	who are headed for a sure and bad end
p. 235	relatively modest in intensity	fairly quiet
p. 236	turn of the century	the years near the beginning of a new century
p. 241	metronome	device that produces a regular sound to indicate tempo
p. 252	principal's office	the office of the head of a school, where children who misbehave sometimes are sent
p. 254	haphazard	not organized, carelessly
p. 260	trial and error	trying different things to see what works

Word Parts

Here are some words that are made up of word parts, and that you can find in this chapter. After you've looked at these, you can look for others in the chapter using the same word parts.

WORD	WORD PART IT USES	MEANING
temporary	temp = time	not lasting long
recur	re = again cur = to run, to move through	to come or occur again
contact	con = together, with, against tact = touch	to get together with; to get in touch; to touch together
provide	pro = forward, before vid, vis = to see	to place before, to offer
aversion	a, an = not, away vers, vert = to turn	distasteful, to make one turn away from
distort	dis = take away, not tort = to twist	to twist improperly, to change something's form in a bad way

Knowing the word parts listed above, you can also create the following words. You can get an idea of their meanings from the word parts they use.

reverse	_____ + _____	to turn around, to change direction completely
contemporary	_____ + _____	belonging to the same time
revise	re + vis	_____
converse	_____ + _____	opposite

Pronunciation

p. 249   reinforcement   ree-in-force'-ment   p. 243   extinction   ex-stink'-shun

Answers and Explanations

To find relevant material in your textbook, consult the pages cited with each answer. Also, PN and PT citations refer to modules in *PsychNow!* and *Psyk.trek* materials, respectively.

Mastering the Concepts

1. permanent (p. 232)
2. behavior (p. 232)
3. experience (p. 232)
4. orienting (p. 234)
5. Habituation (p. 234)
6. sensitization (p. 235)
7. signal (p. 236)
8. classical (p. 236)
9. Pavlov (p. 236)
10. unconditioned (p. 237)
11. unconditioned (p. 237)
12. conditioned (p. 237)
13. conditioned (p. 237)
14. before (p. 238)

15. new (p. 238)
16. blocking (p. 238)
17. passive (p. 238)
18. substitute (p. 241)
19. aversions (p. 240)
20. second-order (p. 241)
21. generalization (p. 242)
22. discrimination (p. 243)
23. extinction (p. 243)
24. habituation (p. 244)
25. recovery (p. 244)
26. inhibition (p. 245)
27. instrumental (p. 247)
28. operant (p. 247)

29. effect (p. 248)
30. strengthened (p. 248)
31. weakened (p. 248)
32. discriminative (p. 249)
33. generalization (p. 249)
34. discrimination (p. 249)
35. reinforcement (p. 249)
36. Positive (p. 249)
37. deprivation (p. 250)
38. negative (p. 250)
39. escape (p. 251)
40. avoidance (p. 251)
41. conditioned (p. 252)
42. positive (p. 252)

43. negative (p. 252)
44. schedules (p. 254)
45. continuous (p. 254)
46. partial (p. 254)
47. fixed ratio (p. 254)
48. variable ratio (p. 254)
49. Fixed interval (p. 255)
50. extinction (p. 254)
51. faster (p. 254)
52. predictability (p.255)
53. shaping (p. 257)
54. observational (p. 260)
55. models (p. 261)
56. vicarious (p. 261)

Evaluating Your Progress

Preview & Learning About Events: Noticing and Ignoring

1.   c   a. Wrong.   An orienting response is an *inborn* tendency to shift attention toward a novel stimulus.
  (p. 232)   b. Wrong.   Performance is any overt behavior, not a change in behavior.
             d. Wrong.   Knowledge is a by-product of learning.

2.   b   a. Wrong.   Modeling is imitation of other people's actions and is not relevant here.
  (p. 234)   c. Wrong.   Spontaneous recovery is the reappearance of a CR after extinction has occurred.
             d. Wrong.   Sensitization is an increase in responsiveness to a stimulus that has been repeated.

3.   **a**   b. Wrong.   Sensitization increases the orienting response. Habituation decreases it.
  (p. 234)   c. Wrong.   Stimulus generalization is responding to stimuli that are similar to the original stimulus.
            d. Wrong.   Reinforcement *increases* a response.

Learning What Events Signal: Classical Conditioning

1.   **c**   a. Wrong.   Instrumental conditioning involves learning about the consequences of voluntary actions.
  (p. 237)   b. Wrong.   Sensitization involves an increased orienting response to a stimulus that is repeated.
            d. Wrong.   Habituation involves the reduction of an orienting response with repeated stimulation.

2.   **b**   a. Wrong.   A conditioned stimulus produces a response after training has occurred.
  (p. 237)   c. Wrong.   A discriminative stimulus indicates whether a response will be reinforced or not.
  (PN5A)   d. Wrong.   Associate stimulus is not a term used in learning and conditioning.

3.   **c**   a. Wrong.   The unconditioned stimulus was the loud noise.
  (p. 242)   b. Wrong.   The unconditioned response was Albert's crying in response to the noise.
            d. Wrong.   The conditioned response was Albert's crying in response to the rat presented alone.

4.   **c**   a. Wrong.   Unconditioned stimuli elicit *unconditioned* responses and are not involved in
  (p. 243)   discrimination.
            b. Wrong.   This describes stimulus generalization, the opposite of discrimination.
            d. Wrong.   This describes second-order conditioning.

5.   **a**   b. Wrong.   Second-order conditioning uses a CS to condition another CS. There is no extinction.
  (p. 244)   c. Wrong.   Sensitization is an increase in an orienting response, not a return of a CR.
  (PT5B)   d. Wrong.   Generalization involves a CR to a new stimulus, not the return of an extinguished CR.

6.   **c**   a. Wrong.   This describes conditioned inhibition.
  (p. 238)   b. Wrong.   The new stimulus is simultaneous with the old CS, so timing wouldn't be a problem.
            d. Wrong.   The new stimulus and the old CS are paired, so both would be equally reliable sources.

7.   **d**   a. Wrong.   Second-order conditioning requires a second CS be conditioned by an established CS.
  (p. 240)   b. Wrong.   In conditioned inhibition a CS signals the non-occurrence of a US.
            c. Wrong.   In discrimination, stimuli other than the original CS do not yield the CR.

8.   **a**   b. Wrong.   Blocking requires that the US be presented.
  (p. 243)   c. Wrong.   Discrimination doesn't occur based on US elimination. It involves new stimuli.
            d. Wrong.   Generalization occurs when stimuli other than the CS elicit a CR. Not when the US ends.

Learning About the Consequences of Behavior: Operant Conditioning

1.   **b**   a. Wrong.   Extinction is the elimination of a response by ending reinforcement or ending the US.
  (p. 248)   c. Wrong.   Shaping (method of successive approximations) is a method for teaching a response.
            d. Wrong.   Observational learning is learning by observing the responses of others.

2.   **b**   a. Wrong.   Classical conditioning is learning a stimulus signals an event, not what outcome follows.
  (p. 247)   c. Wrong.   Extinction occurs when reinforcement or the US is terminated.
            d. Wrong.   Sensitization is the strengthening of an orienting response to stimuli that are repeated.

3.   **c**   a. Wrong.   Shaping involves reinforcing responses that are increasingly similar to the target response.
  (p. 249)   b. Wrong.   Punishment would decrease the likelihood of the response.
            d. Wrong.   Discrimination involves signals concerning when a response will produce reinforcement.

4. **a**   b. Wrong. Shaping is a method of training a response, not the generalization of responses.
    (p. 249)   c. Wrong. Extinction is the elimination of a response when reinforcement or a US is terminated.
                d. Wrong. Spontaneous recovery is the reemergence of a formerly extinguished response.

5. **c**   a. Wrong. Response increase or decrease determines reinforcement vs. punishment.
    (p. 249)   b. Wrong. Reinforcers always come after the response. They're the consequences of a response.
                d. Wrong. Intrinsic vs. acquired value differentiates primary and secondary (acquired) reinforcement.

6. **b**   a. Wrong. Reinforcement increases the response. Punishment decreases it.
    (p. 252)   c. Wrong. Shaping is a method used to teach a response.
    (PN5B)   d. Wrong. Generalization occurs when a response is made to stimuli other than the original one.

7. **c**   a. Wrong. This describes partial reinforcement.
    (p. 252)   b. Wrong. This describes a discriminative stimulus.
                d. Wrong. This describes a variable-ratio schedule of reinforcement.

8. **a**   b. Wrong. In conditioned inhibition, a stimulus signals when a US will not occur.
    (p. 254)   c. Wrong. A postreinforcement pause is a period after reinforcement when no responses are made.
                d. Wrong. Shaping is the reinforcing of responses that are increasingly similar to the desired response.

9. **c**   a, b, & d.   Wrong.   Their experiences addressed the interaction of natural tendencies and learned
    (p. 259)   relationships, making some relationships easier to learn than others.

10. **d**   a. Wrong. The dog treat is a primary reinforcer (food).
    (p. 257)   b. Wrong. She reinforces every "response"--a continuous schedule.
    (PT5C)   c. Wrong. She is giving reinforcement, so extinction is not in effect.

11. **a**   b.   Wrong.   A variable ratio requires a variable number of responses, not exactly 6, for example.
    (p. 254)   c & d.   Wrong.   Interval schedules are based on the *time* elapsing since last reinforcement.
    (PT5D)

12. **d**   a.   Wrong.   Continuous reinforcement does not produce great resistance to extinction.
    (p. 254)   b & c.   Wrong.   Fixed schedules, ratio or interval, aren't as resistant to extinction as variable ones.

Learning From Others: Observational Learning

1. **b**   a, c, & d.   Wrong.   Observational learning is sometimes called social learning.
    (p. 260)

2. **c**   a. Wrong. Shaping is reinforcement of responses increasingly like a desired response, not imitation.
    (p. 261)   b. Wrong. Discrimination occurs when responses become increasingly selective. No imitation occurs.
    (PN5C)   d. Wrong. Generalization occurs if responses are made to similar stimuli. Imitation is not involved.

3. **a**   b. Wrong. Attractiveness, likeability, status, etc. are influential in observational learning.
    (p. 260)   c. Wrong. If a person doesn't believe he/she can imitate the act, observational learning is not likely.
                d. Wrong. Vicarious reinforcement or punishment influence observational learning.

4. **b**   a. Wrong. Accidental reinforcement is reinforcement that accidentally follows a response.
    (p. 261)   c. Wrong. Partial reinforcement involves reinforcing only some, not all, appropriate responses.
                d. Wrong. Secondary reinforcement uses a reinforcer with acquired value, rather than intrinsic value.

MAKING FINAL PREPARATIONS

Short Essay Questions

1. Habituation is a reduction of an orienting response after a stimulus has occurred repeatedly without significant consequences. Extinction is a reduction of a conditioned response due to repeated absence of the unconditioned stimulus. For both, responses are reduced when stimuli no longer signal notable consequences. (p. 244)

2. Stimulus generalization is adaptive because what is learned with one specific stimulus is transferred to other similar stimuli. Learning is not required for all stimulus variations. This improves interaction with the environment because every variation doesn't require new learning. To open a door with a slightly different knob doesn't require a separate trial and error procedure. Rather than approaching a black snake to see if it bites like the brown one did, the organism can use prior learning to avoid a potentially dangerous situation. (p. 242)

3. Nausea that occurs following eating or drinking becomes associated with whatever was ingested, particularly new or distinctive items. The illness (US) actually produces the nausea/taste aversion (UR). The food or drink becomes a conditioned stimulus for the conditioned response of nausea/taste aversion. That is: food (CS)—illness (US) ⟶ nausea (UR) then food (CR) ⟶ nausea/taste aversion (CR). (p. 240)

4. The varying time interval or number of responses involved in variable schedules makes extinction more difficult for the organism to identify than when the intervals and responses are constant, as in fixed schedules. (p. 258)

5. If a response is accidentally followed by a common reinforcer, the organism can mistakenly consider the reinforcer a consequence of the response. This increases the likelihood the response will be made again. If circumstances cause the response to be followed by the reinforcer again (using a "lucky" pen on a test and doing well) the behavior will be maintained on a partial reinforcement schedule and will resist extinction. (p. 258)

6. Although punishment can quickly eliminate a response, it has limitations. These include failing to teach an appropriate response (it teaches what not to do, not what to do), being difficult to gauge in terms of intensity, and may cause anger, aggression, and resentment. (pp. 252-253)

7. Observational learning allows learning without the organism directly participating. The organism can quickly, and perhaps more safely, learn the consequences of a behavior. It can learn from the mistakes and success of others and more effectively interact with the environment. (pp. 260-261)

8. An FI schedule reinforces the first response made after some set time interval has passed since reinforcement. A VI schedule is similar, but it varies the interval required. FI schedules produce low levels of response in a scalloped pattern, due to the tendency to respond only near the end of the interval. A VI schedule produces a higher and more consistent rate of response. The VI schedule is also more resistant to extinction. (pp. 255-256)

Matching

1. **o** (p. 245)	4. **j** (p. 254)	7. **m** (p. 244)	10. **a** (p. 261)	13. **e** (p. 257)	16. **p** (p. 247)
2. **f** (p. 250)	5. **d** (p. 248)	8. **b** (p. 261)	11. **h** (p. 241)	14. **k** (p. 251)	
3. **i** (p. 235)	6. **l** (p. 242)	9. **c** (p. 236)	12. **n** (p. 250)	15. **g** (p. 234)	

Multiple Choice Pretest 1

1. **d**   a, b, & c.   Wrong.   Sensitization occurs for repeated, intense stimuli, regardless of sensory system. (p. 235)

2. **c**   a. Wrong. This describes observational learning.
    (p. 236)   b. Wrong. This describes respondent (operant) conditioning.
                  d. Wrong. Although not learned, this is most similar to an orienting response.

3. **a**   b. Wrong. The unconditioned response was the dog's salivation in response to food being presented.
    (p. 237)   c. Wrong. The conditioned stimulus was the bell, or the footsteps that elicited salivation after training.
    (PT5A)   d. Wrong. The conditioned response was the dog's salivation to the bell or to the footsteps.

4. **d**   a. Wrong. The noise was the unconditioned stimulus. Crying is a response.
    (p. 242)   b. Wrong. Crying when the noise was presented was the unconditioned response.
    (PN5A)   c. Wrong. The rat was the conditioned stimulus. Crying is a response.

5. **d**   a. Wrong. This is backward conditioning and is unlikely to result in good conditioning.
    (p. 241)   b. Wrong. The tone will not add information, so blocking will occur.
                  c. Wrong. The CS and US usually need to be presented closer together in time.

6. **b**   a. Wrong. The law of effect involves response consequences, not a signal that a stimulus won't
    (p. 245)   appear.
                  c. Wrong. Escape conditioning requires a response that ends an event. The rat's response doesn't.
                  d. Wrong. Avoidance conditioning requires a response prevent a stimulus. The rat's response doesn't.

7. **a**   b. Wrong. There is no second neutral stimulus being added here.
    (p. 240)   c. Wrong. Spontaneous recovery is the reappearance of a CR that has previously been extinguished.
                  d. Wrong. There is no second neutral stimulus being added here.

8. **c**   a. Wrong. If inhibition had occurred, fear would have been inhibited.
    (p. 245)   b. Wrong. Second-order conditioning uses a CS to establish a new CS.
                  d. Wrong. The disappearance, not the reappearance, of the fear would represent extinction.

9. **a**   b. Wrong. Both types of conditioning involve learning.
    (p. 240)   c. Wrong. Both types of conditioning apply to animals and humans.
                  d. Wrong. Discrimination and generalization occur in both types of conditioning.

10. **b**   a.   Wrong. Positive reinforcement is the presentation of an event, not the removal of one.
    (p. 244)   c & d.   Wrong. The response increases, so this isn't punishment of any type.

11. **a**   b.   Wrong. It's reinforcement, but something is added (essay requirement), not removed.
    (p. 247)   c & d.   Wrong. The response (using obscenity) increased, so it isn't punishment.

12. **b**   a.   Wrong. Escape and avoidance involve *removing* (ending or preventing) an event.
    (p. 251)   c & d.   Wrong. Escape and avoidance involve *increasing* a response, so it isn't punishment.

13. **c**   a & b.   Wrong. The response (running into street) was reduced, so reinforcement isn't involved.
    (p. 252)   d.   Wrong. An aversive event (spanking) was added, so it's not negative punishment.

14. **d**   a. Wrong. There is no variable reinforcer. Were you thinking of variable schedule of reinforcement?
    (p. 252)   b. Wrong. Primary reinforcers have intrinsic value, like food or water. Tickets must acquire value.
                  c. Wrong. Tickets are given; an aversive event is not taken away if they act properly.

15. **c**   a. Wrong. Because the requirements for reinforcement are variable, it isn't a fixed schedule.
    (p. 254)   b. Wrong. Payoffs are based on number of plays, not time. The number isn't constant, so it's not FI.
                  d. Wrong. Payoffs are based on number of plays (responses), not time, so it isn't an interval schedule.

16. **c**   a, b, & d.   Wrong.   A scalloped pattern is characteristic of a fixed interval schedule.
   (p. 255)

17. **a**   b. Wrong.   Partial reinforcement is reinforcing some responses, not changing the required response.
   (p. 257)   c. Wrong.   Discrimination involves responding only when a signal indicates reinforcement is possible.
                 d. Wrong.   Sensitization is an increase in an orienting response to a stimulus that is repeated.

18. **d**   a, b, & c.   Wrong.   The key is being a model for politeness, not reinforcing or conditioning it.
   (p. 260)

19. **a**   b & c.   Wrong.   Although this might be true, it doesn't relate to the cited studies.
   (p. 259)   d.   Wrong.   This is not necessarily true and doesn't relate to the cited studies.

Multiple Choice Pretest 2

1. **c**   a. Wrong.   There was no increase in the bell's ability to capture her attention.
   (p. 234)   b. Wrong.   Katrina's behavior did not develop due to experience.
                 d. Wrong.   There was no decrease in the bell's ability to capture her attention.

2. **a**   b. Wrong.   Sensitization would have increased her response to the elevator bell.
   (p. 234)   c. Wrong.   Observational learning is learning by watching others. She didn't do this.
                 d. Wrong.   Spontaneous recovery is the reappearance of an extinguished conditioned response.

3. **c**   a. Wrong.   Spontaneous recovery is the reappearance of a previously extinguished CR.
   (p. 243)   b. Wrong.   Pat didn't learn by observing the behavior of other people.
   (PT5B)   d. Wrong.   No stimulus signals when a dog won't bite as required by conditioned inhibition.

4. **b**   a. Wrong.   There is no voluntary response being affected by its consequences here.
   (p. 236)   c. Wrong.   Sela didn't learn to be queasy by watching someone else be queasy.
                 d. Wrong.   Extinction is the *elimination* of a response.

5. **c**   a. Wrong.   Taste aversions often develop with one exposure.
   (p. 240)   b. Wrong.   Chemotherapy patients know the source, but still develop taste aversions.
                 d. Wrong.   Taste aversions in chemotherapy are not adaptive.

6. **d**   a. Wrong.   Spontaneous recovery is the reappearance of an extinguised CR. A new CS doesn't occur.
   (PT5B)   b. Wrong.   Discrimination would require the CR to occur only to the rat.
                 c. Wrong.   The other animals have not been paired with the rat, so this isn't second-order conditioning.

7. **a**   b. Wrong.   The nurse is not similar to the syringe, so this isn't generalization.
   (p. 241)   c. Wrong.   Key here is the chain of stimuli that signal the upcoming shot, not a narrowing of stimuli.
                 d. Wrong.   The bliss point is a baseline level of satisfaction proposed to explain reinforcement effects.

8. **c**   a. Wrong.   The law of effect involves the results of an action influencing future action, not signaling
   (pp. 248-252)   events prior to a response.
                 b. Wrong.   The law of effect involves operant principles, but not classical conditioning.
                 d. Wrong.   Habituation and sensitization don't relate to the results of a response, as in the law of effect.

9. **b**   a. Wrong.   The alarm is the unconditioned stimulus for the response of waking up.
   (p. 237)   c. Wrong.   A positive reinforcer is a stimulus that, when presented after a response, increases the
   (PN5A)   likelihood of that response occurring again.
                 d. Wrong.   Blocking occurs when a second stimulus fails to give new signaling information and fails
                              to become a conditioned stimulus.

10. **c**   a. Wrong. Shaping is a method for teaching a response, not a sign that reinforcement is possible.
   (p. 249)   b. Wrong. Negative reinforcement is an event that, if removed after a response, increases responding.
             d. Wrong. An FI schedule is a schedule of reinforcement, not a signal that reinforcement might occur.

11. **a**   b.   Wrong. A response (complaining) led to the presentation of an event (grade change) and an
   (p. 249)   increased likelihood of response.
   (PN5B)   c & d. Wrong. A response *increased*, not decreased, so punishment isn't involved.

12. **b**   a. Wrong. Social learning is learning by observation, not changing the reinforcement requirements.
   (p. 257)   c. Wrong. An FR schedule is based on the number of responses, not the form of the responses.
             d. Wrong. Tom's father didn't imitate or demonstrate. Key here is the changing requirements.

13. **c**   a. Wrong. The bliss point relates to reinforcement, not shaping.
   (p. 250)   b. Wrong. The partial reinforcement effect is increased resistance to extinction, not a bliss point.
             d. Wrong. Social learning theory proposes learning by observation, not bliss points.

14. **b**   a. Wrong. The mother's schedule is based on time, so it is an interval schedule (FI 10 min).
   (p. 255)   c. Wrong. The mother's schedule is based on time, and is fixed, so it is an FI 10 minute schedule.
             d. Wrong. The mother's schedule is fixed, not variable.

15. **a**   b. Wrong. A conditioned reinforcer acquired its reinforcing characteristics. Pain avoidance is
   (p. 251)   naturally reinforcing.
   (PT5F)   c. Wrong. Sara's response wasn't learned by observing others.
             d. Wrong. There is no inhibition. Sara makes a response.

16. **b**   a.   Wrong. Continuous reinforcement produces the fastest extinction.
   (p. 254)   c & d. Wrong. Extinction is faster after fixed schedules than after variable schedules.

17. **d**   a & b. Wrong. The response (hitting) has decreased, so reinforcement is not involved.
   (p. 252)   c.   Wrong. An event (dessert) is removed, not added, so this is not positive punishment.

18. **d**   a & c. Wrong. An interval schedule is based on the time since reinforcement, not the number of
   (p. 254)   responses.
             b.   Wrong. Variable schedules reinforce after a variable (average) number of responses.

19. **d**   a. Wrong. Adventitious reinforcement relates to superstitious behavior, not modeling research.
   (p. 260)   b. Wrong. Orienting responses involve shifts of attention to novel stimuli, not effects of violence.
             c. Wrong. Bandura's research involved modeling, not the issue of natural vs. learned reinforcers.

20. **a**   b. Wrong. Reinforcement did not occur and then end. The key is observational learning.
   (p. 261)   c. Wrong. Conditioned inhibition occurs when a stimulus signals a US won't occur. There is no US.
             d. Wrong. Accidental reinforcement follows a behavior but is not a result of that behavior.

CHAPTER 8: REMEMBERING AND FORGETTING

ESTABLISHING LEARNING GOALS

Use these learning goals as a preview of the chapter, a guide for active reading, and to evaluate your mastery of the material. Review the relevant goals as you begin and end your reading of each major section of the chapter.

I. Define memory, and describe the role of encoding, storage, and retrieval.

II. Solve the adaptive problem of how to remember information over the short term.
   A. Discuss how visual and auditory sensory memories can be measured.
      1. Define sensory memory and distinguish it from short-term memory.
      2. Describe Sperling's research on iconic memory, and discuss its conclusions.
      3. Identify the type of code and the duration of echoic memory.
      4. Discuss the adaptive value of sensory memory.
   B. Describe how information is represented, maintained, and forgotten over the short term.
      1. Describe the nature of the code used in short-term memory.
      2. Evaluate the question of whether mental images are the same as perceptual images.
      3. Discuss short-term forgetting and evaluate the role of rehearsal.
      4. Discuss why short-term memory has a limited capacity and explain how chunking may help.

III. Solve the adaptive problem of how to store information for the long term.
   A. Define episodic, semantic, and procedural memories.
   B. Explain why it is important to form an elaborate and distinctive memory record.
   C. Describe some simple mnemonic techniques.
      1. Describe the method of loci, pegword techniques, and linkword systems.
      2. Discuss flashbulb memories.

IV. Solve the adaptive problem of how to retrieve information from memory.
   A. Discuss the importance of retrieval cues in remembering.
      1. Discuss the idea that forgetting is mostly cue-dependent.
      2. Explain the encoding specificity principle and transfer-appropriate processing.
   B. Discuss the differences between explicit and implicit memory.
   C. Explain the role of schemas in reconstructive memory.
      1. Provide evidence that long-term memory is reconstructive.
      2. Explain both the adaptive value and the costs of memory schemas.

V. Solve the adaptive problem of how to update and manage memory.
   A. Discuss the contributions of Ebbinghaus, and explain why forgetting is often adaptive.
   B. Describe the mechanisms that cause forgetting including decay and retroactive and proactive interference.
   C. Discuss motivated forgetting and the case for repression.
   D. Describe retrograde and anterograde amnesia and explain where memories might be stored in the brain.

MASTERING THE MATERIAL

Preview & Remembering Over the Short Term (pp. 268-277)

Mastering the Vocabulary. Define or explain each of the following terms. To check your answers, consult the text pages listed.

1. memory (p. 268)

2. encoding (p. 268)

3. storage (p. 268)

4. retrieval (p. 569)

5. sensory memory (p. 269)

6. short-term memory (p. 270)

7. iconic memory (p. 270)

8. echoic memory (p. 270)

9. rehearsal (p. 274)

10. memory span (p. 275)

11. chunking (p. 275)

Mastering the Concepts. Fill in the blanks to create a summary of the section. Answers are on page 195.

Memory is the capacity to _____(1) and _____(2) information. Memory involves three processes: _____(3), storage, and _____(4). This chapter considers four adaptive problems:

How do we remember over the short term? How do we store information for the long term? How is information recovered appropriately? How do we keep memory current?

_____(5) memory retains a replica of the stimulus for a few seconds to assist perceptual processing. Visual sensory memory is _____(6) memory. By comparing recall in _____(7) and _____(8) procedures, Sperling concluded iconic memory is brief (.5 sec). _____(9) memory for audition has a duration of less than a second, although some data suggest 5-10 seconds.

_____(10) memory, or working memory, briefly stores and manipulates information. Information is mostly recoded in an inner voice, but other codes are possible. Errors often sound like the original input. Imagery has properties of both memory and perception. Detail is incomplete, as in memory, but neurological data suggest processes used in perception are also used in imagery.

If short-term memories are not _____(11) they are lost within 1-2 seconds (older estimates suggested 10-15 sec) due to _____(12), interference from new input, or both. Short-term memory span is 7, plus or minus 2, and represents memory's _____(13). The time needed to rehearse input might limit the span; memory span is lower for input that takes longer to say. _____(14), rearranging input into meaningful groups, speeds rehearsal and increases memory span. The _____(15) memory model is a common approach to short-term memory. It includes several mechanisms, including a phonological loop, a visuospatial sketchpad, and a central _____(16), and it helps explain memory problems.

Evaluating Your Progress. Select the one best response. Answers are on page 196. If you make any errors, reread the relevant material before proceeding.

1. A psychologist who is studying how memories are formed and represented is studying the process of
   a. encoding.
   b. storage.
   c. retrieval.
   d. interference.

2. Iconic memory is an example of
   a. short-term memory.
   b. auditory memory.
   c. sensory memory.
   d. repressed memory.

3. Sperling concluded that poor whole report performance is caused by
   a. losing a large amount of the stimulus information before it ever enters iconic memory.
   b. an inability to retain all the stimulus array due to iconic memory's very limited storage capacity.
   c. failure to develop adequate retrieval cues for the information in the array.
   d. the fading of information before all of it can be processed and reported.

4. Information in short-term memory can be encoded in several forms, but the most common code is
    a. acoustic.
    b. visual.
    c. abstract (not related to any sense).
    d. episodic.

5. To keep information in short-term memory for more than a few seconds requires
    a. retrieval cues.
    b. chunking.
    c. rehearsal.
    d. partial report.

6. Organizing input into meaningful units so as to increase the capacity of short-term memory is called
    a. chunking.
    b. the memory span.
    c. cued recall.
    d. rehearsal.

7. A common estimate of the short-term memory span is
    a. 1-5 items.
    b. 5-9 items.
    c. 9-15 items.
    d. more than 20 items.

8. A popular view of short-term memory is
    a. iconic memory.
    b. working memory.
    c. echoic memory.
    d. whole report memory.

Storing Information for the Long Term (pp. 278-285)

Mastering the Vocabulary. Define or explain each of the following terms. To check your answers, consult the text pages listed.

1. long-term memory (p. 278)

2. episodic memory (p. 278)

3. semantic memory (p. 278)

4. procedural memory (p. 278)

5. elaboration (p. 279)

6.   distinctiveness (p. 280)

7.   flashbulb memories (p. 280)

8.   visual imagery (p. 281)

9.   primacy effect (p. 282)

10. recency effect (p. 282)

11. distributed practice (p. 282)

12. mnemonic devices (p. 283)

13. method of loci (p. 283)

14. peg-word method (p. 284)

Mastering the Concepts. Fill in the blanks to create a review of the section. Answers are on page 195.

Long-term memory maintains information for extended periods. Long-term memories can be _____(17) memories, which are memories of personal events, _____(18) memories, factual memories not related to personal events, or _____(19) memories, memories about how to do something.

Several techniques improve long-term memory. _____(20) links new items to existing memories, forming connections that act as retrieval cues. Elaboration is encouraged by thinking about meaning, using _____(21) processing, noting distinctiveness of input, and using visual _____(22). Spacing repetitions of information and using _____(23) rather than massed practice creates rich retrieval cues that aid memory. An item's place in a list also affects its recall, producing a _____(24) curve. The first and last items are recalled best, the _____(25) and recency effects. Being more distinctive might produce these effects. Emotional content influences memory. _____(26) memories are detailed memories of emotionally significant events. People confidently recall many details, but these memories are not very accurate.

Many _____(27) devices or memory aids emphasize imagery, thus increasing distinctiveness and retrieval cues. In the _____(28) technique items are imaged along a path which later acts as a retrieval cue. The _____(29) method uses imagery to link items to memory cues, or pegs, such as a familiar rhyme. The _____(30) system for learning foreign vocabulary uses imagery to link a foreign word with a rhyming known word.

Evaluating Your Progress. Select the one best response. Answers are on page 196. If you make any errors, reread the relevant material before proceeding.

1. Semantic memory includes
    a. events or episodes in one's personal history.
    b. information about how to do something.
    c. a personal memory of a surprising or emotional event.
    d. facts that make little or no reference to one's personal life.

2. Elaboration
    a. increases the number of cues available to assist retrieval.
    b. decreases distinctiveness and thus, reduces the likelihood of retrieval.
    c. involves the simple repetition of an item to be remembered.
    d. adds material that increases the likelihood of interference.

3. Forming images of items in specific places and revisiting those places at retrieval describes
    a. the pegword method.
    b. the chunking method.
    c. the method of loci.
    d. the linkword method.

4. The primacy effect in memory is improved recall for items
    a. at the beginning of a list.
    b. at the end of a list.
    c. given relational processing.
    d. that have emotional content.

5. Grady describes his study technique as "distributed practice." This means that he
    a. creates several visual images for each item he needs to learn.
    b. studies for each class a little bit several times a week.
    c. studies the most important material first in each study session.
    d. devotes one long night to studying a single subject.

6. Barry has a detailed memory of what he was doing when he heard that the World Trade Center had been destroyed. His memory is an example of a(n)
    a. repressed memory.
    b. flashbulb memory.
    c. iconic memory.
    d. procedural memory.

Recovering Information from Cues (pp. 286-292)

Mastering the Vocabulary. Define or explain each of the following terms. To check your answers, consult the text pages listed.

1. free recall (p. 286)

2. cued recall (p. 286)

3. transfer-appropriate processing (p. 288)

4. implicit memory (p. 289)

5. explicit memory (p. 289)

6. schema (p. 290)

Mastering the Concepts. Fill in the blanks to create a summary of the section. Answers are on page 195.

Retrieval is guided by internal or external _____(31). If retrieval cues are presented externally, as in a _____(32) task, recall is better than if no external cues are given, as in free recall. Researchers believe most _____(33) is due to inadequate or inaccessible retrieval cues, not loss of input. To be effective, a cue needs to match at _____(34) and at retrieval. This is most likely to occur with _____(35) -appropriate processing, using the same processes at learning as at testing.

Not all memories are conscious, or _____(36), memories. Remembering without conscious awareness is _____(37) memory. Picture or word fragment completion tests show implicit memory influences behavior, but without the person's awareness. Retrieval cues are important for both types of memory, but conscious strategies are not effective for implicit memory.

Memories are _____(38), not replayed, and _____(39), clusters of related facts, are used to fill in gaps in memory. Although adaptive, this can distort memory. Research also shows memories are influenced by the form of the _____(40) used in testing. Thus, eyewitness memories can be influenced by the interview itself.

Evaluating Your Progress. Select the one best response. Answers are on page 197. If you make any errors, reread the relevant material before proceeding.

1. Comparison of free recall and cued recall performance suggests that most memory failures are due to
   a. information no longer being in memory due to decay.
   b. information no longer being in memory due to interference.
   c. repression of the information so that it cannot be brought to consciousness.
   d. a failure to use an appropriate retrieval cue.

2. Information should be learned using the processes to be used at testing. That is, learners should use
   a. widely distributed practice.
   b. mnemonic techniques based on visual imagery.
   c. transfer appropriate processing.
   d. implicit memory, not explicit memory.

3. Organized clusters of facts assist recall from long-term memory when actual memories are limited. These knowledge structures are called
   a. the inner voice.
   b. schemas.
   c. episodic memories.
   d. working memories.

4. Loftus and Palmer's research on memories for accident details clearly demonstrates that
   a. people usually can recall minor details with high accuracy because of the visual nature of events.
   b. people realize what they know about an accident and what they don't know about an accident.
   c. memory is dependent on primarily bottom-up processes.
   d. the way questions about memories are asked significantly influences the memories reported.

5. Remembering without conscious awareness or willful intent is
   a. explicit memory.
   b. implicit memory.
   c. schematic memory.
   d. reconstructive memory.

6. Remembering is not a literal replay of past events. Instead, it is partly a creative process that blends information from schemas with memories about the event. In other words, long-term memory is
   a. reconstructive.
   b. distinctive.
   c. transfer-appropriate.
   d. primarily iconic.

Updating Memory (pp. 292-298)

Mastering the Vocabulary. Define or explain each of the following terms. To check your answers, consult the text pages listed.

1. forgetting (p. 292)

2. decay (p. 294)

3. retroactive interference (p. 294)

4. proactive interference (p. 295)

5. repression (p. 295)

6. amnesia (p. 296)

7. retrograde amnesia (p. 297)

8. anterograde amnesia (p. 297)

Mastering the Concepts. Fill in the blanks to create a summary of the section. Answers are on page 195.

Forgetting, the loss in _____(41) of stored material, is adaptive because it reduces memory "clutter." By testing relearning after various delays, the _____(42) method, Ebbinghaus developed a "forgetting curve." Most forgetting occurs _____(43) after initial learning and continues gradually.

Forgetting was first attributed to _____(44), a loss due to the passage of time, but current theories emphasize _____(45), disruption caused by other material. When new material disrupts old material, _____(46) interference occurs. When old material disrupts new material, _____(47) interference occurs. Interference theory suggests material is not necessarily eliminated but becomes harder to access.

Forgetting can occur for emotionally adaptive, or motivated reasons. _____(48), a defense mechanism proposed by Freud in which memories are pushed out of consciousness, may reduce anxiety. Retrieval failure is accepted, but repression's scientific validity is unclear. Apparent cases of repression might be due to reconstructive memory, differential rehearsal, or other factors.

_____(49) is forgetting caused by physical problems. Head injuries can lead to a loss of memory for events that occurred before the injury, _____(50) amnesia. Brain damage also can lead to the loss of memory for events after the injury, _____(51) amnesia. Implicit memory tests show memories might be formed but not consciously accessible. A cause of this amnesia is _____(52) syndrome, due to alcoholism. The _____(53) is critical for memory, but other areas are also.

Evaluating Your Progress. Select the one best response. Answers are on page 197. If you make any errors, reread the relevant material before proceeding.

1. Ebbinghaus' forgetting curve shows that forgetting occurs
   a. very slowly at first, and then rapidly after a week.
   b. very rapidly at first, and then continues gradually for a long time.
   c. very rapidly at first, but then stops quickly.
   d. at about the same moderate pace for at least the first 6 months, then stops.

2. If previously learned material disrupts memory for recently learned material _____ has occurred.
   a. retrograde amnesia
   b. anterograde amnesia
   c. retroactive inhibition
   d. proactive inhibition

3. The view that simply the passage of time, nothing else, causes forgetting to occur is known as
   a. interference theory.
   b. decay theory.
   c. cue-dependence theory.
   d. distinctiveness theory.

4. Freud proposed traumatic events are pushed from conscious awareness as a defense mechanism in
   a. anterograde amnesia.
   b. overwriting.
   c. repression.
   d. Korsakoff's syndrome.

5. Korsakoff's syndrome, a disorder due to brain damage from chronic alcoholism, causes
   a. anterograde amnesia.
   b. retrograde amnesia.
   c. repression of drinking memories.
   d. total loss of memory for both old and new pasts.

6. Recent research on anterograde amnesia suggests that the amnesia occurs because
   a. new input is not passed from sensory memory to short-term memory.
   b. the memory span of working memory is reduced drastically, preventing learning.
   c. the storage processes of long-term memory are destroyed, preventing any learning.
   d. new input is stored in long-term memory, but direct conscious retrieval is not possible.

7. The _____ appears to be very important for normal memory activity.
   a. occipital lobe
   b. parietal lobe
   c. pons
   d. hippocampus

MAKING FINAL PREPARATIONS

Complete these sections without consulting your book or notes. For a more accurate estimate of how well you know this material, wait at least a day or two after studying the chapter before working on the questions. Some of the material you "know" immediately after working with the chapter will be quickly forgotten. Immediate tests will overestimate what you know well.

Short Essay Questions. Write a brief answer to each question. Sample answers are on page 198.

1. What is the adaptive value of sensory memory?

2. Compare the characteristics and functions of sensory memory and short-term memory.

3. Nick spent three days before each multiple choice test reading and rereading the text but failed the test. Give at least two responses his instructor might make that are based on principles of memory.

4. Explain why memory is described as "reconstructive," and why this might be adaptive.

5. Compare the interference and decay views of forgetting. Which view is currently favored?

6. Why is forgetting adaptive?

Matching. Select the correct definition or description for each item. Answers are on page 198.

_____ 1. Ebbinghaus	**a.** must recall items without explicit retrieval cues
_____ 2. chunking	**b.** studied sensory memory
_____ 3. Sperling	**c.** short-term memory capacity
_____ 4. memory span	**d.** must report cued row of stimulus array
_____ 5. relational processing	**e.** determined forgetting curve
_____ 6. whole report	**f.** technique to improve retrieval, e.g., pegword
_____ 7. phonological loop	**g.** compares time to learn with time to relearn
_____ 8. Peterson & Peterson	**h.** studied duration of short-term memory
_____ 9. mnemonic device	**i.** must report entire stimulus array
_____ 10. free recall	**j.** system that very briefly retains a replica of input
_____ 11. short-term memory	**k.** component of working memory
_____ 12. Loftus & Palmer	**l.** studied the influence the question has on memory
_____ 13. partial report task	**m.** "how to" memory
_____ 14. savings method	**n.** reorganizing input into meaningful units
_____ 15. sensory memory	**o.** looking for common characteristics; elaboration
_____ 16. procedural memory	**p.** working memory

Multiple Choice Pretest 1. Select the one best response. Answers are on page 199.

1. Memory is the capacity to preserve and recover information. Information is recovered through
   a. encoding processes.
   b. storage processes.
   c. retrieval processes.
   d. transduction processes.

2. Iconic memory and echoic memory are two types of
   a. procedural memory.
   b. short-term memory.
   c. long-term memory.
   d. sensory memory.

3. Mistakes in short-term memory are likely to involve responses that sound like one of the original items even if the items were presented visually. From this, researchers conclude that short-term memory
   a. retains information for 1-2 seconds.
   b. has a limited capacity of 5 to 9 items.
   c. mostly uses an inner voice to code information.
   d. can be disrupted by either decay or interference.

4. Although disputed by recent studies, the Peterson & Peterson distractor task experiment was thought to show the duration of short-term memory is
   a. 0.5 second.
   b. 1-2 seconds.
   c. 10-15 seconds.
   d. 30-40 seconds.

5. Kim formed images of the to-be-remembered items with the objects in the nursery rhyme, "One is a bun, two is a shoe, three is a tree..." (a cat in a bun, a chicken wearing shoes, etc.). This illustrates
   a. the method of loci.
   b. a pegword method.
   c. the inner voice.
   d. a distributed practice method.

6. Brenda told Eric the nine streets to take to her apartment. He remembers the first streets, but not the rest. Eric's pattern of memory is similar to
   a. flashbulb memory.
   b. the method of loci.
   c. the primacy effect.
   d. transfer-appropriate processing.

7. In a short-term memory task, chess masters organized a view of a chess board in terms of recognizable patterns rather than individual pieces. The technique being used is
   a. chunking.
   b. method of loci.
   c. transfer appropriate processing.
   d. distributed practice.

8. You don't really remember your 14th birthday, but you give a fairly close description by using the season, where you lived, and other schemas. This illustrates the _____ nature of long-term memory.
   a. cue-dependent
   b. transfer-appropriate
   c. reconstructive
   d. distributed

9. Carl repeats, "555-6739, 555-6739..." Carl is keeping the number in short-term memory by using
   a. rehearsal.
   b. the distractor task.
   c. elaboration.
   d. implicit memory.

10. Koby is asked to pick the bank robber out of a line-up. This is most similar to
    a. a partial report procedure.
    b. a free recall test.
    c. an implicit memory test.
    d. a recognition test.

11. Recent research suggests that memory span is determined not so much by space limitations, but by
    a. the distinctiveness of the information being placed in memory.
    b. the number of retrieval cues that are developed at input.
    c. the emotional content of the items being placed in memory.
    d. the rate at which items can be rehearsed in the inner voice.

12. To answer the question, "Where did you park this morning?" requires primarily
    a. episodic memory.
    b. procedural memory.
    c. semantic memory.
    d. flashbulb memory.

13. The mnemonic devices known as method of loci, pegword methods, and linkword methods all utilize
    a. imagery.
    b. distributed practice.
    c. episodic memory.
    d. rhymes.

14. After studying for Exam 2, Al couldn't remember the Exam 1 material. This is an example of
    a. motivated forgetting.
    b. retroactive interference.
    c. proactive interference.
    d. anterograde amnesia.

15. An example of an implicit memory test is
    a. Sperling's partial report test.
    b. a recognition test.
    c. a cued recall test.
    d. a word fragment test.

16. Following a rape, the victim had no memory of the rape, but became very anxious if approached by a man. According to Freud's concept of defense mechanisms and memory, this would be a case of
    a. anterograde amnesia.
    b. proactive interference.
    c. Korsakoff's syndrome.
    d. repression.

17. Football players often have no memory of what happened just before they "get their bell rung" from a hard hit to the head. Their memory loss would be considered
    a. repression.
    b. Korsakoff's syndrome.
    c. retrograde amnesia.
    d. anterograde amnesia.

18. The benefits of distributed practice are mostly due to
    a. the inner voice.
    b. transfer-appropriate processing.
    c. imagery.
    d. elaboration.

19. The current view of forgetting emphasizes
    a. decay.
    b. interference.
    c. repression.
    d. physical problems.

20. Working memory is popular because it helps explain
    a. some effects of brain damage.
    b. the difference in implicit and explicit memory.
    c. the advantage of distributed practice.
    d. repression.

Multiple Choice Pretest 2. Select the one best response. Answers are on page 200.

1. Sperling found partial report performance was no better than whole report performance if the cue was presented about half a second after the array was removed. From this he concluded that
    a. iconic memory contains a raw, unprocessed, sensory image of the input.
    b. iconic memory contains a fairly complete replica of the sensory input.
    c. iconic memory information disappears in less than a second.
    d. memory span is limited by the time required to repeat it with the inner voice.

2. Sperling found that whole report performance was 30-40% accurate, but immediate partial report performance was nearly perfect. From this he concluded that iconic memory
    a. contains a raw, unprocessed, sensory image of the input.
    b. contains a fairly complete replica of the sensory input.
    c. holds information for less than a second.
    d. uses an acoustic (auditory) code even though the input is visual.

3. Anna yells, "Don't talk to me!" as she reaches for a piece of paper on which to write the important information she just heard. Anna seems to believe that forgetting in short-term memory is caused by
   a. encoding specificity.
   b. decay of information.
   c. transfer appropriate processing.
   d. interference from other input.

4. A short term memory task requires that Chris remember CRLMQ. Chris' most likely error would be
   a. **Z**RLMQ.
   b. **O**RLMQ.
   c. CRLM**S**.
   d. CRLM**O**.

5. Evidence that mental imagery is similar to normal visual perception includes all of the following EXCEPT:
   a. Large objects are easier to "see" in images than small objects.
   b. Similar brain areas are active in visual perception and visual imagery.
   c. Partial report patterns are found in both visual perception and imagery.
   d. Brain damaged people sometimes show deficits in both normal perception and imagery.

6. Naki's argument is based on ten significant facts, but one is especially important. To be sure the jurors remember this one fact, Naki leaves it until last in his closing review. Naki is relying on
   a. flashbulb memory.
   b. the recency effect.
   c. the distributed practice effect.
   d. the primacy effect.

7. Memory for the word "horse" will be best if the person
   a. repeats "horse, horse, horse, horse" several times.
   b. realizes "horse" begins with the letter h and remembers that.
   c. thinks of a rhyme for "horse" such as "course."
   d. identifies "horse" as an animal that is ridden for transportation or fun.

8. Which mechanism in working memory controls how processing is allocated?
   a. the visuospatial sketch pad.
   b. the phonological loop.
   c. the dichotic control.
   d. the central executive.

9. Based on memory research, which student is most likely to earn the highest grade on the vocabulary test?
   a. Laura, who spent three hours studying vocabulary the night before the test
   b. Hannah, who spent only 15 minutes each of the last 12 days (3 hours total) studying vocabulary
   c. Theresa, who studied the words for three hours one night two weeks ago
   d. Kristen, who looked at the words once, right before walking into the classroom

10. You studied the habitat and leaves of 100 species of trees on your tree hikes. You can name the tree if given those cues. When given bark samples on your quiz, you were lost. Your problem illustrates
    a. an encoding-retrieval match failure.
    b. relational processing.
    c. a distinctiveness failure.
    d. retroactive interference.

11. Research on flashbulb memories confirms all of the following EXCEPT:
    a. Flashbulb memories usually concern emotional or surprising events.
    b. Flashbulb memories are reported with great confidence, even after significant time.
    c. Flashbulb memories are highly accurate because they are like a picture of the event.
    d. Flashbulb memories include vivid details about the event.

12. Knowing how to play the violin depends most on
    a. episodic memory.
    b. semantic memory.
    c. iconic memory.
    d. procedural memory.

13. Wanda struggles in college Spanish because her high school French comes out instead. This illustrates
    a. decay theory.
    b. memory overwriting.
    c. retroactive interference.
    d. proactive interference.

14. You are on the jury in a trial involving a fight in a bar. Based on what you know about Loftus & Palmer's research, as you listen to the various eyewitnesses you would be wise to
    a. accept their memories of the event as trustworthy and highly accurate.
    b. accept their memories as highly accurate as long as they are very confident about their memories.
    c. listen very carefully to the questions that are asked each person.
    d. believe absolutely nothing they say because eyewitness testimony is never correct.

15. Firefighters visit schools to lecture about what to do in a fire. Some take the process farther and have children "escape" from a smoke-filled fire education trailer. This approach is based on the principle of
    a. reconstructive remembering.
    b. transfer-appropriate processing.
    c. proactive interference.
    d. cue-dependent forgetting.

16. If your recognition of the mugger is influenced by the clothes, race, or "attitude" of the people in a line-up because they fit your idea of "criminal" you are demonstrating the role of _____ in memory.
    a. schemas
    b. elaboration
    c. interference
    d. encoding specificity

17. People remember more if they sleep 4 hours after learning a list of nonsense syllables than if they engage in normal daily activities for 4 hours. These data support the _____ theory of forgetting.
    a. cue-dependent
    b. decay
    c. interference
    d. encoding specificity

18. After a head injury, Bill seems to have no ability to form new memories and knows only the immediate present and his pre-injury past. Bill is suffering from
    a. anterograde amnesia.
    b. retrograde amnesia.
    c. flashbulb memory.
    d. cue-dependent forgetting.

19. Iris' head injury resulted in very serious anterograde amnesia. Her brain damage most likely includes
    a. the hypothalamus.
    b. the hippocampus.
    c. the parietal lobe.
    d. the cerebellum.

LANGUAGE DEVELOPMENT GUIDE

Core Terms

In this chapter, your instructor will probably talk about the ***practical applications*** of what we know about memory -- that is, how you can use the information day-to-day. And then they might use the term ***pragmatic***. That's another term that means, "to focus on *uses* of something." You could say that a pragmatic person looks for practical applications. You might also hear the term ***implications***, as in, "So what are the *implications* of this research finding?" That means something like, "What does this mean in the real world? How can these findings be applied? What further ideas do they lead to?"

A *pragmatic* person is likely to be interested in ***strategies*** -- ways to actually use something. In a lecture on learning strategies, you are likely to hear three words: ***rote, repetition*** and ***simple rehearsal***. As you can probably guess, they all have to do with practicing something over and over. Those terms will be contrasted with ***elaboration***, which means adding detail. It's ***counterintuitive*** (not what you'd expect), but the more detail you add to what you want to remember, the better you will remember it. But the key is that the details have to be interesting. So the practical application here is that if you are studying, the more interesting details and examples you can pay attention to, the better you will remember the material!

Idioms

p. 269   devoid of   without any

p. 271   fleeting image   very brief view

p. 269	snapshot		quick picture or photograph; quick impression
p. 273	temporal order of occurrence		the order in which it happened
p. 274	internal repetition		saying it over and over in your mind
p. 278	athletic prowess		skill at sports
p. 279	an involved sequence of events depicting		a complicated mental image of what happened
p. 281	mediocre at best		only average, or even worse
p. 290	undergraduates		college students
p. 291	just prior to		just before
p. 294	cardiopulmonary resuscitation		CPR, a lifesaving technique for heart attacks
p. 294	indefinitely		for an unknown, perhaps long, period of time
p. 295	conceivable that		it could be that
p. 295	retain the capacity		keep the ability to
p. 295	in the conventional sense		the usual meaning or approach
p. 296	cast themselves in a positive light		make themselves seem as good as possible

Word Parts

Here are some words that are made up of word parts, and that you can find in this chapter. After you've looked at these, you can look for others in the chapter that use the same word.

WORD	WORD PART IT USES	MEANING
retroactive	retro = back	to act on something in the past
proactive	pro = forward	to act on something in the future
amnesia	a = not mne = memory	lost memory
revert	re = again vert = to turn	to turn back to

locate	loc = place	to find
mediocre	med, mid = middle	not very good or very bad
introduce	intro = inward duc = to carry, bring	to bring into

Knowing the word parts listed above, you can also create the following words. You can get an idea of their meanings from the word parts they use.

retrograde	retro + grade	_____
avert	_____ + _____	to prevent, to turn away
dislocate	dis (not) + loc	_____
introvert	_____ + _____	one who is turned inward

Pronunciation

p. 270	iconic	eye-kon'-ick		p. 290	schema	skee'-muh
p. 270	echoic	eh-ko'-ick		p. 297	anterograde	an-tair'-o-grade
p. 283	mnemonic	nee-mon'-ick				

ANSWERS AND EXPLANATIONS

To find relevant material in your textbook, consult the pages cited with each answer. Also, PN and PT citations refer to modules in *PsychNow!* and *Psyk.trek* materials, respectively.

Mastering the Concepts

1. preserve (p. 268)
2. recover (p. 268)
3. encoding (p. 268)
4. retrieval (p. 269)
5. Sensory (p. 269)
6. iconic (p. 270)
7. partial report (p. 271)
8. whole report (p. 271)
9. Echoic (p. 270)
10. Short-term (p. 272)
11. rehearsed (p. 274)
12. decay (p. 275)
13. capacity (p. 275)
14. Chunking (p. 275)
15. working (p. 277)
16. executive (p. 278)
17. episodic (p. 278)
18. semantic (p. 278)
19. procedural (p. 278)
20. Elaboration (p. 279)
21. relational (p. 279)
22. imagery (p. 281)
23. distributed (p. 282)
24. serial position (p. 282)
25. primacy (p. 282)
26. Flashbulb (p. 280)
27. mnemonic (p. 283)
28. method of loci (p. 283)
29. pegword (p. 284)
30. linkword (p. 284)
31. retrieval cues (p. 286)
32. cued recall (p. 286)
33. forgetting (p. 287)
34. encoding (p. 287)
35. transfer (p. 288)
36. explicit (p. 289)
37. implicit (p. 289)
38. reconstructed (p. 290)
39. schemas (p. 290)
40. questions (p. 291)
41. accessibility (p. 292)
42. savings (p. 293)
43. soon (p. 293)
44. decay (p. 294)
45. interference (p. 294)
46. retroactive (p. 294)
47. proactive (p. 295)
48. Repression (p. 295)
49. Amnesia (p. 296)
50. retrograde (p. 297)
51. anterograde (p. 297)
52. hippocampus (p. 298)
53. neurotransmitter (p. 298)

Evaluating Your Progress

Remembering Over the Short Term

1. **a**   b. Wrong. Storage is a maintenance, not a representation, process.
(p. 268)   c. Wrong. Retrieval concerns how information is recovered and is translated into performance.
             d. Wrong. Interference is a process by which information is "forgotten."

2. **c**   a. Wrong. Iconic memory is a sensory memory.
(p. 270)   b. Wrong. Iconic memory is visual, not auditory.
(PT6B)   d. Wrong. Repressed memories have been hidden in the unconscious. Iconic memory is accessible.

3. **d**   a & b. Wrong. Sperling concluded iconic memory contains the entire array, but only briefly.
(p. 271)   c.   Wrong. Retrieval cues aren't used here. They're used for retrieval from long term memory.

4. **a**   b. Wrong. Iconic memory has a visual code; STM is acoustic.
(p. 272)   c. Wrong. STM errors are acoustic, not abstract/semantic.
(PT6A)   d. Wrong. Episodic relates to time-linked memories in LTM, not a STM code.

5. **c**   a. Wrong. Retrieval accesses memories; it doesn't help retain them.
(p. 274)   b. Wrong. Chunking improves storage efficiency, not memory duration.
             d. Wrong. Partial report is a memory test, not a way to maintain memories longer.

6. **a**   b. Wrong. Memory span is the number of items that can be recalled from short-term memory.
(p. 311)   c. Wrong. Cued recall involves giving retrieval cues to assist the person in recalling information.
             d. Wrong. Rehearsal is the repetition of input to improve later recall, not to increase capacity.

7. **b**   a, c, & d.   Wrong.   Most people can recall 7, plus or minus 2, items.
(p. 275)
(PN5D)

8. **b**   a. Wrong. Iconic memory is visual sensory memory, not short-term memory.
(p. 277)   c. Wrong. Echoic memory is auditory sensory memory, not short-term memory.
             d. Wrong. Whole report is one of the recall tasks used in Sperling's sensory memory research.

Storing Information for the Long Term

1. **d**   a. Wrong. This describes episodic memory.
(p. 278)   b. Wrong. This describes procedural memory.
(PN5D)   c. Wrong. This describes a flashbulb memory.

2. **a**   b. Wrong. This is the opposite effect.
(p. 279)   c. Wrong. This is simple rehearsal; elaboration expands input.
             d. Wrong. Elaboration improves memory. Interference does not increase.

3. **c**   a. Wrong. Pegword methods link images with a familiar rhyme or word, not with locations.
(p. 283)   b. Wrong. Chunking involves regrouping into meaningful units, not imagery.
             d. Wrong. Linkword methods use imagery to link an unfamiliar item with a familiar one.

4. **a**   b. Wrong. This is the recency effect.
(p. 282)   c. Wrong. The primacy effect relates to serial position, not elaboration.
             d. Wrong. The primacy effect relates to serial position, not flashbulb memories.

5. **b**   a. Wrong.   Distributed practice refers to the spacing of rehearsal, not imagery.
   (p. 282)   c. Wrong.   This relates to the primacy effect, not distributed (spaced) practice.
            d. Wrong.   This is massed practice, not distributed (spaced) practice.

6. **b**   a. Wrong.   Repressed memories are pushed out of consciousness and not easily retrieved..
   (p. 280)   c. Wrong.   Iconic memories are sensory memories that are very, very brief.
            d. Wrong.   Procedural memories are "how to" memories, not memories of events.

Recovering Information from Cues

1. **d**   a & b.   Wrong.   Cued recall shows an item is present, so it hasn't been eliminated by decay or
   (p. 286)   interference.
            c.   Wrong.   Repression would not allow cued recall, and most "forgetting" is not repression.

2. **c**   a. Wrong.   Distributed practice is beneficial, but it doesn't relate to encoding-retrieval matching.
   (p. 288)   b. Wrong.   Imagery is often good, but it doesn't relate to encoding-retrieval matching.
            d. Wrong.   An explicit-implicit distinction is not relevant unless the test format will be implicit.

3. **b**   a. Wrong.   The inner voice relates to short-term memory encoding, not long-term memory retrieval.
   (p. 290)   c. Wrong.   Episodic memories relate to personal events, not knowledge structures.
   (PT6B)   d. Wrong.   Working memory is a short-term memory concept, not a long-term memory concept.

4. **d**   a. Wrong.   Long-term memory is not highly visual. Loftus's work emphases its reconstructive aspect.
   (p. 291)   b. Wrong.   Loftus showed that people could be made to think they saw something they didn't.
            c. Wrong.   Loftus' work emphasized the top-down (e.g., expectancy, schema) processes.

5. **b**   a. Wrong.   Explicit memory involves conscious, strategic memory processes.
   (p. 289)   c. Wrong.   Schemas are information structures. Key here is "without willful intent."
            d. Wrong.   Reconstructive means constructed from memories and schemas. Key here is
                        "unconscious" or unintentional.

6. **a**   b. Wrong.   Distinctiveness relates to which information is recalled, but not the description given here.
   (p. 290)   c. Wrong.   Transfer-appropriate processing is learning material in a way similar to the way it will be
                        recalled. This does not relate to the current description.
            d. Wrong.   Iconic refers to sensory memory, not long-term memory.

Updating Memory

1. **b**   a, c, & d.   Wrong.   Forgetting is very rapid initially, then slows to a very gradual loss.
   (p. 293)

2. **d**   a & b.   Wrong.   Amnesia is not due to the influence of other learning. It is physically determined.
   (p. 295)   c.   Wrong.   In retroactive inhibition new material interferes with previously learned material.
   (PN5E)

3. **b**   a. Wrong.   Interference assumes factors other than time.
   (p. 294)   c. Wrong.   Cue-dependent forgetting concerns whether information is gone vs. difficult to access.
            d. Wrong.   Distinctiveness as an influence on forgetting is not limited to time passing.

4. **c**   a. Wrong.   Anterograde amnesia is due to brain damage, not psychological trauma.
   (p. 295)   b. Wrong.   Overwriting is not a defense mechanism, but proposes old memories are obscured by new.
            d. Wrong.   Korsakoff's syndrome is amnesia caused by brain damage from alcoholism.

5. **a**
(p. 297)
  b. Wrong. Korsakoff's primarily impairs memories for events after the brain damage, not before.
  c. Wrong. Repression isn't involved, and the amnesia is not selective to drinking-related events.
  d. Wrong. Korsakoff's primarily impairs memories for events after the brain damage.

6. **d**
(p. 298)
  a, b, & c. Wrong. Indirect memory tests show new input is stored in long-term memory. The problem is one of direct, conscious retrieval of new input, not storage failure.

7. **d**
(p. 298)
(PT6C)
  a. Wrong. The occipital lobe is important for visual processing, not memory.
  b. Wrong. The parietal lobe is important for touch and spatial relations, not memory.
  c. Wrong. The pons is responsible for some life support systems and arousal, not memory.

MAKING FINAL PREPARATIONS

Short Essay Questions

1. Sensory memory retains a fairly complete replica of the original sensory input for a short period after the stimulus ends. This allows more time for initial processing and thus, allows more complete processing. Sensory memory may be very important for audition, where stimuli (e.g., speech) must be integrated over time. (p. 270)

2. Sensory memory contains the original sensory input, its duration is less than a second for vision (perhaps a little longer for audition), and it holds the entire stimulus display. Short term memory contains processed information, mostly encoded acoustically, it has a longer duration (1-2 sec), although older estimates suggest it might be only 15-30 sec), and is limited in its capacity. (pp. 270-276)

3. The amount of time studied is not always as important as when you study and how you study. First, you should study for shorter periods throughout the entire period before the exam, not just at the end. This is distributed practice, which is better than massed practice (cramming). Second, by waiting until the last minute you might have thought you had learned something that night but find you had forgotten it by the exam. Most forgetting occurs soon after initial learning. Third, you need to use elaboration to form the rich, distinctive retrieval cues you'll need for the exam; don't just read. Fourth, you should use transfer-appropriate processing--learn the material using the processes you'll use to retrieve it: Practice with multiple-choice questions. (pp. 279-288, 293)

4. Long-term memories are not exact versions of the original material. They contain the general idea, but specific details are reconstructed based on expectations and schema. This is adaptive because incomplete memories can be supplemented to allow the organism to act. (pp. 290-291)

5. Decay theory proposes that memories are lost or forgotten spontaneously due to the passage of time. No other processes are involved. Interference theory, currently favored, proposes that memories are disrupted by other processes---loss of distinctiveness as more material enters memory, loss of good retrieval cues as they are reused with other material, new material overwriting old, etc. (pp. 294-295)

6. Forgetting is adaptive because it reduces the "clutter" of memory. Unneeded or outdated information becomes less accessible so more important information can be accessed more easily. It is usually not necessary to remember every instance of something, and interference is reduced with less material. (p. 292)

Matching

1. **e** (p. 293)	4. **c** (p. 275)	7. **k** (p. 277)	10. **a** (p. 286)	13. **d** (p. 271)	16. **m** (p. 278)
2. **n** (p. 275)	5. **o** (p. 279)	8. **h** (p. 274)	11. **p** (p. 272)	14. **g** (p. 293)	
3. **b** (p. 271)	6. **i** (p. 271)	9. **f** (p. 283)	12. **l** (p. 291)	15. **j** (p. 269)	

Multiple Choice Pretest 1

1. **c**
   (p. 269)
   - a. Wrong. Encoding is the initial formation of memories, not their recovery.
   - b. Wrong. Storage processes maintain, rather than recover, information.
   - d. Wrong. Transduction is the transformation of physical energy into neural activity.

2. **d**
   (p. 270)
   - a, b, & c. Wrong. Iconic and echoic are visual and auditory sensory memory, respectively.

3. **c**
   (p. 272)
   - a, b, & d. Wrong. Although true concerning STM, these are not conclusions from the data cited.

4. **c**
   (p. 274)
   - a. Wrong. This is an estimate of the duration of iconic memory.
   - b. Wrong. This is an estimate of the duration of echoic memory.
   - d. Wrong. This is longer than any short-term memory estimate.

5. **b**
   (p. 284)
   - a. Wrong. Method of loci uses places along a path, not a rhyme.
   - c. Wrong. The inner voice relates to short-term memory encoding, not mnemonic techniques.
   - d. Wrong. Distributed practice refers to spacing practice, rather than massing it all at once.

6. **c.**
   (p. 282)
   - a. Wrong. Flashbulb memories are detailed memories about emotionally important events.
   - b. Wrong. The method of loci is a mnemonic technique that improves memory.
   - d. Wrong. Related encoding and retrieval processes are not relevant here; serial position is.

7. **a**
   (p. 275)
   - b. Wrong. The method of loci uses imagery involving familiar places, not meaningful patterns.
   - c. Wrong. The chess masters are not matching encoding and retrieval processes.
   - d. Wrong. Distributed practice is spaced practice.

8. **c**
   (p. 290)
   - a. Wrong. A "memory" is created (constructed) here, in spite of having no direct retrieval cues.
   - b. Wrong. A "memory" is created (constructed) here. Learning vs. testing processes are not key here.
   - d. Wrong. Distributed means spaced, which does not relate to schema.

9. **a**
   (p. 274)
   - b. Wrong. Carl is rehearsing. Distractor tasks prevent rehearsing short-term memory items.
   - c. Wrong. Elaboration involves forming connections to other items. Carl isn't doing that.
   - d. Wrong. Implicit memory is remembering without conscious awareness or intent.

10. **d**
    (p. 289)
    - a. Wrong. Partial report is used to study sensory memory, not long-term memory.
    - b. Wrong. Free recall would involve Koby describing the person.
    - c. Wrong. Koby is consciously, intentionally using his memory, an explicit test.

11. **d**
    (p. 275)
    - a, b, & c. Wrong. Recent research centers on the length of time required to rehearse the items. The longer it takes to say an item, the smaller the memory span seems to be.

12. **a**
    (p. 278)
    - b. Wrong. Procedural memory is "how to" memory.
    - c. Wrong. Semantic memory involves facts unrelated to one's personal history.
    - d. Wrong. Flashbulb memories are highly detailed memories of emotionally charged events.

13. **a**
    (p. 283)
    - b. Wrong. Distributed practice refers to spacing practice rather than massing it all at once.
    - c. Wrong. These do not all use information about events in one's personal past.
    - d. Wrong. Pegwords use rhymes, but the method of loci doesn't.

14. **b**　　a. Wrong.　Motivated forgetting, like repression, is not likely without anxiety involved.
(p. 294)　　c. Wrong.　If proactive, Al would have trouble with the new material due to the old material.
　　　　　　　d. Wrong.　Even if Al had brain damage, the pattern fits retrograde, not anterograde amnesia.

15. **d**　　a, b, & c.　Wrong.　These all require conscious, willful use of memory; they are explicit tests.
(p. 289)

16. **d**　　a. Wrong.　Anterograde amnesia isn't a defense mechanism. It is caused by brain injury.
(p. 295)　　b. Wrong.　This isn't a defense mechanism. It is interference of new memories by old ones.
　　　　　　　c. Wrong.　This isn't a defense mechanism. It is an amnesia caused by alcoholism.

17. **c**　　a. Wrong.　Repression is due to emotional trauma, not physical trauma to the brain.
(p. 297)　　b. Wrong.　Korsakoff's syndrome is due to alcoholism and involves problems forming new memories.
(PT6C)　　 d. Wrong.　Anterograde amnesia is loss of memory for events after the injury, not those before.

18. **d**　　a. Wrong.　The inner voice is a short-term memory concept. Distributed practice relates to long-term
(p. 282)　　　　　　　　memory.
　　　　　　　b. Wrong.　Distributed processing doesn't ensure encoding will satisfy the needs at retrieval.
　　　　　　　c. Wrong.　Imagery is not necessarily a part of distributed processing, which is defined by timing.

19. **b**　　a. Wrong.　Decay is given much less emphasis, although some researchers do not rule it out.
(p. 294)　　c. Wrong.　Repression is a special case of forgetting, and its scientific validity is questioned.
　　　　　　　d. Wrong.　Physical problems certainly affect memory, but not the usual forgetting.

20. **a**　　b. Wrong.　Working memory is short-term memory. Implicit memory is considered long-term.
(p. 277)　　c. Wrong.　Distributed practice involves long-term memory, not working memory.
　　　　　　　d. Wrong.　Repression is a long-term memory concept, not a working (short-term memory) concept.

Multiple Choice Pretest 2

1. **c**　　a & b.　Wrong.　This is true concerning iconic memory, but it is not based on the data cited.
(p. 271)　　d.　　　Wrong.　The inner voice relates to short-term memory, not iconic memory.

2. **b**　　a & c.　Wrong.　This is true concerning iconic memory, but it is not based on the data cited.
(p. 271)　　d.　　　Wrong.　Short-term memory and echoic memory use acoustic codes, not iconic memory.

3. **d**　　a. Wrong.　Key here is Anna's avoidance of new input. New input might interfere with the old.
(p. 294)　　b. Wrong.　Anna is avoiding new input that might interfere with the old. Decay is time-based.
(PN5E)　　 c. Wrong.　Key here is avoiding new, interfering input, not matching encoding and retrieval processes.

4. **a**　　b, c, & d.　Wrong.　Short-term memory errors are usually substitutions of similarly sounding items.
(p. 273)
(PT6B)

5. **c**　　a, b, & d.　Wrong.　These are true.
(p. 273)

6. **b**　　a. Wrong.　Flashbulb memories are emotionally influenced memories.
(p. 282)　　c. Wrong.　Distributed practice improves memory but isn't related to item position in a list.
　　　　　　　d. Wrong.　A primacy effect is improved memory for the first items presented.

7. **d**   a.   Wrong.   Simple repetition is valuable, but not as much as elaboration.
(p. 279)   b & c.   Wrong.   These involves only limited elaboration.

8. **d**   a. Wrong.   The visuospatial sketch pad maintains and processes visual input.
(p. 277)   b. Wrong.   The phonological loop maintains and processes acoustic input.
            c. Wrong.   The dichotic task is not a working memory mechanism.

9. **b**   a. Wrong.   Laura massed her practice, which is not the most effective approach.
(p. 282)   c. Wrong.   Massed practice and large delay is not a good idea.
            d. Wrong.   Kristen has recency going for her, but no repetition. She's likely to forget several terms.

10. **a**   b. Wrong.   Relational processing is elaboration. Key here are the cues during encoding vs. testing.
(p. 288)   c. Wrong.   Distinctiveness was present. Key here are the cues during encoding vs. testing.
            d. Wrong.   Retroactive = new items disrupt old items. Key here are cues during encoding vs. testing.

11. **c**   a, b, & d.   Wrong.   These are all true statements. Flashbulb memories are not necessarily accurate.
(p. 281)

12. **d**   a. Wrong.   Episodic memory involves personal events, not "how to."
(p. 278)   b. Wrong.   Semantic memory involves word meanings, not "how to."
            c. Wrong.   Iconic memory is sensory memory, not "how to" memory.

13. **d**   a. Wrong.   Decay would reduce the impact of French, not cause it to interfere.
(p. 295)   b. Wrong.   In overwriting, new material overwrites (obscures) old memories, the opposite of here.
            c. Wrong.   Retroactive interference here would be the Spanish wiping out the French she knew.

14. **c**   a. Wrong.   Although not completely inaccurate, they can be far from correct.
(p. 291)   b. Wrong.   Confidence does not ensure accuracy of memory.
            d. Wrong.   Although far from perfect, the memories are not entirely inaccurate.

15. **b**   a. Wrong.   Reconstructive memory suggests memories are constructed, not just replayed. Key here,
(p. 288)   though, is learning using the processes to be used during testing, a fire.
            c. Wrong.   Proactive interference is memory disruption caused by previously learned items. Key here,
                         though, is learning using the processes to be used during testing, a fire.
            d. Wrong.   Cue-dependent forgetting occurs when items are in memory but appropriate retrieval cues
                         are not available. Key here is learning that uses the same processes that will be used for
                         testing, a fire.

16. **a**   b. Wrong.   Elaboration is the expansion of to-be-remembered items to improve later recovery.
(p. 290)   c. Wrong.   Interference is a possible cause of forgetting.
            d. Wrong.   Encoding specificity relates the cues at encoding with the effective cues for retrieval.

17. **c**   a. Wrong.   Free recall vs. cued recall comparisons support cue-dependent forgetting.
(p. 294)   b. Wrong.   Decay would predict no difference because the time interval was the same.
            d. Wrong.   There's no reason to involve encoding. The difference is the activity during the delay.

18. **a**   b. Wrong.   Retrograde amnesia disrupts retrieval of old memories, not forming of new ones.
(p. 297)   c. Wrong.   Flashbulb memories are detailed memories of emotionally-charged event.
            d. Wrong.   Cue-dependent forgetting is forgetting due to having inappropriate retrieval cues.

19. **b**   a, c, & d.   Wrong.   Damage here doesn't usually cause amnesia. Damage to the hippocampus does.
(p. 298)
(PT6C)

CHAPTER 9: THOUGHT AND LANGUAGE

ESTABLISHING LEARNING GOALS

Use these learning goals as a preview of the chapter, a guide for active reading, and to evaluate your mastery of the material. Review the relevant goals as you begin and end your reading of each major section of the chapter.

I. Solve the adaptive problem of how to communicate with others.
    A. Explain the structure of language.
        1. Define phoneme, morpheme, phonology, syntax, and semantics.
        2. Differentiate the surface structure and deep structure of language.
    B. Discuss the factors that contribute to language comprehension.
    C. Name the major milestones of language development.
    D. Describe efforts to produce language in nonhuman species.
        1. Describe the language skills of the animals studied.
        2. Discuss the criticisms of the claims that nonhuman species learned a language.
    E. Evaluate the possibility that language is an adaptation.

II. Solve the adaptive problem of how to classify or categorize objects.
    A. Define "category," and discuss some of the factors that confirm category membership.
        1. Discuss the idea that categories have defining features.
        2. Discuss the idea that categorization is based on family resemblance.
    B. Distinguish between prototype and exemplar views of categorization.
    C. Explain the hierarchical organization of categories.

III. Solve the adaptive problem of solving problems effectively.
    A. Distinguish between well- and ill-defined problems.
    B. List the steps in the IDEAL problem-solving technique.
    C. Describe factors that influence how a problem is identified and defined.
        1. Define problem representation.
        2. Define functional fixedness, and explain its adaptive value.
    D. Compare algorithms and heuristics, and give examples of each.
        1. Describe the means-ends heuristic.
        2. Describe the working backward heuristic.
        3. Describe the searching for analogies heuristic and when analogies will be recognized.
    E. Explain the importance of assessing your problem-solving strategy.

IV. Solve the adaptive problem of making effective decisions.
    A. Discuss how framing alternatives influence decision making.
    B. Discuss some common decision-making biases.
    C. Describe the common decision-making heuristics.
        1. Explain the role of base rate and conjunction errors in the representativeness heuristic.
        2. Describe how the availability and anchoring and adjustment heuristics influence decisions.
    D. Discuss the pros and cons of using heuristics.

MASTERING THE MATERIAL

Preview & Communicating with Others (pp. 304-314)

Mastering the Vocabulary. Define or explain each of the following terms. To check your answers, consult the text pages listed.

1. thinking (p. 304)

2. grammar (p. 306)

3. phonology (p. 306)

4. syntax (p. 306)

5. semantics (p. 306)

6. phonemes (p. 306)

7. morphemes (p. 307)

8. surface structure (p. 308)

9. deep structure (p. 308)

10. pragmatics (p. 308)

Mastering the Content. Fill in the blanks to create a summary of this section. Answers are on page 220.

Thinking, or _____(1), involves the processes used to mentally manipulate knowledge and is the focus of study for the field of cognitive _____(2). This chapter examines four adaptive problems concerning thinking: How do individuals communicate? How do they categorize things? How do people solve problems? How do people make decisions?

To be a language, the communication system must have _____(3), rules for combining symbols to convey meaning. Grammar involves three parts: _____(4), the rules for combining sounds,

_____(5), the rules for combining words, and semantics, the rules for meaning. Words are composed of phonemes, the smallest speech sounds, and _____(6), the smallest units of meaning. Words are combined using syntax to form phrases and sentences. Language can be ambiguous because one surface structure can have multiple _____(7) structures. These meanings are evaluated by top-down processes, including _____(8), the practical knowledge used to judge a speaker's intent.

The universal stages of development suggest language is not entirely determined by _____(9). Babies coo at 3-5 weeks, _____(10) by 4-6 months, produce single words by 1 year, and multiple words by 2 years. Environment affects language after _____(11), shaping accent and specific words. Early speech is described as _____(12) speech because it omits all unimportant words (Give cup.). The tendency to _____(13) (runned) may indicate children automatically learn language production rules, and supports the role of genetic preparedness for language development. Nonhuman primates have learned to communicate with _____(14) language or plastic symbols. Not all researchers agree this is _____(15). The fact that there are specialized language areas in the brain, a specialized vocal tract, a rapid rate of development, and the universal tendency to make certain errors suggests language is an _____(16).

Evaluating Your Progress. Select the one best response. Answers are on page 220. If you make any errors, reread the relevant material before proceeding.

1. Morphemes are
   a. the smallest unit of sound.
   b. the smallest unit of language that carries meaning.
   c. the rules for combining sounds to make words.
   d. the underlying representation of meaning in language.

2. If you are studying the practical knowledge used to comprehend a speaker's intentions, you are studying
   a. semantics.
   b. grammar.
   c. pragmatics.
   d. phonology.

3. Which is NOT a part of grammar?
   a. semantics
   b. syntax
   c. prototypes
   d. phonology

4. The intended meaning of "Visiting relatives can be a pain" is unclear because it has two
   a. phonemes.
   b. morphemes.
   c. surface structures.
   d. deep structures.

5. English has about 40-45 basic speech sounds that are known as
   a. phonemes.
   b. morphemes.
   c. the surface structure.
   d. the deep structure.

6. Most psychologists believe
   a. the sequence of language development is universal.
   b. there is little innate or genetic influence on language development.
   c. one-word utterances transmit little or no meaning.
   d. humans are the only species to communicate with symbols.

7. Most children first use single words at about
   a. 4-6 months.
   b. 12 months.
   c. 18 months.
   d. 24 months.

8. Telegraphic speech omits
   a. verbs.
   b. nouns.
   c. articles.
   d. intonation or stress ("?," "!")

9. Which of the following is NOT an accurate statement concerning language in nonhuman species?
   a. Chimps have learned to make two-word communications.
   b. Chimps have used new, unique word combinations to describe objects.
   c. Chimps have learned language skills by watching other chimps using language.
   d. Chimps have learned to produce sign language and spoken language.

Classifying and Categorizing (pp. 315-319)

Mastering the Vocabulary. Define or explain each of the following terms. To check your answers, consult the text pages listed.

1. category (p. 315)

2. defining features (p. 315)

3. family resemblance (p. 316)

4. prototypes (p. 317)

5. category exemplars (p. 318)

6. basic-level categories (p. 319)

Mastering the Concepts. Fill in the blanks to create a summary of the section. Answers are on page 220.

A _____(17) is a class of objects that belong together, and that allows inferences about members' characteristics and predictions about the future. Categories are defined in terms of _____(18) features and family _____(19). Using fixed features can work poorly for _____(20) categories with fuzzy _____(21). Members of natural categories have features that are characteristic, not _____(22). In a family resemblance approach, members share many, but not all, of a set of critical features.

Psychologists differentiate the idea of _____(23), an ideal representative of a category, and category _____(24), examples of the category, as means for assigning category membership. The exemplar view suggests all members of the category are stored and used for comparison. The prototype view suggests items are compared to a stored prototype, not the actual members of the category. Because more information is available than prototypes would predict, researchers tend to favor the exemplar view.

Categories are structured in _____(25). _____(26) categories are the first to be learned and give the most useful information. Higher categories, _____(27), are less descriptive.

Evaluating Your Progress. Select the one best response. Answers are on page 221. If you make any errors, reread the relevant material before you proceed.

1. The defining features and family resemblance approaches differ because the defining features approach
   a. requires the object to have all the defining features, but family resemblance doesn't.
   b. uses prototypes, but family resemblance uses category exemplars to assign membership.
   c. is used best with natural concepts, but family resemblance is used best with math concepts.
   d. applies to non-living objects, but family resemblance applies to living objects.

2. Prototype theory proposes that new objects are classified based on a comparison to
   a. each of the individual examples of members of the category.
   b. a list of critical features that define the category.
   c. the abstract "best" example of a category.
   d. the superordinate characteristics of the category.

3. The category level that generates the most useful information, is used most, and is learned first is the
   a. prototype.
   b. superordinate.
   c. basic-level.
   d. fuzzy.

Solving Problems (pp. 320-326)

Mastering the Vocabulary. Define or explain each of the following terms. To check your answers, consult the text pages listed.

1. well-defined problem (p. 320)

2. ill-defined problem (p. 320)

3. functional fixedness (p. 323)

4. algorithms (p. 324)

5. heuristics (p. 324)

6. means-ends analysis (p. 324)

7 working backward (p. 325)

8. searching for analogies (p. 325)

9. mental sets (p. 325)

Mastering the Concepts. Fill in the blanks to create a summary of the section. Answers are on page 220.

Problems are situations in which there is some uncertainty about how to reach a goal. _____(28) defined problems have a clear goal, a starting point, and a way to evaluate success. _____(29) defined problems do not have clear goals, starting points, or ways to evaluate the outcome. The IDEAL Problem Solver outlines effective problem solving: _____(30) the problem; _____(31) the problem efficiently; _____(32) a variety of strategies; Act on the problem strategy; and _____(33) back and evaluate the strategy. Problem _____(34) is critical, but prior beliefs and habits can distort the process. People treat objects and their functions in a fixed and typical way, functional _____(35).

Strategies for solving problems include _____(36), step-by-step instructions that guarantee a solution, and _____(37), "rules of thumb" which are helpful but do not guarantee success. Algorithms are useful only for certain _____(38) problems. Heuristics can be inaccurate, but they allow rapid, logical, decisions. One heuristic is _____(39) analysis, in which actions are chosen to reduce distance to the goal. This often includes breaking a larger problem down into _____(40). The working _____(41) heuristic begins at the goal and works toward the start. In the searching for _____(42) heuristic, similar past problems guide the solution. Mental _____(43) may cause reliance on old strategies and can be a problem. Looking back and evaluating the solution is the critical last step in problem solving.

Evaluating Your Progress. Select the one best response. Answers are on page 221. If you make any errors, reread the relevant material before you proceed.

1. A problem with a specific goal, a specific starting place, and a good way to evaluate a solution is
   a. a well-defined problem.
   b. a heuristic.
   c. a means-ends analysis.
   d. an ill-defined problem.

2. IDEAL is Bransford & Stein's
   a. classification system for different types of problems.
   b. steps to follow for effective problem solving.
   c. artificial intelligence (computer program) problem solver.
   d. algorithm for solving ill-defined problems.

3. The incubation effect is the sudden or easier solution to a problem that occurs when
   a. the searching for analogies heuristic is used.
   b. an ill-defined problem becomes a well-defined problem.
   c. the problem is set aside for a period of time.
   d. the IDEAL system is used.

4. The concept that is most closely related to functional fixedness is
   a. mental set.
   b. IDEAL.
   c. algorithm.
   d. well-defined problem.

5. "Look for similarities between the current problem and a previous problem, and solve the current problem using the procedures that were successful before." This represents
   a. the means ends heuristic.
   b. the availability heuristic.
   c. the working backward heuristic.
   d. the searching for analogies heuristic.

6. Heuristics are
   a. step-by-step instructions for how to solve a problem.
   b. general guidelines or strategies for solving a problem.
   c. strategies that guarantee a correct solution.
   d. only useful with a well-defined problem.

7. Selecting actions to reduce the gap between the current starting point and the desired goal describes
   a. the representativeness heuristic.
   b. the availability heuristic.
   c. the searching for analogies heuristic.
   d. the means-ends heuristic.

Making Decisions (pp. 327-332)

Mastering the Vocabulary. Define or explain each of the following term. To check your answers, consult the text pages listed.

1. decision making (p. 327)

2. framing (p. 327)

3. confirmation bias (p. 329)

4. belief persistence (p. 329)

5. representativeness heuristic (p. 329)

6. availability heuristic (p. 330)

7. conjunction error (p. 330)

8. anchoring and adjustment (p. 331)

Mastering the Concepts. Fill in the blanks to create a summary of the section. Answers are on page 220.

Decision making, choosing from among a set of alternatives, is affected by beliefs and perceptions. How alternatives are presented, their _____(44), is important. Selection is not necessarily rational and based on the _____(45). Perception of possible gain leads to risk avoidance; possible loss leads to risk in order to avoid loss. Personal interpretation of the situation and biases, rather than objective information is critical. For example confirmation bias and _____(46) persistence are biases that tend to cause people to make decisions that maintain pre-existing ideas.

Heuristics can lead to inaccurate evaluations. The _____(47) heuristic, in which alternatives are compared to a prototype, causes decisions that disregard objective facts. Base rates are often ignored. This also causes the _____(48) error, in which a combination of traits is judged more common than a single trait (A+B > A). In the _____(49) heuristic, estimates are inflated if many examples of the concept can be generated easily. In the _____(50) and adjustment heuristic, the starting point is influential. Low starting values lead to _____(51) estimates. Heuristics can distort decisions, but they allow _____(52), often effective, decisions using incomplete information.

Evaluating Your Progress. Select the one best response. Answers are on page 221. If you make any errors, reread the relevant material before proceeding.

1. When treatment outcomes are described in terms of deaths, doctors make different decisions than if treatment outcomes are described in terms of survival. In other words, the decision is influenced by
    a. framing.
    b. the representativeness heuristic.
    c. the availability heuristic.
    d. conjunction errors.

2. If people always acted rationally, decisions would be based on
    a. a means-ends analysis.
    b. the representativeness heuristic.
    c. anchoring and adjustment.
    d. expected value.

3. Judging the probability of an event based on the event's similarity to a typical or average event is
   a. the expected value of the event.
   b. the availability heuristic.
   c. the representativeness heuristic.
   d. the conjunction error.

4. Judging an event's probability based on the ease of recalling an example of a similar event is
   a. the expected value.
   b. anchoring and adjustment.
   c. the representativeness heuristic.
   d. the availability heuristic.

5. In the anchoring and adjustment heuristic, decisions are influenced by
   a. existing opinions or beliefs.
   b. initial estimates or starting points.
   c. ideas about what the typical case is like.
   d. the way the problem is presented or worded.

6. The conjunction error and ignoring the base rate are commonly related to
   a. the framing effect.
   b. the availability heuristic.
   c. the representativeness heuristic.
   d. the anchoring and adjustment heuristic.

MAKING FINAL PREPARATIONS

Complete these sections without consulting your book or notes. For a more accurate estimate of how well you know this material, wait at least a day or two after studying the chapter before working on the questions. Some of the material you "know" immediately after working with the chapter will be quickly forgotten. Immediate tests will overestimate what you know well.

Short Essay Questions. Write a brief answer to each question. Sample answers are on page 222.

1. Cite some reasons why most researchers believe language has a strong genetic component.

2. Summarize the language capabilities of nonhuman species.

3. Compare the prototype and category exemplar theories of categorization, and explain why researchers tend to favor the exemplar theory.

4. Why are mental sets such as functional fixedness generally adaptive?

5. Define heuristics and discuss their limitations and adaptive value.

Matching. Select the correct definition or description for each item. Answers are on page 222.

_____ 1. algorithm	**a.** an event's likely frequency in a population
_____ 2. exemplars	**b.** rules used in language to communicate meaning
_____ 3. thinking	**c.** rules of thumb or general strategies
_____ 4. expected value	**d.** most representative member of category
_____ 5. base rate	**e.** rules for how sounds combine to form words
_____ 6. mental sets	**f.** processes of mental manipulation of knowledge
_____ 7. framing	**g.** rules for how words are combined
_____ 8. semantics	**h.** step-by-step rules that guarantee a correct solution
_____ 9. decision making	**i.** processes used to choose from among alternatives
_____ 10. prototype	**j.** specific category members stored in memory
_____ 11. anchors	**k.** well-established habits of perception and thought
_____ 12. syntax	**l.** manner in which problem is presented
_____ 13. heuristics	**m.** (probability of outcome) X (value of outcome)
_____ 14. phonology	**n.** starting points that influence decisions or estimates

Multiple Choice Pretest 1. Select the one best response. Answers are on page 223.

1. The Welsh language allows letter and sound sequences that English does not (e.g., drwy, llwytho). This represents a difference in the two languages'
   a. phonology.
   b. syntax.
   c. semantics.
   d. pragmatics.

2. In the word "unmade," "un" and "made" represent
   a. phonemes.
   b. morphemes.
   c. the surface structure.
   d. the deep structure.

3. Pierre's babbling has begun to sound like French in rhythm and common sounds. Pierre is probably
   a. about 5 weeks old.
   b. about 4 months old.
   c. about 8 months old.
   d. about 1 year old.

4. The speaker's actual intent is not always clear from the specific words used, but listeners use their practical knowledge to accurately comprehend the intent and to reply appropriately. This practical knowledge represents
   a. syntax.
   b. prototypes.
   c. pragmatics.
   d. defining features.

5. "Mommy give cookie Tommy?" is an example of
   a. babbling.
   b. pragmatics.
   c. telegraphic speech.
   d. overgeneralization.

6. All of the following support a strong genetic component in language development EXCEPT:
   a. Language development proceeds through the same stages all around the world.
   b. Children use grammatical forms ("runned") that have not been reinforced.
   c. All children show the same changes in vocalization until 6 months old.
   d. Between 6 and 18 months, children develop the accent associated with their native language.

7. Which of the following is true concerning attempts to teach nonhuman species language?
   a. A few chimps have learned spoken language, although their pronunciation is poor.
   b. Chimps have learned to use single words, but they cannot progress to the two-word stage.
   c. Chimps can use symbols to communicate only if the symbols look like the objects they represent.
   d. Researchers have reported that chimps can produce new word combinations.

8. If an animal must bark and have four legs and a tail to be a dog, the category is defined in terms of
   a. family resemblance.
   b. a prototype.
   c. exemplars.
   d. defining features.

9. If a new object is compared to several individual examples of a category, membership is based on
   a. prototypes.
   b. category exemplars.
   c. the availability heuristic.
   d. fuzzy boundaries.

10. The level of category that provides the most useful and predictive description of an object is
    a. a superordinate category.
    b. a prototype category.
    c. a well-defined category.
    d. a basic-level category.

11. In IDEAL, the A stands for
    a. Allocate.
    b. Algorithm.
    c. Answer.
    d. Act.

12. An example of a well-defined problem would be
   a. getting a vase to your mother by her birthday.
   b. understanding the meaning of life.
   c. selecting the best college to attend.
   d. finding the person who will be a good spouse.

13. A paper-and-pencil maze has six starting positions, only one of which leads to the pot of gold. Cliff visually followed the path leading away from the pot of gold until he had an idea about which path he should choose. Cliff used the problem solving approach known as
   a. means-ends analysis.
   b. searching for analogies.
   c. working backward.
   d. anchoring and adjustment.

14. All of the following are true concerning algorithms EXCEPT:
   a. They guarantee a correct solution if properly followed.
   b. They are step-by-step rules or procedures for solving a problem.
   c. They guarantee the most rapid solution to a problem.
   d. They are more useful with well-defined problems than with ill-defined problems.

15. Jonas always looks for evidence that supports his theory, but he never tries to find evidence that contradicts his theory. Jonas' research approach illustrates
   a. confirmation bias.
   b. the representativeness heuristic.
   c. the working backwards heuristic.
   d. belief persistence.

16. In contest #1, Alice has a 10% chance of winning $1000. In contest #2, she has an 80% chance of winning $50. If she enters only one contest, the rational choice is _____. Based on research, she's likely to enter _____.
   a. #1; #1
   b. #1; #2
   c. #2; #2
   d. #2; #1

17. People usually decide that coin tosses of HHHTTT are less likely than HTHTTH because HHHTTT doesn't seem like an outcome that could be a typical random sequence. This demonstrates
   a. the availability heuristic.
   b. the representativeness heuristic.
   c. functional fixedness.
   d. anchoring and adjustment.

18. Leo used to eat tuna often, but after a case of botulism made headlines, he decided tuna was too risky. His decision appears to have been influenced by
   a. a framing effect.
   b. functional fixedness.
   c. the representativeness heuristic.
   d. the availability heuristic.

19. In the anchoring and adjustment heuristic, the "anchor" is the
    a. initial estimate or starting point.
    b. middle or typical score or estimate.
    c. final estimate or last alternative.
    d. most common similar event that is recalled.

Multiple Choice Pretest 2. Select the one best response. Answers are on page 224.

1. Mary threw the ball. The ball was thrown by Mary. These sentences have the same
    a. surface structure.
    b. deep structure.
    c. phonemes.
    d. pragmatics.

2. The word "cat" has _____ phonemes.
    a. 0
    b. 1
    c. 2
    d. 3

3. A clear example of overgeneralization is
    a. "Daddy sees the mouses."
    b. "Mommy washed cup."
    c. "The cow was kicked by the horse."
    d. "Da-da-da-da."

4. At what age do children typically begin to use single, simple words?
    a. 4 months
    b. 8 months
    c. 1 year
    d. 2 years

5. Overgeneralization demonstrates that
    a. language development is strongly influenced by the environment.
    b. children develop language by imitating their parents.
    c. children have a natural inclination to acquire the rules of language.
    d. language development is not as universal as the genetic view of language development requires.

6. Ruth identifies an object as a peach if it is very similar to some ideal peach. Ruth seems to use
    a. category exemplars.
    b. defining features.
    c. prototypes.
    d. basic-level categories.

7. Deanne is three years old. She is the just learning the concept of categorization. She classifies large, four-legged objects that go "moo" as cows. Her categories are going to be primarily
   a. subordinate categories.
   b. median categories.
   c. basic-level categories.
   d. superordinate categories.

8. Bob has broken his term paper assignment into subgoals that will take him closer to his final goal: collect reference material; develop outline; write rough draft; revise to final draft. He will attack each subgoal one by one. This problem solving approach is most similar to
   a. means-ends analysis.
   b. searching for analogies.
   c. working backward.
   d. the framing effect.

9. Evan had replaced his lawnmower's spark plug to get it running smoothly. When his car started running poorly, he remembered the lawnmower and tried changing his car's sparkplugs. His strategy was most representative of
   a. a means-ends analysis.
   b. working backward.
   c. searching for analogies.
   d. framing.

10. If Fonda follows the kit's step-by-step instructions, the boards will become a bookcase. The instructions represent
    a. heuristics.
    b. analogies.
    c. an algorithm.
    d. prototypes.

11. You expect a class will be hard if the instructor says 35% of the class will get Ds or Fs, but not if the instructor says 65% will get a C or higher. Your expectations illustrate the importance of
    a. the availability heuristic.
    b. expected value.
    c. framing.
    d. mental set.

12. You can easily remember the times that changing an answer was an error. If your memories of bad outcomes influence you to avoid changing answers, you are using
    a. the availability heuristic.
    b. the working backward heuristic.
    c. an algorithm.
    d. the confirmation bias.

13. Monty is considering different approaches to a problem. He is working on the _____ in IDEAL.
    a. I
    b. D
    c. E
    d. A

14. Jibu is out of sand and salt to use on his icy driveway. The 20 lbs of birdseed he has in his garage would be a good substitute, but he doesn't consider that possibility. Jibu's thinking illustrates
    a. the availability heuristic.
    b. a framing effect.
    c. means-ends analysis.
    d. functional fixedness.

15. At first, people came through Tamara's gate at the fair in groups of two or three. Later, group size increased substantially. The same number of people went through Nick's gate, but in the opposite pattern---many large groups at first, then dwindling. Tamara estimated the crowd at 2000, but Nick estimated 7000. The difference in their estimates can best be explained by
    a. the representativeness heuristic.
    b. the availability heuristic.
    c. the anchoring and adjustment heuristic.
    d. the working backward heuristic.

16. "If you don't know the answer to a test question, choose the longest answer." This is an example of
    a. an algorithm.
    b. a heuristic.
    c. an ill-defined problem.
    d. a prototype.

17. Ted is 20 years old, 6 foot 2, and weighs 325 lbs. You decided that Ted is more likely to be a college student and football player than just a college student. This decision illustrates
    a. functional fixedness.
    b. a framing effect.
    c. a conjunction error.
    d. means-ends failure.

18. The adaptive value of heuristics is that they
    a. always produce rational, highly accurate decisions.
    b. keep decision-making objective and fact-oriented.
    c. allow reasonable, quick decisions from limited facts.
    d. provide step-by-step instructions that reduce cognitive demands.

19. Chris continues to have faith in the ability of the local telephone psychic service to foresee the future. Recent news reports showed the "psychics" were just reading from prepared scripts and other information that showed there was nothing psychic involved, but this contradictory information has not changed Chris' thinking. Chris provides a good example of
    a. ignoring the base rate.
    b. confirmation bias.
    c. representativeness heuristic.
    d. belief perseverance.

LANGUAGE DEVELOPMENT GUIDE

Core Terms

In discussing thought, your instructor may talk about *logic*, and how illogical some of our thinking is. We often commit logical *fallacies* -- errors in clear thinking, such as making unfounded assumptions. You may be urged to think *critically*. That means questioning your own assumptions as well as those of others.

In discussing language your instructor may use the terms *bilingual* or *multilingual*. The word part *bi* means two, and the word part *multi* means many, so a *bilingual* person speaks two languages, and a *multilingual* person speaks many. Your instructor might also use the term *non-native*, meaning someone who was not born or raised in the country that they are now in.

Idioms

p. 304	internally based psychological phenomena	things that happen within peoples' minds
p. 304	rationales	reasons
p. 305	knack	special talent or skill
p. 305	*homo sapiens*	human beings
p. 307	decipher	decode; tell what something means
p. 307	nuances	subtle clues or details that provide information
p. 308	to bolster	to increase the support for something
p. 309	trivial	of little importance
p. 312	fine-tune their articulation skills	get better at speaking clearly
p. 312	arbitrary symbols	symbols chosen more or less randomly
p. 312	surrogate children	adopted children
p. 312	effectively mute	unable to speak
p. 313	the jury is still out	it has not yet been definitely decided
p. 324	follow rigid scripts	follow very specific rules about how to behave
p. 324	an arsenal of strategies	a collection of ways to attack a problem
p. 369	ticket scalping	buying tickets, and then selling them for a higher price

Word Parts

Here are some words that are made up of word parts, and that you can find in this chapter. After you've looked at these, you can look for others in the chapter that use the same word parts.

WORD	WORD PART IT USES	MEANING
structure	struct = to build	something that has been built
conclusion	con = together clud, clus = to close	to come together finally; to have a final idea
illogical	il = not, wrong log = reason	not reasonable
influence	in = in flu = to flow	to have an affect on; to have power over
conjunction	con = together junct = to join	something that joins things together; a point of joining
egocentric	ego = self center = center	self-centered

Knowing the word parts listed above, you can also create the following words. You can get an idea of their meanings from the word parts they use.

instruct	_____ + _____	to fill someone with sets of ideas
construct	con + struct	_____
confluence	con + flu	_____
concentric	_____ + _____	coming in toward the center
preclude	pre + clud	_____

Pronunciation

p. 305	linguistic	lin-gwis'-tick	p. 324	heuristics	hure-is'-ticks
p. 306	phonology	fone-ol'-o-gee	p. 324	algorithms	al'-go-ri-thums
p. 307	morphemes	mor'-feem	p. 331	anchoring	ang'-kor-ing

ANSWERS AND EXPLANATIONS

To find relevant material in your textbook, consult the pages cited with each answer. Also, PN and PT citations refer to modules in *PsychNow!* and *Psyk.trek* materials, respectively.

Mastering the Concepts

1. cognition (p. 304)
2. science (p. 304)
3. grammar (p. 306)
4. phonology (p. 306)
5. syntax (p. 306)
6. morphemes (p. 307)
7. deep (p. 308
8. pragmatics (p. 308)
9. experience (p. 310)
10. babble (p. 311)
11. 6 months (p. 311)
12. telegraphic (p. 311)
13. overgeneralize (p. 311)

14. sign (p. 313)
15. language (p. 313)
16. adaptation (p. 314)
17. category (p. 315)
18. defining (p. 315)
19. resemblance (p. 316)
20. natural (p. 316)
21. boundaries (p. 316)
22. defining (p.316)
23. prototypes (p. 317)
24. exemplars (p. 318)
25. hierarchies (p. 318)
26. Basic-level (p. 319)

27. superordinates (p. 319)
28. Well- (p. 320)
29. Ill- (p. 320)
30. identify (p. 321)
31. define (p. 321)
32. explore (p. 321)
33. look (p. 322)
34. representation (p. 322)
35. fixedness (p. 323)
36. algorithms (p. 324)
37. heuristics (p. 324)
38. well-defined (p. 324)
39. means-ends (p. 324)

40. subgoals (p. 324)
41. backward (p. 325)
42. analogies (p. 325)
43. sets (p. 325)
44. framing (p. 327)
45. expected value (p. 328)
46. belief (p. 329)
47. representativeness (p. 329)
48. conjunction (p. 330)
49. availability (p. 330)
50. anchoring (p. 331)
51. lower (p. 331)
52. economical (p. 331)

Evaluating Your Progress

Preview & Communicating with Others

1. **b**
(p. 307)
   - a. Wrong. This describes phonemes, not morphemes.
   - c. Wrong. This describes phonology, not morphemes.
   - d. Wrong. This describes deep structure, not morphemes.

2. **c**
(p. 308)
   - a. Wrong. Semantics are the rule to communicate meaning, but do not include practical knowledge.
   - b. Wrong. The rules of language = grammar.
   - d. Wrong. The rules for combining sounds = phonology.

3. **c**
(p. 306)
   - a. Wrong. Semantics, rules used to communicate meaning, is a part of grammar.
   - b. Wrong. Syntax, rules for combining words, is a part of grammar.
   - d. Wrong. Phonology, rules for combining sounds, is a part of grammar.

4. **d**
(p. 308)
   - a. Wrong. Multiple phonemes, the smallest speech sound units, is not a problem.
   - b. Wrong. Morphemes are the smallest units of meaning. Having two is not a problem.
   - c. Wrong. A sentence has one surface structure (word order); two deep structures is a problem.

5. **a**
(p. 306)
   - b. Wrong. Morphemes are the smallest units of meaning. Phonemes are sound units.
   - c & d. Wrong. These are grammatical characteristics of sentences, not speech sounds.

6. **a**
(p. 310)
   - b. Wrong. The speed and common sequence of development strongly supports a genetic component.
   - c. Wrong. Single words, especially combined with gestures or intonation, communicate a lot.
   - d. Wrong. Although the issue of whether it's a true language isn't clear, chimps do use symbols.

7. **b**
(p. 311)
   - a. Wrong. Babbling begins at about 4-6 months.
   - c. Wrong. Children usually have several words at 18 months.
   - d. Wrong. Children begin putting 2 words together at about 2 years.

8. **c**   a, b, & d.   Wrong.   Telegraphic speech has 2+ words and intonation, but no articles or prepositions.
(p. 311)

9. **d**   a, b, & c.   Wrong.   These are true, but chimps have not learned to produce spoken language.
(p. 312)

Classifying and Categorizing

1. **a**   b. Wrong.   Defining features give a clear definition, so prototypes (and exemplars) are not relevant.
(p. 315)   c. Wrong.   Defining features are not very appropriate for natural categories (with fuzzy boundaries).
             d. Wrong.   Defining features are inappropriate for natural categories, including non-living ones.

2. **c**   a. Wrong.   This describes exemplar theory. A prototype is the "best" example.
(p. 317)   b. Wrong.   This describes the critical features definition of categories. "Best" = prototype.
             d. Wrong.   Superordinate is the most general category. A prototype is the "best " example.

3. **c**   a. Wrong.   A prototype is not a type of category, it is the most representative member of a category.
(p. 319)   b. Wrong.   Superordinate categories are high level categories that are less useful.
             d. Wrong.   Fuzzy is not a category level; it is a description of a type of boundary.

Solving Problems

1. **a**   b. Wrong.   Heuristics are "rules of thumb," not a type of problem.
(p. 320)   c. Wrong.   Means-ends analysis is a way to solve problems, not a type of problem.
(PT6D)   d. Wrong.   Ill-defined problems lack one or more of the listed characteristics.

2. **b**   a, c, & d.   Wrong.   IDEAL describes basic steps (not an algorithm) for effective problem solving.
(p. 321)

3. **c**   a & d.   Wrong.   No particular problem-solving strategy is involved in the incubation effect.
(p. 326)   b.   Wrong.   Problems can't shift from ill-defined to well-defined.

4. **a**   b. Wrong.   IDEAL is a problem solving system, not a tendency to view objects in limited ways.
(p. 325)   c. Wrong.   Algorithms are step-by-step plans that ensure a solution, not ideas about object functions.
             d. Wrong.   A well-defined problem has a clear start and goal. It doesn't relate to an object's function.

5. **d**   a. Wrong.   The means ends heuristic uses subgoals to move closer to a solution.
(p. 325)   b. Wrong.   The availability heuristic is to use ease of recalling examples, not to look for similar cases.
             c. Wrong.   Working backward from a goal is not mentioned.

6. **b**   a. Wrong.   This answer describes algorithms.
(p. 324)   c. Wrong.   Heuristics don't guarantee a solution; algorithms do.
             d. Wrong.   Heuristics can be used for ill-defined problems. Algorithms need well-defined problems.

7. **d**   a. Wrong.   The representativeness heuristic uses ideas of the "representative" case to make decisions.
(p. 324)   b. Wrong.   The availability heuristic involves basing estimates on the ease of generating examples.
             c. Wrong.   Searching for analogies involves considering how similar problems were solved in the past.

Making Decisions

1. **a**   b. Wrong.   Key to this question is the wording of the outcomes, not how representative they are.
(p. 327)   c. Wrong.   Key here is the wording of the outcomes, not how easily an example is generated.
(PN5F)   d. Wrong.   Key to this question is the wording of the outcomes, not missestimating a conjunction.

2. **d**   a. Wrong. Means-ends analyses are not best in all cases.
   (p. 328) b. Wrong. The representativeness heuristic is not always the most rational approach.
            c. Wrong. Anchoring and adjustment is not possible in all cases.

3. **c**   a. Wrong. Expected value = probability of outcome X value, not a comparison to an average event.
   (p. 329) b. Wrong. The availability heuristic bases estimates on ease of generating an example.
            d. Wrong. The failure to see conjunctions as less likely than single characteristics is not relevant here.

4. **d**   a. Wrong. Expected value is not used to estimate event probabilities.
   (p. 330) b. Wrong. In anchoring and adjustment initial events, not the ease of recall, effect estimates.
            c. Wrong. Representativeness involves similarity to a prototype, not ease of recall of a similar event.

5. **b**   a. Wrong. This describes confirmation bias or belief perseverance.
   (p. 331) c. Wrong. This describes the representativeness heuristic.
            d. Wrong. This describes the framing effect.

6. **c**   a, b, & d. Wrong. Conjunction error and base rate occur because the alternative matches a
   (p. 329)   preconceived typical case, leading to an overestimation of likelihood.

MAKING FINAL PREPARATIONS

Short Essay Questions

1. Language development occurs in the same sequence and at approximately the same rate across the world, as predicted by a biological component. The grammar of children differs from adults' and would not be predicted from an environmental view. Overgeneralization of rules occurs, causing the production of word forms that would not have been reinforced. Development also occurs very rapidly. (pp. 310-312)

2. Chimps and other nonhuman primates have been taught to use sign language or plastic symbol keys to communicate. Some have developed significant vocabularies, produced multiple-word constructions, perhaps have generated novel constructions, and have learned language by watching other chimps. The process is difficult and slow, and the anecdotal nature of the data, cause some to question whether their communication should be considered true language. (pp. 312-313)

3. Prototype theory proposes that new items are compared to a prototype, an ideal example of the category. The category exemplar theory proposes that all the members of the category are stored in memory and are used to compare to new items. Researchers favor the exemplar theory because people seem to have more information available about the category than prototype theory would predict. (pp. 317-318)

4. Mental sets develop as a result of experience in the world. They reflect the way the world often works. Thus, they provide a rapid, and usually accurate, means of representing information. (p. 325)

5. Heuristics are "rules of thumb" or general strategies used in reasoning and problem solving. They give guidance, not explicit instructions, and though they often lead to good answers, they don't guarantee success. Organisms don't always have time to evaluate all possible strategies. Heuristics afford a means for making economical, rapid, and fairly accurate responses even with incomplete information. (pp. 324, 331)

Matching

1. **h** (p. 324)	4. **m** (p. 328)	7. **l** (p. 327)	10. **d** (p. 317)	13 **c** (p. 324)
2. **j** (p. 318)	5. **a** (p. 330)	8. **b** (p. 306)	11. **n** (p. 331)	14 **e** (p. 306)
3. **f** (p. 304)	6. **k** (p. 325)	9. **i** (p. 327)	12. **g** (p. 306)	

Multiple Choice Pretest 1

1. **a**   b. Wrong.   Syntax regulates word combinations.
    (p. 306)   c. Wrong.   Semantics are rules for communicating meaning.
                d. Wrong.   Pragmatics involve practical knowledge used to guide language comprehension.

2. **b**   a.   Wrong.   Phonemes are the basic speech sounds (\n\). "Un" and "made" are units of meaning.
    (p. 307)   c & d.   Wrong.   Sentences, not words, have surface and deep structures.

3. **c**   a. Wrong.   Babbling doesn't begin by 5 weeks. Cooing does.
    (p. 311)   b. Wrong.   Babbling begins now, but similarity to a specific language occurs later.
                d. Wrong.   Pierre would probably be using words at one year.

4. **c**   a. Wrong.   Syntax is rules for combining words, not practical knowledge used in comprehension.
    (p. 308)   b. Wrong.   Prototypes are ideal representation of category members, not aspects of comprehension.
                d. Wrong.   Defining features is an approach to categorization, not language comprehension.

5. **c**   a. Wrong.   Babbling does not include words.
    (p. 311)   b. Wrong.   Pragmatics, use of practical knowledge, might be needed here, but this doesn't represent
                             pragmatics.
                d. Wrong.   Overgeneralization is applying rules of grammar too broadly, not omitting function
                             words.

6. **d**   a, b, & c.   Wrong.   These all support a genetic view.
    (p. 310)

7. **d**   a. Wrong.   This is false. Attempts to teach spoken language were totally unsuccessful.
    (pp. 313)   b. Wrong.   This is false. Washoe and others do combine "words."
                c. Wrong.   This is false. The symbols can be abstract (triangle = banana).

8. **d**   a. Wrong.   Family resemblance does not require all attributes to be present.
    (p. 315)   b. Wrong.   A prototype is an ideal member, but other members don't have to have all attributes.
                c. Wrong.   Exemplars are the particular members of a category, not really a way to define it.

9. **b**   a. Wrong.   A prototype is an ideal member, and each category has only one.
    (p. 318)   c. Wrong.   The availability heuristic bases estimates on the ease of generating examples.
                d. Wrong.   Fuzzy boundaries are characteristics of natural categories, not examples of members.

10. **d**   a. Wrong.   Superordinate categories are too general to contain much information.
    (p. 319)   b. Wrong.   Prototypes are not category levels.
                c. Wrong.   Well-defined is not a category level.

11. **d**   a, b, & c.   Wrong.   A stands for Act on the strategy.
    (p. 322)

12. **a**   b, c, & d.   Wrong.   These have no easily defined or evaluated goal.
    (p. 320)

13. **c**   a. Wrong.   Cliff worked backward from the goal. He did not use subgoals.
    (p. 325)   b. Wrong.   There were no analogous problems here. He worked backward from the goal.
                d. Wrong.   Anchoring and adjustment is an estimation procedure. There were no estimates required.

14. **c**   a, b, & c.   Wrong.   These are true. Algorithms don't always give quick solutions, only correct ones.
(p. 324)

15. **a**   b.   Wrong.   He is not basing a decision on a "typical" example. Key here is looking only for one type
(p. 329)   of information.
         c.   Wrong.   He is not working backwards from a goal. He is seeking only facts that fit his ideas.
         d.   Wrong.   He is not ignoring disconfirming evidence, because he is not even looking for it.

16. **b**   a.   Wrong.   #1 is rational (expected value = $100 vs. $40), but people avoid risk (choose #2).
(p. 328)   c & d.   Wrong.   #2 is not a rational choice. Expected value = $40 vs. $100.

17. **b**   a.   Wrong.   Availability is based on ease of generating examples, not similarity to a typical outcome.
(p. 329)   c.   Wrong.   Key here is the comparison to typical randomness, not an object's usual function.
(PT6E)   d.   Wrong.   Starting points are not relevant; comparison to a typical situation is.

18. **d**   a.   Wrong.   Framing effects involve the influence of wordings. This decision was influenced by a
(p. 330)   recent example of a bad outcome.
         b.   Wrong.   Functional fixedness involves not seeing new uses. Key here is the recent bad outcome.
         c.   Wrong.   The representativeness heuristic involves decisions based on similarity to a standard
                      example. Key here is the recent example of a bad outcome.

19. **a**   b, c, & d.   Wrong.   An initial estimate or starting point is the anchor. Adjustments are made from
(p. 331)   there.

Multiple Choice Pretest 2

1. **b**   a.   Wrong.   Each has a different word order (surface structure) but the same meaning (deep structure).
(p. 308)   c.   Wrong.   Each has different phonemes (speech sounds).
         d.   Wrong.   Sentences don't have pragmatics (knowledge used to understand intent), the listener does.

2. **d**   a, c, & d.   Wrong.   Cat has 1 morpheme (meaning unit) and 3 phonemes(\k\ \a\ \t\ ).
(p. 307)

3. **a**   b.   Wrong.   This is telegraphic speech.
(p. 311)   c.   Wrong.   The grammar is fine. A 4-year-old might misunderstand this, however.
         d.   Wrong.   This is babbling, not the overgeneralization of a grammatical rule.

4. **c**   a.   Wrong.   Babbling, not word use, usually begins at about 4 months.
(p. 311)   b.   Wrong.   Babbling resembles a particular language at 8 months, but no words are used.
         d.   Wrong.   Children begin using two words together by age 2.

5. **c**   a & b.   Wrong.   Environmental reinforcement models for overgeneralization are not likely.
(p. 311)   d.   Wrong.   Overgeneralization is used to support the natural predisposition for language.

6. **c**   a.   Wrong.   Using exemplars requires comparing the object to all memories of each peach she's seen.
(p. 317)   b.   Wrong.   Defining features compares the object to a list of specific features, not to an ideal example.
         d.   Wrong.   Basic-level categories describe a level in the hierarchy, not a way to assign categories.

7. **c**   a.   Wrong.   Basic-level categories are acquired first.
(p. 319)   b.   Wrong.   Median is not a valid level. Basic-level categories are acquired first.
         d.   Wrong.   Basic-level categories are acquired first. Cow is not a superordinate category.

8. **a**
(p. 324)

b.	Wrong.	There is no consideration of analogous problems. Key here was attacking subgoals.
c.	Wrong.	Bob worked from "start" toward a goal, not the reverse. Key here are the subgoals.
d.	Wrong.	Framing is the way a problem is stated. Key here are the subgoals.

9. **c**
(p. 325)

a.	Wrong.	There were no subgoals.
b.	Wrong.	He didn't begin at the goal; he used a similar problem as a guide to the solution.
d.	Wrong.	The way the problem was presented was not an issue.

10. **c**
(p. 324)

a.	Wrong.	Heuristics are rules of thumb, not detailed instructions. Key here is "step-by-step."
b.	Wrong.	Analogies are similarities between problems. Key here is "step-by-step."
d.	Wrong.	Prototypes are ideal members of a category. Key here is "step-by-step."

11. **c**
(p. 327)

a.	Wrong.	There is no difference in the ability to generate examples. Key here is the wording.
b.	Wrong.	Expected value is not relevant. Key here is the different wording of the outcomes.
d.	Wrong.	Habits are not relevant. Key here is the different wording of the outcomes.

12. **a**
(p. 330)

b.	Wrong.	You didn't work backward from a goal. You used memories to influence a decision.
c.	Wrong.	There is no step-by-step process ensuring a correct outcome.
d.	Wrong.	The emphasis here was the ease of recalling cases of making an error, not looking only for evidence that confirms a belief.

13. **c**
(p. 321)

a.	Wrong.	I = Identify the problem. Monty is exploring different strategies.
b.	Wrong.	D = Define the problem. Monty is exploring different strategies.
d.	Wrong.	A = Act on the problem strategy. Monty is exploring different strategies.

14. **d**
(p. 323)

a.	Wrong.	The question involved a restricted view of an object's function, not ease of recalling events.
b.	Wrong.	Wording is not an issue. Seeing only the usual function of an object is the key here.
c.	Wrong.	No subgoals were involved. Seeing only the usual function of an object is the key here.

15. **c**
(p. 331)

a.	Wrong.	There's no mention of differing ideas of a typical crowd. Key is the initial flow.
b.	Wrong.	If ease of recall is used, estimates would use last crowd pattern, not first.
d.	Wrong.	If worked backward, estimates would be reversed.

16. **b**
(p. 324)

a.	Wrong.	This doesn't guarantee a correct solution, so it can't be an algorithm.
c.	Wrong.	This isn't a problem at all; it's a strategy for solving a problem.
d.	Wrong.	Prototypes are the most representative members of categories, not a strategy.

17. **c**
(p. 330)

a.	Wrong.	Functional fixedness involves considering only the object's usual function. Key here is selecting two attributes, rather than one as most likely.
b.	Wrong.	The way the problem was posed was not important. Key here is selecting two attributes.
d.	Wrong.	Means-ends analysis is a problem solving, not a decision-making procedure.

18. **c**
(p. 331)

a.	Wrong.	Heuristics do not always produce rational or highly accurate decisions.
b.	Wrong.	Heuristics involve subjective factors (memory, interpretation, "typical").
d.	Wrong.	Heuristics don't give step-by-step instructions.

19. **d**
(p. 329)

a.	Wrong.	Key in this question is ignoring contradictory facts, not the expected rate of an event.
b.	Wrong.	Chris is ignoring contradictory facts, not just failing to look for it.
c.	Wrong.	The key to this question is ignoring contradictory facts, not the use of a "typical" case.

CHAPTER 10: INTELLIGENCE

ESTABLISHING LEARNING GOALS

Use these learning goals as a preview of the chapter, a guide for active reading, and to evaluate your mastery of the material. Review the relevant goals as you begin and end your reading of each major section of the chapter.

I. Solve the conceptual problem of defining intelligence.
   A. Discuss the psychometric approach to conceptualizing intelligence, including Spearman's two-factor theory.
      1. Describe how Galton applied the psychometric approach in measuring intelligence.
      2. Explain Spearman's two-factor theory, and discuss its contribution.
      3. List Thurstones primary mental abilities and how they were identified.
   B. Define fluid intelligence and crystallized intelligence.
   C. Explain how the speed of neural transmission might influence intelligence.
   D. Discuss Gardner's theory of multiple intelligences.
      1. Explain why a multiple intelligences approach has been proposed and its impact.
      2. List and describe Gardner's seven kinds of intelligence.
   E. Explain Sternberg's triarchic theory of intelligence.
      1. List and describe Sternberg's three types of intelligence.
      2. Evaluate Sternberg's theory.

II. Solve the practical problem of measuring individual differences.
   A. Discuss the components of a good test: reliability, validity, and standardization.
   B. Discuss IQ, and explain how it is interpreted.
      1. Describe the purpose of Binet and Simon's IQ test and how IQ is computed.
      2. Define deviation IQ, and discuss its advantages.
   C. Define mental retardation and giftedness.
      1. Describe the behavioral characteristics of individuals with high IQ scores.
      2. Describe the behavioral characteristics of individuals with low IQ scores.
   D. Discuss the validity of IQ tests and the effects of labeling.
      1. Describe how the validity of intelligence tests is evaluated and the outcome of the evaluation.
      2. Discuss labeling effects and why they occur.
   E. Discuss creativity, emotional intelligence, and tacit knowledge.

III. Solve the practical problem of discovering the sources of intelligence.
   A. Evaluate the stability of IQ, and explain why IQ might change.
   B. Explain why twin studies are used to evaluate genetic contributions to intelligence.
      1. Discuss the evidence for a genetic influence in intelligence.
      2. Explain heritability, and describe the heritability of intelligence.
   C. Discuss environmental influences on intelligence, and explain how they interact with genetic influences.
      1. Discuss the evidence that environment influences intelligence.
      2. Identify factors that might account for group differences in intelligence test scores.

Mastering the Material

Preview & Conceptualizing Intelligence (pp. 228-247)

Mastering the Vocabulary. Define or explain each of the following terms. To check your answers, consult the text pages listed.

1. intelligence (p. 339)

2. psychometrics (p. 340)

3. factor analysis (p. 341)

4. g (general intelligence) (p. 341)

5. s (specific intelligence) (p. 341)

6. fluid intelligence (p. 343)

7. crystallized intelligence (p. 343)

8. multiple intelligences (p. 345)

9. triarchic theory (p. 345)

Mastering the Concepts. Fill in the blanks to create a summary of the section. Answers are on page 234.

Intelligence is a concept used to account for individual _____(1) in mental test performance. This chapter considers three conceptual and practical problems: How should intelligence be conceptualized? How can it be measured? What are the sources of intelligence?

The _____(2) approach analyzes performance on mental tests to understand intelligence.

_____(3) first proposed that some single intellectual ability causes _____(4) performance across a variety of psychological and physical tests. _____(5) is a mathematical technique to find relationships between scores on several tests. _____(6) concluded two factors explain test performance: *g*, or _____(7) intelligence, and *s*, or a _____(8) factor. Spearman's _____(9) theory has been criticized, with Thurstone proposing seven "_____(10) mental abilities" instead. Modifications of general intelligence include hierarchical models, with _____(11) at the top and sub-factors, such as Cattell and Horn's _____(12) and crystallized intelligence, at lower levels. Fluid and crystallized intelligence help explain differences in intelligence due to culture and age.

_____(13) transmission speed also has been proposed as a determinant of mental ability. Faster speed means faster processing and more efficient resource allocation. The latency of the _____(14) signal relates to intelligence test scores.

Gardner's theory of _____(15) intelligences proposes eight different intelligences, rather than one general intelligence. Based on case studies of exceptional talents, the theory includes traditional types of intelligence (logical-mathematical) that are measured by conventional tests and others (bodily-kinesthetic, musical, intrapersonal, naturalist) that are not. Although many agree with a _____(16) view of intelligence, some view Gardner's theory as a study of talents, not intelligence, and criticize its lack of scientific support.

Sternberg's _____(17) theory proposes three major components and includes not only information processing activities, but also adaptive and practical components. _____(18) intelligence refers to analytical skills and information processing, the skills measured by most psychometric tests.

_____(19) intelligence applies to coping with new tasks. _____(20) intelligence involves the ability to adapt to the environment, or "street smarts." Triarchic theory is limited by the difficulty of defining and measuring the practical and creative components.

Evaluating Your Progress. Select the one best response. Answers are on page 243. If you make any errors, reread the relevant material before proceeding.

1. Spearman proposed that intelligence can be accounted for by
    a. general intelligence and a test-specific factor.
    b. fluid intelligence and crystallized intelligence.
    c. verbal intelligence and spatial intelligence.
    d. analytical intelligence and practical intelligence.

2. If you are very high in Spearman's *g* factor, you would be expected to
    a. perform very well on general knowledge tests, but poorly on more specific tests.
    b. perform very well on a wide variety of mental tests.
    c. have some special skill such as musical ability or artistic talent.
    d. have great insight into your own feelings and emotions.

3. In the psychometric approach to studying intelligence, the main focus is on
    a. neural transmission and processing speed.
    b. performance on mental tests.
    c. adaptation to the environment.
    d. the interaction of mental ability, creativity, and adaptability.

4. Thurstone suggested that intelligence can be accounted for by _____ primary mental abilities.
    a. 2
    b. 3
    c. 5
    d. 7

5. Fluid intelligence is best described as
    a. the natural ability to solve problems and reason.
    b. bodily-kinesthetic intelligence.
    c. knowledge and mental ability acquired from experience.
    d. practical intelligence.

6. Researchers who use the P100 signal believe intelligence is related to
    a. the dominant hemisphere of the brain.
    b. the efficiency of muscle contractions.
    c. the speed of neural processing.
    d. the size of the brain area activated by mental tests.

7. Bodily-kinesthetic intelligence and intrapersonal intelligence are included in
    a. Thurstone's primary mental abilities theory of intelligence.
    b. Sternberg's triarchic theory of intelligence.
    c. Gardner's multiple intelligences theory.
    d. Spearman's two-factor theory of intelligence.

8. According to the triarchic theory, a person who does well on traditional intelligence tests is high in
    a. general intelligence.
    b. practical intelligence.
    c. analytical intelligence.
    d. creative intelligence.

Measuring Individual Differences (pp. 347-357)

Mastering the Vocabulary. Define or explain each of the following terms. To check your answers, consult the text pages listed.

1. achievement tests (p. .48)

2. aptitude tests (p. .18)

3.   reliability (p. 348)

4.   validity (p. 348)

5.   standardization (p. 349)

6.   intelligence quotient (p. 350)

7.   mental age (p. 350)

8.   deviation IQ (p. 351)

9.   mental retardation (p. 352)

10. gifted (p. 352)

11. creativity (p. 355)

12. emotional intelligence (p. 356)

13. tacit knowledge (p. 356)

Mastering the Concepts. Fill in the blanks to create a summary of the section. Answers are on page 243.

Psychological tests measure individual differences. Some, _____(21) tests, measure current status. Others, _____(22) tests, measure the ability to learn. Regardless of what is measured, all good tests need _____(23), _____(24), and standardization. Reliability is a measure of _____(25) and often is evaluated in terms of _____(26) reliability, the correlation of scores from two separate testings. Validity is a measure of whether the test measures what it is supposed to measure. _____(27) validity evaluates whether the test provides a broad measure of the characteristic. _____(28) validity evaluates how well the test predicts future behavior. _____(29) validity measures how well the test relates to a theoretical view or concept. Standardization is the use of _____(30) procedures on all occasions.

The most famous index of intelligence is the intelligence _____(31) or IQ. Binet and Simon developed an intelligence test to identify children who would have difficulty in school. A child's _____(32) was determined based on a comparison of his or her performance with the performance of children of specific ages. A child with a mental (not actual) age of 8 performs as well as an average 8-year-old. Later, Terman developed the formula, (_____(33) age / chronological age) X 100 = IQ, which creates an "average" score of _____(34).

Modern tests compute a _____(35) IQ, based on a score's location in the distribution for others of the same age, to avoid problems created by comparisons based on mental age. Most people have IQs between _____(36). Scores below 70 suggest mental _____(37); scores above 130 suggest _____(38). Mental retardation is caused by both genetic and environmental influences and varies from mild to profound. Giftedness is associated with many aspects of success.

Major intelligence tests (Stanford-Binet, WAIS, etc.) are valid for predicting _____(39) success. Because of criticisms that previous tests failed to broadly sample intelligence, _____(40) items were included in the Weschler tests. Testing dangers include _____(41) effects and misinterpretation.

_____(42) is the ability to generate original, useful ideas. Creativity is not highly correlated with traditional IQ scores. _____(43) intelligence is the ability to perceive, understand, and express emotion in useful ways, and might be a better predictor of social or career success than IQ.

Standard intelligence assessments focus on well-defined, academic material, and do not predict job success well. Wagner & Sternberg suggest job performance can be predicted by evaluating _____(44) knowledge, unspoken practical "know how" that is rarely taught, but is gained through _____(45) people's behavior. Tacit knowledge is assessed using scenarios of decision-making situations. Criticisms of the tacit knowledge concept include questions about its _____(46) validity, its separate identity, and its ability to predict job performance better than general intelligence can.

Evaluating Your Progress. Select the one best response. Answers are on page 244. If you make any errors, reread the relevant material before proceeding.

1. A reliable test is a test that
   a. gives approximately the same result from one administration to the next.
   b. is administered the same way each time it is given.
   c. accurately predicts a future outcome.
   d. measures what it is supposed to measure.

2. High scores on the new test used to select new candidates for the police academy accurately predict high achievement on the job two years later. This finding provides evidence that the new test is
   a. an achievement test.
   b. reliable.
   c. standardized.
   d. valid.

3. An IQ of 100 corresponds to
   a. very high intelligence.
   b. average intelligence.
   c. mild retardation.
   d. severe retardation.

4. Binet's original IQ test was designed to
   a. quantify the genetic determinant of intelligence.
   b. quantify the environmental determinants of intelligence.
   c. predict job success in adulthood.
   d. identify children who would do poorly in traditional schools.

5. Ed, age 10, has a raw score of 110. To compute his deviation IQ score the psychologist will
   a. compare the location of 110 relative to the average score in the 10-year-olds' distribution.
   b. find the age associated with an average score of 110 and compare that "mental age" to Ed's age.
   c. test Ed twice and compute the difference between the two scores.
   d. compare this test score with other ratings (from teachers, parents, etc.) of his intelligence.

6. Lee has been classified as mentally retarded. Lee's IQ score is probably
   a. between 90 and 100.
   b. between 85 and 90.
   c. below 70.
   d. below 50.

7. Comparison of intelligence test scores and later school performance shows intelligence tests have
   a. good content validity.
   b. poor content validity.
   c. good predictive validity.
   d. poor predictive validity.

8. Tacit knowledge is best described as
   a. innate.
   b. "book learning."
   c. practical "know how."
   d. "hard-wired."

9. Which is true concerning creativity?
   a. Creativity is highly correlated with IQ.
   b. Creativity is not really measured by intelligence tests.
   c. Creativity requires the ability to understand and express emotion.
   d. Creativity is also known as tacit knowledge.

Discovering the Sources of Intelligence: The Nature-Nurture Issue (pp. 358-366)

Mastering the Vocabulary. Define or explain the following terms. To check your answers, consult the text pages listed.

1. heritability (p. 362)

Mastering the Concepts. Fill in the blanks to create a summary of the section. Answers are on page 243.

Strong genetic determinants predict stable intelligence, whereas strong environmental determinants predict changing intelligence. Some evidence suggests fast habituation in infancy relates to intelligence, but reliable measurements of intelligence cannot be obtained until age _____(47). A longitudinal study found _____(48) in IQ throughout adulthood, but a slight decline begins at age 60.

_____(49) intelligence, basic information processing, declines but crystallized intelligence, acquired knowledge, remains constant or increases. The Flynn effect, a general increase in test scores over the past 70 years, is usually explained in terms of changes in _____(50).

Twin studies suggest that genetic factors are important determinants of intelligence. _____(51) twins have the most similar IQs, even if reared apart. Twin studies indicate _____(52), the amount of the variation in IQ scores within a population that is due to genetics, may be 50 - 70%. Still, separated twins have less similar IQs than twins reared together, showing that _____(53) influences intelligence.

Racial differences in IQ occur, but why is unclear. They reflect average IQs, and cannot be applied to individuals. Economic differences exist and these environmental factors are hard to separate from genetic factors. Test _____(54) can contribute to the difference, but they do not account for all of it. Studies of minority children adopted into advantaged homes find higher IQs than the racial average, supporting an _____(55) factor. Most see IQ resulting from an _____(56) of genetics and environment. Genetics may establish a reaction range in which IQ is pushed up or down by environmental factors.

Evaluating Your Progress. Select the one best response. Answers are on page 244. If you make any errors, reread the relevant material before proceeding.

1. According to the Seattle Longitudinal study, the first modest reductions in intelligence occur at age
    a. 40.
    b. 50.
    c. 60.
    d. 70.

2. Based on research on the origins of intelligence, which of the following relatives would have the most similar IQ scores?
   a. same-sex fraternal twins raised together
   b. identical twins raised apart
   c. fathers and biological sons living together
   d. non-twin siblings raised together

3. The Flynn Effect is
   a. the higher heritability found for certain ethnic groups.
   b. the tendency to label groups based on their IQ.
   c. the change in an IQ score that is due to test bias.
   d. an increase in the typical IQ scores over the past several decades.

4. If a trait has high heritability, we can conclude that
   a. much of the change in the trait over time can be attributed to genetics.
   b. much of the variability of the trait within a population can be attributed to genetics.
   c. much of any between-group differences found for the trait can be attributed to genetics.
   d. much of an individual's score for the trait can be attributed to genetics.

5. Which is true concerning racial differences in IQ?
   a. The range of IQ scores for a race is much greater than the difference in IQ scores between races.
   b. The heritability of intelligence is high, so racial differences must be due to genetic differences.
   c. The racial differences in IQ almost entirely are due to racially biased intelligence tests.
   d. Minority children adopted into white homes perform the same as children from minority homes.

MAKING FINAL PREPARATIONS

Complete these sections without consulting your book or notes. For a more accurate estimate of how well you know this material, wait at least a day or two after studying the chapter before working on the questions. Some of the material you "know" immediately after working with the chapter will be quickly forgotten. Immediate tests will overestimate what you know well.

Short Essay Questions. Write a brief answer to each question. Sample answers are on page 245.

1. Explain what is meant by general intelligence (g) and why Spearman proposed this concept.

2. Discuss the contributions and limitations of the multiple intelligences theory and the triarchic theory.

3. Explain why standardization is necessary in a good test.

4. Define validity, and discuss the apparent validity of intelligence tests.

5. Discuss the possible dangers of IQ labeling.

6. Discuss the stability of intelligence in adulthood, including the roles of fluid and crystallized intelligence.

7. Summarize the current thought concerning the role of genes and the environment as determinants of intelligence, citing evidence relevant to each factor.

Matching. Select the correct definition or description for each item. Answers are on page 246.

_____	1. Sternberg	**a.** used for standard comparison of scores
_____	2. achievement test	**b.** proposed 7 primary mental abilities instead of *g*
_____	3. crystallized intelligence	**c.** intelligence based on acquired knowledge
_____	4. Galton	**d.** the age that best fits a child's test performance
_____	5. heritability	**e.** unspoken practical knowledge
_____	6. aptitude test	**f.** proposed triarchic theory
_____	7. fluid intelligence	**g.** basic reasoning & information processing skill
_____	8. test-retest reliability	**h.** proposed multiple intelligences theory
_____	9. tacit knowledge	**i.** index of trait variability in a group due to genetics
_____	10. Spearman	**j.** similarity of scores on two administrations of a test
_____	11. Thurstone	**k.** proposed two-factor theory
_____	12. practical intelligence	**l.** one of first to use the psychometric approach
_____	13. Terman	**m.** revised Binet's test and developed IQ formula
_____	14. mental age	**n.** measures current status of knowledge
_____	15. norm group	**o.** "street smarts" in triarchic theory
_____	16. Gardner	**p.** measures ability to learn

Multiple Choice Pretest 1. Select the one best response. Answers are on page 246.

1. The psychometric approach to intelligence
   a. examines the environmental and biological factors that determine intelligence.
   b. uses factor analysis to measure relationships between scores on mental tests.
   c. measures the speed of neural processing in the brain to predict intelligence.
   d. uses reaction times and error rates on mental tests to predict intelligence.

2. Thurstone's theory of primary mental abilities suggests
   a. a high score on one primary mental ability will be accompanied by high scores on the others.
   b. that differences in intelligence are best described by 3 factors or abilities.
   c. the primary mental abilities are fairly independent abilities.
   d. most athletes would score high in the kinesthetic primary mental ability.

3. Crystallized intelligence is best described as
   a. the natural ability to solve problems and reason.
   b. the ability to adapt to an environment ("street smarts").
   c. the ability to infer other people's moods and motivations.
   d. knowledge and mental ability acquired from experience.

4. The brain activity that is used to measure indirectly the speed of neural transmission is the
   a. *g* wave.
   b. P100 signal.
   c. alpha wave.
   d. triarchic complex.

5. Gardner's theory of multiple intelligences has been criticized for all of the following except:
   a. It is primarily descriptive.
   b. It really deals with talents, not intelligences.
   c. It is supported by little scientific evidence.
   d. It broadens the way intelligence is conceptualized.

6. Analytical, practical, and creative intelligence are part of
   a. Spearman's general intelligence theory.
   b. Gardner's multiple intelligences theory.
   c. Sternberg's triarchic intelligence theory.
   d. Thurstone's primary mental abilities theory.

7. Tara got about the same score on the SAT the two times she took it last year. This indicates the SAT
   a. is reliable.
   b. is standardized.
   c. has high construct validity.
   d. has high content validity.

8. Mica's on the job experiences have allowed him to develop a good understanding of how to identify good workers and other management skills. Mica probably will score high on tests of
   a. *g*.
   b. intrapersonal intelligence.
   c. analytic intelligence.
   d. tacit knowledge.

9. Tito is 5 and scored as well as the average 8-year-old. Terman would compute his IQ score to be
   a. 63
   b. 113
   c. 130
   d. 160

10. Approximately 68% of the population have a deviation IQ score of
    a. 100 or lower.
    b. 85 - 115.
    c. 70 - 130.
    d. above 130

11. To evaluate the content validity of a new test for depression, a psychologist might check to see if
    a. it predicts who will develop depression within the next six months.
    b. its scores tend to vary the way an accepted theory of depression would predict.
    c. it samples a wide range of behaviors associated with depression.
    d. it gives about the same result if taken twice in a relatively short period of time.

12. To be classified as "gifted," an individual must have an IQ at or above approximately
    a. 115.
    b. 130.
    c. 145.
    d. 160.

13. Terman's study of gifted children found
    a. they grew up to be more likely to commit suicide than "normal" people.
    b. they were less socially adept and more withdrawn than "normal" people.
    c. they were more likely to be divorced than "normal" people.
    d. they were more successful in adult occupations than "normal" people.

14. The most common intelligence tests have good predictive validity for
    a. academic performance.
    b. success in a career.
    c. the difference in fluid and crystallized intelligence.
    d. the ability to adapt to environmental demands.

15. The earliest time at which reliable estimates of IQ can be obtained is
    a. sometime between age 6 months and 1 year.
    b. sometime between age 2 and 3 years.
    c. sometime between age 4 and 7 years.
    d. sometime between age 8 and 12 years.

16. The heritability for intelligence is estimated to be
    a. 70 - 90%.
    b. 50 - 70%.
    c. 30 - 50%.
    d. 10 - 30%.

17. Sternberg and Wagner suggest that tacit knowledge is a good predictor of
    a. job success.
    b. IQ.
    c. satisfaction in life.
    d. academic performance.

18. Gardner's interpersonal and intrapersonal intelligences are most similar to the new idea of
    a. emotional intelligence.
    b. creativity.
    c. tacit knowledge.
    d. fluid intelligence.

Multiple Choice Pretest 2. Select the one best response. Answers are on page 247.

1. Positive correlations between scores on several very different mental tests support
   a. Spearman's two-factor theory of intelligence.
   b. Gardner's multiple intelligences theory.
   c. Sternberg's triarchic theory of intelligence.
   d. Cattell's concept of crystallized and fluid intelligence.

2. In modern psychometric theories, general intelligence is considered
   a. a totally worthless concept without support from any data.
   b. at the top of a hierarchy of factors that are involved in intelligence.
   c. one of three equally important factors that are involved in intelligence.
   d. to be the sole factor determining differences in performance on mental tests.

3. Verbal fluency, verbal comprehension, numerical ability, spatial ability, memory, perceptual speed, and reasoning are
   a. Catell's crystallized intelligence factors.
   b. Thurstone's primary mental abilities.
   c. Gardner's multiple intelligences.
   d. Sternberg's triarchic intelligences.

4. Jill, age 20, scores high in crystallized intelligence. Jill probably
   a. inherited her crystallized intelligence from her parents.
   b. has had a great deal of education.
   c. will show a large drop in crystallized intelligence by age 60.
   d. has very fast reaction times.

5. Hank can quickly size up a situation and turn it to his advantage, making him a very successful businessman. In terms of the triarchic theory of intelligence, Hank is high in
   a. analytical intelligence.
   b. creative intelligence.
   c. practical intelligence.
   d. intrapersonal intelligence.

6. Pat's raw score is 120, which corresponds to a score one standard deviation above the mean for her age group. Her deviation IQ score must be
   a. 90
   b. 100
   c. 115
   d. 135

7. The deviation IQ was developed to avoid the problems created by
   a. using "mental age" as the critical comparison.
   b. a lack of predictive validity for the Stanford-Binet IQ test.
   c. a lack of reliability in the Stanford-Binet IQ test.
   d. the complex mathematics involved in computing the IQ score.

8. To allow fair comparisons of scores across individuals, a test must be
   a. high in predictive validity.
   b. high in content validity.
   c. an aptitude test.
   d. standardized.

9. Concern about using the P100 signal to evaluate intelligence include all of the following EXCEPT:
   a. The relationship is a correlation.
   b. Differences in the P100 signal account for a small part of the differences in intelligence scores.
   c. The P100 might correlate with IQ scores, but not be directly related to intelligence.
   d. People differ in the amount of time required for the P100 signal to appear.

10. Clinical psychologists need the ability to read people's emotions and motivation. They need high
    a. general intelligence (g).
    b. creative intelligence.
    c. interpersonal intelligence.
    d. intrapersonal intelligence.

11. Although Terman's study found general benefits of being gifted, recent research has suggested a increased emotional problems and social isolation for a subgroup of the gifted population. This subgroup is primarily
    a. the moderately gifted (IQ = 130-150.
    b. the profoundly gifted (IQ > 180).
    c. female.
    d. from high socioeconomic backgrounds.

12. An individual with an IQ of 60 would be expected to
    a. eventually graduate from high school and become fully self-supporting.
    b. develop academic skills at the 6th grade level and become self-supporting.
    c. develop academic skills at the 2nd grade level and become semi-independent.
    d. have limited speech and be able to learn only simple tasks.

13. By developing intelligence tests that include a wider variety of tasks (e.g., WISC, WAIS) to reflect multiple intelligences, psychologists are addressing the criticisms of intelligence tests'
    a. content validity.
    b. predictive validity.
    c. standardization.
    d. reliability.

14. Scarr and Weinberg have found that the average IQ of African American children raised in white, middle-class homes is higher than the average IQ of all African Americans. From this we can conclude
    a. genetic differences between races cause racial differences in IQ.
    b. racially biased tests are the cause of the racial differences in IQ.
    c. discrimination is the cause of the racial differences in IQ.
    d. environmental factors may contribute to the racial differences in IQ.

15. A genetic determinant of intelligence would be supported most by high correlations between the IQ scores of
    a. identical twins raised together.
    b. identical twins raised apart.
    c. fraternal twins raised together.
    d. fraternal twins raised apart.

16. During adulthood, fluid intelligence usually _____, and crystallized intelligence _____.
    a. stays the same or increases; stays the same or increases
    b. stays the same or increases; decreases
    c. decreases; decreases
    d. decreases; stays the same or increases

17. Having no styrofoam packing materials, Pat used popcorn instead. Pat probably would score high in
    a. analytic thinking.
    b. crystallized intelligence.
    c. fluid intelligence.
    d. creativity.

18. Most psychologists believe that intelligence is determined by
    a. genetics, almost exclusively.
    b. the environment, almost exclusively.
    c. a significant interaction of genetics and environment.
    d. some yet-to-be-discovered factor.

LANGUAGE DEVELOPMENT GUIDE

Core Terms

One of the central questions about intelligence is whether it is one thing or many things, and you are likely to hear terms like *comprehensive, multifaceted,* and *multimodal*. A *comprehensive* test covers all the relevant material, so a comprehensive intelligence test would have many questions of different kinds. *Multifaceted* and *multimodal* are very similar; a multifaceted test would have many different parts, and a multimodal one would measure something in many different ways

Your instructor may talk about various levels of education using unfamiliar terms. *Primary* school is from kindergarten to about 6th grade. *Secondary* school is 7th through 12th grade. *Higher education* is all that follows graduation from high school. *Undergraduates* are college students seeking bachelor's degrees.

Graduate students are pursuing master's degrees or doctorates, and we would say that they are in graduate school. *Postgraduate* work is academic work done after receiving a doctorate.

Idioms

p. 338	cocky grin	a smile that says that he is very self-confident
p. 338	furrowed brows	wrinkled foreheads, suggesting worry or concentration
p. 338	secret caches	valuable things hidden away in various spots
p. 339	cartography school	a school for map-makers
p. 339	granted that	given that; let's assume that
p. 341	in a more rigorous way	with more standardization, more careful control, etc.
p. 341	mathematically inclined	very good at and interested in math
p. 343	socioeconomic classes	your social level, based upon your income
p. 345	*savant*	short for *idiot savant*, a person with low mental ability except in one spectacular area
p. 351	appropriate curriculum adjustments	helpful changes in what is being taught to a child
p. 353	socially adept	good at making friends and talking with people
p. 353	bookworm	someone who reads a lot
p. 353	pass with flying colors	perform very well
p. 356	cut and dried	easy to understand; clear and simple
p. 357	intuitively plausible	possible, based on common sense
p. 359	airtight	perfect; impossible to damage
p. 360	test battery	group of tests
p. 362	irrespective	no matter which one

Word Parts

Here are some words that are made up of word parts, and that you can find in this chapter. After you've looked at these, you can look for others in the chapter with the same word parts.

WORD	WORD PART IT USES	MEANING
multiple	mult = many	several, many
triarchic	tri = three arch = rule	rule of threes
logical	log = reason	reasonable; clearly thought
concept	con = together cept = to take	a group of ideas, or an idea that explains several things
psychometric	psych = mind meter = to measure	tools and techniques for measuring the mind and its abilities
predict	pre = before dict = to say	to foretell
excel	ex = out of cel = to move	to move beyond, to pass up
component	com = together pon, pos = to put	a part of some larger whole

Knowing the word parts listed above, you can also create the following words. You can get an idea of their meanings from the word parts they use.

multiply	multi + ply (to fold over)	_____
precept	_____ + _____	a basic rule; a foundational idea on which one builds
monarch	mon (one) + arch	_____
composition	com + pos	_____
dictate	_____	to say to someone
psychological	_____ + _____	_____

Pronunciation

p. 345	triarchic	try-ark'-ick		p. 356	tacit	ta'-sit
p. 350	quotient	kwo'-shint		p. 362	heritability	hair-i-ta-bil'-i-ty

ANSWERS AND EXPLANATIONS

To find relevant material in your textbook, consult the pages cited with each answer. Also, PN and PT citations refer to modules in PsychNow! and Psyk.trek materials, respectively.

Mastering the Concepts

1. differences (p. 339)
2. psychometric (p. 340)
3. Galton (p. 340)
4. similar (p. 341)
5. Factor analysis (p. 341)
6. Spearman (p. 341)
7. general (p. 341)
8. specific (p. 341)
9. two-factor (p. 341)
10. primary (p. 341)
11. g (p. 342)
12. fluid (p. 343)
13. Neural (p. 343)
14. P100 (p. 343)
15. multiple (p. 344)
16. broad (p. 345)
17. triarchic (p. 345)
18. Analytical (p. 346)
19. Creative (p. 346)
20. Practical (p. 346)
21. achievement (p. 348)
22. aptitude (p. 348)
23. reliability (p. 348)
24. validity (p. 348)
25. consistency (p. 348)
26. test-retest (p. 348)
27. Content (p. 348)
28. Predictive (p. 348)
29. Construct (p. 349)
30. the same (p. 349)
31. quotient (p. 350)
32. mental age (p. 350)
33. mental (p. 351)
34. 100 (p. 351)
35. deviation (p. 351)
36. 85 and 115 (p. 352)
37. retardation (p. 352)
38. giftedness (p. 352)
39. academic (p. 353)
40. nonverbal (p. 354)
41. labels (p. 354)
42. Creativity (p. 355)
43. Emotional (p. 356)
44. tacit (p. 356)
45. observing (p. 356)
46. scientific (p. 357)
47. 4 - 7 years (p. 359)
48. stability (p. 360)
49. Fluid (p. 360)
50. environment (p. 360)
51. Identical (p. 361)
52. heritability (p. 362)
53. environment (p. 362)
54. biases (p. 364)
55. environmental (p. 364)
56. interaction (p. 365)

Evaluating Your Progress

Preview & Conceptualizing Intelligence

1. **a** (p. 343)
   - b. Wrong. These are Cattell and Horn's units of intelligence.
   - c. Wrong. These are 2 of Gardner's 7 multiple intelligences.
   - d. Wrong. These are 2 of the 3 types of intelligence in the triarchic theory.

2. **b** (p. 341)
   - a, c, & d. Wrong. General intelligence (g) is a broad ability, but not limited to general information.

3. **b** (p. 340)
   - a. Wrong. Biological measures are not usually considered part of the psychometric approach.
   - c. Wrong. This is closer to Sternberg's Triarchic approach.
   - d. Wrong. This describes Sternberg's Triarchic approach.

4. **d** (p. 341)
   - a, b, & c. Wrong. There are 7 primary mental abilities.

5. **a** (p. 343) (PN6D)
   - b. Wrong. This represents one of Gardner's intelligences, not Cattell's fluid intelligence.
   - c. Wrong. This represents one of the triarchic intelligences, not Cattell's fluid intelligence.
   - d. Wrong. This represents one of the triarchic intelligences, not Cattell's fluid intelligence.

6. c   a. Wrong. The P100 doesn't indicate the dominant hemisphere.
(p. 343)   b. Wrong. The P100 is an electrical waveform generated by the brain.
             d. Wrong. The P100 does not reflect the size of an active brain area.

7. c   a. Wrong. Thurstone's primary abilities are traditional mental skills.
(p. 344)   b. Wrong. Sternberg proposes similarly unique dimensions, but not these.
             d. Wrong. Spearman proposed g and s, not these.

8. c   a. Wrong. General intelligence is not part of the triarchic theory.
(p. 346)   b. Wrong   Practical intelligence is the ability to adapt to the environment or "street smarts."
             d. Wrong. Creative intelligence is the ability to deal with new tasks or situations quickly.

Measuring Individual Differences

1. a   b. Wrong. This describes standardization.
(p. 348)   c. Wrong. This describes predictive validity.
(PT7B)   d. Wrong. This describes validity in general.

2. d   a. Wrong. Achievement tests measure current status, not future performance.
(p. 348)   b. Wrong. Reliability doesn't involve predictions, just consistency if retested.
             c. Wrong. Standardization doesn't use prediction, only constant conditions.

3. b   a. Wrong. Giftedness is an IQ above 130. Think about what it means if real age = mental age.
(p. 350)   c. Wrong. Mild retardation is classified as IQs of 50-70.
             d. Wrong. Severe retardation is classified as IQs of 20-35.

4. d   a, b, & c.   Wrong.   The French government wanted to identify "dull" children who needed a
(p. 350)   different academic experience.

5. a   b. Wrong. This is how Terman's original IQ was computed.
(p. 351)   c. Wrong. Deviation refers to difference from the average for that age.
(PT7C)   d. Wrong. The deviation is in relation to the performance of others, not other people's opinions.

6. c   a, b, & d.   Wrong.   Mental retardation is assigned when IQ is below 70. IQ of 70-130 is normal.
(p. 352)

7. c   a & b.   Wrong.   These data don't really address content validity, only predictive validity.
(p. 348)   d.   Wrong.   Tests scores and school performance are correlated, so predictive validity isn't poor.

8. c   a. Wrong. Tacit knowledge is mostly acquired through experience.
(p. 356)   b. Wrong. Tacit knowledge is not taught directly in school or elsewhere.
             d. Wrong. Hard-wired implies innate, which is incorrect. Tacit knowledge is acquired.

9. b   a. Wrong. The correlation of creativity & IQ is low.
(p. 355)   c. Wrong. This is emotional intelligence.
(PN5G)   d. Wrong. Tacit knowledge is implicit, practical "know-how."

Discovering the Sources of Intelligence: The Nature-Nurture Issue

1. c   a, b, & d.   Wrong.   Intelligence is quite stable throughout, but limited declines occur after age 60.
(p. 360)

2. b   a, c, & d.   Wrong.   The stronger the genetic link, the higher the correlation, even if environment
(p. 362)   differs.

3. **d**   a. Wrong. The Flynn effect relates to change in the population's mean IQ over time, not heritability.
    (p. 360) b. Wrong. The Flynn effect relates to change in the population's mean IQ over time, not labeling.
              c. Wrong. The Flynn effect relates to change in the population's mean IQ over time, not test bias.

4. **b**   a, c, & d. Wrong. Heritability is an index of the *variability* of a trait *within* a group that is due to
    (p. 362)   genetic factors. It does not involve a change over time.
    (PT7D)

5. **a**   b. Wrong. Remember, heritability only pertains to within-group differences in IQ.
    (p. 363) c. Wrong. Racial differences remain even when biased questions are removed.
              d. Wrong. Adoption studies show higher IQs for minorities if raised in white middle-class homes.

MAKING FINAL PREPARATIONS

Short Essay Questions

1. Spearman considered general intelligence to be the primary intellectual ability responsible for individual differences in IQ. Spearman analyzed performance on several different mental tests using factor analysis and found that people who performed well on one test usually performed well on most other tests. That is, one common ability (he called general intelligence) seemed to control performance. (p. 341)

2. Both Gardner's and Sternberg's theories broadened what intelligence is conceptualized to be. They included aspects of behavior which previous theories had not, and they extended intelligence to include interpersonal and "real world," nonacademic abilities. These additions are difficult to define or test scientifically, and critics ask whether they are part of intelligence or only specific talents. (pp. 344-347)

3. Standardization, maintaining the same procedures for all administrations of the test, is needed if scores are to be compared across individuals or groups. If procedures differ, differences in IQ scores could be due to the procedural differences rather than individual differences in intelligence. (p. 349-350)

4. Validity is an assessment of how well a test measures what it is supposed to measure. Intelligence tests are considered to be valid, at least relating to academic performance. They predict academic performance well, giving them good predictive validity. Researchers have questioned their content validity, but the Weschler tests added performance scales so that a broader range of activities are sampled. (pp. 348-349, 353-354)

5. Labels of "smart" or "slow" are difficult to change and lead to different treatment. Teachers treated "smart" children with more respect and expose them to more opportunities than "slow" children, further delaying possible advancement of the "slow" children. Mislabeling due to misuse of IQ tests resulted in immigration laws designed to keep out "defective" groups early in the 20th century. (pp. 354-355)

6. The Seattle Longitudinal study suggests that IQ remains quite steady throughout adulthood, with only a slight decline after age 60. Individual differences are large in later years, possibly due to physical problems. Fluid intelligence seems to decline, but crystallized intelligence remains constant or increases. (pp. 359-360)

7. Intelligence is determined by an interaction of genes and environment. Genetic factors are supported by twin studies that show genetic similarity predicts IQ similarity. Even if environments differ, identical twins have more similar IQs than same-sex fraternal twins reared together. Adoption studies of minority children reared in "advantaged" homes find they have higher IQs than average, supporting environmental factors. (pp. 361-366)

Matching

Multiple Choice Pretest 1

1. **b**   a.   Wrong.   The conceptualization, not origin, of intelligence is key to the psychometric view.
(p. 340)   c & d.   Wrong.   The psychometric approach uses standard tests, not neural measures or reaction time.

2. **c**   a. Wrong.   The factors are fairly independent, so one test score doesn't predict another.
(p. 341)   b. Wrong.   Thurstone proposed 7 primary mental abilities, not 3.
          d. Wrong.   Gardner proposed kinesthetic intelligence, not Thurstone.

3. **d**   a. Wrong.   This is fluid intelligence, as opposed to crystallized intelligence.
(p. 343)   b. Wrong.   This is Sternberg's practical intelligence.
(PN6D)   c. Wrong.   This is Gardner's interpersonal intelligence.

4. **b**   a & d.   Wrong.   These are not types of brain activity.
(p. 343)   c.   Wrong.   Alpha waves are associated with relaxation, not mental activity.

5. **d**   a, b, & c.   Wrong.   These are all points of criticism.
(p. 345)

6. **c**   a. Wrong.   Spearman proposed g and s.
(p. 346)   b. Wrong.   Gardner proposed 8 different intelligences, but not these.
          d. Wrong.   Thurstone proposed 7 different abilities, but not these.

7. **a**   b. Wrong.   A test is standardized if it is *administered* the same way for all people, every time.
(p. 348)   c. Wrong.   A test has construct validity if it taps into a theoretical construct.
          d. Wrong.   A test has content validity if it samples broadly from the domain of interest.

8. **d**   a. Wrong.   These are tacit knowledge skills, which do not relate to g.
(p. 356)   b. Wrong.   Intrapersonal intelligence is insight about one's own feelings and emotions.
          c. Wrong.   Analytic intelligence involves standard intelligence skills.

9. **d**   a, b, & c.   Wrong.   IQ = (mental age/chronological age) X 100 = (8/5) X 100 = 160.
(p. 351)
(PT7C)

10. **b**   a. Wrong.   100 is the average, so about 50% of the scores are at or below 100.
(p. 352)   c. Wrong.   About 96% of the scores fall between 70 and 130.
          d. Wrong.   Only about 2% of the population have scores of 130 or above.

11. **c**   a. Wrong.   This answer describes predictive validity.
(p. 348)   b. Wrong.   This answer describes construct validity.
          d. Wrong.   This answer describes reliability.

12. **b**   a, c, & d.   Wrong.   The usual score is 130 or above.
(p. 352)

13. **d**   a, b, & c.   Wrong.   Terman found gifted children were at least as stable and sociable as "normals."
(p. 353)

14. **a**   b. Wrong.   Intelligence tests were designed for, and currently are evaluated in terms of predicting
(p. 353)   academic performance. They do not predict career success well.

               c. Wrong.   Intelligence tests were designed for, and currently are evaluated in terms of predicting
                                  academic performance. They do not predict fluid vs. crystallized intelligence well.

               d. Wrong.   Intelligence tests were designed for, and currently are evaluated in terms of predicting
                                  academic performance. They do not relate to practical intelligence.

15. **c**   a, b, & d.   Wrong.   Reliability is poor in infancy and toddlerhood, but good by early school-age.
(p. 359)

16. **b**   a, c, & d.   Wrong.   The most common estimate is 50%, but some suggest 70% is more accurate.
(p. 362)
(PT6D)

17. **a**   b, c, & d.   Wrong.   Tacit knowledge is correlated with job success.
(p. 356)

18. **a**   b. Wrong.   Inter-and intra-personal intelligence deals with emotions, not novel ideas.
(p. 356)   c. Wrong.   Inter-and intra-personal intelligence deals with emotions, not practical "know how."
               d. Wrong.   Inter-and intra-personal intelligence deals with emotions, not basic reasoning skills.

Multiple Choice Pretest 2

1. **a**   b & c.   Wrong.   This correlation supports a single factor view. These are multifactor.
(p. 341)   d.   Wrong.   This correlation would have nothing to say about the fluid vs. crystallized issue.

2. **b**   a & d.   Wrong.   General intelligence hasn't been discarded or accepted totally.
(p. 342)   c.   Wrong.   Triarchic theory proposes 3 aspects of intelligence, but none is *g*.

3. **b**   a. Wrong.   These are closer to what Cattell described as fluid intelligence than to crystallized.
(p. 341)   c. Wrong.   Gardner proposed musical, bodily-kinesthetic, logical-mathematical, linguistic, spatial,
                                  interpersonal, & intrapersonal intelligences.
               d. Wrong.   Sternberg proposed analytical, practical, and creative intelligences.

4. **b**   a. Wrong.   Crystallized is related to experience.
(p. 343)   c. Wrong.   Crystallized intelligence doesn't decline significantly with age.
(PN6D)   d. Wrong.   Fluid intelligence, a more biologically based ability, might be related to reaction times.

5. **c**   a. Wrong.   Analytical intelligence involves traditional mental skills and reasoning.
(p. 346)   b. Wrong.   Creative intelligence involves learning novel tasks quickly.
               d. Wrong.   Intrapersonal intelligence is not part of the triarchic theory.

6. **c**   a. Wrong.   Pat's score is above the mean, but 90 is below the mean of 100.
(p. 351)   b. Wrong.   Pat's score is above the mean, but 100 is the mean.
               d. Wrong.   135 is more than 2 standard deviations above; 1 standard deviation = 15 deviation IQ pts.

7. **a**   b. Wrong.   The Stanford-Binet test has good predictive validity.
(p. 351)   c. Wrong.   The Stanford-Binet test has good reliability.
               d. Wrong.   Computing deviation IQ is not less complex than computing Terman's IQ score.

8. **d**   a. Wrong.   Comparisons could be fair, but the test would not be useful for predicting anything.
    (p. 349)   b. Wrong.   Comparison could be fair, but the test would not provide a good measure of the attribute.
               c. Wrong.   Aptitude tests are not the only tests that allow comparisons across people.

9. **d**   a, b, & c.   Wrong.   These are all reasons for caution in using the P100 signal to predict intelligence.
    (p. 344)   The fact that individual differences occur in P100 is the reason it might be useful.

10. **c**   a. Wrong.   General intelligence involves basic mental skills, not these skills.
    (p. 345)   b. Wrong.   Creative intelligence involves coping well with new tasks, not these skills.
               d. Wrong.   Intrapersonal intelligence involves insight into one's own emotions, not other people's.

11. **b**   a. Wrong.   Moderately gifted people had no greater problems than "normals."
    (p. 353)   c. Wrong.   No sex differences are reported in your text.
               d. Wrong.   High socioeconomic background has been proposed as a reason for *greater* success.

12. **b**   a. Wrong.   People with IQs of 60 are unlikely to progress past a 6th grade level.
    (p. 353)   c. Wrong.   This describes IQs of 35-50, moderate retardation. IQ = 60 is mild retardation.
               d. Wrong.   This describes IQs of 20-35, severe retardation. IQ = 60 is mild retardation.

13. **a**   b. Wrong.   Predictive validity relates to predicting some criterion behavior, not sampling broadly.
    (p. 349)   c. Wrong.   Standardization involves using the same procedures for all people, not sampling broadly.
               d. Wrong.   Reliability relates to whether there is test-retest similarity, not sampling broadly.

14. **d**   a.   Wrong.   The data address environmental influences, not genetic factors in racial differences.
    (p. 364)   b & c.   Wrong.   The data don't address these issues, only predictions about environmental factors

15. **b**   a. Wrong.   If raised together, both environment and genes are the same, so either could be critical.
    (p. 361)   c. Wrong.   This would support environmental factors (genes different, same environment).
    (PT7D)   d. Wrong   This would favor neither--both genes and environment differs.

16. **d**   a, b, & c. Wrong.   Fluid intelligence decreases, while crystallized intelligence remains stable.
    (p. 360)

17. **d**   a. Wrong.   Analytic thinking involves traditional intellectual skills. Key here is the unusual, new idea.
    (p. 355)   b. Wrong.   Crystallized intelligence is acquired abilities. Key here is the unusual, new idea.
               c. Wrong.   Fluid intelligence involves inborn reasoning abilities. Key here is the unusual, new idea.

18. **c**   a, b, & d.   Wrong.   Data clearly show both environment and genes influence intelligence.
    (p. 365)
    (PT7D

CHAPTER 11: MOTIVATION AND EMOTION

ESTABLISHING LEARNING GOALS

Use these learning objectives as a preview of the chapter, a guide for active reading, and to evaluate your mastery of the material. Review the relevant objectives as you begin and end your reading of each major section of the chapter.

I.   Solve the adaptive problem of activating behavior.
   A. Discuss the roles of instincts and drive in activating behavior.
   B. Define incentive motivation, and describe how it activates behavior.
   C. Distinguish between achievement motivation and intrinsic motivation.
   D. Discuss how each need in Maslow's hierarchy influences behavior.

II. Solve the adaptive problem of meeting the biological need for food.
   A. Describe the internal factors that influence when and why we eat.
      1. Describe the role of glucose and insulin levels in hunger and eating.
      2. Discuss the role of the hypothalamus and other brain areas in the control of eating.
   B. Describe the external factors that influence when and why we eat.
   C. Explain how body weight is regulated.
   D. Discuss anorexia nervosa and bulimia nervosa.

III. Solve the adaptive problem of meeting the biological need for sexual activity.
   A. Describe the characteristics of the human sexual response cycle.
   B. Discuss the role of hormones in sexual behavior.
   C. List some external influences on sexual behavior.
   D. Discuss the factors that influence mate selection.
   E. Discuss the factors that may determine sexual orientation.

IV. Solve the adaptive problem of expressing and experiencing emotion.
   A. Discuss the evidence for and against basic emotions.
      1. Discuss the cross-cultural research concerning facial expressions and emotion.
      2. Explain the facial-feedback hypothesis.
   B. Discuss the role of arousal in emotional experience.
      1. Explain the basic logic behind using physiological arousal to signal dishonestly.
      2. Discuss the limitations and problems of polygraph exams.
   C. Describe the subjective experiences of anger, happiness, and disgust.
   D. Differentiate among the James-Lange, Cannon-Bard, and two-factor theories of emotion.
      1. Describe Schachter & Singer's research and the resulting conclusions.
      2. Critique each theory.

MASTERING THE MATERIAL

Preview & Activating Behavior (pp. 372-380)

Mastering the Vocabulary. Define or explain each of the following terms. To check your answers, consult the text pages listed.

1. motivation (p. 372)

2. emotions (p. 372)

3. instincts (p. 374)

4. drive (p. 375)

5. homeostasis (p. 375)

6. incentive motivation (p. 375)

7. achievement motive (p. 376)

8. intrinsic motivation (p. 377)

9. need hierarchy (p. 379)

Mastering the Concepts. Fill in the blanks to create a summary of the section. Answers are on page 267.

Motivation, the set of factors that initiate and _____(1) behavior toward a goal, and emotion are closely linked. Emotions include a _____(2) reaction, a _____(3) experience, and an expressive reaction. Four adaptive problems are discussed: What factors activate goal-directed action? What factors create hunger and control eating? What factors promote sexual behavior? How and why do emotions occur?

Motivation is the result of both internal and external events. _____(4), unlearned characteristic responses, are internal motivators that influence animal, and possibly human, behavior. The concept of

_____(5), a psychological state due to an internal physiological need, is an alternative to the idea of instincts. Drives maintain _____(6), but unlike instincts, drives are flexible in format.

_____(7) motivation involves the value of an external factor. Internal and external factors interact, as in the case of _____(8) motivation, a drive for success or accomplishment. Experience with failure, cultural attitudes, and other external factors influence achievement behaviors.

_____(9) motivation, self-motivated behavior without external reward or homeostatic influence, can be reduced by rewards. Explanations include a loss of _____(10) when rewarded and the possibility the _____(11) is perceived to be the source of motivation (overjustification). This occurs only if rewards are _____(12), so the promise of reward might be critical, not the reward itself.

Maslow proposed a _____(13) that prioritizes needs. _____(14) and safety needs are most basic, and _____(15), reaching one's full potential, is the final need. Maslow's hierarchy is criticized for its lack of scientific rigor, but it has had wide impact.

Evaluating Your Progress. Select the one best response. Answers are on page 268. If you make any errors, reread the relevant material before proceeding.

1. Which is true concerning the current view of human instincts?
   a. Instincts play no role in goal-directed human behavior.
   b. Instincts are not a widely applied explanation for goal-directed human behavior.
   c. Seventeen instincts account for much goal-directed human behavior.
   d. Twelve instincts account for much goal-directed human behavior.

2. A psychological state that arises in response to an internal physiological need is
   a. an instinct.
   b. an emotion.
   c. homeostasis.
   d. drive.

3. Incentives differ from drives because
   a. incentives involve physiological needs, but drives do not.
   b. incentives "pull" behavior, but drives "push" behavior.
   c. incentives are unlearned, but drives are learned.
   d. incentives are internal, but drives are external.

4. Homeostasis is
   a. an internal drive or need for success.
   b. goal-directed behavior that seems to be entirely self-motivated.
   c. a psychological state that arises in response to an internal physiological need.
   d. the process through which the body maintains a steady state.

5. People who work hard to accomplish some task are said to be high in
   a. self-actualization.
   b. intrinsic motivation.
   c. achievement motivation.
   d. homeostasis.

6. Beverly spends every spare minute playing her violin. This behavior is best explained in terms of
   a. intrinsic motivation.
   b. the two-factor theory.
   c. need for homeostasis.
   d. a musical drive.

7. The most important and most accepted aspect of Maslow's hierarchy of needs is
   a. the idea that need for self-actualization is the most important need of all.
   b. the clear definitions given for newly proposed needs.
   c. the idea that some needs are more important or basic than others.
   d. the suggestion that need for achievement is the most important need of all.

8. Jim is open, spontaneous, and has fulfilled his personal potential. Maslow would say he has achieved
   a. self-actualization.
   b. incentive motivation.
   c. homeostasis.
   d. his set point.

Meeting Biological Needs: Hunger and Eating (pp. 380-386)

Mastering the Vocabulary. Define or explain each of the following terms. To check your answers, consult the text pages listed.

1. glucose (p. 381)

2. insulin (p. 381)

3. ventromedial hypothalamus (p. 381)

4. lateral hypothalamus (p. 382)

5. set point (p. 384)

6. obesity (p. 385)

7. anorexia nervosa (p. 386)

8. bulimia nervosa (p. 386)

Mastering the Content. Fill in the blanks to create a summary of this section. Answers are on page 267.

Internal conditions, including stomach contents, are monitored to control eating. Receptors monitor blood _____(16), a sugar required for energy production. As levels increase, hunger decreases. _____(17), a pancreatic hormone required for glucose utilization, also is monitored. The glucose-insulin interaction is critical, but other internal factors (body fat level) are important.

The _____(18) is important in the control of eating. Damage to the _____(19) hypothalamus results in overeating; stimulation of this area inhibits eating. Damage to the _____(20) hypothalamus inhibits eating; stimulation initiates eating. These areas were once considered the satiety and initiation centers for eating, but recent data suggest the situation is more complex. Other data suggest the _____(21) and _____(22) also are involved in eating behavior. Eating is also influenced by learned eating _____(23), the presence of food cues, and other external factors.

Both internal and external factors regulate weight. The _____(24) theory states individuals have a natural weight the body tries to maintain. _____(25) factors may control the number of fat cells and _____(26) rate to establish a set point. Excessive body fat, _____(27), is not just a matter of poor willpower. Metabolic rate, set point, cultural habits, and stress also influence eating and weight.

Culturally-influenced "ideal" weights and inaccurate body images affect eating. _____(28) nervosa, in which an abnormally low weight is maintained, can include the perception of being fat even while starving. In _____(29) nervosa, _____(30) eating is followed by purging. Both disorders have serious medical consequences and are most common in women with an obsessive desire to be thin.

Evaluating Your Progress. Select the one best response. Answers are on page 268. If you make any errors, reread the relevant material before proceeding.

1. Hunger increases as the blood level of _____ decreases.
    a. fat.
    b. salt.
    c. glucose.
    d. estrogen.

2. The part of the brain once thought to be the satiety center (to control the termination of eating) is the
   a. hippocampus.
   b. brainstem.
   c. ventromedial hypothalamus.
   d. lateral hypothalamus.

3. After eating a meal of sweet foods, sweet foods lose their appeal, but food of other flavors do not. Psychologists explain this effect in terms of
   a. glucose-insulin interaction.
   b. a set point.
   c. homeostasis.
   d. sensory-specific satiety.

4. The set point is
   a. the fixed amount of glucose needed for cellular activity.
   b. the natural weight the body tries to maintain.
   c. the insulin level that stimulates a desire to eat.
   d. the weight that is viewed as ideal in a specific culture.

5. Anorexia nervosa is an eating disorder
   a. most common in young men.
   b. in which the person eats massive quantities of food at one time.
   c. characterized by an irrational fear of being overweight.
   d. that is most common in middle-aged women.

Meeting Biological Needs: Sexual Behavior (pp. 387-393)

Mastering the Vocabulary. Define or explain each of the following terms. To check your answers, consult the text pages listed.

1. excitement phase (p. 388)

2. plateau phase (p. 388)

3. orgasmic phase (p. 388)

4. resolution phase (p. 388)

5. sexual scripts (p. 390)

6. sexual orientation (p. 392)

Mastering the Concepts. Fill in the blanks to create a summary of the section. Answers are on page 267.

Sexual behavior ensures continuation of the species and may lead to companionship, love and protection. The sexual response follows a fixed sequence. In the _____(31) phase, physiological arousal begins, leading to erection in men and lubrication in women. In the _____(32) phase, these processes continue to develop, but slowly. Sexual release occurs during the _____(33) phase, then arousal returns to normal in the _____(34) phase. Men have a _____(35) period in which further sexual response is impossible.

Animals' sexual behavior is controlled by _____(36) and often limited to a period of fertility. Human sexual behavior is mostly under the control of the _____(37), although estrogens and androgens are influential. Loss of sex hormones does not necessarily eliminate all sexual motivation in humans. Touch and other external stimuli affect human sexual behavior. Animals respond to certain scents or _____(38), but little evidence supports an effect on sexual desire.

Exactly how, when, and why people have sex is influenced by _____(39), learned tendencies and attitudes. Some sex differences in sexual scripts are cross-cultural. Men do not link sex and marriage, are more likely to engage in _____(40) strategies, and prefer young, attractive partners, not financially secure partners. Some of these behaviors may be adaptations.

A person's sexual _____(41) involves whether the same or different sex is found sexually and emotionally attractive. _____(42) are predominantly attracted to the same sex; _____(43) are predominantly attracted to the opposite sex. Orientation should be considered a continuum, rather than distinct categories. Homosexuality once was thought to be caused by a dominant mother and passive father. Recent research refutes this and suggests _____(44) factors influence orientation. Differences in the _____(45) have been found. Twin studies support a _____(46) factor, and a "gay gene" has been proposed. However, the data are _____(47) which complicates interpretation, and genetic factors clearly are not the entire story.

Evaluating Your Progress. Select the one best response. Answers are on page 269. If you make any errors, reread the relevant material before proceeding.

1. The role of sex hormones in the sexual behavior of humans can be described as
   a. highly important. They strictly determine when people seek sexual activity.
   b. moderately important. They are more important than some things, but they don't have total control.
   c. minimally important. Hormones have some influence, but the individual maintains control.
   d. totally unimportant. Hormones have no influence on sexual behavior.

2. The first phase in the human sexual response is the
   a. plateau phase.
   b. orgasmic phase.
   c. resolution phase.
   d. excitement phase.

3. Cross-cultural studies show that in most cultures
   a. men are more likely than women to pursue long-term sexual strategies.
   b. men place more value on their long-term partner's attractiveness than women do.
   c. women place less value on the financial status of a prospective partner than men do.
   d. men are less concerned than women with having a young sexual partner.

4. Pheromones are
   a. sexual odors-producing chemicals.
   b. sex hormones.
   c. tactile (touch) stimuli that produce arousal.
   d. a biological determinant of sexual orientation.

5. The learned programs that instruct people on how, why, and what to do in their sexual interactions are
   a. sexual menus.
   b. sexual orientations.
   c. sexual instincts.
   d. sexual scripts.

6. Recent research suggests that homosexuality is at least partially determined by
   a. sexual molestation during early childhood.
   b. having a domineering mother and passive father.
   c. single parent families with no father or other role model present.
   d. biological factors.

Expressing and Experiencing Emotion (pp. 393-404)

Mastering the Vocabulary. Define or explain each of the following terms. To check your answers, consult the text pages listed.

1. facial-feedback hypothesis (p. 394)

2. polygraph test (p. 397)

3. James-Lange theory (p. 401)

4. Cannon-Bard theory (p. 402)

5.　two-factor theory (p. 454)

Mastering the Concepts. Fill in the blanks to create a summary of the section. Answers are on page 267.

　　　Emotions involve a _____(48) reaction, an expressive reaction, and _____(49) experience. Ekman found six basic emotions (fear, happiness, _____(50), sadness, anger, and disgust/contempt) associated with cross-cultural _____(51) expressions, suggesting a genetic origin of the expression of emotion. The facial _____(52) hypothesis suggests input from facial muscles influence emotion. Others view basic emotions as shared components of many emotions.

　　　Physiological arousal prepares the body to make a response. Performance declines at very low and high levels of arousal. Arousal is the basis of _____(53) tests. Lying is assumed to lead to emotionality, which causes physiological changes. Lying is inferred if arousal differs on relevant and control questions. Problems include the ease of "beating" the test and a high false _____(54) rate. Certain events (being restrained, expectations violated) are linked to anger, but happiness is influenced by social _____(55) and adaptation level. The emotion of _____(56) is often food-related, but relates to contamination. Disgust is not innate, and may be irrational due to "sympathetic magic."

　　　Different theories of emotion handle the three components of emotion differently. The common sense view states a stimulus causes an emotion, which causes physical changes. The _____(57) theory states a stimulus causes physical changes, which determine an emotion. This theory requires different patterns for each emotion and a _____(58) of emotion if feedback about physical changes is eliminated. Some research confirms these predictions. The _____(59) theory states a stimulus independently produces both the emotional experience and physical changes. The _____(60) theory, currently the most accepted theory, states the stimulus causes physical changes, but the emotion is the result of cognitive appraisal or interpretation of the physical changes in context. This is supported by Schachter & Singer's data showing expectations about physical reactions affect emotion.

Evaluating Your Progress. Select the one best response. Answers are on page 269. If you make any errors reread the relevant material before proceeding.

1.　Jess' heart was racing, she felt afraid, and she was screaming. Her screams represent the emotion's
　　a.　physiological response.
　　b.　expressive reaction.
　　c.　subjective experience.
　　d.　unconscious experience.

2. Some facial expressions are recognized across cultures and occur in early infancy. This supports
   a. the facial feedback hypothesis.
   b. the James-Lange theory of emotion.
   c. a genetic origin for expressions of emotion.
   d. the two-factor theory of emotion.

3. The facial feedback hypothesis states that
   a. information from facial muscles to the brain influences what emotion is experienced.
   b. people evaluate the emotional impact they have on someone by noting facial expressions.
   c. people tend to adopt the facial expressions shown by the people around them.
   d. the experience of an emotion determines facial expression.

4. Which of the following best represents the relationship between performance and level of arousal?
   a. As arousal increases, performance increases.
   b. As arousal increases, performance decreases.
   c. As arousal increases, performance decreases and then increases.
   d. As arousal increases, performance increases and then decreases.

5. The basic assumption behind the polygraph exam is that lying causes
   a. delayed response time to relevant questions.
   b. changes in vocal intensity during responses to relevant questions.
   c. increased emotionality which is accompanied by physiological reactions.
   d. a specific pattern of physiological activity that is distinct from other situations.

6. Dan believes that a specific emotion is experienced because a stimulus has caused specific physical changes to occur. Dan's view of emotion is most similar to
   a. the commonsense view.
   b. the James-Lange theory.
   c. the sympathetic magic theory.
   d. the two-factor theory.

7. According to the Cannon-Bard theory, emotions are
   a. the result of specific patterns of physiological arousal.
   b. determined by a cognitive appraisal process.
   c. determined by the feedback from the facial muscles.
   d. independent of the physiological changes.

8. The two-factor theory is very different from other approaches because it
   a. adds a cognitive component to the experience of emotion.
   b. places more emphasis on specific physiological patterns than other theories.
   c. proposes emotions precede any physiological changes.
   d. proposes that emotions are independent of physiological changes.

9. Which of the following is true concerning happiness?
   a. Happiness is explained in terms of sympathetic magic.
   b. Overjustification explains why rewards produce happiness.
   c. Happiness produces activity in the lateral hypothalamus.
   d. Happiness is greatly influenced by social comparisons and adaptation level.

MAKING FINAL PREPARATIONS

Complete these sections without consulting your book or notes.

Matching. Select the correct definition or description for each item. Answers are on page 270.

_____ 1. Cannon-Bard	**a.** set of factors that initiate and direct behavior
_____ 2. incentive motivation	**b.** unlearned behaviors controlled by triggering stimuli
_____ 3. refractory period	**c.** eating disorder in which binge eating occurs
_____ 4. James-Lange	**d.** external factor that exerts a pulling effect on actions
_____ 5. sexual orientation	**e.** cause of intrinsic motivation-reward relationship
_____ 6. polygraph	**f.** proposed need hierarchy
_____ 7. intrinsic motivation	**g.** self-motivated goal directed behavior
_____ 8. instinct	**h.** added cognitive evaluation to the emotion sequence
_____ 9. sympathetic magic	**i.** proposed body reactions precede and drive emotion
_____ 10. anorexia nervosa	**j.** eating disorder associated with very low weight
_____ 11. bulimina nervosa	**k.** physical and emotional responses are independent
_____ 12. Maslow	**l.** measurement of physiological activity to detect lies
_____ 13. plateau phase	**m.** idea that objects in contact acquire "like" properties
_____ 14. motivation	**n.** sexual/emotional attraction to same or different sex
_____ 15. overjustification	**o.** second stage in sexual response cycle
_____ 16. Schachter & Singer	**p.** time when stimulation can't result in sexual arousal

Short Essay Questions. Write a brief answer to each question. Sample answers are on page 270.

1. Compare incentive motivation and drive.

2. Describe how external factors influence eating behavior.

3. Discuss the possible determinants of the weight set point.

4. Compare the determinants of sexual behavior for animals and humans.

5. Describe the three basic components of all emotions.

6. Explain the basic assumption of polygraph exams, and discuss why polygraphs may be inaccurate.

7. Discuss how expectations and adaptation level influence happiness.

Multiple Choice Pretest 1. Select the one best response. Answers are on page 271.

1. The idea of human instincts has been replaced by the concept of
    a. incentives.
    b. intrinsic motivation.
    c. drive.
    d. emotion.

2. Ben just ate a large dinner and wishes he could discreetly loosen his belt, but when the dessert cart rolls by, he selects a beautiful piece of cheesecake. Taking the dessert is an example of the power of
    a. drives.
    b. instincts.
    c. incentives.
    d. needs.

3. Children will be most likely to show high achievement motivation and attempt to accomplish a task if
    a. they have a history of failing at the task, driving up their need to achieve.
    b. their parents show they value the task.
    c. they are never rewarded for their effort.
    d. they are working at the lowest levels of Maslow's hierarchy.

4. Scott has always volunteered to walk his neighbor's dog because he thinks it is fun. When his neighbor went on vacation, he paid Scott to walk the dog each day. According to research on intrinsic motivation, it is likely that when being paid, Scott found walking the dog to be
    a. more fun than before.
    b. as fun as before.
    c. less fun than before.
    d. less fun for a week, then more fun than before.

5. Deanna's parents are worried about her refusal to eat. She weighs 80 lbs., but still thinks she is too fat for a 5 ft-6 inch 17-year-old. A health professional should advise her parents that
    a. Deanna probably has anorexia nervosa, a serious eating disorder.
    b. Deanna probably has bulimia nervosa, a serious eating disorder.
    c. Deanna will begin eating again when she reaches her normal set point.
    d. Deanna is just going through a growth spurt that is nothing to worry about.

6. Of the following needs, the one that is most basic in Maslow's hierarchy and the first to be satisfied is
    a. self-actualization needs.
    b. belongingness needs.
    c. self-esteem needs.
    d. biological needs.

7. Destruction to the lateral hypothalamus causes
   a. abnormal sexual behavior.
   b. bulimia nervosa.
   c. loss of emotional response.
   d. reduction of eating and body weight.

8. You are likely to feel hungry and seek food when
   a. your glucose level decreases.
   b. insulin is released.
   c. your estrogen decreases.
   d. your pheromone level increases.

9. Brain areas that have been linked to the control of eating include the
   a. brainstem and hippocampus.
   b. cerebellum and pons.
   c. amygdala and midbrain.
   d. parietal lobe and occipital lobe.

10. A person's set point probably is determined by
    a. cultural attitudes.
    b. willpower.
    c. food preferences.
    d. genetics.

11. According to Masters and Johnson, increased heart rate and blood pressure and penile erection begins in
    a. the orgasmic phase.
    b. the resolution phase.
    c. the excitement phase.
    d. the plateau phase.

12. For humans, sexual motivation is best described as
    a. a hormone-based drive.
    b. incentive motivation.
    c. a process of self-actualization.
    d. a physiological need.

13. Compared to men, when exposed to sexually explicit images women
    a. are less likely to report sexual arousal, and show no physiological signs of arousal.
    b. are less likely to report sexual arousal, but show similar physiological arousal.
    c. are as likely to report sexual arousal, but show few physiological signs of arousal.
    d. are as likely to report sexual arousal, and show similar physiological arousal.

14. Autopsies on the brains of homosexual and heterosexual men found differences in the
    a. hypothalamus.
    b. hippocampus.
    c. frontal lobes.
    d. temporal lobes.

15. Dot's friend tells her, "Smile. You'll feel better." Her advice is consistent with the
    a. Cannon-Bard theory.
    b. the two-factor theory.
    c. the facial feedback hypothesis.
    d. the James-Lange theory.

16. Psychologists who believe that there are 4-6 basic emotions support their argument with
    a. twin studies showing identical emotional reactions to a stimulus.
    b. the fact that all babies show emotions very early.
    c. the cross-cultural data on recognition of facial expressions.
    d. the results of polygraph exams.

17. Firecrackers exploded behind Kim. To explain Kim's fear, the Cannon-Bard theory would suggest
    a. the firecrackers made Kim feel afraid, and being afraid makes her heart beat rapidly.
    b. the firecrackers made Kim feel afraid and made her heart beat rapidly.
    c. Kim felt afraid because she appraised the situation as dangerous.
    d. Kim was afraid because her heart was beating rapidly.

18. Most courts do not accept polygraph exams as evidence for all of the following reasons EXCEPT
    a. polygraph exams result in innocent people being declared liars.
    b. liars sometimes can trick the test.
    c. physiological reactions can occur for reasons other than lying.
    d. estimates of "truthful" physiological reactions cannot be obtained.

19. In Schachter & Singer's study, the subjects most likely to adopt the mood of the accomplice were
    a. the subjects given a stimulant and then told that the drug would cause arousal symptoms.
    b. the subjects given a stimulant but not told that the drug would cause arousal symptoms.
    c. the subjects given saline solution and then told that the "drug" would cause arousal symptoms.
    d. the subjects given saline solution and not told that the "drug" would cause arousal symptoms.

20. A snarling dog approached Rob suddenly. He began to sweat, his heart beat more rapidly, and his muscles tensed. According to the James-Lange theory, Rob first felt the emotion of fear
    a. right after seeing the dog and before physiological arousal began.
    b. at the same time as the physiological arousal began.
    c. right after the physiological arousal began.
    d. right after he evaluated or appraised the physiological arousal.

Multiple Choice Pretest 2. Select the one best response. Answers are on page 272.

1. Tom has weighed 250 lbs. all of his adult life. He lost 20 lbs. while sick one time, but was back up to 250 lbs. within a few weeks of getting well. Tom's experience is best explained by
   a. overjustification.
   b. Maslow's need hierarchy.
   c. the two-factor theory.
   d. set point theory.

2. A male stickleback fish sees a form with a red belly enter the area and immediately attacks. This will occur the first, and every other time a red-bellied form is seen. This behavior is an example of
   a. an instinct.
   b. a drive.
   c. incentive motivation.
   d. homeostasis.

3. Tad hasn't eaten in 12 hours. The psychological state that will cause him go to the pantry for food is
   a. a need.
   b. incentive motivation.
   c. a drive.
   d. intrinsic motivation.

4. Jill pulls on a sweater when she begins to feel chilly. Her behavior is best explained in terms of
   a. incentive motivation.
   b. instinct.
   c. set point.
   d. homeostasis.

5. School breakfast programs make sure children aren't hungry so that they will be interested and able to focus on learning and academic achievement. The view of motivation that is most similar to this is
   a. incentive motivation theory.
   b. Schachter & Singer's two-factor theory.
   c. Maslow's hierarchy of needs.
   d. intrinsic motivation theory.

6. Mandy frequently eats a half-gallon of ice cream, two bags of cookies, a bucket of fried chicken, half a cake and three bags of potato chips in one evening. Afraid of gaining weight, but unable to stop eating, she vomits and uses laxatives to get rid of the food. Mandy's behavior is characteristic of
   a. a lateral hypothalamic lesion or tumor.
   b. diabetes, an insufficiency of insulin.
   c. anorexia nervosa.
   d. bulimia nervosa.

7. In some cultures premarital sex is strictly forbidden, and married couples have sex essentially fully clothed. Other cultures encourage sexual experimentation and have no problems with nudity. According to Gagnon and Simon, these differences are best explained in terms of different
   a. hormones.
   b. genes.
   c. sexual scripts.
   d. sexual orientations.

8. Performing in front of an audience always increases arousal levels, but performing in a championship match increases arousal even more. Which performer is most likely to experience poorer performance in the championship than in non-championship competition?
   a. Becky, who has very low arousal under non-championship conditions.
   b. Gail, who has moderate arousal under non-championship conditions.
   c. Hattie, who has fairly high arousal under non-championship conditions.
   d. All of the performers are equally likely to experience poorer championship performance.

9. The reduction in intrinsic motivation when rewards are given may be due to people's perception that they perform a task because of the reward, rather than because they enjoy it. This represents
   a. overjustification.
   b. learned helplessness.
   c. self-actualization.
   d. adaptation.

10. Mona worked very hard to get As in school, practiced daily to become an expert pianist, and successfully ran for class President. Mona's internal drive to succeed best represents strong
    a. incentive motivation.
    b. basic needs.
    c. need for homeostasis.
    d. achievement motivation.

11. Leroy suddenly began eating a lot and gaining weight. In the unlikely event a brain tumor is to blame, we should suspect the tumor is in the
    a. midbrain.
    b. lateral hypothalamus.
    c. ventromedial hypothalamus.
    d. frontal lobe.

12. Ten minutes after he reached orgasm, Chuck is mentally responding to his partner's sexual advances, but his body isn't responding. Chuck's limitation is probably due to the fact that he
    a. is in the plateau phase of sexual response.
    b. is in the resolution phase of sexual response.
    c. is in the pre-excitement phase of sexual response.
    d. has depleted his testosterone supply.

13. Brain and twin studies are consistent with the idea that sexual orientation is partially determined by biological or genetic factors, but a cause-effect relationship has not been established because
    a. the brain and twin studies data are correlational.
    b. the brain and twin studies do not match other recent data that show no biological factor.
    c. not all of the identical twins have the same orientation.
    d. sexual orientation is too difficult to classify.

14. Which is LEAST likely to represent a male's sexual attitudes?
    a. Attractiveness is highly valued in the choice of a long-term partner.
    b. Sexual intercourse with someone known only briefly is not appealing.
    c. Younger mates are preferred.
    d. Short-term relationships are acceptable or desirable.

15. A rare disorder involving the facial nerves leaves the face expressionless. According to the facial feedback hypothesis, people with this disorder should
    a. be unable to recognize the facial expressions of other people.
    b. not require a cognitive interpretation before experiencing emotion.
    c. experience less emotion.
    d. not show social comparison effects.

16. Babies show a wide range of emotional expressions, and emotional facial expressions are identified across cultures. These data support the idea that
    a. there are 10 basic emotions.
    b. the expression of emotion has a biological or genetic component.
    c. cognitive appraisal is an important part of the emotional experience.
    d. feedback from facial muscles is used to interpret an emotional experience.

17. Hal was smiling and he said he felt unbelievably happy. The missing component of the emotion is
    a. a physiological response.
    b. a subjective experience.
    c. an expressive reaction.
    d. a cognitive reaction.

18. The James-Lange theory predicts that
    a. if physiological feedback is eliminated, emotions should be eliminated, or at least reduced.
    b. expectations about a stimulus or situation should influence the emotion experienced.
    c. fear will produce the same general pattern of physical changes as anger.
    d. physical changes will be slower to occur than the emotional experience.

19. Juan meets a woman as he emerges from climbing three flights of stairs. According to the two-factor theory, Juan will be most likely to report the emotion of sexual attraction or "love at first sight" if
    a. his physiological pattern is specific to love rather than exercise.
    b. he attributes his increased heart rate to the woman, rather than to the stairs.
    c. he receives feedback that he is smiling.
    d. he expects his heart rate to increase as a result of climbing the stairs.

20. Although Mia made a 60 on her paper, she is happy because other people made 50s. This supports the idea that happiness is influenced by
    a. adaptation level.
    b. social comparison.
    c. the relationship between arousal and performance.
    d. sympathetic magic.

LANGUAGE DEVELOPMENT GUIDE

Core Terms

This chapter will approach the subject of emotions and motivation *objectively;* that is, it will not refer to individual experiences, but to what people in general experience. Psychologists are interested in the *universality* of motivation and emotions -- the behaviors, facial expressions, and so on that are common to people all around the world. You will probably find yourself comparing what you read about emotions with your *subjective,* personal experience.

Idioms

p. 372	meltdown	step-by-step breakdown with dangerous results
p. 372	"fix"	a dose of an illegal drug
p. 372	junkie	drug addict
p. 373	shy away	move away to avoid
p. 381	optimal level	best level for good performance
p. 396	rates skyrocket	rates go up very high quickly
p. 398	blowing off steam	expressing anger, such as yelling
p. 399	amorous attentions	flirting, mating activities
p. 399	Holy Grail	a very valuable thing that is sought but not often found (refers to the cup Christ used at the Last Supper, which legendary knights went on quests to find)
p. 400	akin to contagion	like a communicable disease (for example, a cold virus)
p. 400	have no conception	have no idea
p. 400	notions	ideas

Word Parts

Here are some words that are made up of word parts, and that you can find in this chapter. After you've looked at these, you can look for others in the chapter that use the same word parts.

WORD	WORD PART IT USES	MEANING
compel	com = together pel, puls = drive, push, throw	to urge, force
consume	con = together sum = to take, use, waste	to use up
resist	re = again, back sist, stet, sta = to stand	to hold against, withstand
external	ext, extra = outer	outside

266

disrupt	dis = bad, not, apart rupt = to tear, break	to break apart
aversion	a = not, away vers, vert = to turn	strong dislike

Knowing the word parts listed above, you can also create the following words. You can get an idea of their meanings from the word parts they use.

divert	di+ vert	_____
dissatisfied	dis + sat	_____
consist	_____ + _____	to make up all together; to add up to
extrovert	_____ + _____	one who is turned outward; friendly person
repulsive	re + puls	_____

Pronunciation Assistance

p. 375	homeostasis	home-ee-o-stay'-sis	p. 385	obesity	o-bee'-si-tee
p. 381	ventromedial	ven-tro-mee'-dee-al	p. 397	polygraph	pol'-ee-graf

ANSWERS AND EXPLANATIONS

To find relevant material in your textbook, consult the pages cited with each answer. Also, PN and PT citations refer to modules in *PsychNow!* and *Psyk.trek* materials, respectively.

Mastering the Concepts

1. direct (p. 372)
2. physiological (p. 372)
3. subjective (p. 375)
4. Instincts (p. 374)
5. drive (p. 375)
6. homeostasis (p. 375)
7. Incentive (p. 375)
8. achievement (p. 376)
9. Intrinsic (p. 377)
10. control (p. 378)
11. reward (p. 378)
12. expected (p. 379)
13. hierarchy (p. 379)
14. Biological (p. 379)
15. self-actualization (p. 379)
16. glucose (p. 381)
17. Insulin (p. 381)
18. hypothalamus (p. 381)
19. ventromedial (p. 381)
20. lateral (p. 382)
21. brainstem (p. 382)
22. hippocampus (p. 382)
23. habits (p. 382)
24. set point (p. 384)
25. Genetic (p. 385)
26. metabolic (p. 385)
27. obesity (p. 385)
28. Anorexia (p. 386)
29. bulimia (p. 386)
30. binge (p. 386)
31. excitement (p. 388)
32. plateau (p. 388)
33. orgasmic (p. 388)
34. resolution (p. 388)
35. refractory (p. 388)
36. hormones (p. 389)
37. individual (p. 389)
38. pheromones (p. 390)
39. sexual scripts (p. 390)
40. short-term (p. 391)
41. orientation (p. 392)
42. Homosexuals (p. 392)
43. Heterosexuals (p. 392)
44. biological (p. 392)
45. hypothalamus (p. 392)
46. genetic (p. 393)
47. Correlational (p. 393)
48. physiological (p. 393)
49. subjective (p. 393)
50. surprise (p. 394)
51. facial (p. 391)
52. feedback (p. 397)
53. polygraph (p. 397)
54. positive (p. 398)
55. comparisons (p. 397)
56. disgust (p. 399)
57. James-Lange (p. 401)
58. reduction (p. 401)
59. Cannon-Bard (p. 402)
60. two-factor (p. 404)

Evaluating Your Progress

Preview & Activating Behavior

1. **b** a, c, & d. Wrong. Although human instincts might exist, the difficulty of identifying true instincts
(p. 374)   has caused them to lose favor as an explanation of human behavior.

2. **d** a. Wrong. An instinct is a characteristic behavioral response to an external stimulus.
(p. 375) b. Wrong. Emotions are not responses to internal physiological needs.
         c. Wrong. Homeostasis is the process by which the body maintains a steady state.

3. **b** a. Wrong. Drives involve physiological needs, incentives do not.
(p. 376) c. Wrong. Incentives can be learned, and drives are usually unlearned.
         d. Wrong. Incentives are external, and drives are usually internal.

4. **d** a. Wrong. This is a definition of achievement motivation.
(p. 375) b. Wrong. This is a definition of intrinsic motivation.
         c. Wrong. This is a definition of drive.

5. **c** a. Wrong. Self-actualization involves fulfilling your ultimate potential in life.
(p. 376) b. Wrong. Intrinsic motivation is self-motivated behavior, such as painting a picture for pleasure.
(PT8B)   d. Wrong. Homeostasis is the process by which the body maintains a stable state.

6. **a** b. Wrong. This is a theory of emotion, not motivation.
(p. 377) c. Wrong. There is no physiological imbalance here.
         d. Wrong. Drives are psychological states resulting from physiological needs.

7. **c** a. Wrong. Self-actualization and its position are not entirely accepted.
(p. 379) b. Wrong. Critics complain about the lack of clear definition and testability.
(PT10C) d. Wrong. Achievement is not given as the most important need in the hierarchy.

8. **a** b, c, & d. Wrong. Maslow used "self-actualization" to describe the state of fulfilling potential.
(p. 379)
(PN7A)

Meeting Biological Needs: Hunger and Eating

1. **c** a, b, & d. Wrong. Glucose levels are critical for controlling hunger.
(p. 381)
(PT8A)

2. **c** a. Wrong. The hippocampus might be involved in eating, but it wasn't the proposed satiety center.
(p. 381) b. Wrong. The brainstem might be involved in eating, but it wasn't the proposed satiety center.
         d. Wrong. The lateral hypothalamus was the proposed "start-up" center.

3. **d** a. Wrong. A glucose-insulin interaction influences eating, but it doesn't produce this effect.
(p. 384) b. Wrong. A set point might influence the amount eaten, but it doesn't produce this effect.
         c. Wrong. Homeostasis, the process of maintaining a steady state, is not related to this effect.

4. **b** a, c, & d. Wrong. Set point refers to a weight the body tries to maintain.
(p. 384)

5.   **c**   a & d.   Wrong.   Anorexia is most common in young women.
(p. 386)   b.   Wrong.   Binge eating is not common to anorexia. Self-starvation is.
(PT7D)

Meeting Biological Needs: Sexual Behavior

1.   **c**   a.   Wrong.   Even the absence of sex hormones does not necessarily prevent sexual behavior.
(p. 389)   b.   Wrong.   For humans, sexual behavior is primarily determined by personal control.
           d.   Wrong.   Hormone levels can reduce sexual behavior in some cases or increase it.

2.   **d**   a.   Wrong.   The plateau phase is the second phase.
(p. 388)   b.   Wrong.   The orgasmic phase is the third phase.
           c.   Wrong.   The resolution phase is the last phase.

3.   **b**   b, c, & d.   Wrong.   These are all opposite from the actual data.
(p. 391)

4.   **a**   b.   Wrong.   Pheromones are odor-producing chemicals, not hormones.
(p. 390)   c.   Wrong.   Pheromones are odor-producing chemicals, not tactile stimuli.
           d.   Wrong.   Pheromones may be a biological influence of sexual behavior, but not of orientation.

5.   **d**   a.   Wrong.   Sexual menu is not a relevant term.
(p. 390)   b.   Wrong.   Sexual orientations involve the type (sex) of sexual partner selected.
           c.   Wrong.   Instincts are not learned.

6.   **d**   a, b, & c.   Wrong.   Recent research does not confirm these hypotheses.
(p. 392)

Expressing and Experiencing Emotion

1.   **b**   a.   Wrong.   Her heart racing is the physiological response.
(p. 393)   c.   Wrong.   Her feeling of fear is the subjective experience.
(PT8C)   d.   Wrong.   There is no unconscious experience in emotion.

2.   **c**   a.   Wrong.   This hypothesis deals with influences on emotion, not with recognizing facial expressions.
(p. 394)   b.   Wrong.   This theory states physiological responses determine the emotion. Recognizing facial
                         expressions is not relevant.
           d.   Wrong.   The 2-factor theory requires an interpretation of a physiological reaction, but not cross-
                         cultural similarity in facial expression.

3.   **a**   b, c, & d.   Wrong.   These do not represent the facial feedback hypothesis, which states feedback
(p. 394)   from facial muscles is used to interpret the emotion being experienced.

4.   **d**   a.   Wrong.   At high levels of arousal, performance decreases.
(p. 396)   b.   Wrong.   Performance decreases only at high levels of arousal; it increases otherwise.
           c.   Wrong.   This is backward.

5.   **c**   a.   Wrong.   Physiological behavior, not response time is measured during a polygraph exam
(p. 397)   b.   Wrong.   Physiological behavior, not vocal intensity is measured during a polygraph exam.
           d.   Wrong.   Lying doesn't produce changes that are unlike the changes with other emotional events.

6.   **b**   a.   Wrong.   Commonsense view would say stimulus---> emotion---> physical changes.
(p. 401)   c.   Wrong.   Sympathetic magic is a concept to explain disgust when contamination is not a threat.
           d.   Wrong.   The two-factory theory includes a cognitive evaluation, which is absent here.

269

7. **d**   a. Wrong.   This is the James-Lange view.
  (p. 402)   b. Wrong.   This is the two-factor theory.
             c. Wrong.   This is the facial feedback hypothesis.

8. **a**   b. Wrong.   The James-Lange theory places most emphasis on physical change.
  (p. 404)   c. Wrong.   Two-factor theory has emotion following physical change.
  (PT8D)   d. Wrong.   This is the Cannon-Bard theory, not two-factor theory.

9. **d**   a. Wrong.   Sympathetic magic is a factor in disgust.
  (p. 398)   b. Wrong.   Overjustification is one possible factor in the effect of reward on intrinsic motivation.
             c. Wrong.   The lateral hypothalamus relates to eating behavior, not happiness.

MAKING FINAL PREPARATIONS

Matching

1. **k** (p. 402)	4. **i** (p. 401)	7. **g** (p. 377)	10. **j** (p. 386)	13. **o** (p. 388)	16. **h** (p. 404)
2. **d** (p. 375)	5. **n** (p. 392)	8. **b** (p. 374)	11. **c** (p. 386)	14. **a** (p. 372)	
3. **p** (p. 388)	6. **l** (p. 397)	9. **m** (p. 400)	12. **f** (p. 379)	15. **e** (p. 378)	

Short Essay Questions

1. A drive is a psychological state that arises in response to an internal physiological need and pushes the organism into action. Incentive motivation is an external factor that exerts a pulling effect on action. Thus, they differ both in origin and method of activation of behavior. (pp. 375-376)

2. External factors include food cues, eating habits, cultural influences, and social factors. Food cues may provide an incentive to eat even when physiological signals do not indicate hunger. Similarly, eating habits influence when and what we eat, and these are influenced by cultural and social factors. Eating is associated with social situations, and culture determines many attitudes about food. (pp. 382-383)

3. The weight set point is the standard weight the body tries to maintain and is possibly determined by genetically established metabolic rate and body fat. Metabolic rate controls how efficiently calories are utilized. The number of fat cells present varies and constrains weight gain and loss. (p. 384-385)

4. Hormones control animal sexual behavior but only minimally influence humans. Many animals mate during fertile periods, and their sexual behavior is highly specific in form, both determined by hormones. Some animals respond to pheromones, scents which activate sexual behavior. For humans, if hormones are absent, sexual activity often declines, but the normal rhythm of hormones exerts minimal changes in sexual activity. Humans control the timing and form of their sexual behavior. Pheromones exert no clear effect. (pp. 388-391)

5. Emotions involve (1) physiological reaction, an arousal manifest in changes in heart rate, blood pressure, etc.; (2) expressive reactions, such as facial expressions, postures, or vocalization; and (3) subjective reaction, internal thoughts and feelings of fear, sadness, etc. (pp. 372, 393)

6. Polygraph exams are based on the idea that lying leads to emotionality, which in turn produces increased physiological arousal that can be measured. Thus, by comparing responses to control and relevant questions, a lie can be inferred. However, polygraphs can be very inaccurate because they are easy to beat, and other factors besides lies can produce arousal, which may lead to false positive errors, to call the truth a lie. (p. 397)

7.   Happiness can be produced when expectations are exceeded, or can be eliminated when expectations are not met. How high one's expectations are affects the likelihood of being happy. People also become used to certain conditions, and deviations from that adaptation level produce changes in happiness. (pp. 398-399)

Multiple Choice Pretest 1

1. **c**   a. Wrong.   Incentives are external motivators, instincts and drives are internal.
    (p. 375)   b. Wrong.   Intrinsic motivation is self-motivation, not a response to some state or stimulus.
                d. Wrong.   Emotions can act as motivators, but they did not replace the concept of instinct.

2. **c**   a. Wrong.   Ben isn't hungry; there is no physiological need to eat.
    (p. 375)   b. Wrong.   Humans don't have a characteristic, unlearned response to pie.
                d. Wrong.   Needs are states of deprivation. Ben has just eaten and has no need for more food.

3. **b**   a. Wrong.   This reduces the chance they will try, even if they have high achievement motivation.
    (p. 377)   c. Wrong.   Rewards can reduce intrinsic motivation, but they can act as incentives for achievement.
    (PT8B)   d. Wrong.   The lowest levels concern bodily needs, not achievement.

4. **c**   a & b.   Wrong.   Expectation of rewards reduces intrinsic motivation.
    (p. 377)   d.   Wrong.   The reward will further decrease intrinsic motivation, not begin to have less effect.

5. **a**   b.   Wrong.   Bulimia is characterized by relatively stable weight, with binge eating and purging.
    (p. 386)   c & d.   Wrong.   Refusal to eat, excessive weight loss, and distorted body image describe anorexia.

6. **d**   a.   Wrong.   This is the last need to be addressed.
    (p. 379)   b & c.   Wrong.   These are some of the last needs to be addressed.

7. **d**   a. Wrong.   Other areas of the hypothalamus are important for sexual behavior.
    (p. 382)   b. Wrong.   Although weight loss occurs, it is not due to the binge-purge cycle of bulimia.
                c. Wrong.   The lateral hypothalamus is not involved in emotion.

8. **a**   b. Wrong.   Insulin is released in response to food intake, not hunger.
    (p. 381)   c. Wrong.   Estrogen is a female sex hormone and is not related to hunger.
                d. Wrong.   Pheromones are odors that influence sexual behaviors.

9. **a**   b, c, & d.   Wrong.   These areas are not involved in the control of eating.
    (p. 382)

10. **d**   a, b, & c.   Wrong.   These influence eating patterns, but not the set point.
    (p. 385)

11. **c**   a. Wrong.   This is the phase in which orgasm occurs, not the beginning of arousal.
    (p. 388)   b. Wrong.   During resolution, arousal subsides to normal. This is the last phase.
                d. Wrong.   The plateau phase follows initial arousal and includes changes related to reproduction.

12. **b**   a & d.   Wrong.   There is no real physiological need for sex, and hormones are not critical.
    (p. 390)   c.   Wrong.   Self-actualization does not involve sexual behavior.

13. **b**   a.   Wrong.   Women show similar physiological reactions to explicit material.
    (p. 390)   c & d.   Wrong.   Women are less likely to report being aroused by explicit material.

14. **a** b, c, & d. Wrong. An area in the hypothalamus was smaller in homosexuals than in heterosexuals.
(p. 392)

15. **c** a. Wrong. Key here is the idea that one's expression affects subjective experience of emotion, not that physiological and subjective components are simultaneous and independent.
(p. 394) b. Wrong. Key here is the idea that one's expression affects subjective experience, not that physiological responses are cognitively interpreted to yield a particular emotion.
 d. Wrong. Key here is the idea that one's expression affects subjective experience, not that specific patterns of physiological activity identify an emotion.

16. **c** a & b. Wrong. Data such as these would only support a biological origin, not 4-6 basic emotions.
(p. 394) d. Wrong. Polygraph data have no relation to the idea of 6 basic emotions.

17. **b** a. Wrong. This is the commonsense view.
(p. 402) c. Wrong. This is the two-factor view.
 d. Wrong. This is the James-Lange view.

18. **d** a, b, & c. Wrong. These are all problems. "Truthful" estimates are obtainable from measurements for control questions.
(p. 397)

19. **b** a. Wrong. Subjects not expecting arousal, but experiencing arousal, adopted the mood.
(p. 403) c & d. Wrong. Saline did not produce arousal, and thus, nothing to interpret as emotion.

20. **c** a. Wrong. This is the commonsense view. James-Lange uses stimulus--physical change--emotion.
(p. 401) b. Wrong. This is the Cannon-Bard theory. James-Lange uses stimulus--physical change--emotion.
 d. Wrong. This is the two-factor theory. James-Lange uses stimulus--physical change--emotion.

Multiple Choice Pretest 2

1. **d** a. Wrong. Overjustification explains the effect of reward on intrinsic motivation, not weight control.
(p. 384) b. Wrong. Maslow's hierarchy proposes motives are prioritized, but doesn't involve weight control.
 c. Wrong. The 2-factor theory is Spearman's theory of intelligence or Schachter & Singer's theory of emotion, not a theory of weight control.

2. **a** b. Wrong. Drives are responses to internal physiological needs. There is no need here.
(p. 374) c. Wrong. Incentive motivation doesn't produce the same response on all occasions.
 d. Wrong. Homeostasis is a process by which the body maintains a steady state.

3. **c** a. Wrong. A need (physiological) causes the drive (psychological) that gets him to look for food.
(p. 375) b. Wrong. Incentive motivation is an external factor "pulling" behavior, not a psychological state.
 c. Wrong. He seeks food because of a biological need. Intrinsic motivation isn't a response to a need.

4. **d** a. Wrong. The sweater is a means to an end (keeping warm), not the cause of the behavior.
(p. 375) b. Wrong. Sweaters do not naturally cause a person to put them on.
 d. Wrong. Set point relates to weight control, not temperature.

5. **c** a & d. Wrong. Incentive and intrinsic motivation do not emphasize satisfying basic needs first.
(p. 379) b. Wrong. Two-factor theory relates to emotion. Prioritizing needs is Maslow's idea.

6. **d** a. Wrong. Damage to the lateral hypothalamus would more likely cause her to quit eating.
(p. 386) b. Wrong. Diabetes would keep glucose high, leading to less hunger and less eating.
 c. Wrong. Anorexia nervosa involves self-starvation.

7. **c**   a. Wrong.   Hormones do not determine sexual attitudes or behaviors in humans.
    (p. 390)   b. Wrong.   Genes do not determine sexual attitudes.
                d. Wrong.   Sexual orientation relates to heterosexuality or homosexuality, not habits like these.

8. **c**   a. Wrong.   Increases from low arousal will probably not push arousal past optimal levels.
    (p. 396)   b. Wrong.   Increases from moderate arousal are less likely to hurt than increases from high levels.
                d. Wrong.   Performance increases as arousal moves from low to moderate, but then decreases.

9. **a**   b. Wrong.   Learned helplessness is giving up after repeated failure.
    (p. 378)   c.. Wrong.   Self-actualization is fulfilling one's potential performing a task.
                d. Wrong.   Adaptation relates to becoming accustomed to a particular situation.

10. **d**   a. Wrong.   Incentive motivation depends on external factors, but Mona's need to succeed is internal.
    (p. 376)   b. Wrong.   Basic needs include food, water, safety, not a need to succeed.
    (PT8B)   c. Wrong.   Homeostasis is a process of maintaining a steady state, not a need to succeed.

11. **c**   a & d. Wrong.   These areas do not control eating.
    (p. 381)   b.   Wrong.   Damage to this area usually results in reduction of intake and weight loss.

12. **b**   a. Wrong.   Stimulation produces arousal during the plateau phase. Key here is the recent orgasm.
    (p. 388)   c. Wrong.   This is not a true phase of sexual response. Key here is the recent orgasm.
                d. Wrong.   Sexual activity does not deplete testosterone. Key here is the recent orgasm.

13. **a**   b, c, & d. Wrong.   The brain and twin studies were correlational and can't prove cause-effect. Data
    (p. 393)   for other factors wouldn't eliminate biological factors as *partial* determinants.

14. **b**   a, c, & d. Wrong. These are all characteristic of male sexual attitudes.
    (p. 391)

15. **c**   a. Wrong.   Facial expression affects one's own experience, not the interpretation of others' emotions.
    (p. 394)   b. Wrong.   A lack of facial feedback would be more likely to increase the role of cognitive evaluation.
                d. Wrong.   Social comparison, using others' emotions to judge your own, doesn't rely on expression.

16. **b**   a. Wrong.   These data don't support a certain number of basic emotions, and 4-6, not 10, is accurate.
    (p. 394)   c. Wrong.   These data don't relate to the two-factor theory. Cognitive factors are not involved here.
                d. Wrong.   These data don't relate to facial feedback hypothesis. No mention of feedback is made.

17. **a**   b & d. Wrong.   Feeling happy is the subjective (or cognitive) reaction.
    (p. 393)   c.   Wrong.   Smiling is an expressive reaction.
    (PT8C)

18. **a**   b. Wrong.   This is predicted by the two-factor theory. James-Lange doesn't include expectations.
    (p. 401)   c. Wrong.   James-Lange predicts different physical responses for each different emotion.
                d. Wrong.   James-Lange has physical changes preceding emotion, not following emotion.

19. **b**   a. Wrong.   Two-factor theory doesn't require different physical patterns for different emotions.
    (p. 404)   c. Wrong.   Two-factor theory isn't based on facial expression feedback.
                d. Wrong.   Here, the heart rate would be attributed to the stairs, rather than attraction to a woman.

20. **b**   a. Wrong.   The issue isn't the frequency of getting low grades, but how the other people did.
    (p. 398)   c. Wrong.   Arousal was not an issue. The relationship of her grade to other people's was key.
                d. Wrong.   Sympathetic magic relates to acquiring similar properties, not comparative status.

CHAPTER 12: PERSONALITY

ESTABLISHING LEARNING GOALS

Use these learning goals as a preview of the chapter, a guide for active reading, and to evaluate your mastery of the material. Review the relevant goals as you begin and end your reading of each major section of the chapter.

I. Solve the practical problem of defining and measuring personality.
    A. Discuss how factor analysis is used to identify basic personality traits.
        1. Describe Cattell's source traits and Eysenck's superfactors.
        2. Describe the Big Five and explain why this approach is popular.
    B. Describe how Allport distinguished among cardinal, central, and secondary traits.
    C. Describe self-report inventories and projective personality tests.
        1. Describe three self-report inventories, how they are used, and their strengths and weaknesses.
        2. Compare projective tests to self-report inventories and identify their strengths and weaknesses.

II. Solve the practical problem of determining how personality develops.
    A. Describe Freud's psychodynamic theory of personality and mind.
        1. Define conscious, preconscious, and unconscious mind, and describe their roles.
        2. Define id, ego, and superego, and describe their relationship to each other and to behavior.
        3. Describe repression, denial, projection, sublimation, and reaction formation.
        4. Describe each psychosexual stage, and discuss the concept of fixation.
        5. Describe Jung's, Horney's, Adler's, and the current view of psychodynamic theory.
    B. Summarize and evaluate humanistic approaches to personality, including the specific proposals of Carl Rogers and Abraham Maslow.
        1. Compare the humanistic and psychodynamic approaches.
        2. Describe Roger's theory, and discuss the self-concept, positive regard, and congruence.
        3. Describe Maslow's theory, and discuss the role of self-actualization.
        4. Discuss the criticisms of the humanistic approach to personality.
    C. Describe social-cognitive theories of personality.
        1. Explain the role of classical and instrumental conditioning and observational learning.
        2. Describe how expectations and beliefs influence behavior or personality.
        3. Discuss the criticisms of the social-cognitive approach.

III. Solve the conceptual problem of resolving and person-situation debate.
    A. Define the person-situation debate, and discuss its components.
        1. Evaluate the evidence for within- and across-situation consistency.
        2. Define self-monitoring behavior.
    B. Discuss how genetic factors influence personality.

MASTERING THE MATERIAL

Preview & Conceptualizing and Measuring Personality (pp. 410-418)

Mastering the Vocabulary. Define or explain each of the following terms. To check your answers, consult the text pages listed.

1. personality (p. 410)

2. trait (p. 411)

3. trait theories (p. 412)

4. Big Five (p. 414)

5. cardinal traits (p. 415)

6. central traits (p. 416)

7. secondary traits (p. 416)

8. self-report inventories (p. 416)

9. projective personality test (p. 417)

Mastering the Concepts. Fill in the blanks to create a summary of the section. Answers are on page 293.

_____(1) is one's distinguishing pattern of psychological characteristics. Personality _____(2), tendencies to behave in a particular way, establish an identity. Three conceptual and practical problems are addressed: How should traits be conceptualized and measured? How do traits develop? Are traits independent of the environment?

Trait theories, systems for assessing individual _____(3), use a _____(4) approach in which responses on questionnaires are used to identify traits. _____(5) analysis identifies related behaviors that reflect a disposition or trait. Cattell identified 16 _____(6) traits that vary between two opposites (e.g., reserved-outgoing). Eysenck proposed three superfactors: extroversion, how sociable one is; _____(7), how moody or anxious; and psychoticism, how uncaring or cruel. Most psychologists support the _____(8) traits: extroversion, _____(9), conscientiousness, neuroticism, and openness to experience.   Allport, studying individuals rather than group data, proposed three levels of traits. _____(10) traits are very dominant traits. _____(11) traits are less dominant but enduring. Secondary traits are mostly situation-specific.

There are two main types of personality tests. _____(12) inventories are paper-and-pencil tests involving true-false questions or ratings. These include the 16 Personality Factor, which measures Cattell's 16 primary factors, the NEO-PI-R, which measures the Big 5, and the very popular _____(13), which is also used to diagnose disorders. Self-report inventories are _____(14) tests whose strengths are reliability, standardization, validity and ease of scoring. _____(15) tests, such as the Rorschach test and the _____(16), allow unrestricted responses, often to an ambiguous stimulus. Critics of projective tests cite poor reliability and validity. Critics of inventories cite subject bias and poor predictive validity.

Evaluating Your Progress. Select the one best response. Answers are on page 293. If you make any errors, reread the relevant material before proceeding.

1.   Cattell proposed 16 basic personality traits (timid--venturesome, relaxed--tense) he called
     a.   cardinal traits.
     b.   central traits.
     c.   source traits.
     d.   secondary traits.

2.   In Eysenck's trait approach, a person strong in neuroticism is likely to
     a.   be irritable and moody.
     b.   sociable and outgoing.
     c.   cooperative with others.
     d.   rude to other people.

3.   Currently, the most popular trait theory is
     a.   the Big 5 traits.
     b.   Eysenck's three superfactors.
     c.   Allport's trait theory.
     d.   Cattell's 16 factor theory.

4.   "Occasional" traits in Allport's theory are called
     a.   secondary traits.
     b.   source traits.
     c.   central traits.
     d.   cardinal traits.

5. Allport's trait theory was developed based on
   a. the factor analysis of tests from large groups of people.
   b. cross-cultural testing of groups of people with many languages.
   c. comparing the Rorschach test results of normal and disturbed groups.
   d. detailed studies of particular individuals.

6. All of the following are self-report inventories EXCEPT
   a. the MMPI.
   b. the NEO-PI-R.
   c. the Rorschach test.
   d. the 16 Personality Factor test.

7. Projective personality tests
   a. have very high validity and reliability.
   b. use a true-false or rating scale format in most cases.
   c. use an unstructured or ambiguous stimulus in most cases.
   d. use an objective scoring technique.

Determining How Personality Develops (pp. 471-433)

Mastering the Vocabulary. Define or explain each of the following terms. To check your answers, consult the text pages listed.

1. psychodynamic theory (p. 420)

2. conscious mind (p. 420)

3. preconscious mind (p. 420)

4. unconscious mind (p. 420)

5. id (p. 421)

6. superego (p. 421)

7. ego (p. 421)

8. defense mechanisms (p. 422)

9. repression (p. 422)

10. denial (p. 422)

11. rationalization (p. 422)

12. projection (p. 422)

13. reaction formation (p. 422)

14. sublimation (p. 423)

15. oral stage (p. 423)

16. anal stage (p. 423)

17. phallic stage (p. 423)

18. latency period (p. 424)

19. genital stage (p. 424)

20. collective unconscious (p. 425)

21. humanistic psychology (p. 426)

22. self-concept (p. 426)

23. positive regard (p. 426)

24. conditions of worth (p. 426)

25. incongruence (p. 427)

26. self-actualization (p. 427)

27. social-cognitive theories (p. 429)

28. locus of control (p. 430)

29. self-efficacy (p. 430)

30. reciprocal determinism (p. 431)

Mastering the Concepts. Fill in the blanks to create a summary of the section. Answers are on page 293.

Freud's _____(17) theory proposes behavior is influenced by unconscious forces, and that the mind includes the conscious mind, holding current thoughts, the _____(18) mind, containing inactive but accessible memories, and the _____(19) mind, containing memories, urges, and conflicts that are inaccessible, but still influence behavior. Items in the unconscious are revealed in the symbolic, or latent content, of _____(20).

Freud suggested personality has three parts. The _____(21), residing in the unconscious, is driven by innate urges and the need for immediate gratification. It operates by the _____(22) principle, without regard to morals. The _____(23) contains morals defined by parents and society and acts as a conscience. It follows an _____(24) principle. The _____(25) operates by the _____(26) principle. It tries to satisfy the id while staying within the limits set by the superego.

To reduce anxiety, the ego uses _____(27) mechanisms. The most important is _____(28), burying uncomfortable, often sexual, thoughts in the unconscious. In denial, a person refuses to believe anxiety producing facts, and rationalization explains away those facts. In _____(29) unacceptable ideas are attributed to others. Reaction formation involves transforming anxiety-producing thoughts into an _____(30) form of behavior (e.g., hate to floods of affection). In _____(31) unacceptable behaviors are channeled into socially acceptable forms.

Freud proposed psychosexual stages of development, each associated with an _____(32) zone of the body. In the first year, the _____(33) stage, pleasure is obtained by the mouth. The second year begins the _____(34) stage, and pleasure is obtained by passing feces. The _____(35) stage begins at age 3 and is focused on the genitals. At this time sexual feelings are directed toward the opposite sex parent, which causes the conflict of the _____(36) complex (boys) or Electra complex (girls).

Failure to resolve this conflict causes later sexual problems. After age 5 and until puberty, sexuality is suppressed, and the _____(37) stage focuses on friendships. At puberty, sexuality reemerges in an adult form in the _____(38) stage. Failure to satisfy the needs of a stage (or overindulgence) leads to a _____(39) and adult behavior characteristic of that childhood stage. An oral fixation retains excessive oral activities (e.g., smoking); anal fixation results in excessive neatness or messiness.

Adler, Jung, and Horney, disagreed with Freud's emphasis on sexuality. Adler viewed feelings of _____(40) as the force behind behavior. Jung replaced sexuality with a general life force and added the idea of a _____(41) unconscious that contains _____(42), symbols passed down through generations. Horney argued against the concept of penis envy and for a balanced view of women. Freud's theory has lost much of its influence, although some basic ideas, such as the impact of the conflict between personal and societal demands still are accepted. Criticisms include a lack of scientific rigor and testability, and continued concern about his view of women.

The _____(43) approach stresses people's positive qualities and potential for growth. Actions are influenced by the environment and a person's _____(44) of reality. Rogers stressed the need for a _____(45) self-concept which develops when _____(46) is given without conditions of worth. Maslow believed personality reflects the person's position in the need hierarchy. Inappropriate behavior results from being unable to satisfy basic needs and self-actualization. Critics argue humanistic theories are vague, incomplete, based on subjective data, and too optimistic, but this approach remains popular.

The social-_____(47) approach emphasizes experience and cognitive factors. Classically conditioned or reinforced behaviors become "traits." Modeling theories say traits come from _____(48) others' behavior, especially if the behavior is reinforced. The social-cognitive view also considers people's beliefs. Some people see outcomes as based on chance, an _____(49) locus of control, while others feel they control the outcome, an _____(50) locus of control. Feelings of competence, or _____(51) also effect behavior. Critics argue social-cognitive theories are insufficient and focus too much on the situation and too little on biological factors and the whole person.

Evaluating Your Progress. Select the one best response. Answers are on page 294. If you make any errors, reread the relevant material before proceeding.

1. According to Freud, the part of the mind that contains inactive, but accessible, thoughts is the
    a. preconscious mind.
    b. conscious mind.
    c. unconscious mind.
    d. collective unconscious mind.

2. According to Freud, the superego
   a. operates according to the reality principle.
   b. is located entirely in the unconscious mind.
   c. contains society's rules about right and wrong.
   d. desires immediate, total satisfaction of needs.

3. The defense mechanism of repression
   a. transforms an anxiety-producing desire into a behavior that expresses the opposite desire.
   b. channels an inappropriate behavior into a more socially appropriate one.
   c. attributes an unacceptable thought or desire to someone else.
   d. submerges troubling thoughts deep into the unconscious mind.

4. Each of Freud's stages of development are based on the
   a. body region that provides pleasure or sexual gratification.
   b. defense mechanism that the ego tends to employ the most.
   c. part of the personality that is dominant at that time (ego, id, superego).
   d. level of congruence that has been achieved for the self-concept at that time.

5. According to Freud, when the needs of a particular psychosexual stage are frustrated
   a. incongruence is likely to develop.
   b. a fixation will occur.
   c. the Oedipal complex will occur.
   d. the id will be overwhelmed by the superego.

6. Jung's archetypes are
   a. a general life force.
   b. mystical, inherited concepts.
   c. traits produced by reciprocal determinism.
   d. located in the personal unconscious.

7. Which of the following is false?
   a. Despite some criticism, Freud's theory gained influence during the past several decades.
   b. Many of the important and unique concepts in Freud's theory lack scientific rigor.
   c. Many of the important and unique concepts in Freud's theory are almost impossible to test.
   d. Freud's theory is very male-oriented and views women as weaker psychologically.

8. The theory that stresses the human's capacity for self-awareness, choice, responsibility and growth is
   a. the social-cognitive theory of personality.
   b. the humanistic theory of personality.
   c. the social learning theory of personality.
   d. the psychodynamic theory of personality.

9. The humanistic theorist, Carl Rogers, suggests that for a healthy personality to develop
   a. the Electra or Oedipal complex must be resolved.
   b. love should be given only when the person is acting appropriately.
   c. the self-concept must be congruent.
   d. conditions of worth must be present.

10. The social-cognitive approach to personality emphasizes
   a. self-actualization.
   b. biological urges that drive behavior.
   c. learning and expectations.
   d. the innate goodness of human nature.

11. After watching the baseball team win the game on a double-play, B.J. said, "I don't think I'd ever want to be a professional athlete. Whether you win or lose is a matter of luck. You can practice all you want and be the best player, but if the other guy is luckier, he wins the game." B.J. would be described as having
   a. high self-efficacy.
   b. internal locus of control.
   c. unmet conditions of worth.
   d. external locus of control.

Resolving the Person-Situation Debate (pp. 433-437)

Mastering the Vocabulary. Define or explain each of the following terms. To check your answers, consult the text pages listed.

1. person-situation debate (p. 433)

2. self-monitoring (p. 433)

Mastering the Concepts. Fill in the blanks to create a summary of the section. Answers are on page 293.

The person-situation debate involves the question of whether behavior is _____ (52) across situations, as a definition of personality based on enduring traits requires. Mischel found behavior was fairly _____ (53) across situations. Within similar situations, Hartshorne & May found consistent behavior, supporting a social-cognitive view. Apparent inconsistency might be due to the number of observations, or it might reflect a personality trait, _____ (54). Those high in this trait monitor the situation and change their behavior to fit it; those low in the trait act consistently regardless of the context. Self-monitoring may be associated with good _____ (55) performance and position in social networks. Most psychologists assume both the situation and the person interact to produce behavior. Certain situations compel inconsistency; others allow consistency.

Twin studies of personality traits support a _____ (56) factor. Although the environment is influential, genetic influences are also very important, at least for some traits. This allows enduring traits.

Evaluating Your Progress. Select the one best response. Answers are on page 294. If you make any errors, reread the relevant material before proceeding.

1. The person-situation debate involves the basic question of whether
    a. behavior is consistent across situations.
    b. personality is innate or learned.
    c. self-monitoring is a genetic trait or a learned trait.
    d. personality tests reflect the conscious or unconscious aspects of the mind.

2. Mischel's research on the consistency of behavior found
    a. weak correlations for the MMPI profiles of identical twins.
    b. weak correlations for behavior across situations.
    c. strong correlations for behavior across situatuions, but only for the Big 5 traits.
    d. strong correlations for behavior across situations for Cattel's 16 source traits.

3. People who evaluate the situation and change their behavior to fit it
    a. are high self-monitors.
    b. are low self-monitors.
    c. have an internal locus of control.
    d. have an external locus of control.

4. Twin studies suggest that personality traits are determined
    a. entirely by genetics.
    b. entirely by the environment or experience.
    c. by both the environment and genetics, but genetics probably play a greater role.
    d. by both the environment and genetics, with each equally important.

MAKING FINAL PREPARATIONS

Complete these sections without consulting your book or notes. For a more accurate estimate of how well you know this material, wait at least a day or two after studying the chapter before working on the questions. Some material you "know" immediately after working with the chapter will be quickly forgotten. Immediate tests will overestimate what you know well.

Short Essay Questions. Write a brief answer for each question. Sample answers are on page 295.

1. Compare source traits and superfactors.

2. Compare projective personality tests and self-report inventories.

3. Explain the Oedipal and Electra complexes and their role in personality development.

4. Compare the psychodynamic and humanistic views of personality.

5. Explain Ron's very quiet personality in terms of operant conditioning and modeling.

6. Discuss the criticism of the social-cognitive approach to personality and behavior.

7. Explain how psychologists resolve the person-situation debate.

Matching. Select the correct definition or matching accomplishment for each. Answers are on page 295.

_____ 1. Karen Horney
_____ 2. Raymond Cattell
_____ 3. Gordon Allport
_____ 4. Alfred Adler
_____ 5. Hans Eysenck
_____ 6. Carl Jung
_____ 7. Walter Mischel
_____ 8. self-efficacy
_____ 9. Abraham Maslow
_____ 10. Carl Rogers
_____ 11. Sigmund Freud
_____ 12. Rorschach
_____ 13. Electra complex
_____ 14. positive regard
_____ 15. reciprocal determinism
_____ 16. conditions of worth

a. found 16 source traits of personality
b. proposed self-actualization
c. proposed cardinal, central, & secondary traits
d. added collective unconscious
e. beliefs about our own ability
f. expectations people believe others place on them
g. girl's anxiety over sexual attraction to father
h. beliefs, behavior, environment affect what's learned
i. idea that people value others' approval
j. found three trait superfactors of personality
k. stressed the self-concept
l. found inconsistency of behavior across situations
m. proposed fixation and psychosexual stages
n. projective personality test
o. argued against idea of penis envy in women
p. proposed inferiority complex

Multiple Choice Pretest 1. Select the one best response. Answers are on page 296.

1. Beth completed a personality inventory intended to identify "normal" personality traits. The test assessed the dimensions of reserved vs. outgoing, controlled vs. uncontrolled, and others. The test probably was the
   a. Rorschach test.
   b. 16 Personality Factor test.
   c. MMPI (Minnesota Multiphasic Personality Inventory).
   d. NEO-PI-R.

2. The Big 5 traits are extroversion, neuroticism, openness to experience, agreeableness, and
   a. conscientiousness.
   b. psychoticism.
   c. hysteria.
   d. intelligence.

3. Allport proposed that most people may be described in terms of 5-10 representative traits known as
   a. cardinal traits.
   b. source traits.
   c. secondary traits.
   d. central traits.

4. Jerry is telling a story about a rather ambiguous picture he was shown. He is taking
   a. the 16 Personality Factor test.
   b. the MMPI.
   c. a self-report personality inventory.
   d. a projective test.

5. Critics of self-report inventories such as the MMPI have complained that
   a. it is easy for subjects to bias their answers to make themselves look good.
   b. the scoring procedures are much too subjective.
   c. two people scoring the same test often give different interpretations.
   d. they allow too much freedom in the person's response.

6. Tom feels anxious anytime he is out in public, but he can't figure out why. According to Freud, Tom's anxiety probably originates with some past conflict now hidden in
   a. the preconscious mind.
   b the unconscious mind.
   c. the superego.
   d. the reaction formation.

7. As a young boy, Rick would spy on the girls in locker rooms and peep in neighbors' windows to satisfy his need to look at female bodies. As an adult, Rick is a professional photographer, a profession that allows him great opportunities to look at beautiful women. Freud might suggest that his choice of profession is an example of the defense mechanism of
   a. repression.
   b. sublimation.
   c. reaction formation.
   d. projection.

8. According to Freud, the id
   a. uses defense mechanisms to reduce anxiety produced by the superego.
   b. develops from experience with parents and society.
   c. follows the idealistic principle.
   d. seeks immediate satisfaction of animalistic urges.

9. Bill, age 21, is a true slob. His sink is always full of dirty dishes, and his apartment is filled with trash. Freud would probably suggest that Bill is fixated at
   a. the oral stage.
   b. the anal stage.
   c. the phallic stage.
   d. the latency stage.

10. According to Freud's psychosexual stages view of development, children from about age 6 to puberty are in
    a the phallic stage and are undergoing the Oedipal or Electra complex.
    b. the genital stage and are deriving sexual pleasure more directly with the opposite sex.
    c. the latency stage and are forming solid friendships rather than seeking sexual gratification.
    d. the anal stage and are deriving pleasure from expelling or retaining feces.

11. Adler proposed that the important factor in abnormal personality development is
    a. developing irrational, rather than rational, beliefs.
    b. developing incongruence and conditions of worth during childhood.
    c. how people deal with a basic sense of inferiority.
    d. having many models of unhealthy personalities during childhood.

12. Karen Horney disagreed with Freud's view that women are dissatisfied with their sex and that they have
    a. the Oedipus complex.
    b. weak superegos.
    c. an inferiority complex.
    d. penis envy.

13. Carl Rogers, the humanistic theorist, believes that people have an inborn need for
    a. conditions of worth.
    b. incongruence.
    c. positive regard.
    d. defense mechanisms.

14. The view that personality traits are influenced by genetic factors is supported by higher correlations on the MMPI for
    a. identical twins reared together than for identical twins reared apart.
    b. identical twins reared apart than for fraternal twins reared together.
    c. fraternal twins reared together than for fraternal twins reared apart.
    d. fraternal twins reared apart than for identical twins reared apart.

15. According to Maslow, people are inherently good and only act aggressively or unkindly when
    a. they have reached self-actualization.
    b. they have not satisfied their basic survival needs.
    c. the conflict between the id and superego gets out of control.
    d. they have been reinforced for this behavior.

16. The humanistic view of personality and behavior has been criticized for all of the following EXCEPT
    a. proposing humans have control over their behavior, rather than being driven by animalistic urges.
    b. the fact that many of the concepts in their theories are vague and not clearly developed.
    c. the problem of testing a theory that emphasizes subjective experiences.
    d. the highly optimistic view that all humans will achieve lofty goals if not blocked in their pursuit.

17. To explain Ted's very aggressive personality, a social-cognitive theorist probably would suggest that
    a. Ted learned to be aggressive by being reinforced for aggression.
    b. Ted's natural biological inheritance includes strong urges to be aggressive.
    c. Ted has been frustrated in his attempt to reach full self-actualization.
    d. Ted's self concept is incongruent, leading to feelings of conflict.

18. The idea that beliefs, behavior, and the environment interact to shape what is learned from experience is
    a. self-efficacy.
    b. self-actualization.
    c. reciprocal determinism.
    d. conditions of worth.

19. Based on Hartshorne and May's research on dishonesty, if Kim stole a dollar from a classmate
    a. Kim will probably steal money from another classmate if given the opportunity.
    b. Kim will probably steal again and is likely to cheat on tests at school.
    c. Kim will show dishonest behavior in all aspects of life from childhood to adulthood.
    d. Kim is no more likely to steal again or show dishonesty in any aspect of life than anybody else.

20. Self-monitoring behavior may help explain.
    a. whether genetic background or experience is most critical in personality development.
    b. why different theorists propose very different numbers of personality traits.
    c. why mental disorders develop.
    d. patterns of behavioral consistency or inconsistency.

Multiple Choice Pretest 2. Select the one best response. Answers are on page 297.

1. Marisha is competitive in every aspect of her life. She had to be first in her class, go to the best school, win every game, and have the nicest car. She feels badly if anybody beats her at anything. Marisha's competitiveness is characteristic of Allport's concept of
    a. a primary trait
    b. a cardinal trait.
    c. a secondary trait.
    d. a central trait.

2. "How can you use that test?" Ed asked. "Don't you know that two psychologists are probably going to give two different interpretations, and the validity is questionable?" The test probably is
    a. the 16 Personality Factor.
    b. the Rorschach test.
    c. the NEO-PI-R.
    d. the MMPI.

3. Harry is carefree, relaxed, and stable. In Eysenck's view, Harry is low in
   a. extroversion.
   b. neuroticism.
   c. conscientiousness.
   d. psychoticism.

4. The Big 5 traits are more popular than Cattell's or Eysenck's traits because the Big 5
   a. aren't sex-biased and the Cattell's and Eysenck's approaches are biased.
   b. consistently have been found in many cultures and using many languages.
   c. were identified by studying individuals instead of using factor analysis of group data.
   d. give a more specific, detailed description of personality than either Cattell's or Eysenck's traits.

5. To diagnose Fritz's psychological problem, a psychologist is most likely to have him take
   a. the MMPI.
   b. the 16 Personality Factor test.
   c. the NEO-PI-R.
   d. any of the above; all are primarily used to diagnose mental disorders.

6. Sociopaths are sometimes described as having no conscience or morality. Freud would say that sociopaths lack
   a. an ego.
   b. and id.
   c. a superego.
   d. a libido.

7. Claire was sexually abused 10 years ago. She hasn't thought about it in years. However, she can describe what happened asked a question about it. Claire's memory of her abuse was kept in her
   a. unconscious mind.
   b. preconscious mind.
   c. collective unconscious.
   d. reaction formation.

8. Roy, age 4, has unconscious sexual feelings for his mother. Roy is currently in Freud's
   a. oral stage.
   b. genital stage.
   c. anal stage.
   d. phallic stage.

9. Jung proposed that the collective unconscious contains
   a. all the forbidden desires and traumas accumulated over the person's life.
   b. the ego and its defense mechanisms.
   c. a driving force to overcome inferiority and to achieve superiority.
   d. archetypes, symbols of enduring concepts passed from one generation to the next.

10. The aspect of Freud's psychodynamic theory that is most accepted today is
    a. the important role of repression.
    b. the concept of penis envy.
    c. the impact of the need to satisfy biological processes and the demands of society.
    d. his views on the nature and role of human sexuality.

11. Lester is always accusing his wife of being attracted to other men, but in reality, it is Lester who has frequent thoughts about having affairs with other women. Freud might suggest that Lester is dealing with the anxiety that these unacceptable wishes create by using the defense mechanism of
    a. repression.
    b. sublimation.
    c. projection.
    d. reaction formation.

12. Tanisha has undergone a peak experience that has allowed her to clearly understand her place in the universe and the meaning of her existence. Maslow would say she has
    a. developed strong conditions of worth.
    b. reached an internal locus of control.
    c. attained self-actualization.
    d. found her collective unconscious.

13. Cal thinks he is very smart and creative, but in college he has gotten mediocre grades and has gotten no praise for his papers or presentations. Carl Rogers might predict Cal will become anxious because of
    a. incongruence.
    b. the elimination of conditions of worth.
    c. self-actualization.
    d. high self-efficacy.

14. Dr. Geltic believes personalities are made, not born. That is, a specific personality is the result of conditioning and an interpretation of how the world works. Dr. Geltic's view is most similar to that of
    a. psychodynamic theory.
    b. humanistic theory.
    c. neo-Freudian theory.
    d. social-cognitive theory.

15. A humanistic theorist would agree with all of the following EXCEPT:
    a. Behavior is influenced by the individual's own view of the world.
    b. The environment influences the growth process, but it cannot stop it entirely.
    c. Every person is a unique and individual whole.
    d. Behavior is motivated primarily by unconscious, biological urges.

16. Lee is very nervous about her promotion. She's not sure she can handle the job. Lee seems to have
    a. an internal locus of control.
    b. an external locus of control.
    c. low self-efficacy.
    d. high self-efficacy.

17. The person-situation debate is important for personality theory because
    a. personality is defined in terms of enduring (consistent) psychological characteristics.
    b. none of the current theories have a component that suggests consistent behavior should occur.
    c. personality theories propose factors that supposedly apply to all people, not just a few.
    d. personality theories should explain individual differences, not behavior common to everyone.

18. May believes business success is determined by how hard people work. May has
    a. low self-efficacy.
    b. high self-efficacy.
    c. internal locus of control.
    d. external locus of control.

19. The person most likely to be a low self-monitor is
    a. Ben, who thinks he passed the chemistry test because he worked very hard to learn the material.
    b. Lynn, who dresses conservatively at work, but dresses in wild outfits when going out socially.
    c. Eva, who is as loud and boisterous when dining at a fancy restaurant as when playing racquetball.
    d. Mort, who is very insecure and tries to please whomever he is around at the moment.

20. The social-cognitive theory has been criticized because it
    a. overemphasizes the role of biological and genetic determinants of personality.
    b. tends to neglect the individual as a whole and emphasizes the reactions to specific situations.
    c. doesn't consider the role of operant and classical conditioning as a determinant of personality.
    d. is essentially scientifically untestable.

LANGUAGE DEVELOPMENT GUIDE

Core Terms

In the lectures on this chapter and those that follow, you are likely to hear several related terms that all have to do with a way of organizing ideas. First of all, this process of organizing and classifying ideas can be called 'creating a *taxonomy*.' A familiar taxonomy might be the one that you learned in biology class, classifying different organisms into species. To explain complex concepts like personality (or intelligence or development) we construct a *model* -- a tentative description that shows all the parts we know about and how they relate. There are different kinds of models. One kind is a *hierarchy*, a sort of pyramid or stair-step which has the most basic element at the bottom, and climbs to the more rare or special elements. Maslow's hierarchy works this way. So does a hierarchy of people in a business, or a school. A second common kind of model is a *matrix*. A matrix is a set of boxes arranged in rows and columns -- you might call it a chart. The matrix has a vertical *axis* and a horizontal axis, and it allows you to neatly classify things in relation to one another; you just sort them into the cell to which they belong. Imagine a chart that has 'height' along one side and 'weight' along the bottom. You could put each of your friends into a box between those lines, depending upon their height and weight. The plural of axis is *axes,* and they are also sometimes called *dimensions.*

By the way, using models is a terrific way to study. Sometimes the models are already drawn for you, in the illustrations in the book. That's almost a shame, because it is so helpful to draw them for yourself. To check whether you really understand a concept in the book, you might want to try to reproduce a model that has been described and drawn for you -- such as Freud's model of the personality, or Maslow's hierarchy of needs. How well you do at filling in the various parts will show you exactly what you know well, and where you need to do a little more studying. Try it!

Idioms

p. 410	strict sensibilities	very strong sense of what is proper
p. 410	smoking ebullition	boiling activity
p. 410	thesis	main idea
p. 410	dark side of their nature	unpleasant, evil, or animal-like part of their personality
p. 412	brooding	worrying, especially for a long time, without action
p. 412	an opposing pole	an opposite
p. 420	the nineteenth century	the 1800s
p. 422	rears its ugly head	shows itself
p. 422	dark recesses	back corners; hidden places
p. 422	harboring	keeping, holding
p. 422	anti-Semite	one who hates Jews
p. 424	coining	making for the first time
p. 424	intellectual heir	someone who will carry on one's ideas
p. 433	strikes at the core of	gets at the most important part of
p. 434	chameleon-like	able to change one's appearance; able to change one's behavior to fit in or meet expectations (refers to a lizard that can change its body color for camouflage)

Word Parts

Here are some words that are made up of word parts, and that you can find in this chapter. After you've looked at these, you can look for others in the chapter that use the same word parts.

WORD	WORD PART IT USES	MEANING
psychodynamic	psych = mind dyna, dyno = power	the actions of the mind; that which powers the mind
controversial	contra, contro = against vers, vert = to turn	a dispute; raising arguments against

infer	in = in, into fer = bring into, bear, yield	to carry over a truth from one point to another
presumed	pre = before sum = bring together, add, take	to take for granted; assume to be true
intermediate	inter = between med = middle	being or happening in the middle between two ends
irrational	ir, il, im, in = not rat, ratio = thought	unreasonable, illogical
proposed	pro = before, forth pos = to put	to suggest, put forward
erogenous	ero = sexual love gen = birth, race, kind, origin	coming from sexual love
retention	re = again, back tent, tain = to hold	to hold back
contradict	contra = against dict = to say	to say the opposite as another says
constrain	con = together strain = to bind	to limit freedom, confine

Knowing the word parts listed above, you can also create the following words. You can get an idea of their meanings from the word parts they use.

psychogenic	psych + gen	_____
restrain	_____ + _____	to hold back, to prevent from further movement
prefer	pre + fer	_____
invert	_____ + _____	to turn over; to change into the opposite direction
interpose	inter + pos	_____
mediate	_____	to stand between, to help opposites connect

Pronunciation

p. 420   ego   ee'-go   p. 425   efficacy   eff'-i-kuh-see

ANSWERS & EXPLANATIONS

To find relevant material in your textbook, consult the pages cited with each answer. Also, PN and PT citations refer to modules in *PsychNow!* and *Psyk.trek* materials, respectively.

Mastering the Concepts

1. Personality (p. 410)	15. Projective (p. 417)	29. projection (p. 422)	43. humanistic (p. 426)
2. traits (p. 411)	16. TAT (p. 418)	30. opposite (p. 422)	44. interpretation (p. 426)
3. differences (p. 412)	17. psychodynamic (p. 420)	31. sublimation (p. 423)	45. congruent (p. 427)
4. psychometric (p. 412)	18. preconscious (p. 420)	32. erogenous (p.423)	46. positive regard (p. 426)
5. Factor (p. 412)	19. unconscious (p. 420)	33. oral (p. 423)	47. cognitive (p. 429)
6. source (p. 412)	20. dreams (p. 420)	34. anal (p. 423)	48. modeling (p. 430)
7. neuroticism (p. 413)	21. id (p. 421)	35. phallic (p. 423)	49. external (p. 430)
8. Big 5 (p. 414)	22. pleasure (p. 421)	36. Oedipus (p. 424)	50. internal (p. 430)
9. agreeableness (p. 414)	23. superego (p. 421)	37. latency (p. 424)	51. self-efficacy (p. 430)
10. Cardinal (p. 415)	24. idealistic (p. 421)	38. genital (p. 424)	52. consistent (p. 434)
11. Central (p. 416)	25. ego (p. 421)	39. fixation (p. 424)	53. inconsistent (p. 434)
12. Self-report (p. 416)	26. reality (p. 421)	40. inferiority (p. 424)	54. self-monitoring (p. 434)
13. MMPI (p. 416)	27. defense (p. 422)	41. collective (p. 425)	55. job (p. 435)
14. objective (p. 417)	28. repression (p. 422)	42. archetypes (p. 425)	56. genetic (p. 436)

Evaluating Your Progress

Preview & Conceptualizing and Measuring Personality

1. **c**   a, b, & d.   Wrong.   These are Allport's types of traits.
   (p. 412)

2. **a**   b.   Wrong.   This relates to the extroversion factor.
   (p. 413)   c & d.   Wrong.   These relate to the psychoticism factor.

3. **a**   b, c, & d.   Wrong.   These are not the most popular.
   (p. 413)

4. **a**   b. Wrong.   Source traits are Cattell's idea.
   (p. 416)   c. Wrong.   Central traits are "representative" traits.
   (PN7A)   d. Wrong.   Cardinal traits are "dominant" traits.

5. **d**   a, b, & c.   Wrong.   Allport used an ideographic (case study) approach, not group data.
   (p. 415)

6. **c**   a, b, & d.   Wrong.   These are self-report inventories; the Rorschach is a projective test.
   (p. 418)

7. **c**   a. Wrong.   The validity and reliability have been questioned.
(p. 417)   b. Wrong.   Self-report personality inventories (objective tests) use these formats, not projective tests.
(PT7A)   d. Wrong.   Self-report inventories are scored objectively. Projective tests use subjective scoring.

Determining How Personality Develops

1. **a**   b. Wrong.   The conscious mind has active, current thoughts.
(p. 420)   c. Wrong.   The unconscious contains only inaccessible information.
           d. Wrong.   The collective unconscious is Jung's idea, and it is inaccessible.

2. **c**   a.   Wrong.   This answer describes the ego.
(p. 421)   b & d.   Wrong.   These answers describe the id.
(PN7A)

3. **d**   a. Wrong.   This is reaction formation. Repression pushes forbidden desires into the unconscious.
(p. 422)   b. Wrong.   This is sublimation. Repression pushes forbidden desires into the unconscious.
(PT10A)   c. Wrong.   This is projection. Repression pushes forbidden desires into the unconscious.

4. **a**   b, c, & d. Wrong.   Freud proposed psychosexual stages, based on the part of the body from which
(p. 423)   sexual pleasure is derived at a particular time.

5. **b**   a. Wrong.   Incongruence is a term from humanistic personality theories.
(p. 424)   c. Wrong.   Freud believed all boys face the Oedipal complex during the phallic period.
           d. Wrong.   Failure to satisfy needs results in fixation, not a strong superego.

6. **b**   a. Wrong.   Jung preferred a general life force to Freud's sexual one, but archetypes are not a life force.
(p. 425)   c. Wrong.   This is an interaction of belief, behavior, and environment in social-cognitive theory.
           d. Wrong.   Archetypes are found in the collective unconscious, not the personal unconscious.

7. **a**   b, c, & d. Wrong.   These are all true, but Freud's theory has *lost* influence.
(p. 425)

8. **b**   a. Wrong.   This approach stresses learning and thought. Humanistic theory stresses growth.
(p. 426)   c. Wrong.   This approach stresses observational learning. Humanistic theory stresses growth.
           d. Wrong.   Freud's theory takes a negative, deterministic view. Humanistic theory stresses growth.

9. **c**   a. Wrong.   This is a Freudian concept, not humanistic.
(p. 427)   b. Wrong.   This describes conditional love, which is not healthy.
           d. Wrong.   Conditions of worth lead to an incongruent self-concept, an unhealthy situation.

10. **c**   a & d.   Wrong.   These are stressed in humanistic theories.
(p. 429)   b.   Wrong.   This is a Freudian view.

11. **d**   a. Wrong.   Key here is the feeling about luck vs. effort (locus of control), not competency.
(p. 430)   b. Wrong.   Internal locus of control would emphasize the importance of one's own effort, not luck.
           c. Wrong.   Key here is luck vs. effort (locus of control), not others' expectations.

Resolving the Person-Situation Debate

1. **a**   b. Wrong.   The person-situation debate involves behavioral consistency and does not involve the
(p. 434)   issue of genetic vs. learned influences.
           c. Wrong.   Self-monitoring has been suggested as a concept that might help explain inconsistency of
                         behavior, but it is not the basic issue in the debate.
           d. Wrong.   The person-situation debate involves behavioral consistency, not levels of consciousness.

2. **b**   a. Wrong.   Mischel examined behavior across situations, not twin MMPI data.
   (p. 434)   c. Wrong.   Mischel didn't differentiate the Big 5 from other possible traits.
               d. Wrong.   Mischel didn't differentiate source traits from other possible traits.

3. **a**   b.   Wrong.   Low self-monitors do not alter their behavior to fit a situation.
   (p. 434)   c & d.   Wrong.   Locus of control is the perceived source of control, not behavioral consistencey.

4. **c**   a. Wrong.   Fraternal twins reared apart were less similar than fraternal twins reared together.
   (p. 437)   b. Wrong.   Identical twins reared apart were more similar than fraternal twins reared together.
   (PT10D)   d. Wrong.   For some traits at least, identical twins were no less similar if raised apart.

MAKING FINAL PREPARATIONS

Short Essay Questions

1. Cattell's source traits are 16 trait dimensions that account for individual differences in behavior. Eysenck, using a different version of factor analysis found 3 superfactors (neuroticism, psychoticism, and extroversion) that he felt described the basics of personality. Source traits provide a finer analysis than superfactors. (pp. 412-413)

2. Projective tests do not constrain the possible answers and often involve ambiguous stimuli, allowing the unconscious to project its contents onto the answer. Interpretation of responses is partly subjective. Self-report inventories ask the individual to rate themselves. Questions are direct and involve limited response options (true-false, etc.). Scoring is objective, but subjects may bias their answers to look good. (pp. 416-418)

3. Freud felt that children in the phallic stage had unconscious sexual desires for the opposite sex parent. This causes anxiety known as the Oedipus complex for boys and the Electra complex for girls. Failure to resolve this conflict results in sexual problems in adulthood. (p. 424)

4. The psychodynamic view is based on negative, animalistic biological urges, conflicts, and anxiety. Unconscious sexuality and aggression battle the need to be moral. The humanistic view is a positive view of people that stresses their innate goodness, control over their behavior, self-awareness, and potential for growth. In this view, people strive to achieve their full potential. (p. 426)

5. An instrumental conditioning view of personality would suggest that Ron often had been reinforced when quiet in the past. A modeling (observational learning) approach would add that he might have observed another person's quiet behavior and its consequences. In both cases, he learned that the consequence of being quiet is reinforcement, so he developed and maintained his quiet ways. (pp. 429-430)

6. The social-cognitive approach has been criticized as being insufficient. By focusing on what is learned about particular situations, this approach ignores the person as a whole. Also, biological influences are neglected. (pp. 431-432)

7. Psychologists solve the debate by assuming that both the person and the situation must be considered because people interact with situations. Current conditions will influence behavioral traits, causing some traits to appear in one context and not in others. Also, some situations can force modification of behavior. (pp. 435-436)

Matching

1. **o** (p. 425)	4. **p** (p. 424)	7. **l** (p. 434)	10. **k** (p. 426)	13. **g** (p. 424)	16. **f** (p. 426)
2. **a** (p. 412)	5. **j** (p. 413)	8. **e** (p. 430)	11. **m** (p. 424)	14. **i** (p. 426)
3. **c** (p. 416)	6. **d** (p. 425)	9. **b** (p. 427)	12. **n** (p. 418)	15. **h** (p. 431)

Multiple Choice Pretest 1

1. **b**   a. Wrong.   The Rorschach is a projective test, not a personality inventory.
    (p. 416)   c. Wrong.   The MMPI often is used to diagnose disorders, and it doesn't address the dimensions listed.
                d. Wrong.   The NEO-PI-R measures the Big 5, not Cattel's source traits.

2. **a**   b Wrong.   This is one of Eysenck's 3 superfactors, not one of the Big 5.
    (p. 414)   c. Wrong.   This is an MMPI scale, not one of the Big 5.
                d. Wrong.   This is one of Cattell's 16 factors.

3. **d**   a. Wrong.   Allport's cardinal traits are single traits that dominate all of a person's behavior.
    (p. 416)   b. Wrong.   Source traits are Cattell's 16 personality traits.
    (PN7A)   c. Wrong.   Allport's secondary traits are noticeable only occasionally.

4. **d**   a, b, & c. Wrong.   Personality inventories (e.g., MMPI, 16PF) do not allow unstructured answers.
    (p. 417)

5. **a**   b. Wrong.   Self-report tests are objectively scored, often by computer. Projective test scoring is fairly
    (p. 417)   subjective.
                c. Wrong.   Inter-scorer differences is a problem of projective tests, not objective tests.
                d. Wrong.   Self-report tests limit responses (e.g., true/false). Projective tests are open-ended.

6. **b**   a. Wrong.   The conscious and preconscious are accessible. The unconscious is not.
    (p. 417)   c. Wrong.   The superego defines and strives for ideal behavior. It does not contain hidden conflicts.
                d. Wrong.   Reaction formation is a defense mechanism, not a storehouse for conflicts.

7. **b**   a. Wrong.   Nothing is being forgotten. Key here is the socially acceptable outlet for his urges.
    (p. 420)   c. Wrong.   There is no opposite behavior. Key here is the socially acceptable outlet for his urges.
                d. Wrong.   There is no attribution of his urges to another person. Key here is the socially acceptable
                            outlet for his urges.

8. **d**   a. Wrong.   The ego uses defense mechanisms.
    (p. 423)   b. Wrong.   The id is innate. The superego develops with experience.
                c. Wrong.   The superego follows the idealistic principle.

9. **b**   a. Wrong.   Oral fixations involve oral activities (eating, smoking...), not issues of order or disorder.
    (p. 424)   c. Wrong.   A phallic fixation would involve sexual relationships, not being a slob.
                d. Wrong.   A fixation in latency might involve a disinterest in sex, not issues of order or disorder.

10. **c**   a. Wrong.   The phallic stage runs from about age 3 to 5.
    (p. 424)   b. Wrong.   The genital stage runs from puberty to adulthood.
    (PN7A)   d. Wrong.   The anal stage runs from the second year of life to about age 3.

11. **c**   a. Wrong.   This is Horney's view. Adler stressed overcoming inferiority.
    (p. 424)   b. Wrong.   This is Roger's humanistic view. Adler stressed overcoming inferiority.
                d. Wrong.   This is a social learning view. Adler stressed overcoming inferiority.

12. **d**   a. Wrong.   Freud proposed the Oedipus complex for males, not females.
    (p. 424)   b. Wrong.   This is not one of Freud's views. Horney took issue with Freud's concept of penis envy.
                c. Wrong.   Freud didn't propose the inferiority complex. Horney disliked his concept of penis envy.

13. c   a & b.   Wrong.   These are not needs; they inhibit growth.
(p. 426)   d.   Wrong.   This a Freudian concept, not a needed condition in Rogers' theory.
(PT10C)

14. b   a & c.   Wrong.   These are accurate data, but they support an environmental component.
(p. 437)   d.   Wrong.   These are inaccurate data, and they would not really favor either view.

15. b   a. Wrong.   Self-actualization involves fulfilling a potential, associated with positive behavior.
(p. 428)   c. Wrong.   This is a Freudian concept, not something Maslow would consider.
            d. Wrong.   Maslow was a humanistic theorist. Reinforcement is central to the social-cognitive view.

16. a   b, c, & d.   Wrong.   These are all points of criticism. Personal control is well accepted.
(p. 428)

17. a   b. Wrong.   This is a Freudian view. Reinforcement is important in the social-cognitive approach.
(p. 429)   c. Wrong.   This is a humanistic view. Reinforcement is important in the social-cognitive approach.
            d. Wrong.   Incongruence is a humanistic view. Reinforcement is important in social-cognitive theory.

18. c   a. Wrong.   Self-efficacy is the belief a person holds about their own ability to perform a task.
(p. 431)   b. Wrong.   Self-actualization is the ingrained desire to reach one's true potential.
            d. Wrong.   Conditions of worth are the expectations that people believe others place on them.

19. a   b & c.   Wrong.   Dishonesty is likely to reoccur in similar situations, but not in different situations.
(p. 434)   d.   Wrong.   Dishonesty is likely to reoccur in similar situations.

20. d   a. Self-monitoring, modifying behavior to fit a situation, says little about the nature-nurture issue.
(p. 434)   b. Self-monitoring, modifying behavior to fit a situation, says little about factor analysis.
            c. Self-monitoring, modifying behavior to fit a situation, does not relate to psychopathology.

Multiple Choice Pretest 2

1. b   a. Wrong.   Allport did not propose "primary" traits.
(p. 415)   c. Wrong.   Secondary traits are traits that occur occasionally, not in all aspects of behavior.
            d. Wrong.   Central traits are characteristic of the person but are not evident in all aspects of behavior.

2. b   a, c, & d.   Wrong.   These are criticisms of projective tests (Rorschach), not self-report inventories.
(p. 418)

3. b   a. Wrong.   Extroversion relates to sociability.
(p. 412)   c. Wrong.   This is the Big 5 trait, not Eysenck's, showing dependability, productivity, etc.
            d. Wrong.   Low psychoticism would be sensitive, caring, and kind.

4. b   a. Wrong.   Sex bias is not an issue for these approaches.
(p. 415)   c. Wrong.   The Big 5 did come from factor analysis. Allport used an ideographic approach.
            d. Wrong.   The most detailed description is Cattell's 16 factor approach.

5. a   b, c, & d.   Wrong.   The 16 PF and NEO-PI-R are used for describing *normal* personality.
(p. 416)

6. c   a. Wrong.   The ego does not involve the conscience or morality. It is the mediator or executive.
(p. 421)   b. Wrong.   The id does not have a conscience or morality. It follows the pleasure principle.
            d. Wrong.   The libido is Freud's concept of sexual energy.

7. **b**   a. Wrong.   Things in the unconscious are not directly accessible.
    (p. 420)   c. Wrong.   The collective unconscious contains ancestral, not personal memories.
                   d. Wrong.   Reaction formation is a defense mechanism characterized by behavior opposite to one's
                                true feelings.

8. **d**   a, b, & c.   Wrong.   Roy is experiencing the Oedipus complex, a hallmark of the phallic stage,
    (p. 423)   involving children ages 3-5.

9. **d**   a. Wrong.   One's personal traumas are placed in the personal unconscious.
    (p. 425)   b. Wrong.   The collective unconscious contains concepts passed through generations, not the ego.
    (PN7A)   c. Wrong.   Adler stressed inferiority/superiority, not Jung.

10. **c**   a. Wrong.   Some question the reality of repression, and others do not view it as a major factor.
    (p. 425)   b. Wrong.   The concept of penis envy is considered unrealistic and even distasteful by many.
                   d. Wrong.   Even other psychodynamic theorists disagreed with Freud's view of sexuality's role.

11. **c**   a. Wrong.   He's attributing (projecting) the feelings to someone else, not "forgetting" them.
    (p. 422)   b. Wrong.   He's attributing the feelings to his wife, not channeling them to acceptable forms.
                   d. Wrong.   He's attributing (projecting) the feelings to his wife, not acting in an opposite way to them.

12. **c**   a. Wrong.   Conditions of worth are expectations we believe others have of us, and they don't relate to
    (p. 428)   peak experiences.
                   b. Wrong.   Internal locus of control is the belief that one has some control over what happens. It is not
                                Maslow's concept, and it is not related to peak experiences.
                   d. Wrong.   Jung proposed the collective unconscious. It does not relate to peak experiences.

13. **a**   b, c, & d.   Wrong.   These are good situations. Key here is the mismatch between his self-concept
    (p. 427)   and his experiences.
    (PT10C)

14. **d**   a, b, & c.   Wrong.   These theories all emphasize inborn tendencies, not conditioning and
    (p. 429)   interpretation.

15. **d**   a, b, & c.   Wrong.   These are all characteristic of the humanistic view of behavior. The view that
    (p. 426)   behavior is motivated by unconscious urges is a Freudian view.

16. **c**   a & b.   Wrong.   Lee's concern is about her ability, not whether her efforts make a difference.
    (p. 430)   d.   Wrong.   High self-efficacy involves high confidence in one's ability to do the job.

17. **a**   b. Wrong.   Most theories assume consistency (e.g., if the self-concept is stable, so is behavior;
    (p. 433)   conditioning produces consistency).
                   c. Wrong.   The debate questions behavioral consistency across situations, not across people.
                   d. Wrong.   The debate questions consistency across situations, not across people.

18. **c**   a & b.   Wrong.   Nothing is said about how May feels about her own personal chance for success.
    (p. 430)   d.   Wrong.   An external locus of control focuses on luck or external factors, not personal effort.

19. **c**   a.   Wrong.   Ben has an internal locus of control, but we can't tell about self-monitoring.
    (p. 434)   b & d.   Wrong.   Lynn and Mort adjust their behavior to fit the situation--high self-monitoring.

20. **b**   a. Wrong.   Social-cognitive theories are criticized for not considering biological factors sufficiently.
    (p. 431)   c. Wrong.   Social-cognitive theories do include conditioning as an important determinant.
                   d. Wrong.   Freud's theory is the considered difficult to test scientifically, not social-cognitive theories.

CHAPTER 13: SOCIAL PSYCHOLOGY

ESTABLISHING LEARNING GOALS

Use these learning goals as a preview of the chapter, a guide for active reading, and to evaluate your mastery of the material. Review the relevant goals as you begin and end your reading of each major section of the chapter.

I.   Solve the adaptive problem of social cognition, interpreting the behavior of others.
   A. Discuss how physical attractiveness, stereotypes, and social schemas influence our impressions of others.
     1. Describe the impact of attractiveness and social schemas.
     2. Identify common types of stereotypes and explain factors that influence stereotyping.
     3. Describe self-fulfilling prophecy, and discuss how it can influence behavior.
     4. Define and discuss prejudice.
   B. Discuss how we attribute causality to the behavior of others, explaining the biases and errors that we show.
     1. Define attribution, and describe the covariation model of attribution.
     2. Compare internal and external attributions, and describe the fundamental attribution effect, the actor-observer effect, and the self-serving bias.
   C. Explain how attitudes are formed and changed.
     1. Describe the cognitive, affective, and behavioral components of attitudes.
     2. Explain how exposure, conditioning, and observational learning influence attitudes.
     3. Describe the elaboration likelihood model of persuasion.
     4. Define cognitive dissonance, and discuss the research on its effect on attitudes.
     5. Describe the self-perception theory of the relationship between behavior and attitude.

II. Solve the adaptive problem of how social influence affects behavior.
   A. Define and discuss social facilitation and interference.
   B. Describe the bystander effect, and the concept of diffusion of responsibility.
   C. Describe how behavior changes in a group setting.
     1. Describe social loafing and deindividuation, and explain their possible causes.
     2. Describe Asch's research on conformity, and discuss the factors that increase conformity.
   D. Discuss some aspects of group decision making.
     1. Describe group polarization.
     2. Describe groupthink.
   E. Describe the Milgram experiment, and discuss what it implies about authority.
   F. Discuss how culture affects social influence.

III. Solve the adaptive problem of establishing relations with others.
   A. Describe the factors that influence our perception of facial attractiveness.
   B. Explain the factors that influence us to like or love others.
   C. Define the components of romantic love, and explain the triangular theory of love.

MASTERING THE MATERIAL

Preview & Interpreting the Behavior of Others: Social Cognition (pp. 444-460)

Mastering the Vocabulary. Define or explain each of the following terms. To check your answers, consult the text pages listed.

1. social psychology (p. 445)

2. social cognition (p. 446)

3. social schema (p. 447)

4. stereotypes (p. 447)

5. self-fulfilling prophecy (p. 448)

6. prejudice (p. 449)

7. discrimination (p. 449)

8. attributions (p. 450)

9. external attribution (p. 451)

10. internal attribution (p. 452)

11. fundamental attribution error (p. 452)

12. actor-observer effect (p. 453)

13. self-serving bias (p. 453)

14. attitude (p. 454)

15. elaboration likelihood model (p. 456)

16. source characteristics (p. 457)

17. cognitive dissonance (p. 458)

18. self-perception theory (p. 458)

Mastering the Concepts. Fill in the blanks to create a summary of the section. Answers are on page 319.

_____(1) psychology is the study of how people perceive, influence and relate to other people. Three adaptive problems are discussed: How do people interpret the behavior of others? How do people behave in the presence of others? How do people establish relations with other people?

Social _____(2) is the study of how people use cognitive processes to understand other people and themselves. Impressions of other people are influenced by that person's physical appearance and the observer's _____(3) about the person. Expectations are based on _____(4), knowledge structures about social experiences, and influence action.

_____(5) are schemas about the traits and behavior of people that belong to a group, especially groups based on race, gender, or _____(6). Stereotypes cause self-fulfilling _____(7) effects in which expectations lead to behaviors which themselves cause the person to behave in ways matching the expectations. Prototype and exemplar theories have been proposed to explain stereotypes. Stereotypes may be adaptive heuristics, but they may lead to rigid interpretations, increase the chance of _____(8) and discrimination. Prejudice is reduced with repeated, _____(9) social interactions with representative individuals from the group.

According to Kelly's covariation model, inferences about the cause of a behavior, _____(10), are based on events occurring with a behavior, and the consistency, distinctiveness, and consensus of the relationship. _____(11), or situational, attributions are likely if these factors are strong. If consistency is high, but the others are low, an _____(12), trait-based, attribution is made. The _____(13) attribution error is a bias to make internal attributions about someone else's behavior. The actor-observer effect is the tendency to make _____(14) attributions about one's own behavior. The _____(15) bias is the tendency to make internal attributions about one's successes, but external ones about failures. Attribution biases allow quick decisions but possibly inaccurate decisions.

_____(16), beliefs held about something, have three parts: a _____(17) part involving knowledge; an _____(18) part involving feelings; and a _____(19) part involving a predisposition to act. Attitudes develop through mere _____(20), classical and instrumental conditioning, and _____(21) learning.

The elaboration likelihood model of attitude change states change occurs through a _____(22) route where the content of a persuasive message is processed, or through a peripheral route where superficial cues are influential and the message is not processed directly. In peripheral processing _____(23) characteristics and heuristics are important influences. Festinger's cognitive _____(24) theory states behavior inconsistent with attitude creates dissonance (tension) that the person seeks to reduce, usually by changing the _____(25). People asked to lie changed their attitudes to fit the lie more if paid a little than if paid a lot. Bem's self-perception theory states people use their _____(26) to infer their _____(27). The _____(28) technique shows that people who behave in small ways implying an attitude later engage in larger behaviors implying the attitude because self-perception is triggered. The low balling technique works similarly.

Evaluating Your Progress. Select the one best response. Answers are on page 319. If you make any errors, reread the relevant material before proceeding.

1. Dan's first impression of his new roommate will be most strongly influenced by his roommate's
   a. name.
   b. apparent intelligence.
   c. physical appearance.
   d. first words.

2. When one's expectations about a person actually cause that person to behave in the expected way,
   a. a self-fulfilling prophecy effect has occurred.
   b. a social schema has been violated.
   c. a fundamental attribution error has been made.
   d. cognitive dissonance has developed.

3. The most common types of stereotypes are based on race, age, and
   a. gender.
   b. intelligence.
   c. hair color.
   d. occupation.

4. Kelly's covariation model of attribution states that attributions are influenced by
   a. originality, familiarity, and personality.
   b. intelligence, mood, and age.
   c. race, age, and gender.
   d. consensus, distinctiveness, consistency.

5. If everyone that ate the mushrooms got sick, the relationship has
   a. high distinctiveness.
   b. high consistency.
   c. high consensus.
   d. low consistency.

6. When the surgeon's patient died, the intern decided the surgeon was incompetent. This illustrates
   a. an internal attribution.
   b. an external attribution.
   c. self-serving bias.
   d. cognitive dissonance.

7. The fundamental attribution error is the tendency to make
   a. internal attributions about oneself for good outcomes, and external attributions for bad outcomes.
   b. external attributions about oneself for good outcomes, and internal attributions for bad outcomes.
   c. internal attributions about other people's behavior more readily than external attributions.
   d. external attributions about other people's behavior more readily than internal attributions.

8. When people explain their successes in terms of their personal characteristics, but explain their failures in terms of environmental events or situations, they are demonstrating
   a. the fundamental attribution error.
   b. the self-serving bias.
   c. self-perception theory.
   d. a self-fulfilling prophecy effect.

9. The affective component of an attitude is
   a. the person's thoughts about the object of the attitude.
   b. the person's strength of commitment to the object of the attitude.
   c. the person's behavioral predispositions concerning the object of the attitude.
   d. the person's feelings about the object of the attitude.

10. An example of mere exposure as a means of attitude formation is
    a. liking a car because the music in the ads makes you feel happy.
    b. liking a brand of shoes because an athlete endorses them.
    c. liking a song after hearing it several times.
    d. liking a charity because it sent you a nice thank you letter.

11. The central route of persuasion involves
    a. focusing attention on processing the persuasive message itself.
    b. superficial cues in the persuasive message that are not processed directly.
    c. basing attitudes on emotional responses to an ad or persuasive message.
    d. creating a state of tension as a result of mismatched attitudes and behavior.

12. Attitudes shift due to the tension produced by attitudes and behaviors that do not match, according to
    a. the elaboration likelihood theory.
    b. the cognitive dissonance theory.
    c. the self-perception theory.
    d. the triangular theory.

13. Festinger paid some subjects $1 and some $20 to lie about a boring task. Others were not asked to lie. Festinger found the greatest positive shift in attitudes about the task occurred in the subjects
   a. paid $20 to lie.
   b. paid $1 to lie.
   c. paid $20 or $1 (equal shift, but greater than non-liars).
   d. not asked to lie.

14. The alternative to cognitive dissonance theory is Bem's self-perception theory, which states
   a. behaviors and attitudes that don't match create a tension that the person seeks to reduce.
   b. people give more emphasis to internal factors when explaining someone else's behavior.
   c. attitudes form either from evaluation of the message or based on superficial cues in the message.
   d. people examine their behavior and infer their attitudes based on those behaviors.

Behaving in the Presence of Others: Social Influence (pp. 461-473)

Mastering the Vocabulary. Define or explain each of the following terms. To check your answers, consult the text pages listed.

1. social influence (p. 461)

2. social facilitation (p. 461)

3. social interference (p. 462)

4. altruism (p. 463)

5. bystander effect (p. 463)

6. diffusion of responsibility (p. 464)

7. social loafing (p. 465)

8. deindividuation (p. 465)

9. conformity (p. 466)

10. in-group (p. 467)

11. group polarization (p. 467)

12. groupthink (p. 468)

13. obedience (p. 469)

Mastering the Concepts. Fill in the blanks to create a summary of the section. Answers are on page 319.

Social _____ (29) involves how the presence of others affects behavior. Audiences may enhance performance, social _____ (30), or disrupt performance, social _____ (31). Task difficulty influences whether performance improves or declines; difficult or new tasks show _____ (32) because the audience increases arousal.

In the _____ (33) effect the presence of others inhibits helping behavior, altruism, because of _____ (34) of responsibility. Helping increases if the person has watched others be helpful. Diffusion of responsibility can explain _____ (35), working less hard when in a group, and might influence _____ (36), a depersonalization that can lead to destructive behavior.

People in groups often show _____ (37), behavior that shifts toward the group norm. Asch's research shows that people will give a wrong answer if everyone else does so, especially if the group contains 3-5 people for whom the person has respect or a sense of identification, as in an _____ (38). In _____ (39) social influence, conformity is an attempt to get approval or avoid rejection, but in _____ (40) social influence, the group is a source of information.

Group decisions differ from those of individuals. With time, a group decision grows more extreme, the group _____ (41) effect. Close-knit groups make bad decisions when they value obtaining a consensus more than considering all the facts, a situation known as _____ (42).

As shown by Milgram's research, orders given by an authority often lead to _____ (43). Sixty-five percent of Milgram's subjects obeyed and gave what they thought were severe shocks to another person. Obedience is reduced when the prestige of the setting or the authority is low, and when the authority figure _____ (44) the room. This study has been criticized as _____ (45).

Whether a person has an independent or interdependent sense of self is influenced by cultural factors. As a result, social phenomena like conformity may vary across cultures.

Evaluating Your Progress. Select the one best response. Answers are on page 320. If you make any errors, reread the relevant material before you proceed.

1. Zajonc suggests that social facilitation and interference effects occur because an audience
   a. decreases arousal and causes the most recent response to occur.
   b. decreases arousal and causes the most dominant response to occur.
   c. increases arousal and causes the most recent response to occur.
   d. increases arousal and causes the most dominant response to occur.

2. In the bystander effect
   a. performance of a task improves when there are a large number of observers.
   b. people are reluctant to help someone if a large number of people are present.
   c. decisions made in a group tend to be more extreme than those made in isolation.
   d. one person in a group task doesn't do his or her fair share of the work.

3. Decisions about the invasion of Cuba and the launching of the Challenger space shuttle were disastrous because the group was most concerned about reaching a consensus and ignored dissenting views and information. This close-mindedness and overestimation of the uniformity of opinion is known as
   a. groupthink.
   b. group polarization.
   c. social loafing.
   d. informational social influence.

4. The bystander effect is explained in terms of
   a. increased arousal created by the presence of other people.
   b. greater obedience that is created by being a bystander in a group.
   c. the feeling that responsibility is shared by the other people present.
   d. the feeling that one shares certain characteristics with other members of a group.

5. Feeling anonymous, less self-conscious, and possibly depersonalized, and being willing to do things you normally wouldn't do are characteristic of
   a. social loafing.
   b. normative social influence.
   c. groupthink.
   d. deindividuation.

6. An individual will be most likely to conform if
   a. the group contains 10 people or more, rather than 4 or 5 people.
   b. the individual shares common features with the group members.
   c. at least one person in the group does not conform.
   d. the group is made up of people the person doesn't respect.

7. Normative social influence stimulates conformity based on
   a. the desire to receive approval from others and to avoid rejection.
   b. the information group members can give about an unfamiliar situation.
   c. the power exerted by an authority figure.
   d. the perception that group members share the responsibility for a decision.

8. Group polarization involves the tendency
   a. to act like the other members of the group because they have important information.
   b. for a group decision to grow more extreme with increasing time.
   c. for a group to emphasize reaching a consensus rather than considering dissenting views.
   d. to separate into leaders and workers in groups working on a specific project.

9. In Milgram's experiment on obedience, 65% of the people
   a. refused to begin the experiment after hearing they would have to shock someone.
   b. began the experiment, but quit when they were faced with actually having to shock someone.
   c. participated in most of the experiment, but quit when the "learner" started screaming with pain.
   d. participated in the entire experiment, giving the highest level of shocks to the "learner."

Establishing Relations with Others (pp. 474-481)

Mastering the Vocabulary. Define or explain each of the following terms. To check your answers, consult the text pages listed.

1. reciprocity (p. 479)

2. passionate love (p. 480)

3. companionate love (p. 480)

Mastering the Concepts. Fill in the blanks to create a summary of the section. Answers are on page 319.

Physical appearance influences social relations. An evolutionary view of attractiveness predicts attractiveness should be related to _____ (46) capacity (youth and health) and be similar across cultures. Attractive faces tend to be _____ (47) or prototypical faces. Although cross-cultural similarities in attractiveness exist, culture-specific attitudes are important also.

Primary determinants of relationships include _____ (48), the physical distance between the people's homes, _____ (49), the number of shared interests or characteristics, and _____ (50), a tendency to return feelings received. Physical nearness encourages relationships through mere exposure or a sense of connectedness developing from repeated contact. Similarity influences relationships by _____ (51) a person's beliefs, because people dislike others that do not share their views, or because personal characteristics limit the range of choices.

Love can be _____ (52) love, which is an intense desire, or _____ (53) love, which is a less intense, but a more enduring feeling of trust and warmth. Sternberg's _____ (54) theory of love classifies love based on three dimensions: passion or erotic attraction, _____(55) or the sharing of feelings, and _____(56) to remaining in the relationship. Passion may develop first, but often fades. Commitment and intimacy develop later, but are more likely to endure.

Evaluating Your Progress. Select the one best response. Answers are on page 321. If you make any errors, reread the relevant material before proceeding.

1. The most accurate summary of research on facial attractiveness is:
    a. Universal, innate factors entirely determine what types of faces are most attractive.
    b. Cultural factors entirely determine what types of faces are most attractive.
    c. Both universal and cultural-specific factors determine what faces are most attractive.
    d. Attractiveness is entirely an individual matter; there is little consistency in choices.

2. Interpersonal attraction is primarily determined by
    a. proximity, similarity, and reciprocity.
    b. income, proximity and attractiveness.
    c. reciprocity, education, and attractiveness.
    d. income, education, and attractiveness.

3. Ralph Waldo Emerson wrote in *Friendship*, "To have a friend, you must be a friend." He seems to be referring to the determinant of love and friendship that social psychologists call
    a. similarity.
    b. proximity.
    c. reciprocity.
    d. conformity.

4. The type of love most likely to lead to self-disclosure and enduring feelings of trust and warmth is
    a. passionate love.
    b. companionate love.
    c. empty love.
    d. infatuated love.

5. Sternberg's triangular view of love is based on
    a. proximity, similarity, and reciprocity.
    b. growth, duration, and arousal.
    c. loving, liking, and desiring.
    d. passion, intimacy, and commitment.

MAKING FINAL PREPARATIONS

Complete these sections without consulting your book or notes. For a more accurate estimate of how well you know this material, wait at least a day or two after studying the chapter before working on the questions. Some material you "know" immediately after working with the chapter will be quickly forgotten. Immediate tests will overestimate what you know well.

Short Essay Questions. Write a brief answer to each question. Sample answers are on page 321.

1. Explain the adaptive value and disadvantages of stereotypes.

2. Compare Festinger's cognitive dissonance theory and Bem's self-perception theory.

3. Compare social facilitation and social interference and explain why each occurs.

4. Describe the bystander effect and give one primary explanation.

5. Explain why similarity might promote friendship.

6. Compare passionate and companionate love.

Matching. Select the correct definition or description for each item. Answers are on page 322.

_____	1. reciprocity	**a.**	compliance in response to an authority
_____	2. social interference	**b.**	get attitude shift by inducing attitude-consistent act
_____	3. elaboration likelihood model	**c.**	impaired performance in the presence of others
_____	4. obedience	**d.**	knowledge structures relating to social experiences
_____	5. social cognition	**e.**	conducted obedience experiments
_____	6. Daryl Bem	**f.**	proposed theory of cognitive dissonance
_____	7. social facilitation	**g.**	conducted conformity experiments
_____	8. Solomon Asch	**h.**	how thoughts help people understand people
_____	9. foot-in-the-door technique	**i.**	proposes central & peripheral route to attitude
_____	10. Stanley Milgram	**j.**	beliefs about traits of a particular group
_____	11. stereotypes	**k.**	enhanced performance in the presence of others
_____	12. self-fulfilling prophecy	**l.**	tendency to return feeling shown toward oneself
_____	13. Leon Festinger	**m.**	positive or negative evaluation of something
_____	14. social schemas	**n.**	expectation leads to behavior matching expectation
_____	15. attitude	**o.**	emphasizes consistency, distinctiveness, consensus
_____	16. covariation model	**p.**	proposed self-perception theory of attribution

Multiple Choice Pretest 1. Select the one best response. Answers are on page 322.

1. An evolutionary approach to attractiveness would suggest people are attracted to people
    a. who look like them (share the same gene pool).
    b. who are youthful and healthy looking.
    c. who have unusual features.
    d. who fit their cultural definition of beauty.

2. Research indicates that when people first see an attractive person, they tend to assume the person is
    a. less intelligent than people with an average appearance.
    b. more self-centered than people with an average appearance.
    c. better adjusted than people with an average appearance.
    d. greater trouble-makers than people with an average appearance.

3. All of the following are true EXCEPT:
    a. Stereotypes are activated by recent exposure to stereotypic beliefs.
    b. The most common stereotypes involve age, gender, and race.
    c. Stereotypes produce an overemphasis on within-group differences.
    d. Repeated, widespread exposure to representative members of a group reduces stereotyping.

4. In Kelly's covariation model of attribution, behaviors that occur only in one situation have
    a. high consensus.
    b. high distinctiveness.
    c. low consistency.
    d. low consensus.

5. According to Kelly's covariation model, internal attributions are most likely when there is
    a. low consistency, high consensus, and high distinctiveness.
    b. low consistency, low consensus, and low distinctiveness.
    c. high consistency, high consensus, and high distinctiveness.
    d. high consistency, low consensus, and low distinctiveness.

6. The view that persuasion can involve a central route or a peripheral route is
    a. the cognitive dissonance theory.
    b. the elaboration likelihood model.
    c. the self-perception theory.
    d. the social schema model.

7. According to your text, positive or negative evaluations of a group and its members defines
    a. discrimination.
    b. altruism.
    c. prejudice.
    d. source characteristics.

8. Who would experience the most cognitive dissonance, according to Festinger?
    a. Harry, who buys drinks for his friends.
    b. Ron, who drives an ugly car he was given as a gift.
    c. Walter, a vegetarian, who eats chicken at a dinner at his boss' house.
    d. Pete, who smokes cigarettes, knowing they are bad for his health.

9. Social interference is common if a difficult task is performed with an audience. A common explanation for this is increased
   a. deindividuation.
   b. conformity.
   c. reciprocity.
   d. arousal.

10. Dee is most likely to get help quickly if she has an accident where there are
    a. 1 or 2 witnesses.
    b. 5-10 witnesses.
    c. 10-20 witnesses.
    d. 20-40 witnesses.

11. When a student gets up and leaves during the middle of his lecture, Dr. Marsh always thinks, "That student is a rude, inconsiderate fool!" Dr. Marsh's thoughts illustrate
    a. altruism.
    b. a self-fulfilling prophesy.
    c. the fundamental attribution error.
    d. cognitive dissonance.

12. When the quarterback threw a game-winning pass, he attributed his success to his great skill. When he threw a disastrous interception, he attributed his failure to a gust of wind. This pattern represents
    a. the fundamental attribution error.
    b. a self-fulfilling prophesy.
    c. elaboration likelihood.
    d. the self-serving bias.

13. Nancy hates cigarettes. She knows they cause lung disease, and she feels ill when she smells them, so she will not sit in an area in which smoking is allowed. The cognitive component of this attitude is
    a. hating the cigarettes.
    b. knowing they cause lung disease.
    c. feeling ill when she smells them.
    d. refusing to sit in a smoking area.

14. Rob barely sings the national anthem when he is in a large group. Rob's behavior is most similar to
    a. the bystander effect.
    b. group polarization.
    c. lowballing.
    d. social loafing.

15. Everyone thinks blue carpet is a great idea except Don, but he votes for it, too. Don's behavior reflects
    a. conformity.
    b. group polarization.
    c. obedience.
    d. social facilitation.

16. Paul hates football, but he went to all the games with his fraternity brothers and yelled and cheered with enthusiasm like they did. Paul's behavior is an example of
    a. the actor-observer effect.
    b. normative social influence.
    c. group polarization.
    d. groupthink.

17. The university president began the meeting by stating that tuition should be increased by $1000 for all new students to provide money for faculty raises. The group knew that this move might cause a reduction in enrollment, but they chose to ignore this and other possible problems and concentrated only on getting a consensus. Their behavior illustrates
    a. informational social influence.
    b. social interference.
    c. group polarization.
    d. groupthink.

18. Research on obedience has shown that
    a. very few people obey orders to hurt someone unless the study is carried out in a highly prestigious location.
    b. most of the people who gave the highest shock in Milgram's study had figured out the hoax.
    c. obedience is most likely if the person giving the orders leaves the room afterward.
    d. Milgram's basic results can be replicated in many countries.

19. Which of the following sayings is best supported by research on friendships?
    a. Birds of a feather flock together.
    b. Absence makes the heart grow fonder.
    c. Familiarity breeds contempt.
    d. Opposites attract.

20. Mike and Carol share an incredibly strong need to be with each other and strong emotional arousal when together. Their relationship is an example of
    a. companionate love.
    b. empty love.
    c. passionate love.
    d. friendship.

Multiple Choice Pretest 2. Select the one best response. Answers are on page 324.

1. Jill heard that Sue, her freshman "little sister," was unfriendly. As a result, Jill didn't try to make friends. Hurt by Jill's coldness, Sue wasn't friendly either, confirming Jill's expectations. This illustrates
    a. cognitive dissonance.
    b. social interference.
    c. a self-fulfilling prophecy effect.
    d. the self-serving bias.

2. Brad believes students of Asian heritage are excellent students and especially good at math and science. Brad's belief is an example of
   a. cognitive dissonance.
   b. the actor-observer effect.
   c. an external attribution.
   d. a stereotype.

3. Before deciding Dan's failing grade was due to his lack of knowledge rather than the nature of the test, you asked how his classmates did on the exam. Your decision emphasized
   a. consistency.
   b. consensus.
   c. distinctiveness.
   d. expectation.

4. When Pat was late, Lee decided Pat's tardiness was due to car trouble. Lee's belief is an example of
   a. the fundamental attribution error.
   b. the self-serving bias.
   c. an external attribution.
   d. an internal attribution.

5. If Anne makes the fundamental attribution error, she will explain her favorite politician's loss in the election by saying,
   a. "He just didn't have the campaign skills necessary to get his ideas across."
   b. "His opponent ran a dirty campaign that turned the voters away from the real issues."
   c. "He didn't have big money behind him, so he couldn't buy the advertising time he needed to win."
   d. "The voters were determined to get rid of all the incumbents, no matter how good they were."

6. The head of marketing often claimed, "Say it often enough, and people will start to believe it." This suggests she believes attitudes are influenced by
   a. mere exposure.
   b. classical conditioning.
   c. instrumental conditioning.
   d. deindividuation.

7. Sid is an Indianapolis Pacers basketball fan. He knows the team's win-loss record and the achievements of the individual players. He buys season tickets every year, and gets angry if anyone says they aren't the best. The behavioral component of Sid's attitude is
   a. knowing the team's win-loss record.
   b. knowing the achievements of the individual players.
   c. buying season tickets every year.
   d. getting angry at people who disagree with him.

8. Candidate Smith distributes summaries of his views and accomplishments. Candidate Smith is using
   a. cognitive dissonance as a means of persuasion.
   b. instrumental conditioning as a means of persuasion.
   c. the central route as a means of persuasion.
   d. the peripheral route as a means of persuasion.

9. Kit, a volunteer, and Tom, a highly paid staff member, work on Candidate Smith's campaign. Although Candidate Smith recently admitted he has a criminal conviction, both Kit and Tom have continued to work for him. According to cognitive dissonance theory, how are Kit's and Tom's attitudes about Candidate Smith likely to have changed since the news about his criminal record?

   a. Both Kit's and Tom's attitudes became less favorable, but Kit's changed more.
   b. Both Kit's and Tom's attitudes became less favorable, but Tom's changed more.
   c. Both Kit's and Tom's attitudes became less favorable by an equal amount.
   d. Kit's attitude became less favorable, but Tom's attitude became more favorable.

10. Members of the Residence Hall Council initially felt that some minor changes were needed in the visitation policies. After a very lengthy, well-balanced, thorough discussion, they produced a very extreme proposal restricting visitation to 1:00-7:00 pm. Their shift to a more extreme view illustrates
   a. groupthink.
   b. social facilitation.
   c. normative social influence.
   d. group polarization.

11. Charities emphasize getting any kind of donation at first, no matter how small. They know that having complied with a small request makes a person much more likely to comply with a large request later. This represents
   a. behavioral consensus.
   b. a self-fulfilling prophesy.
   c. normative social influence.
   d. the foot in the door technique.

12. Georgia just met a woman who is like a twin sister. She likes the same things Georgia likes, she looks a little like Georgia, and she often starts to say the same thing as Georgia. Based on the research on interpersonal relationships, Georgia will probably
   a. feel really creepy about finding someone so similar to her and will avoid her in the future.
   b. very quickly become lasting friends with this person.
   c. become friends for a short while before becoming bored with someone so like her.
   d. become friends for a short while before the small differences cause her to lose interest.

13. Ben realized that every time he had an open elective, he took a psychology class. Based on his observation, Ben has decided he must like psychology. Ben's attitude is best explained by
   a. self-perception theory.
   b. cognitive dissonance theory.
   c. the fundamental attribution error model.
   d. the elaboration likelihood model.

14. A victory rally Fred attended turned into a wild riot by hundreds of students, Fred included. Afterward, Fred said, "It was weird. I didn't feel like me. I just felt like a part of the crowd, and everybody else was tearing up the Quad, so I did too. Fred seems to have experienced
   a. group polarization.
   b. social facilitation.
   c. deindividuation.
   d. reciprocity.

15. Kit saw a boy fall out of a tree in the crowded park, but he didn't help immediately. This is similar to
    a. the group polarization effect.
    b. the self-fulfilling prophecy effect.
    c. the mere presence effect.
    d. the bystander effect.

16. All of Nan's friends ride bikes to school. Nan hates bikes, but she wants her friends' approval, so she starts riding a bike to school. Nan's conformity seems to involve
    a. group polarization.
    b. obedience.
    c. normative social influence.
    d. informational social influence.

17. "He told me to do it." "Everybody else did it too!" "Nobody else did anything either." These are comments likely to be heard when explaining behavior in situations like Milgram's experiment, riots, and the Kitty Genovese case. Each comment illustrates the importance of
    a. self-perception theory.
    b. diffusion of responsibility.
    c. internal attributions.
    d. reciprocity.

18. Sal and Carol tell each other their private thoughts and feelings. They score high on the dimension of
    a. passion.
    b. commitment.
    c. intimacy.
    d. companionship.

19. He knew it might cause a fire, but Jacob used the wire the foreman told him to use. Jacob's behavior is best explained in terms of
    a. social loafing.
    b. social interference.
    c. obedience.
    d. normative social influence.

20. Research has found that people tended to rate as most attractive the pictures of
    a. people who look similar to themselves.
    b. people who have very distinctive features.
    c. people who were blends of many other people.
    d. people who had asymmetrical faces.

LANGUAGE DEVELOPMENT GUIDE

Core Terms

In the lectures on social psychology, your instructor may refer to ***pro-social*** behaviors, such as ***philanthropy,*** or charity. These are behaviors that help others.

Your instructor may also use the terms *legal, ethical* and **moral**. These terms are not quite interchangeable. Something that is *illegal* breaks a specific law in a society; something that is *unethical* breaks the principles that guide conduct in a profession, such as those research psychologists must follow in designing their studies. Finally, something that is *immoral* violates public standards for good behavior.

One term that you may hear in the lecture on conformity and obedience is **compliance**. Psychologists make a careful distinction between these three terms. Conformity is doing what you see others like you do, like dressing in clothes like those your friends wear. Obedience is doing what you are told to do by an authority figure. Compliance is sort of in-between; it is doing what you are asked to do (either explicitly or implicitly) by others around you who are *not* in a position of authority.

Idioms

p. 444	itching for	wanting, restlessly waiting for
p. 444	spearheaded by	led by, directed by
p. 444	shortcomings	faults
p. 444	save one	except one
p. 444	locale	location
p. 447	judging a book by its cover	making assumptions about someone or something based upon its outward appearance
p. 447	seedy characters	people who seem to be likely to cause trouble or who are dressed poorly
p. 450	channel surfing	flipping from one television (TV) channel to another
p. 451	sour disposition	unpleasant personality
p. 453	bearing down on your bumper	coming closer and closer to the back of your car
p. 453	tailgated	followed very closely by another car
p. 453	switch gears	change topics or approaches to a topic
p. 455	landlord	owner of a rented property, such as a house or apartment
p. 455	pet deposit	money some landlords require pet owners to pay in order to keep their pets in the house with them
p. 455	classified ads	short advertisements in newspapers

Word Parts

Here are some words that are made up of word parts, and that you can find in this chapter. After you've looked at these, you can look for other words in the chapter that use the same word parts.

WORD	WORD PART IT USES	MEANING
apathy	a = not path = feeling	feeling nothing
attractive	a, ad = to, toward tract = to pull	having the power to draw others closer; pleasing
dissonance	dis = not son = sound	conflict; harsh, disagreeable sound
exposure	ex = out of, away from pos, pon = place, set, put	left visible; left out in the open
expressing	ex = out of, away from press = to press, send out	showing, sending out
inclined	in = in, into, toward clin, lin = line, level	angled toward, tending toward
prejudice	pre = before jud = to judge, decide	a decision made before evidence is presented
project	pro = forward ject = to throw	send out beforehand; that which goes before
prototypical	proto = first typ = kind	first of its kind
speculate	pect, spec, spect = to look at	to think about; to see what is happening or about to happen

Knowing the word parts listed above, you can also create the following words. You can get an idea of their meanings from the word parts they use.

sympathy	sym (together) + pathy	_____
expect	_____ + _____	to look forward to, to see ahead
inject	in + ject	_____
contract	_____ + _____	that which pulls or ties together

propose	pro + pos	_____
atypical	_____ + _____	not like others of its kind
prospect	pro + spect	_____

Pronunciation

p. 465   deindividuation   dee-in-di-vi′-ju-ay′-shun   p. 479   reciprocity   re-si-prah′-si-tee

ANSWERS AND EXPLANATIONS

To find relevant material in your textbook, consult the pages cited with each answer. Also, PN and PT citations refer to modules in *PsychNow!* and *Psyk.trek* materials, respectively.

Mastering the Concepts

1. Social (p. 445)
2. cognition (p. 446)
3. expectations (p. 446)
4. social schemas (p. 447)
5. Stereotypes (p. 447)
6. age (p. 447)
7. prophecy (p. 448)
8. prejudice (p. 449)
9. widespread (p. 450)
10. attributions (p. 450)
11. External (p. 451)
12. internal (p. 452)
13. fundamental (p. 452)
14. external (p. 453)
15. self-serving (p. 453)
16. Attitudes (p. 454)
17. cognitive (p. 455)
18. affective (p. 455)
19. behavioral (p. 455)
20. exposure (p. 455)
21. observational (p. 456)
22. central (p. 457)
23. source (p. 457)
24. dissonance (p. 458)
25. attitude (p. 458)
26. behavior (p. 458)
27. attitudes (p. 458)
28. foot-in-the-door (p. 459)
29. influence (p. 461)
30. facilitation (p. 461)
31. interference (p. 462)
32. interference (p. 462)
33. bystander (p. 463)
34. diffusion (p. 464)
35. social loafing (p. 465)
36. deindividuation (p. 465)
37. conformity (p. 466)
38. in-group (p. 467)
39. normative (p. 467)
40. informational (p. 467)
41. polarization (p. 467)
42. groupthink (p. 468)
43. obedience (p. 469)
44. leaves (p. 472)
45. unethical (p. 471)
46. reproductive (p. 475)
47. average (p. 475)
48. proximity (p. 478)
49. similarity (p. 478)
50. reciprocity (p. 479)
51. validating (p. 479)
52. passionate (p. 480)
53. companionate (p. 480)
54. triangular (p. 480)
55. intimacy (p. 480)
56. commitment (p. 480)

Evaluating Your Progress

Preview & Interpreting the Behavior of Others: Social Cognition

1. **c**   a, b, & d.   Wrong.   First impressions are most strongly influenced by physical appearance.
    (p. 446)

2. **a**   b. Wrong.   Expectations are upheld, not violated.
    (p. 448)   c. Wrong.   The fundamental attribution error is making internal attributions about other's behavior.
                d. Wrong.   Cognitive dissonance is tension produced when attitudes and actions don't match.

3. **a**   b, c, & d.   Wrong.   Although stereotypes can include these, race, age, and gender are most common.
    (p. 447)

4. **d**   a, b, & c.   Wrong.   These are not part of the covariation model.
    (p. 451)
    (PT12A)

5. **c**   a.   Wrong.   There is no information about whether people get sick only after eating mushrooms.
    (p. 451)   b & d. Wrong.   There is no information about whether the same reaction has occurred before.

6. **a**   b. Wrong.   Incompetence is an internal trait, not an external situation.
    (p. 452)   c. Wrong.   The intern isn't making attributions about himself and gains nothing here.
    (PN8B)   d. Wrong.   There is no tension due to a mismatch of attitude and behavior here.

7. **c**   a. Wrong.   This is self-serving bias. Fundamental attribution error involves attributions for others.
    (p. 452)   b. Wrong.   Fundamental attribution error deals with attributions about others, not oneself.
                 d. Wrong.   This is the opposite pattern found with fundamental attribution error.

8. **b**   a. Wrong.   Attributions in this question are for people's own behavior, not someone else's.
    (p. 453)   c. Wrong.   Nobody is examining their own behavior to determine what their beliefs are.
                 d. Wrong.   Nobody's expectations are resulting in later behavior that matches their expectations.

9. **d**   a. Wrong.   This answer describes the cognitive component. Affect concerns emotions.
    (p. 455)   b. Wrong.   This is not considered a component of an attitude, and affect concerns emotions.
                 c. Wrong.   This answer describes the behavioral component. Affect concerns emotions.

10. **c**   a. Wrong.   This is classical conditioning in action.
    (p. 455)   b. Wrong.   This is a source characteristic in action.
                 d. Wrong.   This is instrumental conditioning in action.

11. **a**   b & c. Wrong.   These involve the peripheral route of persuasion.
    (p. 457)   d.   Wrong.   This describes cognitive dissonance, not the central route to persuasion.

12. **b**   a. Wrong.   Elaboration likelihood proposes central and peripheral routes to persuasion, not tension.
    (p. 458)   c. Wrong.   Self-perception theory states we use behavior to infer our attitudes. Tension isn't involved.
                 d. Wrong.   The triangular theory is Sternberg's theory of love.

13. **b**   a, c, & d.   Wrong.   Those paid $1 had the greatest shift in attitude.
    (p. 457)

14. **d**   a. Wrong.   This describes the cognitive dissonance theory.
    (p. 458)   b. Wrong.   This describes the fundamental attribution error.
                 c. Wrong.   This describes the elaboration likelihood model.

Behaving in the Presence of Others: Social Influence

1. **d**   a, b, & c.   Wrong.   Arousal is increased, causing the best learned, dominant response to occur.
    (p. 462)

2. **b**   a. Wrong.   This describes social facilitation.
    (p. 463)   c. Wrong.   This describes the group polarization effect.
                 d. Wrong.   This describes social loafing.

3. **a**   b. Wrong.   The decision didn't become more extreme. Note the suppression of dissenting views.
    (p. 468)   c. Wrong.   The decision didn't involve some members working less. Key is suppression of dissension.
                 d. Wrong.   The decision didn't involve conformity because the group was perceived to know more.

4. **c**
(p. 464)

- a. Wrong. This is the explanation of social facilitation and social interference.
- b. Wrong. Obedience isn't relevant; the person is reluctant to help due to diffusion of responsibility.
- d. Wrong. This describes an in-group. In the bystander effect the key is diffusion of responsibility.

5. **d**
(p. 465)

- a. Wrong. Social loafing is not doing your share of work when in a group. Anonymity and depersonalization are not typical.
- b. Wrong. Normative social influence involves conformity in order to fit in or be liked. Depersonalization, etc. is not involved.
- c. Wrong. Groupthink involves an emphasis on consensus and a failure to consider all information.

6. **b**
(p. 466)
(PN8C)

- a. Wrong. Group sizes above 5 don't increase conformity further, and can decrease it.
- c. Wrong. One person dissenting dramatically decreases conformity in others.
- d. Wrong. Conformity is decreased if the group is not respected.

7. **a**
(p. 467)

- b. Wrong. This answer describes informational social influence as a factor in conformity.
- c. Wrong. Normative relates to being average or typical of a group. No authority figure is needed.
- d. Wrong. Acting like others (the norm) reduces rejection. Diffusion of responsibility isn't an issue.

8. **b**
(p. 467)

- a. Wrong. This describes informational social influence.
- c. Wrong. This describes groupthink.
- d. Wrong. Group polarization involves the nature of group decisions, not division of labor.

9. **d**
(p. 471)

- a, b, & c. Wrong. Most people were distressed, but continued to the highest shock level.

Establishing Relations with Others

1. **c**
(p. 477)

- a. Wrong. Culture is influential.
- b. Wrong. Universal tendencies have been found.
- d. Wrong. General tendencies have been found.

2. **a**
(p. 478)

- b, c, & d. Wrong. Income, education, and attractiveness are not primary determinants.

3. **c**
(p. 479)

- a, b, & d. Wrong. The quote suggests one person must act friendly for another to be friendly-- reciprocity.

4. **b**
(p. 480)

- a. Wrong. Passionate love is usually low in commitment and enduring trust and warmth.
- c. Wrong. Empty love has commitment, but little passion or intimacy.
- d. Wrong. Infatuated love is low in intimacy (self-disclosure).

5. **d**
(p. 480)
(PT12B)

- a, b, & c. Wrong. The sides of the triangle are passion, intimacy, and commitment.

MAKING FINAL PREPARATIONS

Short Essay Questions

1. Stereotypes act as "rules of thumb" for how to organize the social world and how to act with new people. Stereotypes can be relatively accurate, although not always. The danger of stereotypes is that they emphasize differences between groups rather than differences within groups, and they may lead to prejudice and self-fulfilling prophesies. (pp. 447-450)

2. Festinger's cognitive dissonance is a tension created by a mismatch of attitudes and behavior. The person then tries to reduce dissonance, mostly by adjusting the attitude to match the behavior. Bem's theory doesn't involve dissonance. Bem suggests that rather than trying to reconcile existing attitudes and behavior, people determine their attitude on the spot by examining their recent behavior. "If I did this, I must like that." (pp. 458-459)

3. The presence of other people can improve (social facilitation) or impair (social interference) performance. These effects occur due to the increased arousal an audience produces. If the task is easy and well-learned, performance improves because arousal tends to result in the dominant response being made. If the task is difficult or new, the dominant response is not usually desired, leading to impaired performance. (pp. 461-462)

4. The bystander effect is the reluctance to help when other people are present. The primary explanation is that responsibility for helping (or the consequences of not helping) are shared by all present, a diffusion of responsibility. Thus, the person feels less responsible for helping; someone else can help. (pp. 463-464)

5. Similarity might promote friendship because similar views validate our views, which is valued. We might associate with similar people to avoid associating with people who don't agree with us. Physical factors might limit the range of possible mates. Unattractive people might be limited to other unattractive people as companions, and economic or social similarity can restrict exposure to different people. (pp. 478-479)

6. Passionate love involves an intense erotic attraction to, and longing for, another person. It has intimacy but low commitment. Companionate love has less passion, but is high in intimacy and commitment. (p. 480)

Matching

1. l (p. 479)	4. a (p. 469)	7. k (p. 461)	10. e (p. 469)	13. f (p. 458)	16. o (p. 451)
2. c (p. 462)	5. h (p. 445)	8. g (p. 466)	11. j (p. 447)	14. d (p. 447)	
3. i (p. 457)	6. p (p. 458)	9. b (p. 459)	12. n (p. 448)	15. m (p. 454)	

Multiple Choice Pretest 1

1. **b**   a, c, & d.   Wrong.   Evolutionary theory stresses reproductive and protective value.
(p. 457)

2. **c**   a, b, & d.   Wrong.   Physical attractiveness is associated with positive first impressions.
(p. 446)

3. **c**   a, b, & d.   Wrong.   These are all true.
(p. 449)

4. **b**   a & d.   Wrong.   Consensus involves whether other people show the behavior in the situation.
(p. 451)   c.   Wrong.   Consistency involves whether the behavior occurs every time the situation is present.

5. **d**   a & b.   Wrong.   These patterns are not strongly associated with a particular type of attribution.
(p. 452)   c.   Wrong.   This pattern is associated with external attributions.

6. **b**   a. Wrong.   Cognitive dissonance theory states that attitudes shift to match discrepant behavior.
(p. 456)   c. Wrong.   Self-perception theory states that behavior is used to infer attitudes.
          d. Wrong.   A social schema model concerns the knowledge base that influences social experiences.

7. **c**　　a. Wrong.　Discrimination is *behavior* that is directed against members of a group.
(p. 449)　b. Wrong.　Altruism is acting in a way that shows unselfish concern for the welfare of others.
　　　　d. Wrong.　Source characteristics are features of the person presenting a persuasive message.

8. **d**　　a. Wrong.　Harry's doing something nice to people he likes--no dissonance.
(p. 458)　b. Wrong.　Rod doesn't have to like a free car--little or no dissonance.
(PT12C)　c. Wrong.　Walter can justify eating meat because it's dinner with the boss--little or no dissonance.

9. **d**　　a. Wrong.　Deindividuation leads to atypical behavior, but not impaired behavior.
(p. 462)　b. Wrong.　Conformity involves copying behavior. Social interference doesn't involve conformity.
　　　　c. Wrong.　Reciprocity relates to friendships, not audience effects.

10. **a**　　b, c, & d.　Wrong.　Reluctance to help increases as the number of people present increases.
(p. 463)

11. **c**　　a. Wrong.　Altruism is helping behavior, not assigning blame for a failure.
(p. 452)　b. Wrong.　Dr. Marsh is making an attribution, not letting expectations affect his behavior.
　　　　d. Wrong.　Dr. Marsh is making an attribution. There is no mismatch of belief and behavior.

12. **d**　　a. Wrong.　He did not make an internal attribution about someone else's behavior.
(p. 453)　b. Wrong.　He didn't change his behavior based on his expectations.
(PM8B)　c. Wrong.　The elaboration likelihood model concerns attitude change, not attribution.

13. **b**　　a. Wrong.　This is the attitude itself, not one of the components.
(p. 455)　c. Wrong.　This is the affective component.
　　　　d. Wrong.　This is the behavioral component.

14. **d**　　a. Wrong.　The bystander effect is the reluctance to help if others are present.
(p. 465)　b. Wrong.　Group polarization is the tendency to make more extreme decisions in a group.
　　　　c. Wrong.　Low-balling is a technique related to attitude-behavior relationships.

15. **a**　　b. Wrong.　Group polarization causes extreme decisions. Don going along with the group is key here.
(p. 466)　c. Wrong.　Obedience is following an order. Don wasn't ordered to do anything.
　　　　d. Wrong.　Social facilitation is improved performance in the presence of others.

16. **b**　　a. Wrong.　The actor-observer effect relates to attributions, not conformity.
(p. 467)　c. Wrong.　Group polarization is a shift to a more extreme view when a group makes a decision.
　　　　d. Wrong.　Groupthink involves group decisions. No decision is involved in this question.

17. **d**　　a. Wrong.　There is no conformity based on information value. Key is the rush to consensus.
(p. 468)　b. Wrong.　Performance does not decrease due to an audience. Key is the rush to consensus.
　　　　c. Wrong.　The decision did not become more extreme with time. Key is the rush to consensus.

18. **d**　　a. Wrong.　Obedience is reduced but is still quite common when the setting is not prestigious.
(p. 472)　b. Wrong.　The fact that they were very upset disproves the idea they knew about the hoax.
　　　　c. Wrong.　*Less* obedience occurs if the authority figure leaves.

19. **a**　　b. Wrong.　Friendships are facilitated by proximity and mere exposure.
(p. 478)　c. Wrong.　Friendships are facilitated by proximity, mere exposure, and similarity.
　　　　d. Wrong.　Friendships are less likely when people are dissimilar.

20. **c**　　a, b, & d.　Wrong.　These do not involve the intense arousal of passionate love.
(p. 480)

Multiple Choice Pretest 2

1. **c**   a. Wrong.   Cognitive dissonance would occur if Jill's actions and attitudes didn't match.
(p. 448)   b. Wrong.   Social interference is impaired performance due to the presence of others.
          d. Wrong.   Self-serving bias is making internal attributions for your success, external ones for failures.

2. **d**   a. Wrong.   There is no mismatch in attitude and behavior, because only a belief is stated here.
(p. 447)   b. Wrong.   The actor-observer effect is the tendency to make external attributions about our own behavior, but internal attributions about others' behavior.
          c. Wrong.   This is an internal attribution.

3. **b**   a. Wrong.   If you decide based on whether Dan always fails, consistency is involved.
(p. 451)   c. Wrong.   If you decide based on whether Dan only failed this exam, distinctiveness is involved.
          d. Wrong.   Checking what other people did involves consensus. Expectancy is not a factor.

4. **c**   a. Wrong.   Fundamental attribution error is a bias to make internal attributions, not external ones.
(p. 451)   b. Wrong.   Self-serving bias would require an internal attribution in this situation.
(PN8B)   d. Wrong.   Car trouble is an event, not a trait, so the attribution is external, not internal.

5. **a**   b, c, & d.   Wrong.   These are all external attributions. Fundamental attribution error is a bias to
(p. 452)   make internal attributions about someone else.

6. **a**   b. Wrong.   The emphasis is on repetition, not an association of neutral and unconditioned stimuli.
(p. 455)   c. Wrong.   The emphasis is on repetition. Responses (attitudes) are not being reinforced or punished.
          d. Wrong.   Deindividuation occurs in a large group. The saying doesn't involve group influences.

7. **c**   a & b.   Wrong.   These are cognitive components.
(p. 455)   d.   Wrong.   These are affective components.

8. **c**   a. Wrong.   There is no mismatch of behavior and attitude here. Key is his use of direct information.
(p. 457)   b. Wrong.   There is no reward here. His use of direct information is the critical factor.
(PT12C)   d. Wrong.   He is using direct information, not source characteristics.

9. **b**   a.   Wrong.   Tom can justify his work because he is paid. Disapproval won't produce dissonance.
(p. 458)   c & d.   Wrong.   Kit has more dissonance than Tom. She is freely supporting Smith, so her attitude will remain more positive to better match her behavior.

10. **d**   a. Wrong.   The discussion was well balanced, so groupthink didn't occur.
(p. 467)   b. Wrong.   An audience didn't improve performance. Positions became more extreme.
          c. Wrong.   Conformity to be like the group is not an issue. The issue is the shift to an extreme view.

11. **d**   a. Wrong.   Consensus relates to whether others behave similarly.
(p. 459)   b. Wrong.   Self-fulfilling prophesy involves the effect of one person's attitudes on another person's behavior, not the effect of compliance with small requests.
          c. Wrong.   There is no indication that conforming to a group's standard is relevant in this question.

12. **b**   a, c, & d.   Wrong.   Similarity is a strong determinant of friendship.
(p. 478)

13. **a**   b. Wrong.   Ben is basing his attitude on his behavior, not changing it due to dissonance.
(p. 458)   c. Wrong.   Ben is not making an internal attribution about someone's behavior.
(PT12A)   d. Wrong.   Ben's attitude is based on an evaluation of his past behavior, not central or peripheral routes.

14. **c**   a. Wrong. Key here is not feeling like an individual, not a more extreme decision after discussion.
(p. 465) b. Wrong. There was no improved performance due to an audience here.
          d. Wrong. Fred did not return the feelings shown toward him. Key here is loss of individuality.

15. **d**   a. Wrong. This doesn't involve a group making a more extreme decision than an individual.
(p. 463) b. Wrong. This doesn't involve expectations leading to behavior matching those expectations.
          c. Wrong. This doesn't involve forming an attitude based on simple exposure to the item.

16. **c**   a. Wrong. Group polarization is a shift to an extreme position, not a tendency to conform.
(p. 467) b. Wrong. Nan was not ordered to ride a bike, she just wanted to avoid rejection.
          d. Wrong. Nan is not gaining information from the group, she just wants approval.

17. **b**   a. Wrong. Self-perception theory relates to attitude change, not the situations described.
(p. 464) c. Wrong. These statements do not explain the cause of behavior in terms of personal traits.
          d. Wrong. The focus of the statements is on other people's participation in events, not on returning feelings shown by others toward oneself.

18. **c**   a. Wrong. Passion involves intense erotic feelings.
(p. 480) b. Wrong. Commitment is a decision to remain in the relationship.
          d. Wrong. Companionship is not a dimension.

19. **c**   a. Wrong. Jacob didn't work less in a group. Key here is Jacob obeying an authority's orders.
(p. 469) b. Wrong. Jacob's performance didn't suffer due to an audience. Jacob obeyed an authority.
          d. Wrong. Jacob didn't conform his behavior to the norm of a group. He obeyed an authority.

20. **c**   a, b, & d.   Wrong.   Blended, prototypical faces were preferred.
(p. 475)

CHAPTER 14: PSYCHOLOGICAL DISORDERS

ESTABLISHING LEARNING GOALS

Use these learning goals as a preview of the chapter, a guide for active reading, and to evaluate your mastery of the material. Review the relevant goals as you begin and end your reading of each major section of the chapter.

I. Solve the conceptual problem of defining abnormality.
    A. Evaluate the various criteria that have been used to define abnormality.
    B. Discuss the legal definition of insanity.
    C. Explain how the medical model classifies and categorizes abnormality.
    D. Discuss the effects of diagnostic labeling.

II. Solve the conceptual problem of classifying psychological disorders.
    A. Describe the DSM-IV.
    B. Describe the common anxiety disorders.
        1. Compare the symptoms of generalized anxiety disorder, panic disorder, and specific phobias.
        2. Describe obsessive-compulsive disorder.
    C. Describe the somatoform disorders.
    D. Describe the common dissociative disorders.
        1. Compare dissociative amnesia and dissociative fugue.
        2. Describe dissociative identity disorder, and discuss why this disorder is controversial.
    E. Describe the common mood disorders.
        1. Describe the symptoms of a major depressive episode.
        2. Describe bipolar disorder.
        3. Discuss the risk factors for suicide and how suicide can be prevented.
    F. Describe the characteristics of schizophrenia.
        1. Differentiate positive and negative symptoms and give examples of each.
        2. Explain how schizophrenia differs from dissociative identity disorder.
    G. Describe the common personality disorders.
        1. Compare paranoid, dependent, and antisocial personality disorders.
        2. Explain why personality disorders are not listed as Axis I disorders.

III. Solve the practical problem of understanding the origin of psychological disorders.
    A. Explain how biological and genetic factors can contribute to psychological disorders.
        1. Describe the role of neurotransmitters in schizophrenia and mood disorders.
        2. Describe structural changes in the brain associated with psychological disorders.
        3. Describe the evidence for a genetic predisposition for schizophrenia and mood disorders.
    B. Explain how maladaptive thoughts can contribute to psychological disorders.
        1. Describe the types of attributions that are characteristic of psychological disorders.
        2. Explain the learned helplessness theory of depression.
    C. Explain how environmental factors can contribute to psychological disorders.

MASTERING THE MATERIAL

Preview & Conceptualizing Abnormality: What is Abnormal Behavior?

(pp. 489-495)

Mastering the Vocabulary. Define or explain each of the following terms. To check your answers, consult the text pages listed.

1. statistical deviance (p. 490)

2. cultural deviance (p. 491)

3. emotional distress (p. 491)

4. dysfunction (p. 491)

5. insanity (p. 492)

6. medical model (p. 493)

7. diagnostic labeling effects (p. 494)

Mastering the Concepts. Fill in the blanks to create a summary of the section. Answers are on page 343.

Three conceptual and practical problems are explored: How should abnormal behavior be defined? How can psychological disorders be classified? What are the underlying causes of psychological disorders?

Abnormality can be defined in terms of _____(1) deviance or infrequency, _____(2) deviance, emotional _____(3), or _____(4), a breakdown in normal functioning. Any one definition is insufficient to define abnormality, and some disorders involve exaggerations of normal behavior. Normal and abnormal behavior are considered to form a continuum, not clear-cut categories.

_____(5) is a legal concept and is usually defined based on the person's ability to understand whether an action is right or wrong. The insanity defense began in the 1800's in the M'Naughten case. It is used in only 1% of felony cases and is successful only 26% of the time.

The _____(6) model views abnormality as a symptom of disease. Support for this includes _____(7) abnormalities found in some disorders and the fact that disorders may be classified in terms of symptoms. Criticisms focus on a lack of identifiable physical causes for some disorders, the idea that some problems are "problems in living," and the stigma of diagnostic _____(8). Rosenhan's pseudopatient study shows that labels affect the interpretation of later behavior.

Evaluating Your Progress. Select the one best response. Answers are on page 343. If you make any errors, reread the relevant material before proceeding.

1. Behaviors that violate the accepted rules might be classified as abnormal using the criterion of
   a. statistical deviance.
   b. cultural deviance.
   c. dysfunction.
   d. emotional distress.

2. Who is most likely to be considered psychologically abnormal?
   a. Fred, who cried for two days nonstop after hearing his father died
   b. Nathan, who screams obscenities at the umpires at the baseball game
   c. Tom, who sits immobile for hours in his room for no apparent reason
   d. Roy, who can calculate the day of the week for any date in the last 1200 years

3. The primary criterion for a judgment of insanity is whether the person
   a. violated the cultural norms for behavior due to a "mental disease."
   b. acted in dysfunctional or maladaptive ways due to a "mental disease."
   c. showed intense emotional distress due to a "mental disease."
   d. had no understanding of the wrongfulness of the behavior due to a "mental disease."

4. Some psychological disorders can be treated with drugs that affect neurotransmitters, and many psychological disorders may be reliably classified in terms of measurable symptoms. These facts support
   a. the legal definition of insanity.
   b. the medical model of abnormality.
   c. the need to consider the context of a behavior before labeling a person psychologically abnormal.
   d. the need for more than one type of deviance to declare a person psychologically abnormal.

5. Rosenhan's pseudopatient study is important because it showed
   a. psychologists are incompetent in most cases.
   b. patients in mental hospitals receive inhumane treatment.
   c. the medical model of psychological disorders is most appropriate.
   d. expectations and labels influence the interpretation of behavior.

Classifying Psychological Disorders: DMS-IV (pp. 496-510)

Mastering the Vocabulary. Define or explain each of the following terms. To check your answers, consult the text pages listed.

1. DSM-IV (p. 496)

2. anxiety disorders (p. 498)

3. generalized anxiety disorder (p. 498)

4. panic disorder (p. 499)

5. agoraphobia (p. 499)

6. obsessive-compulsive disorder (p. 499)

7. specific phobic disorder (p. 500)

8. somatoform disorders (p. 501)

9. hypochondriasis (p. 501)

10. somatization disorder (p. 502)

11. conversion disorder (p. 502)

12. dissociative disorders (p. 502)

13. dissociative amnesia (p. 503)

14. dissociative fugue (p. 503)

15. dissociative identity disorder (p. 503)

16. mood disorders (p. 504)

17. major depressive episode (p. 504)

18. bipolar disorder (p. 505)

19. manic state (p. 505)

20. schizophrenia (p. 507)

21. personality disorders (p. 510)

22. paranoid personality disorder (p. 510)

23. dependent personality disorder (p. 510)

24. antisocial personality disorder (p. 510)

Mastering the Concepts. Fill in the blanks to create a summary of the section. Answers are on page 343.

DSM-IV is a _____(9) system based on objective, measurable criteria without reference to therapy. Axis I, clinical syndromes, and Axis II, _____(10) disorders, classify abnormal behavior. Axis III notes _____(11) conditions, Axis IV notes _____(12) problems, and Axis V evaluates current daily functioning.

Persistent and intense anxiety that interferes with behavior characterizes the _____(13) disorders. In _____(14) anxiety disorder, the anxiety is free-floating and unrealistic and may cause physical symptoms related to the autonomic nervous system. In _____(15) disorder, anxiety is sudden, relatively brief, but intense. If an attack occurs in public, the person may develop _____(16), a fear of going into public places. Obsessive-compulsive disorder involves obsessions, persistent _____(17), and compulsions, a need to perform an action. A specific, irrational fear is found in specific _____(18) disorder.

_____(19) disorders focus on the body. In hypochondriasis, normal bodily reactions are interpreted as serious medical conditions. In somatization disorder, the focus is on _____(20) without a physical cause, rather than the possible disease. In _____(21) disorder, the person has a true symptom but no real physical disorder, such as paralysis when the nervous system is normal.

The _____(22) disorders involve a separation of conscious awareness from memories. Dissociative amnesia involves memory loss not due to head injury. Dissociative _____(23) involves a loss of memory for identity and a flight from the home. Dissociative _____(24) disorder involves more than one personality. This disorder is controversial, and not all psychologists accept it.

The mood disorders involve prolonged, disabling disruptions of emotional state, including depressive disorders and _____(25) disorder. A major depressive episode involves behavioral changes, low mood, and a pessimistic outlook. Milder, more chronic depression is dysthymic disorder. _____(26) depression is disthymic disorder with a major depressive episode. In bipolar disorder, mood swings from depression to a _____(27) of hyperactivity and abnormal thought. The risk factors for suicide include depression, sudden stress, suicidal _____(28), and prior attempts. Suicide among young adults can be reduced through gatekeeper training, _____(29) skills training, and increased media awareness.

_____(30) involves disordered thoughts, emotion, and behavior, but symptoms vary across cases. Symptoms are classified as _____(31) if they involve an excess or added behavior, and _____(32) if they involve a deficit. Schizophrenia often involves hallucinations, _____(33) without a sensory cause, and _____(34), thoughts with inappropriate content. Speech may be disordered, thoughts may be disconnected, emotions may be flat, and bizarre postures may be held for long periods, _____(35).

Axis II describes personality disorders, chronic patterns of behavior that lead to impaired _____(36) function. People with _____(37) personality disorder show a pervasive distrust of others, _____(38) personality disorder involves the need to be taken care of, and _____(39) personality disorder involves no respect for social customs and an absence of guilt. Personality disorders are more ingrained and inflexible than Axis I disorders, and some psychologists argue they are not true disorders, only extreme versions of personality traits.

Evaluating Your Progress. Select the one best response. Answers are on page 344. If you make any errors, reread the relevant material before proceeding.

1. The purpose of the DSM-IV is
    a. to provide a definition of insanity that is based on objective criteria.
    b. to indicate the appropriate treatment for common psychological disorders.
    c. to provide an objective classification system for psychological disorders.
    d. to eliminate the problems associated with diagnostic labeling effects.

2. Axis III and Axis IV of DSM-IV involve
   a. an evaluation of the person's current level of adaptive functioning.
   b. the medical and psychosocial context in which the behavioral symptoms should be considered.
   c. objective and measurable definitions of all the major clinical syndromes.
   d. evaluation of pervasive behavioral characteristics such as mental retardation and personality.

3. The disorders characterized by persistent, intense apprehension that interferes with functioning are
   a. the anxiety disorders.
   b. the schizophrenias.
   c. the mood disorders.
   d. the dissociative disorders.

4. The disorder in which a particular object or situation produces an intense, unrealistic fear is
   a. panic disorder.
   b. obsessive-compulsive disorder.
   c. manic state.
   d. specific phobic disorder.

5. A strong need to perform some behavior, usually in a repetitive manner, is
   a. a phobia.
   b. an obsession.
   c. a delusion.
   d. a compulsion.

6. Hypochondriasis and conversion disorder are
   a. somatoform disorders.
   b. personality disorders.
   c. dissociative disorders.
   d. anxiety disorders.

7. Dissociative fugue most specifically involves
   a. a loss of personal identity that is accompanied by flight from the home.
   b. mood shifts from deep depression to a manic state.
   c. chronic, free-floating anxiety.
   d. the alternation of two or more apparently distinct identities or personalities.

8. Bipolar disorder is characterized by
   a. hallucinations and language disorders.
   b. alternation between depression and a manic state.
   c. dysthymia and a major depressive episode.
   d. two or more personalities.

9. All of the following are characteristic of schizophrenia except
   a. disordered thoughts.
   b. disordered language.
   c. inappropriate emotions.
   d. multiple personalities.

10. Tina thinks that she is Joan of Arc. This is an example of
   a. an hallucination.
   b. a delusion.
   c. catatonia.
   d. dysthymia.

11. Axis II personality disorders differ from Axis I clinical syndromes because personality disorders
   a. generally seem to be due to a specific brain dysfunction, unlike the clinical syndromes.
   b. are more ingrained and inflexible, and are resistant to treatment, unlike the clinical syndromes.
   c. come and go without treatment much more often than the clinical syndromes.
   d. involve statistically deviant behavior, but not maladaptive behavior.

Understanding Psychological Disorders: Biological, Cognitive, or Environmental? (pp. 511-517)

Mastering the Vocabulary. Define or explain each of the following terms. To check your answers, consult the text pages listed.

1. bio-psycho-social perspective (p. 511)

2. learned helplessness (p. 516)

Mastering the Content. Fill in the blanks to create a summary of the section. Answers are on page 343.

The bio-psycho-social perspective recognizes the multiple causes of abnormality. Signs of abnormal brain chemistry or brain structures and evidence for a genetic component to disorders support a biological explanation of some psychological disorders. Schizophrenia may involve an excess of _____(40) or an interaction between dopamine and other neurotransmitters. Drugs that affect dopamine affect the symptoms of schizophrenia. Schizophrenia is associated with low activity in the frontal lobes and enlarged _____(41). For mood disorders, the monoamine neurotransmitters _____(42), norepineprine and dopamine may be involved. The true role of these abnormalities is unclear, however.

There is a strong _____(43) predisposition for schizophrenia and mood disorders. Concordance rates for identical twins with schizophrenia are very high and also very high for _____(44) disorders. Children whose parents have these disorders are at greater risk, even if adopted into healthy homes.

Thought patterns also may be a determinant of mood disorders. People prone to depression tend to make attributions that are _____(45), stable, and global. If repeated failures occur, learned _____(46) can occur, leading to passive behavior and depression.

Evidence suggests some disorders may be learned or influenced by cultural factors. _____(47) might be classically conditioned, and abnormal behaviors, if reinforced, can be acquired through _____(48) conditioning. Observational learning also may contribute to the development of phobias.

Evaluating Your Progress. Select the one best response. Answers are on page 345. If you make any errors, reread the relevant material before proceeding.

1. The neurotransmitter that seems to be involved in schizophrenia is
   a. dopamine.
   b. norepinephrine.
   c. acetylcholine.
   d. epinephrine.

2. If one identical twin develops schizophrenia, the other twin's odds of developing schizophrenia are
   a. 1 in 100.
   b. 1 in 50.
   c. 1 in 20.
   d. 1 in 2.

3. The data concerning genetic influences on mood disorders shows that
   a. mood disorders have no significant genetic component.
   b. mood disorders have a significant genetic component, but it is weaker than that for schizophrenia.
   c. mood disorders have a genetic component at least as strong as that for schizophrenia.
   d. mood disorders are almost entirely due to genetic factors.

4. Instead of pointing to genetic determinants, some psychologists suggest depression is a matter of
   a. maladaptive attributions.
   b. defective parenting.
   c. classical conditioning.
   d. poor diet and too little sleep.

5. Research with monkeys suggests that a disorder likely to develop due to learning is
   a. schizophrenia.
   b. dissociative disorder.
   c. bipolar disorder.
   d. specific phobic disorder.

6. Which neurotransmitter is affected by Prozac, an antidepressant, and may be involved in mood disorders?
   a. acteylcholine
   b. serotonin
   c. GABA
   d. lithium carbonate

MAKING FINAL PREPARATIONS

Complete these sections without consulting your book or notes. For a more accurate estimate of how well you know this material, wait at least a day or two after studying the chapter before working on the questions. Some material you "know" immediately after working with the chapter will be quickly forgotten. Immediate tests will overestimate what you know well.

Short Essay Questions. Write a brief answer to each question. Sample answers are on page 345.

1. Identify the four criteria for abnormality and discuss why classifying abnormal behavior is difficult.

2. Discuss the purpose of Axes III, IV, and V of the DSM-IV.

3. Explain how insanity differs from psychological abnormality.

4. Compare generalized anxiety disorder and specific phobic disorder.

5. Explain what positive and negative symptoms are, and give an example of each.

6. Explain how classical conditioning, instrumental conditioning and observational learning could influence the development of specific phobic disorder.

Matching. Select the correct definition or description for each item. Answers are on page 346.

_____	1. dependent personality disorder	**a.**	belief that others are plotting against you
_____	2. catatonia	**b.**	disorder with thought, emotion, & behavior defects
_____	3. double depression	**c.**	chronic behavior causing impaired social function
_____	4. delusion of persecution	**d.**	lack of emotion
_____	5. anxiety disorders	**e.**	disorders that focus on the body
_____	6. dysthymic disorder	**f.**	involves excessive need to be cared for
_____	7. delusion of grandeur	**g.**	chronic, moderate depression
_____	8. personality disorders	**h.**	tendency to hold strange postures for a long time
_____	9. dissociative disorder	**i.**	sense of helplessness after repeated failures
_____	10. flat affect	**j.**	prolonged and disabling disruption of emotion
_____	11. mood disorders	**k.**	major depressive episode added to dysthymia
_____	12. somatoform disorders	**l.**	the thought you are someone famous
_____	13. learned helplessness	**m.**	disorders with separation of awareness & memory
_____	14. schizophrenia	**n.**	disorders with excessive, prolonged apprehension

Multiple Choice Pretest 1. Select the one best response. Answers are on page 346.

1. If a behavior is classified as abnormal because it occurs infrequently, abnormality is being defined by
   a. cultural deviance.
   b. dysfunction.
   c. emotional distress.
   d. statistical deviance.

2. Which of the following is true concerning the insanity defense in felony cases?
   a. It is attempted in about 25% of felony cases, and it is often successful.
   b. It is attempted in about 25% of felony cases, and it is rarely successful.
   c. It is attempted in less than 1% of felony cases, and it is often successful.
   d. It is attempted in less than 1% of felony cases, and it is rarely successful.

3. Criticisms of the medical model of psychological disorders include the idea that
   a. the medical model sees many disorders as problems with living.
   b. the medical model puts too much emphasis on cultural context.
   c. some mental disorders have no well-defined physical cause.
   d. behavioral symptoms allow reliable classification of many disorders.

4. Diagnostic labeling effects involve
   a. giving inappropriate diagnoses to individuals who have psychological disorders.
   b. treating a person differently because they have a history of psychological disorder.
   c. spontaneous improvements in a person's symptoms after being given a name for their problem.
   d. excusing criminal behavior by blaming it on psychological problems.

5. Axis I of the DSM-IV
   a. includes the criteria used to define major clinical syndromes.
   b. is used to note major medical conditions that might affect diagnosis.
   c. is used to note environmental problems that might affect diagnosis and treatment.
   d. involves a global assessment of the person's current adaptive functioning.

6. Obsessive-compulsive disorder is an example of
   a. an anxiety disorder.
   b. a somatoform disorder.
   c. a dissociative disorder.
   d. a mood disorder.

7. Terri cannot see, although there is nothing physically wrong with her eyes. Terri's problem might be
   a. hypochondriasis.
   b. dissociative fugue.
   c. panic disorder.
   d. conversion disorder.

8. Which is a negative symptom of schizophrenia?
   a. flat affect
   b. catatonia
   c. delusions
   d. disorganized speech

9. Chris has been having repeated attacks of sudden, overwhelming anxiety in which his heart races and he feels like he's going to die. His doctor has found no physical problem. Chris' diagnosis probably is
   a. generalized anxiety disorder.
   b. specific phobic disorder.
   c. panic disorder.
   d. somatoform disorder.

10. Gary shifts between two other apparently distinct personalities, but he has only incomplete knowledge of his alternate selves. Gary's diagnostic classification would probably be
    a. schizophrenia.
    b. dissociative identity disorder.
    c. somatization disorder.
    d. bipolar disorder.

11. For two months Lenny has been sleeping little. He is extremely restless, can't concentrate, and feels worthless and low. He doesn't even get dressed most days. Lenny's problem would be classified as
    a. schizophrenia.
    b. conversion disorder.
    c. obsessive-compulsive disorder.
    d. major depressive episode.

12. We know that schizophrenia is not entirely due to genetic factors because
    a. children raised apart from their schizophrenic parents have a greater rate of schizophrenia than their adoptive siblings.
    b. children raised apart from their schizophrenic parents have the same rate of schizophrenia as their adoptive siblings.
    c. the concordance rate for fraternal twins is very low.
    d. the concordance rate for identical twins is not 100%.

13. Which of the following will be least useful for improving suicide prevention among young people?
    a. Train teachers and coaches to recognize the warning signs for suicide.
    b. Improve availability of suicide hotline services.
    c. Increase media coverage of suicides when they occur.
    d. Teach coping and general life skills to young people.

14. The physiological factors associated with schizophrenia include
    a. brain swelling.
    b. higher than usual frontal lobe activity.
    c. larger than usual ventricles.
    d. neurofibrillary tangles in the cortex.

15. A pervasive and long-term distrust of others, without evidence of thought or emotional disorders, are symptoms of
    a. antisocial personality disorder.
    b. dependent personality disorder.
    c. paranoid personality disorder.
    d. multiple personality disorder.

16. An imbalance of the monoamines (serotonin, norepinephrine, dopamine) seems to be involved in
    a. antisocial personality disorder.
    b. mood disorders.
    c. somatoform disorders.
    d. dissociative disorders.

17. People prone to depression are likely to make attributions about failures that are
    a. global, stable, and internal.
    b. global, unstable, and internal.
    c. specific, unstable, and external.
    d. specific, stable, and external.

18. Theresa always gets a lot of attention when she screams at the sight of a spider. If she develops a spider phobia, an appropriate explanation will be that the phobia was acquired through
    a. classical conditioning.
    b. instrumental conditioning.
    c. observational learning.
    d. learned helplessness.

Multiple Choice Pretest 2. Select the one best response. Answers are on page 347.

1. Becoming a good chemist is so important to Dot that she constantly studies her chemistry. She sleeps and eats little, she has no friends, and she is failing her other classes. Dot's behavior would be considered abnormal based on
    a. insanity.
    b. dysfunction.
    c. cultural deviance.
    d. personal distress.

2. Ike heard voices telling him the children had put a worm in his brain. He planned for weeks how he would kill them and hide their bodies. His insanity defense failed. The jury must have decided
    a. he did not have serious psychological problems.
    b. he met the cultural deviance and statistical criteria, but not the dysfunction or distress criteria.
    c. he was capable of understanding the wrongfulness of his actions.
    d. a medical problem caused his thought disorders, not a psychological one.

3. Laura thinks psychological disorders are caused by a disease that can be cured with an appropriate treatment. Laura believes in
    a. the medical model.
    b. the DSM-IV.
    c. insanity.
    d. the Rosenhan study.

4. Yan, who has a history of depression, is likely to explain being laid off from work by saying,
    a. "It was just luck, I guess. I was one of the most recently hired, so I'm the first to go."
    b. "That foreman never liked me, no matter how hard I worked."
    c. "I'm just incompetent. I was rotten in school, and now I'm rotten in my job."
    d. "I wasn't very good at my job yet. I'll get more training, and this won't happen again."

5. A past political candidate became emotional and had tears in his eyes while talking about the difficulties of his campaign. Because he had a history of depression, this incident received more negative attention than similar behavior by other candidates without histories of depression. The different reactions to the behavior seems to be an example of
   a. dissociation.
   b. learned helplessness.
   c. a diagnostic labeling effect.
   d. maladaptive attributions.

6. Fran suffered a panic attack in public one day, and since then, she has found it very difficult to leave her home without being overwhelmed by anxiety. Her intense fear of going out is characteristic of
   a. obsessive-compulsive disorder.
   b. agoraphobia.
   c. generalized anxiety disorder.
   d. conversion disorder.

7. Mark woke up and found he didn't know who he was or what he did for a living. The doctor he consulted could find no evidence of a stroke or other physical problem. Mark's problem is probably
   a. dissociative identity disorder.
   b. dissociative fugue.
   c. dissociative amnesia.
   d. conversion disorder.

8. Abe worries unrealistically about everything all the time. He shows high autonomic nervous system activity and a variety of chronic medical complaints. Abe probably would be diagnosed as having
   a. panic disorder.
   b. generalized anxiety disorder.
   c. agoraphobia.
   d. obsessive-compulsive disorder.

9. Woody Allen's characters often interpret minor physical symptoms as major diseases. A headache means a brain tumor, and minor indigestion means stomach cancer. This behavior is characteristic of
   a. a somatoform disorder.
   b. a dissociative disorder.
   c. an anxiety disorder.
   d. a personality disorder.

10. Last month Kiesha's mood was very low, she felt worthless and considered suicide. This month Kiesha has been racing around in a hyperactive state making great plans, none of which are realistic or have been completed. She says she feels great, but her thinking isn't normal, and she tends to jump from one idea to another. Kiesha's symptoms are consistent with
    a. dissociative fugue.
    b. dysthymic disorder.
    c. bipolar disorder.
    d. double depression.

11. The primary difference in hypochondriasis and somatization disorder is that
    a. hypochondriasis focuses on the possible disease and somatization disorder focuses on the symptoms.
    b. the anxiety is very general in hypochondriasis, but it is linked to a specific idea or thing in somatization disorder.
    c. there are actual physical problems in hypochondriasis but not in somatization disorder.
    d. hypochondriasis develops rapidly, but somatization disorder develops more slowly.

12. Clark hears voices in his head and thinks the CIA is watching him. His thoughts are generally disordered, and his emotions are inappropriate. His behavior is so maladaptive that he has been hospitalized several times. Clark is probably classified as having
    a. bipolar disorder.
    b. generalized anxiety disorder.
    c. dissociative identity disorder.
    d. schizophrenia.

13. For years Walter has stolen people's money in fake investment schemes. He never feels guilt, and does not respect laws or moral values. A prison psychologist is likely to diagnose Walter as having
    a. schizophrenia.
    b. a personality disorder.
    c. a dissociative disorder.
    d. conversion disorder.

14. Most drugs used to treat schizophrenia block the activity of
    a. dopamine.
    b. serotonin.
    c. acetylcholine.
    d. norepinephrine.

15. Sue is depressed. Her psychologist suggested that she has simply given up because of the many failures she has experienced. Apparently Sue's psychologist believes depression is the result of
    a. classical conditioning.
    b. modeling.
    c. learned helplessness.
    d. instrumental conditioning.

16. The hyperactive, euphoric periods of bipolar disorder are
    a. delusions.
    b. dissociations.
    c. fugue episodes.
    d. manic states.

17. The "schizo" in schizophrenia means "split." This split refers to
    a. consciousness and memory.
    b. personality or identity.
    c. attributions.
    d. the mind or thoughts.

18. Adam and Wilma both have schizophrenia. Their child, Thea, was raised in a healthy adoptive family without contact with Wilma and Adam. The likelihood that Thea will develop schizophrenia is
    a. equal to the general population's likelihood.
    b. equal to her adoptive siblings' likelihood.
    c. much higher than her adoptive siblings' likelihood.
    d. almost 100%.

19. Which of the following is an Axis II disorder?
    a. dependent personality disorder.
    b. dissociative identity disorder.
    c. schizophrenia.
    d. somatoform disorder.

LANGUAGE DEVELOPMENT GUIDE

Core Terms

In the lectures on this chapter, you are likely to hear terms like *pathology, impaired, dysfunction, lesion, compromised* and *debilitating*. Not surprisingly, these are all words having to do with disease. A *lesion*, as you may remember from chapter 3, is a cut or injury; *pathology* refers to a disease that causes damage. A *lesion* of the brain is likely to cause *impairment* or *dysfunction* -- the injured part of the brain won't work properly anymore. Another way to say it is that the function of that part will be *compromised*. Such an injury would be *debilitating* -- it would destroy the ability of the brain to function properly.

Since there are so many more conditions described in the DSM than are discussed in the book, don't be surprised if you hear about some more in class. Your instructor is also likely to talk about some famous *case studies*, or share *anecdotes* (brief stories) about patients they have heard about or treated. These can be both interesting and helpful when you study. Remember, elaborative thinking improves recall -- so thinking of interesting examples will help you recall the material you need to learn.

Idioms

p. 489	the general public	most people
p. 490	sole criterion for	the only way of judging something
p. 492	the brunt of	the main force of
p. 494	pseudopatient	pretend patient; someone who is pretending to be ill
p. 496	clinicians	doctors and other health professionals
p. 494	jingle	short song used in advertisements

p. 502	colorful types	people with unusual personalities
p. 502	Hollywood	California city where movies and TV programs are made
p. 502	the popular press	magazines or newspapers read by the general public
p. 502	amnesiac	someone suffering from amnesia
p. 504	the community at large	the whole community; most of the people involved
p. 505	grandiosity	a belief that you are much more powerful or important than you really are
p. 505	roller-coaster	a ride which sends you up and down hills very quickly
p. 507	gone awry	gone wrong; gone off course
p. 514	adoptees	those who have been adopted
p. 515	extraterrestrials	'people' from outer space; aliens
p. 516	plays a pivotal role	influences an important change
p. 517	does not preclude	does not rule out

Word Parts

Here are some words that are made up of word parts, and that you can find in this chapter. After you've looked at these, you can look for others in the chapter with the same word parts.

WORD	WORD PART IT USES	MEANING
concurrently	con, com = together cur = to run	to run or happen at the same time
divert	di = two vert, vers = to turn	to split; to make go in a different direction
conspire	con, com = together spir = to breathe	to plan secretly; to whisper together
depressive	de = down, from, away press = to push down	that which pushes down
respond	re = again spon = to promise, to cause to expect	to reply, answer; to act in return

Knowing the word parts listed above, you can also create the following words. You can get an idea of their meanings from the word parts they use.

convert   _____ + _____   change, turn around

revert   re + vert   _____

compress   _____ + _____   to press together

Pronunciation

p. 491	dysfunction	dis-funk′-shun	p. 501	hypochondriasis	hy-po-kon-dry′-uh-sis
p. 497	anxiety	ang-zy′-i-tee	p. 503	fugue	fewg
p. 499	agoraphobia	uh-gore-i-fo′-bee-a	p. 507	schizophrenia	skiz-o-fren′-ee-uh *or* skiz-o-freen′-ee-uh

ANSWERS AND EXPLANATIONS

To find relevant material in your textbook, consult the pages cited with each answer. Also, PN and PT citations refer to modules in *PsychNow!* and *Psyk.trek* materials, respectively.

Mastering the Concepts

1. statistical (p. 490)
2. cultural (p. 491)
3. distress (p. 491)
4. dysfunction (p. 491)
5. Insanity (p. 492)
6. medical model (p. 493)
7. neurotransmitter (p. 493)
8. labeling (p. 494)
9. classification (p. 496)
10. personality (p. 496)
11. medical (p. 496)
12. psychosocial (p. 496)

13. anxiety (p. 498)
14. generalized (p. 498)
15. panic (p. 499)
16. agoraphobia (p. 499)
17. thoughts (p. 499)
18. phobic (p. 500)
19. Somatoform (p. 501)
20. symptoms (p. 502)
21. conversion (p. 502)
22. dissociative (p. 502)
23. fugue (p. 503)
24. identity (p. 503)

25. bipolar (p. 505)
26. Double (p. 505)
27. manic state (p. 505)
28. thinking (p. 505)
29. coping (p. 507)
30. Schizophrenia (p. 507)
31. positive (p. 508)
32. negative (p. 508)
33. perceptions (p. 509)
34. delusions (p. 508)
35. catatonia (p. 508)
36. social (p. 510)

37. paranoid (p. 510)
38. dependent (p. 510)
39. antisocial (p. 510)
40. dopamine (p. 512)
41. ventricles (p. 513)
42. serotonin (p. 512)
43. genetic (p. 513)
44. mood (p. 513)
45. internal (p. 515)
46. helplessness (p. 516)
47. Phobias (p. 516)
48. instrumental (p. 517)

Evaluating Your Progress

Preview & Conceptualizing Abnormality: What is Abnormal Behavior?

1. **b**   a. Wrong.   Statistical deviance relates to frequency, not rule violations, not disruptive behavior.
(p. 491)   c. Wrong.   Dysfunction involves maladaptive behavior that might or might not violate rules.
(PN7C)   d. Wrong.   Emotional distress involves personal feelings of emotional discomfort.

2. **c**   a & b.   Wrong.   The context changes the interpretation of these behaviors.
(p. 491)   d.   Wrong.   Statistical deviance isn't enough to declare psychological abnormality.

3. **d**   a, b, & c.   Wrong.   Insanity requires a lack of appreciation for the wrongfulness of the action.
(p. 492)

4. **b**   a, c, & d.   Wrong.   Biological causes and "symptoms" relate to the medical model.
(p. 493)

5. **d**   a.   Wrong.   Diagnosis was based on reported symptoms. Absence of abnormality was later noted.
(p. 494)   b.   Wrong.   There is no indication of inhumane treatment.
            c.   Wrong.   This study says nothing about the validity of the medical model.

Classifying Psychological Disorders: DMS-IV and Selected Clinical Syndromes

1. **c**   a.   Wrong.   DSM-IV only classifies disorders. It doesn't address insanity.
(p. 496)   b.   Wrong.   DSM-IV says nothing about treatment. It only classifies disorders.
            d.   Wrong.   DSM-IV is a labeling system. It won't eliminate labeling effects.

2. **b**   a.   Wrong.   This is Axis V. Axes III and IV deal with medical and psychosocial conditions.
(p. 496)   c.   Wrong.   This is Axis I. Axes III and IV deal with medical and psychosocial conditions.
            d.   Wrong.   This is Axis II. Axes III and IV deal with medical and psychosocial conditions.

3. **a**   b.   Wrong.   Schizophrenia involves disorders of thought, emotion, and behavior, not necessarily worry.
(p. 498)   c.   Wrong.   Mood disorders involve prolonged disruption of emotion, not necessarily apprehension.
(PT11A)   d.   Wrong.   Dissociative disorders involve separation of conscious awareness from memories.

4. **d**   a.   Wrong.   Panic disorder involves sudden, nonspecific anxiety.
(p. 500)   b.   Wrong.   OCD includes intrusive thoughts and ritualistic behavior.
            c.   Wrong.   A manic state involves hyperactivity, not irrational fear of an object.

5. **d**   a.   Wrong.   Phobias are intense, irrational fears.
(p. 499)   b.   Wrong.   Obsessions are persistent, uncontrollable thoughts.
            c.   Wrong.   Delusions are thoughts with inappropriate content.

6. **a**   b.   Wrong.   Hypochondriasis and conversion disorders are Axis I clinical disorders.
(p. 501)   c.   Wrong.   Dissociative disorders involve consciousness and memory, not concern with the body.
            d.   Wrong.   Hypochondirasis and conversion disorder involve excessive focus on the body, not anxiety.

7. **a**   b.   Wrong.   This describes bipolar disorder.
(p. 503)   c.   Wrong.   This describes generalized anxiety disorder.
            d.   Wrong.   This describes dissociative identity disorder.

8. **b**   a.   Wrong.   Hallucinations and language disorders are characteristic of schizophrenia.
(p. 505)   c.   Wrong.   These are two types of mood states, but bipolar disorder doesn't include both of them.
(PN7D)   d.   Wrong.   Multiple personalities are characteristic of a dissociative disorder.

9. **d**   a, b, & c.   Wrong.   These are common in schizophrenia. Multiple personality is a dissociative
(p. 508)   disorder.

10. **b**   a.   Wrong.   Hallucinations are perceptions with no basis in the external environment.
(p. 508)   c.   Wrong.   Catatonia is the tendency to remain in a bizarre posture for hours.
            d.   Wrong.   Dysthymia is chronic, less intense depression.

11. **b**   a. Wrong.   Personality disorders have not been linked to a specific brain dysfunction.
   (p. 510)   c. Wrong.   Personality disorders are more resistant to treatment than most clinical disorders.
             d. Wrong.   Personality disorders produce maladaptive social behavior.

Understanding Psychological Disorders: Biological, Cognitive, or Environmental?

1. **a**   b, c, & d.   Wrong.   None of these is the primary neurotransmitter involved in schizophrenia.
   (p. 512)
   (PT11C)

2. **d**   a, b, & c.   Wrong.   There is a 50% chance of the other twin developing schizophrenia.
   (p. 513)

3. **c**   a, b, & d.   Wrong.   Mood disorders have at least as strong a genetic component as schizophrenia.
   (p. 513)

4. **a**   b, c, & d.   Wrong.   These are not thought to be important determinants of depression.
   (p. 515)

5. **d**   a, b, & c.   Wrong.   These disorders are unlikely to have a significant learned component.
   (p. 517)

6. **b**   a, c, & d.   Wrong.   Mood disorders involve the monoamine neurotransmitters: serotonin, norepinephrine, and dopamine.
   (p. 512)

MAKING FINAL PREPARATIONS

Short Essay Questions

1. The criteria are: statistical deviance (infrequent), cultural deviance (violates norms), emotional distress, and dysfunction (maladaptive). Problems arise because criteria can be violated, but the behavior might be considered normal, or a person who has a problem might not violate most criteria. Intense distress and maladaptive behavior is "normal" if linked to a death, but thought disorders that indicate mental problems might cause no serious problems, other than slight dysfunction. (pp. 489-492)

2. Axis III (medical conditions), Axis IV (psychosocial and environmental problems) and Axis V (level of function) provide a context in which symptoms are evaluated. This allows a very broad assessment and diagnosis and helps in treatment decisions. (p. 496)

3. Insanity is a legal concept. Most definitions of insanity require the person not understand the wrongfulness of his or her actions as a result of a "mental disease." Thus, abnormality is a requirement, but the emphasis is on the lack of understanding of whether an action is right or wrong. (pp. 492-493)

4. Both generalized anxiety disorder and specific phobic disorder are anxiety disorders and involve anxiety. In generalized anxiety disorder the anxiety is not tied to a specific object or situation; it is free-floating or a general state of anxiety. In specific phobic disorder the anxiety is focused on a specific object or event. (pp. 498, 501)

5. Positive symptoms of schizophrenia are excessive or added behaviors, such as hallucinations (hearing voices) or delusions (thinking you're Napoleon). Negative symptoms are deficits in behavior, such as flat affect, a lack of emotional response. (pp. 508-509)

6. The specific fear found with phobias might be learned. If an object is paired with an US for fear, the object might become a CS for fear, setting the stage for a phobia. That is, if you fall off a high location, the height

might become a CS for the US (sense of falling) for the UR (fear). If fear responses are reinforced by being given attention or other rewards, fear responses in that situation will become more common. Finally, watching someone exhibit fear responses to a situation can result in the observational learning of that behavior. Children who watch fear responses in the parents might learn to act the same way. (pp. 516-517)

Matching

1. **f** (p. 510)
2. **h** (p. 509)
3. **k** (p. 505)

4. **a** (p. 519)
5. **n** (p. 498)
6. **g** (p. 505)

7. **l** (p. 519)
8. **c** (p. 510)
9. **m** (p. 502)

10. **d** (p. 509)
11. **j** (p. 504)
12. **e** (p. 501)

13. **i** (p. 516)
14. **b** (p. 507)

Multiple Choice Pretest 1

1. **d**
   (p. 490)

   a. Wrong. Cultural deviance involves behavior that is not accepted by a particular culture.
   b. Wrong. Dysfunction involves behavior that is not adaptive or prevents normal activities.
   c. Wrong. Emotional distress involves personal feelings of emotional discomfort.

2. **d**
   (p. 493)

   a, b, & c. Wrong. The insanity defense is rarely used (1%) and rarely successful.

3. **c**
   (p. 494)

   a & b. Wrong. These are opposite to the actual criticisms.
   d. Wrong. This is a supporting fact, not a criticism.

4. **b**
   (p. 494)

   a, c, & d. Wrong. Diagnostic labeling effects are the effects of the stigma of mental disorder, often involving viewing people negatively and normal behavior as abnormal.

5. **a**
   (p. 496)

   b. Wrong. This is Axis III. Axis I defines major clinical syndromes.
   c. Wrong. This is Axis IV. Axis I defines major clinical syndromes.
   d. Wrong. This is Axis V. Axis I defines major clinical syndromes.

6. **a**
   (p. 499)

   b. Wrong. The somatoform disorders discussed in the text include hypochondriasis, somatization disorder, and conversion disorder.
   c. Wrong. Dissociative disorders include dissociative amnesia, dissociative fugue, and dissociative identity disorder.
   d. Wrong. Mood disorders include major depressive episode, dysthymic disorder, and biopolar disorder.

7. **d**
   (p. 502)

   a. Wrong. Hypochondriasis involves the preoccupation that one has a serious disease, not the appearance of serious symptoms without physical cause.
   b. Wrong. Dissociative fugue involves breaks in normal conscious awareness and memories.
   c. Wrong. Panic disorder involves sudden, overwhelming anxiety.

8. **a**
   (p. 509)

   b, c, & d. Wrong. These are all overt expressions of abnormal behavior (positive symptoms), rather than the elimination of some behavior (negative symptoms).

9. **c**
   (p. 499)
   (PT11A)

   a. Wrong. His anxiety is sudden and intense. Generalized anxiety disorder involves chronic anxiety.
   b. Wrong. His anxiety is not specific to an object or event.
   d. Wrong. His anxiety is too sudden and intense and is not linked to a preoccupation with his body.

10. **b**
    (p. 502)
    (PN7D)

    a. Wrong. Schizophrenia involves disordered thought, behavior, and emotion, not multiple selves.
    c. Wrong. Somatization disorder is a preoccupation with physical symptoms.
    d. Wrong. Bipolar disorder involves shifting from depression to mania, not between personalities.

11. **d** (p. 504)	a. Wrong.	Lenny doesn't show the serious thought and emotional disorders of schizophrenia.
	b. Wrong.	Lenny doesn't have a physical symptom with no physical basis.
	c. Wrong.	Lenny doesn't have either compulsive behavior or obsessive thoughts.

12. **d** (p. 513)	a. Wrong.	This supports a genetic component but doesn't indicate how complete it is.
	b. Wrong.	This is not true, but it would support a strong environmental component.
	c. Wrong.	A low concordance rate for non-identical twins could be due to genes or environment.

| 13. **c**
(p. 507) | a, b, & d. Wrong. | These are all good proposals, but increased media coverage is likely to increase copycat suicides. |

14. **c** (p. 513)	a. Wrong.	Brain shrinkage, not swelling, is associated with schizophrenia.
	b. Wrong.	Frontal lobe activity is lower than normal.
	d. Wrong.	Neurofibrillary tangles is characteristic of Alzheimer's disease, not schizophrenia.

15. **c** (p. 510)	a. Wrong.	Antisocial personality involves lack of guilt and lack of respect for law or customs.
	b. Wrong.	Dependent personality is characterized by an excessive need to be cared for by others.
	d. Wrong.	Multiple personality disorder involves having more than one personality, not distrust.

| 16. **b**
(p. 512) | a, c, & d. Wrong. | Mood disorders involve monoamines. The other disorders listed are not strongly linked to neurotransmitter problems. |

| 17. **a**
(p. 515) | b, c, & d. Wrong. | Their attributions are global, stable, and internal. |

18. **b** (p. 517)	a. Wrong.	She isn't being hurt by the spider. Key here is the attention (reward?).
	c. Wrong.	She isn't watching someone afraid of a spider. Key here is the attention (reward?).
	d. Wrong.	There is not repeated failure here. Key here is the attention (reward?).

Multiple Choice Pretest 2

1. **b** (p. 491) (PN7C)	a. Wrong.	Insanity is a legal term, not a criterion for determining the abnormality of behavior.
	c. Wrong.	Studying doesn't violate cultural norms, but it is maladaptive.
	d. Wrong.	She shows no distress. Her excessive studying is maladaptive.

2. **c** (p. 492)	a. Wrong.	A person can have serious psychological problems but not be insane.
	b. Wrong.	Dysfunction and distress are not required conditions to be declared insane.
	d. Wrong.	Mental disease is part of the criterion for insanity, but it can be due to medical problems.

3. **a** (p. 493)	b. Wrong.	The DSM-IV is a book describing diagnostic guidelines for mental disorders.
	c. Wrong.	Insanity is a legal concept that makes no assumptions about cause or treatment.
	d. Wrong.	The Rosenhan study examined expectancy or labeling effects.

| 4. **c**
(p. 515) | a & b. Wrong. | These are external attributions. Depression is linked to internal attributions. |
| | d. Wrong. | This is an unstable attribution. Depression is linked to stable attributions. |

5. **c** (p. 494)	a. Wrong.	Dissociation is abnormal consciousness, not reactions to a history of mental disorder.
	b. Wrong.	This is "giving up."
	d. Wrong.	Maladaptive attributions are dysfunctional attributions of one's own behavior.

6. **b**   a. Wrong.   An intense fear linked to a specific source is a phobia, not an obsession or compulsion.
   (p. 499)   c. Wrong.   Generalized anxiety disorder has chronic, non-specific anxiety, not a specific fear.
              d. Wrong.   Conversion disorder involves physical symptoms without a physical cause.

7. **c**   a. Wrong.   Dissociative identity disorder involves multiple personalities.
   (p. 503)   b. Wrong.   There was no travel from home accompanying the amnesia.
              d. Wrong.   Conversion disorder does not involve amnesia.

8. **b**   a. Wrong.   His anxiety is constant and non-specific. Anxiety has a sudden onset in panic disorder.
   (p. 498)   c. Wrong.   His anxiety is non-specific. Agoraphobia involves anxiety in a specific situation.
              d. Wrong.   His anxiety is non-specific. OCD has a more focused anxiety and compulsive behavior.

9. **a**   b. Wrong.   Dissociative disorders involve breaks in normal conscious awareness.
   (p. 501)   c. Wrong.   Anxiety disorders do not usually involve misinterpreting small symptoms as major disease.
              d. Wrong.   Personality disorders involve chronic personality traits, not preoccupation with the body.

10. **c**   a. Wrong.   There's no loss of memory and has no travel.
   (p. 505)   b. Wrong.   Dysthymia is a chronic, relatively mild form of depression.
   (PT11B)   d. Wrong.   Double depression is dysthymia with an added major depressive episode.

11. **a**   b. Wrong.   The anxiety is specific in both, but focuses on different things.
   (p. 502)   c. Wrong.   Physical symptoms or problems are present in both disorders.
              d. Wrong.   These disorders do not differ greatly in rate of development.

12. **d**   a. Wrong.   Clark doesn't swing from depression to mania and back.
   (p. 507)   b. Wrong.   There is no free-floating anxiety, and hallucinations are not found in anxiety disorders.
              c. Wrong.   Clark doesn't have multiple personalities.

13. **b**   a, c, & d.   Wrong.   Key here is the lifelong criminality with no remorse, signs of antisocial
   (p. 510)   personality disorder, not any of these clinical syndromes.

14. **a**   b. Wrong.   Antidepressants, not drugs for schizophrenia, usually increase serotonin activity.
   (p. 510)   c. Wrong.   Acetylcholine is associated with Alzheimer's disease, not schizophrenia.
              d. Wrong.   Some antidepressants, not schizophrenia drugs, influence norepinephrine activity.

15. **c**   a. Wrong.   Failures would not classically condition depression.
   (p. 516)   b. Wrong.   Sue is not observing and copying someone's behavior.
              d. Wrong.   Depression is not being reinforced or punished.

16. **d**   a. Wrong.   Delusions are thoughts, not hyperactive periods.
   (p. 505)   b. Wrong.   Dissociations are a separation of normal consciousness and memory.
              c. Wrong.   Fugue episodes are period of amnesia combined with travel.

17. **d**   a. Wrong.   Consciousness and memory problems are part of dissociative disorders, not schizophrenia.
   (p. 508)   b. Wrong.   Multiple personality is the common description of dissociative identity disorder.
              c. Wrong.   There is no split of attributions in schizophrenia.

18. **c**   a & b.   Wrong.   Schizophrenia involves a significant genetic component.
   (p. 513)   d.   Wrong.   Even identical twins only have a 50% concordance rate.

19. **a**   b, c, & d.   Wrong.   These are all Axis I clinical disorders, not Axis II personality disorders.
   (p. 510)

Chapter 15: Therapy

Establishing Learning Goals

Use these learning goals as a preview of the chapter, a guide for active reading, and to evaluate your mastery of the material. Review the relevant goals as you begin and end your reading of each major section of the chapter.

I. Solve the practical problem of how to treat the biomedical aspects of psychological disorders.
   A. Discuss how drug therapies are used to treat psychological disorders.
      1. Describe how the introduction of drug therapy affected the mental health system.
      2. Identify the uses and limitations of each major category of drugs and explain how they work.
   B. Discuss and evaluate electroconvulsive shock therapy.
   C. Explain why psychosurgery is sometimes used to treat psychological disorders.
      1. Describe prefrontal lobotomy and cingulotomy, and discuss their use.
      2. Summarize the current attitude toward psychosurgery.

II. Solve the practical problem of how to treat the mental aspects of psychological disorders.
   A. Evaluate psychoanalysis as a form of insight therapy.
      1. Discuss the basic philosophy of psychoanalysis.
      2. Discuss the role of free association, dream analysis, transference, and resistance.
      3. Describe how modern psychodynamic therapy differs from the psychoanalysis of Freud's era.
   B. Evaluate cognitive therapies.
      1. Describe rational-emotive therapy, and give examples of common types of irrational thought.
      2. Describe Beck's cognitive therapy, and compare it to rational-emotive therapy.
   C. Evaluate humanistic therapies.
      1. Describe client-centered therapy and the three essential core qualities a therapist should have.
      2. Describe Gestalt and existential therapies.
   D. Discuss group and family therapy.

III. Solve the practical problem of how to treat the environmental aspects of psychological disorders.
   A. Explain how conditioning techniques can be used in therapy.
      1. Describe systematic desensitization.
      2. Describe aversion therapy.
   B. Explain how rewards and punishments can be used in therapy.
      1. Describe token economies.
      2. Describe social skills training.

IV. Solve the practical problem of how to evaluate and choose psychotherapy.
   A. Discuss the major findings of clinical evaluation research.
      1. Describe the results of the Philadelphia study and meta-analytic studies of therapy's effectiveness.
      2. Discuss the controversies concerning studies of the effectiveness of therapy.
   B. Describe the factors that are common across psychotherapies.

MASTERING THE MATERIAL

Preview & Treating the Body: Biomedical Therapies (pp. 524-531)

Mastering the Vocabulary. Define or explain each of the following terms. To check your answers, consult the text pages listed.

1. psychotherapy (p. 524)

2. biomedical therapies (p. 526)

3. antipsychotic drugs (p. 527)

4. antidepressant drugs (p. 528)

5. antianxiety drugs (p. 529)

6. electroconvulsive therapy (p. 530)

7. psychosurgery (p. 531)

Mastering the Concepts. Fill in the blanks to create a summary of the section. Answers are on page 366.

_____(1), treatment for mental, emotional or behavioral problems, can help both severe and more minor problems. This chapter considers the practical and conceptual problems of how to treat mental problems by treating the body, mind, and environment, and how to evaluate and choose a therapy.

_____(2) therapies originated in ancient Greece. _____(3) therapy began in the 1950s with the discovery of chlorpromazine to treat _____(4). Drugs have reduced the need for _____(5).

_____(6) drugs used to treat the positive symptoms of schizophrenia reduce _____(7) activity. They don't affect negative symptoms or work for all people, and they have side effects, including _____(8) dyskinesia, involuntary facial movements. Clozapine affects dopamine and serotonin and often works when chlorpromazine doesn't. Depression is treated with antidepressants. Tricyclics affect _____(9), while fluoxetine (Prozac) affects _____(10). They are effective for over _____(11) of patients but require time to work, and they can have side effects. Bipolar disorder is treated with

_____(12) carbonate. _____(13) drugs, such as benzodiazepine tranquilizers, affect _____(14).

Electroconvulsive therapy is used to treat _____(15) that has not responded to other therapies. It is effective in 50-70% of cases. Controversies include not knowing why it works, reports of temporary _____(16), and the possibility of relapse. _____(17), brain surgery to alter behavior, is rarely performed. In the 1930s, Moniz developed the prefrontal _____(18) procedure to calm patients. Major cognitive deficits occurred. Cingulotomy, an operation that removes a little _____(19) system tissue, occasionally is used today to reduce obsessive-compulsive disorder and depression.

Evaluating Your Progress. Select the one best response. Answers are on page 366. If you make any errors, reread the relevant material before you proceed.

1. Biomedical therapy was proposed as early as
   a. 400 B.C. by Hippocrates for treating depression.
   b. the 16th century by doctors for treating "evil spirits."
   c. the 19th century by doctors for treating the paranoia of syphilis.
   d. the 1930's by Moniz for treating violent disorders.

2. Biomedical therapies include drugs, psychosurgery, and
   a. systematic desensitization.
   b. electroconvulsive shock therapy.
   c. psychodynamic therapy.
   d. rational-emotive therapy.

3. The original, and still popular, drug used to treat schizophrenia is
   a. lithium carbonate.
   b. benzodiazepine (e.g., Xanax).
   c. clozapine (e.g., Clozaril).
   d. chlorpromazine (e.g., Thorazine).

4. Most antipsychotic drugs slow or block the activity of
   a. serotonin.
   b. norepinephrine.
   c. dopamine.
   d. GABA.

5. Tricyclic drugs and fluoxetine (Prozac) are examples of
   a. antipsychotic drugs.
   b. antianxiety drugs.
   c. antidepressant drugs.
   d. antimanic drugs.

6. The side effects associated with antidepressant drugs include
   a. tardive dyskinesia and blurry vision.
   b. drowsiness and psychological dependence.
   c. restlessness and diminished sexual desire.
   d. memory loss and possible brain damage.

7. The benzodiazepines
   a. increase the effectiveness of GABA.
   b. block the reuptake of norepinephrine.
   c. are dopamine antagonists.
   d. block the reuptake of serotonin.

8. Moniz used prefrontal lobotomies to
   a. treat severe depression.
   b. calm violent or agitated behavior.
   c. reduce obsessive thoughts.
   d. treat dissociative identity disorder.

9. Electroconvulsive therapy is most commonly used to treat
   a. generalized anxiety disorder.
   b. schizophrenia.
   c. obsessive-compulsive disorder.
   d. depression.

Treating the Mind: Insight Therapies (pp. 532-541)

Mastering the Vocabulary. Define or explain each of the following terms. To check your answers, consult text pages listed.

1. insight therapies (p. 532)

2. psychoanalysis (p. 532)

3. free association (p. 533)

4. dream analysis (p. 533)

5. resistance (p. 533)

6. transference (p. 534)

7. cognitive therapies (p. 535)

8. rational-emotive therapy (p. 535)

9. humanistic therapy (p. 538)

10. client-centered therapy (p. 539)

11. group therapy (p. 541)

12. family therapy (p. 541)

Mastering the Concepts. Fill in the blanks to create a summary of the section. Answers are on page 366.

_____(20) therapies are based on the idea that disorders involve maladaptive thoughts that can be reduced by self-knowledge. _____(21), originated by Freud, emphasizes insight into conflicts repressed in the _____(22) mind. Dream analysis and _____(23), saying what comes to mind, help determine those conflicts. Anxiety causes _____(24), periods of poor cooperation. When conflicts near consciousness, _____(25) occurs as the client directs emotions felt about other people toward the therapist instead. The fact that classical psychoanalysis is very _____(26) and costly has led to brief forms in which the therapist is more active, focuses on selective problems, and emphasizes _____(27), not sexual drives. This modern version is called _____(28) therapy.

Conscious beliefs are emphasized in _____(29) therapies. In Ellis' _____(30) therapy, the therapist challenges any irrational thoughts to guide the person to insight. In Beck's cognitive therapy, the therapist is not combative, and clients are encouraged to discover negative thinking themselves.

The goal of _____(31) therapy is to help clients understand their self-worth and value. In Rogers' _____(32) therapy the therapist must show _____(33), genuineness, and unconditional positive regard to allow clients to analyze their own feelings freely. In Perl's _____(34) therapy the client's goodness is emphasized, but the therapist is more directive. Emphasis is on the _____(35) and expressing oneself as a "whole" person. Existential therapies encourage clients to take responsibility for their life decisions by providing a supportive environment.

Therapy is also done in a _____(36) setting. This cuts costs and provides insight and support from other people. _____(37) therapy involves the entire family, not just one person.

Evaluating Your Progress. Select the one best response. Answers are on page 367. If you make any errors, reread the relevant material before proceeding.

1. The goal of psychoanalysis is to gain insight into disordered behavior by
    a. challenging the irrational beliefs held by the client.
    b. providing a supportive environment in which clients can explore their true self.
    c. bringing unconscious conflicts and memories into conscious awareness.
    d. having clients take notes about their feelings and behavior each day.

2. When transference occurs, clients
    a. go through periods in which they are uncooperative, skip sessions, refuse to talk, etc.
    b. express their feelings to an empty chair and then respond to those feelings.
    c. take over control of the therapy and the therapist simply reflects back their feelings.
    d. express feelings toward the therapist that represent the way they feel about someone else.

3. Therapists using psychodynamic therapy, a modern version of classical psychoanalysis, are likely to
    a. play a less active role than classical psychoanalysts.
    b. emphasize sexual and aggressive drives more than classical psychoanalysts.
    c. focus on a few specific conflicts most relevant to the client's symptoms.
    d. allow the client to gain insight on his or her own.

4. The therapy that attempts to get clients to stop using "I must" beliefs is
    a. existential therapy.
    b. client-centered therapy.
    c. rational-emotive therapy.
    d. Gestalt therapy.

5. The therapy that stresses the here-and-now and forces clients to express current feelings openly is
    a. classical psychoanalysis.
    b. client-centered therapy.
    c. systematic desensitization.
    d. Gestalt therapy.

6. Which is an advantage of group therapy?
    a. Transference is achieved more quickly.
    b. Group therapy is more cost-effective.
    c. It emphasizes conditions of worth.
    d. It uses two therapists rather than one.

7. An emphasis on getting clients to recognize their irrational beliefs themselves, rather than confronting them with them, is characteristic of
    a. Ellis' rational-emotive therapy.
    b. Perls' Gestalt therapy.
    c. Rogers' client-centered therapy.
    d. Beck's cognitive therapy.

8. To provide genuineness, unconditional positive regard and empathy is the goal of
   a. client-centered therapy.
   b. rational-emotive therapy.
   c. behavioral therapy.
   d. Beck's cognitive therapy.

9. Carl Rogers, a client-centered therapist, suggested psychological problems develop because of
   a. incongruence.
   b. genuineness.
   c. unconditional positive regard.
   d. resistance.

Treating the Environment: Behavioral Therapies (pp. 542-547)

Mastering the Vocabulary. Define or explain each of the following terms. To check your answers, consult the text pages listed.

1. behavioral therapies (p. 542)

2. systematic desensitization (p. 543)

3. aversion therapy (p. 544)

4. token economies (p. 603)

Mastering the Concepts. Fill in the blanks to create a summary of the section. Answers are on page 366.

Behavioral therapy assumes psychological problems can be _____(38), and the _____(39) should be treated, not thoughts or feelings. One type, systematic _____(40), replaces a negative response with a relaxation response. Relaxation is paired with successively higher stimuli in the client's _____(41) hierarchy. This is used to treat _____(42). An unwanted response (e.g., drinking) can be eliminated by _____(43) therapy, in which a pleasant reaction to something harmful is replaced with something unpleasant. Problems include _____(44) if therapy is discontinued and ethical considerations. Rewards are used to modify behavior in token _____(45). Tokens are later exchanged for goods or privileges. This is combined with modeling in _____(46) training to improve the adjustment and social skills of people with schizophrenia. _____(47) modifies behavior, but it can damage the client-therapist relationship, it teaches only what not to do, and it raises ethical concerns.

Evaluating Your Progress. Select the one best response. Answers are on page 368. If you make any errors, reread the relevant material before proceeding.

1. Behavioral therapy treats
    a. unconscious conflicts.
    b. behaviors.
    c. irrational thoughts.
    d. neurotransmitter imbalances.

2. The therapy in which relaxation is paired with anxiety-producing stimuli of increasing intensity is
    a. aversion conditioning.
    b. token economy therapy.
    c. existential therapy.
    d. systematic desensitization therapy.

3. The therapy that replaces a pleasant response with an unpleasant one is
    a. systematic desensitization.
    b. aversion therapy.
    c. token economy.
    d. meta-analysis.

4. Using modeling and rewards to teach appropriate ways of interacting with other people in order to improve the quality of life of individuals with psychological disorders is called
    a. systematic desensitization.
    b. aversion therapy.
    c. social skills training.
    d. insight therapy.

5. Token economies
    a. are used to teach appropriate behaviors.
    b. are based on classical conditioning principles.
    c. involve replacing a pleasant response with an unpleasant one.
    d. are used to develop congruent self-concepts.

Evaluating and Choosing Psychotherapy (pp. 547-552)

Mastering the Vocabulary. Define or explain each of the following terms. To check your answers, consult the text pages listed.

1. meta-analysis (p. 549)

2. spontaneous remission (p. 509)

Mastering the Concepts. Fill in the blanks to create a summary of the section. Answers are on page 366.

Valid evaluations of the effectiveness of therapy requires a _____(48) group and proper experimental procedures. The well-controlled Philadelphia study found that after four months, people receiving therapy were _____(49) improved than those on a waiting list, and that psychodynamic and behavioral therapies were _____(50) effective. After one year the three groups _____(51). Researchers have used _____(52) to examine many therapy evaluation studies. Two conclusions are that therapy is better than no therapy, and therapeutic effects are long lasting. Improvement without therapy, _____(53) remission, has raised questions about defining "treatment." The equal effects of all therapies is also controversial and may reflect the effect of _____(54) variables. The similar results also might be due to therapies having certain shared features: _____(55) factors, learning factors, and action factors. Effective therapy is predicted by the amount of _____(56) between client and therapist, and cultural background can be important

Evaluating Your Progress. Select the one best response. Answers are on page 368. If you make any errors, reread the relevant material before proceeding.

1. According to the results of the Philadelphia study, psychotherapy
    a. has no effect.
    b. speeds up natural improvement.
    c. causes an improvement that is larger and longer lasting than getting no therapy.
    d. causes a significant number of people to get worse rather than better.

2. Based on recent meta-analysis of hundreds of studies, we can reasonably conclude
    a. psychotherapy doesn't work.
    b. therapy helps temporarily, but it has no lasting benefit.
    c. psychoanalysis is more effective than behavioral therapies.
    d. all types of therapy are effective, with no type better than the others.

3. Therapies are said to share the common feature of learning factors. Learning factors involve
    a. giving clients a better understanding as to the cause of their behavior.
    b. giving clients suggestions for how they can improve their behavior.
    c. giving clients a sense of hope and control.
    d. giving clients the feeling that someone is concerned and wants to help them.

4. Possibly the most important factor to consider when choosing a therapist is
    a. their orientation (psychodynamic, behavioral, etc.)
    b. their age.
    c. the school at which they received their training.
    d. their amount of empathy.

Making Final Preparations

Complete these sections without consulting your book or notes. For a more accurate estimate of how well you know this material, wait at least a day or two after studying the chapter before working on the questions. Some material you "know" immediately after working with the chapter will be quickly forgotten. Immediate tests will overestimate what you know well.

Short Essay Questions. Write a brief answer to each question. Sample answers are on page 369.

1. Discuss how drug therapy has affected the mental health system.

2. Discuss the uses and limitations of ECT.

3. Compare Ellis' rational emotive therapy and Beck's cognitive therapy.

4. Compare the basic philosophy of insight therapies and behavioral therapies.

5. Summarize the conclusions about the effectiveness of various forms of psychotherapy.

Matching. Select the correct definition or description for each item. Answers are on page 369.

_____ 1. Jones & Wolpe
_____ 2. anxiety hierarchy
_____ 3. fluoxepine
_____ 4. musterbation
_____ 5. prefrontal lobotomy
_____ 6. genuineness
_____ 7. tricyclics
_____ 8. Egas Moniz
_____ 9. existential therapy
_____ 10. resistance
_____ 11. psychodynamic therapy
_____ 12. Gestalt therapy
_____ 13. Albert Ellis
_____ 14. empathy
_____ 15. benzodiazepines
_____ 16. meta-analysis

a. anti-anxiety tranquilizers affecting GABA
b. Ellis' description of an irrational way of thinking
c. open, honest, without phoniness
d. stresses expressing feelings as a whole person
e. ordered list of fear-inducing stimuli
f. understanding; seeing client's point of view
g. stresses accepting responsibility for decisions
h. technique to compare data from many studies
i. developed prefrontal lobotomy
j. modern, shorter form of psychoanalysis
k. anti-depressants that affects norepinephrine
l. developed systematic desensitization
m. unconscious attempt to hinder therapy
n. psychosurgery to calm patient
o. developed rational-emotive therapy
p. Prozac; anti-depressant affecting serotonin

Multiple Choice Pretest 1. Select the one best response. Answers are on page 369.

1. The number of people requiring institutionalization has decreased greatly due to the development of
   a. the prefrontal lobotomy procedure.
   b. the cingulotomy procedure.
   c. systematic desensitization.
   d. psychoactive drugs.

2. Chlorpromazine and clozapine are examples of
   a. antidepressant drugs.
   b. antipsychotic drugs.
   c. antianxiety drugs.
   d. antimanic drugs.

3. Dopamine antagonist antipsychotic medications are affective primarily for reducing
   a. the positive symptoms of schizophrenia.
   b. the negative symptoms of schizophrenia.
   c. both positive and negative symptoms of schizophrenia.
   d. the tardive dyskinesia that can occur with schizophrenia.

4. May suddenly began to forget her appointments, to misplace her dream diary, and to be unwilling to talk during her therapy sessions. A psychoanalytic therapist would interpret her behavior as
   a. transference.
   b. incongruence.
   c. resistance.
   d. musterbation.

5. Tricyclic antidepressant drugs reduce depression by modulating primarily
   a. dopamine.
   b. norepinephrine.
   c. GABA.
   d. serotonin.

6. Saul is taking lithium carbonate for a psychological disorder. The disorder is most likely
   a. schizophrenia.
   b. obsessive-compulsive disorder.
   c. depression (a major depressive episode).
   d. bipolar disorder.

7. Which of the following is not a concern psychologists have about electroconvulsive therapy (ECT)?
   a. ECT reduces depression in very few people.
   b. ECT causes loss of memory for events surrounding the treatment.
   c. ECT's method of action is unknown.
   d. The long-term effect of repeated ECT treatments is not known.

8. Ali is recovering from a cingulotomy. The outcome that might be expected is a reduction of
   a. obsessive-compulsive behavior.
   b. hallucinations and delusions.
   c. the manic periods in bipolar disorder.
   d. the ability to plan and coordinate actions.

9. Rehan's therapist has him relax and say whatever comes into his mind. This technique is
   a. systematic desensitization.
   b. the empty chair technique.
   c. transference.
   d. free association.

10. Getting the client to change irrational, negative beliefs affecting their behavior is the goal of
    a. psychodynamic therapy.
    b. cognitive therapy.
    c. Gestalt therapy.
    d. humanistic therapy.

11. Genuineness, empathy, and unconditional positive regard are central components of
    a. cognitive therapy.
    b. behavioral therapy.
    c. client-centered therapy.
    d. psychoanalytic therapy.

12. In Ellis' rational-emotive therapy the therapist
    a. aggressively challenges the client's irrational thought processes.
    b. provides a supportive environment in which clients can discover their self-worth.
    c. interprets the free associations of the client to determine the unconscious conflicts present.
    d. helps discover the client's anxiety hierarchy.

13. Joe tends to shout and stare. Because Joe soon will leave the hospital, his therapist is using rewards, modeling and role-playing to teach him to interact more appropriately. In other words, he is applying
    a. systematic desensitization.
    b. social skills training.
    c. aversion therapy.
    d. client-centered therapy.

14. A therapist using systematic desensitization to treat specific phobic disorder probably believes that
    a. phobias are caused by incongruent self-concepts.
    b. phobias are symptoms of unconscious conflicts or traumas.
    c. phobias are learned fear responses.
    d. phobias are the result of irrational thinking.

15. When Beth went for treatment of her alcoholism, she was given a drug that made her sick if she drank alcohol. This type of therapy is
    a. Gestalt therapy.
    b. systematic desensitization.
    c. aversion therapy.
    d. a token economy.

16. The Philadelphia study of the effectiveness of therapy found
    a. people who got therapy of any type were better after 4 months than people put on waiting lists.
    b. people who got therapy of any type were better off after 1 year than people put on waiting lists.
    c. people who got behavioral therapy improved more than people who got psychodynamic therapy.
    d. people who got psychodynamic therapy improved more than people who got behavioral therapy.

17. If June's panic disorder has undergone spontaneous remission it has
    a. responded very rapidly to therapy.
    b. failed to respond to therapy.
    c. increased in severity.
    d. improved without treatment.

18. Smith's early meta-analytic study found the average therapy client
    a. was better off than 80% of the people who did not get therapy.
    b. was better off than 30% of the people who did not get therapy.
    c. was not better off than the people who did not get therapy.
    d. was worse off than the people who did not get therapy.

19. All therapies provide clients with suggestions about how to improve. This common factor is
    a. a support factor.
    b. a learning factor.
    c. an action factor.
    d. empathy.

20. Marta believes that the entire family should receive therapy, not just the person with the psychological problem. Based on her philosophy, Marta is probably
    a. an existential therapist.
    b. a behavioral therapist.
    c. a Gestalt therapist.
    d. a family therapist.

Multiple Choice Pretest 2. Select the one best response. Answers are on page 371.

1. Which of the following is not a biomedical therapy used to treat psychological disorders?
   a. electroconvulsive therapy
   b. systematic desensitization
   c. drug therapy
   d. psychosurgery

2. Because Chad had begun to be very hostile and aggressive toward his therapist and once called him "Dad" by mistake, Chad's therapist felt they were getting close to uncovering the conflict causing Chad's anxiety. In psychoanalytic therapy, Chad's behavior toward his therapist is considered
   a. transference.
   b. free association.
   c. resistance.
   d. incongruence.

3. Barry has hallucinations and delusions with his schizophrenia. A psychiatrist is likely to prescribe
   a. electroconvulsive therapy.
   b. an antipsychotic drug.
   c. systematic desensitization.
   d. cingulotomy.

4. Otto has tardive dyskinesia, a disorder that produces involuntary movements of the face and mouth. Otto probably
   a. has had a prefrontal lobotomy.
   b. has had electroconvulsive therapy.
   c. has taken chlorpromazine for some time.
   d. has had a cingulotomy.

5. Flora is taking a drug that slows the reuptake of serotonin. This drug is most likely
   a. a tranquilizing drug like Xanax.
   b. an antianxiety drug like Valium.
   c. an antipsychotic drug like Thorazine.
   d. an anti-depressant drug like Prozac.

6. Renatta is taking the benzodiazepine drug Xanax. Her psychological problem is likely to be
   a. bipolar disorder.
   b. generalized anxiety disorder.
   c. schizophrenia.
   d. depression.

7. As a result of treatment in 1946 for a violent psychological disorder, Craig is calm, but he has cognitive deficits, including the inability to plan and coordinate actions. The treatment probably was
   a. electroconvulsive therapy (ECT).
   b. drug treatment using chlorpromazine (Thorazine).
   c. prefrontal lobotomy.
   d. benzodiazepine (Xanax) drug treatment.

8. Electroconvulsive therapy works by
   a. blocking reuptake of serotonin.
   b. decreasing utilization of dopamine.
   c. modulating norepinephrine activity.
   d. some yet-to-be-determined action.

9. Adele is undergoing electroconvulsive therapy (ECT). Adele has probably
   a. failed to respond to antidepressive drugs.
   b. developed tardive dyskinesia and must give up drug therapy.
   c. developed very violent behavior as part of her schizophrenia.
   d. developed very severe obsessive-compulsive disorder.

10. How does modern psychodynamic therapy differ from classical psychoanalysis?
    a. Psychodynamic therapy is usually done as group therapy.
    b. Psychodynamic therapy is usually briefer.
    c. Psychodynamic therapy emphasizes working on the entire personality rather than limited issues.
    d. Psychodynamic therapy emphasizes aggression and sexual drives.

362

11. Kim's therapist is very non-judgmental and merely reflects back what Kim says. Kim's therapist is
    a. a behavioral therapist.
    b. a client-centered therapist.
    c. a rational-emotive therapist.
    d. a psychoanalytic therapist.

12. Marko's therapist aggressively challenged him to explain why breaking up with his girlfriend means he is a worthless failure and pointed out the illogical aspects of his belief. The therapy being used is
    a. aversion therapy.
    b. classical psychoanalysis.
    c. client-centered therapy.
    d. rational-emotive therapy.

13. Jackie never thought she'd get homework assigned by her therapist, but she did. She has to keep track of her negative thoughts, why they occurred, and how they make her feel. Jackie's therapy is probably
    a. classical psychoanalysis.
    b. rational-emotive therapy.
    c. Beck's cognitive therapy.
    d. systematic desensitization.

14. The goal of humanistic therapy is to
    a. get the client thinking more logically and rationally.
    b. bring unconscious conflicts into consciousness where they can be resolved.
    c. help the client gain insight into his or her self-worth and value as a person.
    d. condition adaptive behaviors to replace maladaptive ones.

15. Dan's therapist is never critical and is always accepting and respectful of him. His therapist is showing
    a. empathy.
    b. unconditional positive regard.
    c. genuineness.
    d. congruence.

16. Cory learned to stay relaxed while he imagined anxiety-producing stimuli. Cory's treatment was
    a. systematic desensitization therapy.
    b. aversion therapy.
    c. a token economy.
    d. psychoanalytic therapy.

17. What is most likely to occur if aversion therapy is ended too soon?
    a. The aversive response will extinguish.
    b. Incongruence will develop.
    c. The client-therapist relationship will be damaged.
    d. A new psychological problem will develop.

18. Leo was given a poker chip because he got dressed appropriately this morning. He will exchange his poker chips for a chance to go on a trip outside the hospital. Leo is taking part in
    a. systematic desensitization.
    b. existential therapy.
    c. aversion therapy.
    d. a token economy.

19. Ida is in psychodynamic therapy, Jo is in behavioral therapy, and Vi is not in therapy. We should expect
    a. Ida will improve greatly, Jo will improve modestly, and Vi will not improve.
    b. Jo will improve greatly, Ida will improve modestly, and Vi will not improve.
    c. Jo and Ida will show equal improvement, and Vi will not improve.
    d. Jo and Ida will show equal improvement, and Vi may improve, but not as quickly.

20. Rodrigo asked your advice about how to find a good therapist. What advice would be most accurate?
    a. "Find one that uses a cognitive approach. That's the best approach to therapy."
    b. "Pick any therapist. Every therapist is just as effective as the others."
    c. "Find one with whom you feel comfortable and who understands you."
    d. "Find one that uses a behavioral approach. That works best for most problems."

LANGUAGE DEVELOPMENT GUIDE

Core Terms

In the lectures on this chapter, you will be learning about drugs that affect the mind, so you can expect to hear the term *psychoactive drugs*. You already learned a bit about one kind of these in the chapter on consciousness; *psychotropic drugs* like marijuana and LSD alter consciousness. But in this chapter you will be learning about *psychopharmaceuticals* --drugs that are *therapeutic* (helpful in treating illnesses). These drugs are used more often than *psychosurgery* (surgical operations on the brain) because they are *non-invasive*; because there are no cuts, there is no risk of wound infection and other surgery-related problems. The other *non-invasive* treatment is, of course, counseling. In these lectures your instructor may use the terms *counseling, therapy* and *psychotherapy* fairly interchangeably.

One more thing: you may wonder why counselors need to have *empathy* rather than *sympathy* for their clients. The answer to this can be found in the word parts: if one has *sympathy*, then one feels along with the other person. A counselor needs to be a bit more objective; in *empathy*, the emphasis is on understanding the feelings rather than participating in them.

Idioms

p. 529	"even keel"	avoiding extremes; not rocking from one side to the other, stable (a keel is the bottom of a boat)
p. 529	a downside	a negative perspective; reason something is not so good

p. 530	of last resort	the least preferred option
p. 531	cognitive deficits	problems in thinking well
p. 533	maneuver around a number of roadblocks	find a way around many difficulties
p. 534	contemporaries	those who live at the same time
p. 535	streamline	to smooth the edges of something, to make it move more easily through air, water, etc.
p. 538	a more subtle tack	a less direct or forceful way
p. 541	odds of	chances, likelihood, probability of

Word Parts

Here are some words that are made up of word parts, and that you can find in this chapter. After you've looked at these, you can look for others with the same word parts.

WORD	WORD PART IT USES	MEANING
antagonist	ant, anti = against agon = struggle	one who struggles against; enemy
eliminate	limin = threshold, borderline	to put outside awareness, to remove
excess	ex = out of cede, ceed, cess = to go, yield	extra, overflow
resistance	re = again sist, sta, stet = to stand	to stand against an attack
subvert	sub = under vert = to turn	to undermine; to attack from underneath
transference	trans = across fer = bring, bear, yield	to send across
innate	in = in nat = newborn	present at birth, inborn
speculated	spec = to look lat = line	to look "down the line", to predict

Knowing the word parts listed above, you can also create the following words. You can get an idea of their meanings from the word parts they use. You fill in the blanks!

sublimate   _____ + _____   to push down below the line of awareness

consistent   _____ + _____   to be compatible, to go together well

transplant   trans + plant   _____

prenatal   pre (before) + nat   _____

Pronunciation

p. 529   tranquilizer   tran'-kwill-eye-zer   p. 531   lobotomy   low-bot'-o-mee

p. 531   prefrontal   pree-front'-al   p. 551   eclectic   ek-lek'-tik

ANSWERS AND EXPLANATIONS

To find relevant material in your textbook, consult the pages cited with each answer. Also, PN and PT citations refer to modules in *PsychNow!* and *Psyk.trek* materials, respectively.

Mastering the Concepts

1. Psychotherapy (p. 524)
2. Biomedical (p. 526
3. Drug (p. 526)
4. schizophrenia (p. 526)
5. institutionalization (526)
6. Anti-psychotic (p. 527)
7. dopamine (p. 527)
8. tardive (p. 527)
9. norepinephrine (p. 528)
10. serotonin (p. 528)
11. 50% (p. 528)
12. lithium (p. 529)
13. Antianxiety (p. 529)
14. GABA (p. 529)

15. depression (p. 530)
16. memory loss (p. 531)
17. Psychosurgery (p.531)
18. lobotomy (p. 531)
19. limbic (p. 531)
20. Insight (p. 532)
21. Psychoanalysis (p. 533)
22. unconscious (p. 532)
23. free association (p. 533)
24. resistance (p. 533)
25. transference (p. 534)
23. lengthy (p. 535)
27. social skills (p. 535)
28. psychodynamic (p. 535)

29. cognitive (p. 535)
30. rational-emotive (p. 535)
31. humanistic (p. 538)
32. client-centered (p. 539)
33. empathy (p. 539)
34. Gestalt (p. 541)
35. here & now (p. 541)
36. group (p. 541)
37. Family (p. 541)
38. learned (p. 542)
39. behavior (p. 542)
40. desensitization (p. 543)
41. anxiety (p. 543)
42. phobias (p. 543)

43. aversion (p. 544)
44. extinction (p. 544)
45. economies (p. 545)
46. social skills (p. 546)
47. Punishment (p. 545)
48. control (p. 548)
49. more (p. 548)
50. equally (p. 548)
51. were equal (p. 548)
52. meta-analysis (p. 549)
53. spontaneous (p. 550)
54. client (p. 550)
55. support (p. 550)
56. empathy (p. 550)

Evaluating Your Progress

Preview & Treating the Body: Biomedical Therapies

1.   **a**   b, c, & d.   Wrong.   These were much later.
   (p. 526)

2. **b**   a. Wrong.   Systematic desensitization is a kind of behavioral therapy that emphasizes learning.
(p. 526)   c. Wrong.   Psychodynamic therapy is the modern version of psychoanalysis, an insight therapy.
(PN7E)   d. Wrong.   Rational-emotive therapy is a cognitive therapy, a type of insight therapy.

3. **d**   a. Wrong.   Lithium carbonate is used to treat bipolar disorder.
(p. 526)   b. Wrong.   Benzodiazepines are used to treat anxiety disorders.
            c. Wrong.   Although clozapine is also an antipsychotic drug, it was recently developed.

4. **c**   a. Wrong.   Clozapine affects serotonin, but most antipsychotics don't. Prozac affects serotonin.
(p. 527)   b. Wrong.   Tricyclic antidepressants, not antipsychotics, affect norepinephrine.
(PT11E)   d. Wrong.   Antianxiety drugs, not antipsychotics, affect GABA.

5. **c**   a, b, & d.   Wrong.   Tricyclics and fluoxetine (Prozac) are antidepressants.
(p. 528)

6. **c**   a. Wrong.   These are side effects of antipsychotic drugs.
(p. 529)   b. Wrong.   These are side effects of antianxiety drugs.
            d. Wrong.   These are side effects of ECT.

7. **a**   b. Wrong.   Tricyclics increase norepinephrine activity.
(p. 529)   c. Wrong.   Antipsychotics are dopamine antagonists.
            d. Wrong.   Prozac (fluoxetine) blocks reuptake of serotonin.

8. **b**   a. Wrong.   Electroconvulsive therapy, not psychosurgery, is used for depression.
(p. 531)   c. Wrong.   A modern psychosurgery, cingulotomy, is used to treat obsessive compulsive disorder.
            d. Wrong.   Dissociative identity disorder is treated with insight therapy, not psychosurgery.

9. **d**   a. Wrong.   Anti-anxiety drugs and insight therapy is used to treat generalized anxiety disorder.
(p. 530)   b. Wrong.   Anti-psychotic drugs are used to treat schizophrenia.
(PN7E)   c. Wrong.   Anti-anxiety drugs or cingulotomies are used to treat obsessive compulsive disorder.

Treating the Mind: Insight Therapies

1. **c**   a. Wrong.   This describes Ellis' rational-emotive therapy.
(p. 533)   b. Wrong.   This describes Rogers' client-centered therapy.
(PT11D)   d. Wrong.   This describes Beck's cognitive therapy.

2. **d**   a. Wrong.   This describes resistance.
(p. 534)   b. Wrong.   This describes the "empty chair" technique used by Gestalt therapists.
            c. Wrong.   This describes client-centered therapy, a humanistic therapy.

3. **c**   a, b, & d.   Wrong.   Modern versions speed therapy by limiting the focus of therapy, being more
(p. 535)   directive early in therapy, and emphasizing interpersonal skills rather than sex
                                        and aggression.

4. **c**   a, b, & d.   Wrong.   Ellis, of rational-emotive therapy, outlined the problem of "musterbation."
(p. 537)

5. **d**   a. Wrong.   Classical psychoanalysis didn't focus on the here and now.
(p. 541)   b. Wrong.   Client-centered therapy doesn't force clients to do anything. The client has control.
            c. Wrong.   Systematic desensitization is not an insight therapy. It is a behavioral therapy.

6. **b** a. Wrong. Transference is a concept in psychoanalytic therapy, which is not a type of group therapy.
(p. 541) c. Wrong. Conditions of worth are harmful, and they relate to humanistic therapy, not group therapy.
      d. Wrong. Group therapy involves a group of clients, not a group of therapists.

7. **d** a. Wrong. Ellis confronts clients with their illogical thoughts.
(p. 538) b. Wrong. Gestalt therapy doesn't emphasize illogical thoughts. It's a humanistic therapy.
      c. Wrong. Client-centered humanistic therapy doesn't emphasis the role of irrational thoughts.

8. **a** b. Wrong. Rational-emotive therapy is confrontational, not empathetic.
(p. 539) c. Wrong. Behavioral therapy seeks to modify behavior to a more adaptive form, not provide insight.
(PN7E) d. Wrong. Cognitive therapy strives for rational thought, not self-worth.

9. **a** b. Wrong. Genuineness is a desirable, therapeutic condition.
(p. 539) c. Wrong. Unconditional positive regard is a desirable situation.
      d. Wrong. Resistance is a psychoanalytic concept, not a client-centered (humanistic) one.

Treating the Environment: Behavioral Therapies

1. **b** a, c, & d. Wrong. Behavioral therapy treats behaviors, not thoughts, neurotransmitters, or the
(p. 542)   unconscious.

2. **d** a. Wrong. Aversion therapy replaces a pleasant response with an unpleasant one.
(p. 543) b. Wrong. Token economies use rewards to increase desired behaviors.
(PT11E) c. Wrong. Existential therapy encourages people to take responsibility for their decisions.

3. **b** a. Wrong. Systematic desensitization replaces an unpleasant response with a pleasant one.
(p. 544) c. Wrong. Token economies don't replace pleasant responses, they reward appropriate behavior.
(PN7E) d. Wrong. Meta-analysis is a research tool, not a therapy.

4. **c** a. Wrong. Systematic desensitization reduces anxiety. It doesn't each appropriate social behavior.
(p. 456) b. Wrong. Aversion therapy doesn't use modeling or rewards, and it doesn't teach communication.
      d. Wrong. Insight therapy strives for insight into the problem. It doesn't teach social behavior.

5   **a** b. Wrong. Token economies are based on operant conditioning.
(p. 545) c. Wrong. This describes aversion therapy.
      d. Wrong. This describes client-centered therapy.

Evaluating and Choosing Psychotherapy

1. **b** a, c, & d. Wrong. Control groups caught up with therapy groups, so therapy primarily speeds up a
(p. 548)   natural improvement.

2. **d** a. Wrong. Psychotherapy does work.
(p. 549) b. Wrong. Meta-analysis shows there is a lasting benefit of therapy.
      c. Wrong. Meta-analysis finds no particular therapy is consistently better than another.

3. **a** b & c. Wrong. These are part of the action factor.
(p. 550) d.   Wrong. This is part of the support factor.

4. **d** a, b, & c. Wrong. Empathy is one of the best predictors of an effective therapist.
(p. 551)

MAKING FINAL PREPARATIONS

Short Essay Questions

1. Drug therapy has greatly reduced the number of people who are institutionalized for psychological treatment. Drugs reduce symptoms and allow people to be treated in their communities. (p. 526)

2. ECT is used to treat depression that has not responded to other therapies. It is highly effective, but its use has been limited by several concerns. Although reports of serious memory deficits has not been found in controlled research, ECT causes memory loss for events close to the treatment. Because ECT involves several treatments, there is worry that brain damage might occur. Also, why it works is unknown, causing caution. (p. 530)

3. Both therapies view abnormality to be due to irrational thoughts. In Ellis' therapy the client is aggressively confronted concerning irrational thoughts. Beck's therapy is not as confrontational. Clients are encouraged to discover their own irrational thoughts. (pp. 535-538)

4. Insight therapies are based on the idea that by gaining insight into a problem, a person can resolve the problem and become psychologically healthy. The thoughts or conflicts are treated. Behavioral therapies treat behaviors, not thoughts. Any underlying problem is almost irrelevant; if a behavior is unwanted or inappropriate, change the behavior. This assumes that abnormal behavior can be learned, and unlearned. (pp. 532, 542)

5. Repeated evaluations of therapy suggest that any major type of therapy is better than no therapy, but that no one type of therapy is significantly better than the others. Untreated people do improve, and may catch up to treated people eventually, but therapy speeds the improvement. (pp. 548-550)

Matching

1. l (p. 543)	4. b (p. 537)	7. k (p. 528)	10. m (p. 533)	13. o (p. 535)	16. h (p. 549)
2. e (p. 543)	5. n (p. 531	8. i (p. 531)	11. j (p. 535)	14. f (p. 550)	
3. p (p. 528)	6. c (p. 539)	9. g (p. 541)	12. d (p. 541)	15. a (p. 529)	

Multiple Choice Pretest 1

1. **d**   a & b.   Wrong.   Psychosurgery is rare now and has not significantly impacted institutionalization.
    (p. 526)   c.   Wrong.   Systematic desensitization is used in relatively few types of disorders, most of which would not result in institutionalization.

2. **b**   a, c, & d.   Wrong.   Chlorpromazine and clozapine are antipsychotic drugs used for schizophrenia.
    (p. 527)

3. **a**   b & c.   Wrong.   Dopamine antagonists primarily affect the positive symptoms.
    (p. 527)   d.   Wrong.   Dopamine antagonists cause tardive dyskinesia, they don't reduce it.

4. **c**   a. Wrong.   In transference, behavior reflects how the client feels about someone else.
    (p. 533)   b. Wrong.   Incongruence is a concept in humanistic therapy and involves the self-concept.
    (PN7E)   d. Wrong.   Musterbation, holding irrational "I must" ideas, is a cognitive therapy concept.

5. **b**   a. Wrong.   Dopamine is blocked by antipsychotic drugs.
    (p. 528)   c. Wrong.   GABA is increased by antianxiety drugs.
               d. Wrong.   Prozac, an antidepressant, modulates serotonin, but Prozac isn't a tricyclic.

6. **d**   a. Wrong. Schizophrenia doesn't involve mania, the primary target of lithium carbonate.
(p. 529)   b. Wrong. Obsessive-compulsive disorder doesn't involve mania, the primary target of lithium.
             c. Wrong. The major target of lithium is manic behavior.

7. **a**   b, c, & d.   Wrong.   These are all points of concern, but ECT is very effective.
(p. 530)

8. **a**   b & c.   Wrong.   Cingulotomy is used to treat obsessive-compulsive disorder.
(p. 531)   d.   Wrong.   These are side effects of prefrontal lobotomy, not cingulotomy.

9. **d**   a. Wrong. Sytematic desensitization involves relaxation when faced with anxiety-producing stimuli.
(p. 533)   b. Wrong. This technique involves clients projecting their feelings at an empty chair and talking back.
             c. Wrong. This situation involves transferring toward the therapist feelings felt about another person.

10. **b**   a. Wrong. Psychodynamic therapy is based on resolving unconscious conflicts.
(p. 535)   c. Wrong. Gestalt therapy is based on getting the client to function as a "whole" person.
             d. Wrong. Humanistic therapy is based on getting the client to develop congruence.

11. **c**   a, b, & d.   Wrong.   Genuineness, empathy, and unconditional positive regard are the hallmarks of
(p. 539)   humanistic client-centered therapy.

12. **a**   b. Wrong. This describes humanistic (client-centered) therapy.
(p. 535)   c. Wrong. This describes psychoanalytic therapy.
             d. Wrong. Anxiety hierarchies are part of the behavioral therapy, systematic desensitization.

13. **b**   a. Wrong. Systematic desensitization eliminates anxiety responses; it doesn't teach social skills.
(p. 546)   c. Wrong. Aversion therapy replaces pleasant responses with unpleasant ones.
             d. Wrong. Client-centered therapy focuses on thoughts, not behaviors.

14. **c**   a. Wrong. Systematic desensitization is a behavioral therapy. This view is humanistic.
(p. 542)   b. Wrong. Systematic desensitization is a behavioral therapy. This view is psychoanalytic.
(PT11E)   d. Wrong. Systematic desensitization is a behavioral therapy. This view is cognitive.

15. **c**   a. Wrong. Gestalt therapy is a humanistic therapy. It doesn't condition unpleasant responses.
(p. 544)   b. Wrong. Systematic desensitization conditions a pleasant, not an unpleasant response.
             d. Wrong. Token economies reward desired behavior. They don't condition an unpleasant response.

16. **a**   b.   Wrong.   Therapy groups didn't differ from the waiting list people after 1 year.
(p. 548)   c & d.   Wrong.   Type of therapy did not matter.

17. **d**   a, b, & c.   Wrong.   Spontaneous remission is an improvement without treatment.
(p. 550)

18. **a**   b, c & d.   Wrong.   The average therapy patient is better off than 80% of those getting no therapy.
(p. 549)

19. **c**   a. Wrong. Support factors involve someone who wants to help them get better, not how.
(p. 552)   b. Wrong. Learning factors involve understanding why their behavior occurs.
             d. Wrong. Empathy is the understanding of the client's point of view, part of the support factor.

20. **d**   a. Wrong. Existential therapy focuses on the individual accepting responsibility for life choices.
(p. 541)   b. Wrong. Behavior therapy focuses on changing the target behavior, not treating the family.
             c. Wrong. Gestalt therapy focuses on the individual, not the family.

Multiple Choice Pretest 2

1. **b**   a, c, & d.   Wrong.   These are all biomedical therapies.
    (p. 543)
    (PN7E)

2. **a**   b, c, & d.   Wrong.   Chad had begun to express feelings toward his therapist that he actually feels
    (p. 534)   about someone else (Dad). This is transference, a good sign in therapy.

3. **b**   a. Wrong.   ECT is almost exclusively used for depression, not schizophrenia.
    (p. 527)   c. Wrong.   Systematic desensitization is used for specific phobic disorder, not schizophrenia.
               d. Wrong.   Cingulotomies are rare and used for depression and obsessive-compulsive disorder.

4. **c**   a. Wrong.   Prefrontal lobotomy doesn't produce tardive dyskinesia. Some antipsychotic drugs do.
    (p. 527)   b. Wrong.   ECT doesn't produce tardive dyskinesia. Some antipsychotic drugs do.
               d. Wrong.   Cingulotomy doesn't produce tardive dyskinesia. Some antipsychotic drugs do.

5. **d**   a. Wrong.   Tranquilizers affect GABA, not serotonin.
    (p. 528)   b. Wrong.   Antianxiety drugs affect GABA, not serotonin.
    (PT11E)   d. Wrong.   Antipsychotics usually affect primarily dopamine, not serotonin.

6. **b**   a, c, & d.   Wrong.   Benzodiazepines are antianxiety drugs.
    (p. 587)

7. **c**   a.   Wrong.   ECT isn't used to calm people; it's used for depression.
    (p. 531)   b & d.   Wrong.   Drugs weren't available before the 50's, and do not have these side effects.

8. **d**   a, b, & c.   Wrong.   The way ECT works is unknown at this time.
    (p. 530)

9. **a**   b. Wrong.   ECT is a treatment for depression. Tardive dyskinesia occurs with antipsychotic drugs.
    (p. 530)   c. Wrong.   ECT is used to treat depression, not to reduce violence in schizophrenia.
               d. Wrong.   ECT is used to treat depression, not obsessive compulsive disorder.

10. **b**   a. Wrong.   Psychodynamic therapy still involves one client at a time.
    (p. 535)   c. Wrong.   Psychodynamic therapy is more likely to focus on more limited issues.
               d. Wrong.   Psychodynamic therapy is more likely to focus on social skills than on sex or aggression.

11. **b**   a. Wrong.   Behavioral therapists modify behavior. The client's thoughts are not the focus.
    (p. 539)   c. Wrong.   A rational-emotive therapist is judgmental and much more assertive.
               d. Wrong.   Psychoanalysts are more directive and actively interpret the client's comments.

12. **d**   a. Wrong.   Aversion therapy conditions an unpleasant response. Challenging beliefs is not involved.
    (p. 535)   b. Wrong.   Classical psychoanalysis doesn't actively challenge irrational thoughts.
               c. Wrong.   Client-centered therapy provides unconditional positive regard and doesn't aggressively
                             challenge the client's ideas.

13. **c**   a. Wrong.   Homework of this sort is not typical of psychoanalysis.
    (p. 535)   b. Wrong.   Rational-emotive therapy aggressively challenges the client rather than focusing on self-
                             discovery.
               d. Wrong.   Systematic desensitization is characterized by conditioning techniques.

14. **c**
(p. 538)
a. Wrong. This is the goal of cognitive therapy.
b. Wrong. This is the goal of psychodynamic therapy.
d. Wrong. This is the goal of behavioral therapy.

15. **b**
(p. 539)
a. Wrong. Empathy is seeing things from a client's perspective.
c. Wrong. Genuineness is openness, honesty, and an absence of phoniness.
d. Wrong. Congruence occurs when the self-concept and reality match.

16. **a**
(p. 544)
(PN7E)
b. Wrong. Aversion therapy uses an unpleasant response, not relaxation, a pleasant one.
c. Wrong. A token economy uses rewards for appropriate behavior.
d. Wrong. Psychoanalysis doesn't teach relaxation responses.

17. **a**
(p. 544)
b. Wrong. Incongruence involves the self-concept. Aversion therapy doesn't deal with self-concept.
c. Wrong. Damage to the client-therapist relations is a problem when punishment is used, not when aversion therapy is brief.
d. Wrong. The old problem might reappear, but a new one would not be expected to develop.

18. **d**
(p. 545)
a. Wrong. Systematic desensitization conditions relaxation. It doesn't reward appropriate behavior.
b. Wrong. Existential therapy focuses on responsibility in decision-making, not reinforcement.
c. Wrong. Aversion therapy conditions an unpleasant response. It doesn't reward behavior.

19. **d**
(p. 548)
a, b, & c. Wrong. Studies consistently find equal improvements across therapies and a greater effect for therapy than for no therapy.

20. **c**
(p. 550)
a, b, & d. Wrong. Empathy and trust are primary determinants of successful therapy.

CHAPTER 16: STRESS AND HEALTH

ESTABLISHING LEARNING GOALS

Use these learning goals as a preview of the chapter, a guide for active reading, and to evaluate your mastery of the material. Review the relevant goals as you begin and end your reading of each major section of the chapter.

I. Solve the conceptual problems of defining stress and describing how it is experienced
   A. Describe the stress response.
      1. Define stress, and explain how it is an adaptive reaction.
      2. Discuss Seyle's General Adaptation Syndrome view of the physiological components of stress.
      3. Describe the psychological aspects of stress and gender differences.
   B. Explain the function of cognitive appraisal as part of the stress response.
   C. Discuss external sources of stress.
      1. Describe the Holmes and Rahé Social Readjustment Rating Scale and explain what it predicts.
      2. Define daily hassles, and compare their effects to those of life events.
      3. Identify other external stressors likely to be studied by environmental psychologists.
   D. Discuss internal sources of stress.
      1. Specify the relationship between perceived control and stress.
      2. Specify the relationship between explanatory styles and stress.
      3. Identify the personality characteristics related to stress and their possible health outcomes.

II. Solve the practical problem of identifying the physical and psychological effects of prolonged stress.
   A. Describe the physical consequences of prolonged stress.
      1. Discuss the link between stress and the immune system.
      2. Discuss the link between stress and cardiovascular problems.
   B. Describe the psychological consequences of prolonged stress.
      1. Describe the symptoms of posttraumatic stress disorder.
      2. Describe the symptoms of burnout and the conditions likely to produce burnout.

III. Solve the adaptive problem of how to cope with stress.
   A. Explain how relaxation techniques can be used to reduce stress.
   B. Explain how stress can be managed through cognitive reappraisal of the stressful situation.

IV. Solve the adaptive problem of how to live a healthy lifestyle.
   A. Discuss the physical and psychological benefits of aerobic exercise.
   B. Discuss the consequences of tobacco use, and explain why quitting smoking is so difficult.
   C. Discuss the value of proper nutrition.
   D. Describe the different types of prevention programs and explain how they're used to target AIDS.

MASTERING THE MATERIAL

Preview & Experiencing Stress (pp. 558-569)

Mastering the Vocabulary. Define or explain each of the following terms. To check your answers, consult the text pages listed.

1. health psychology (p. 558)

2. stress (p. 559)

3. stressors (p. 559)

4. general adaptation syndrome (p. 560)

5. cognitive appraisal (p. 562)

6. environmental psychology (p. 566)

7. perceived control (p. 567)

8. Type A (p. 567)

9. Type B (p. 567)

Mastering the Concepts. Fill in the blanks to create a summary of the section. Answers are on page 389.

_____(1) psychology, part of behavioral medicine, studies the role of biological, psychological, environmental, and cultural factors in promoting physical health. Four adaptive problems are considered: What are the causes and effects of stress? What are the effects of prolonged stress? How can people reduce or cope with stress? What factors promote physical and psychological health?

Stress is the physical and psychological _____(2) to demanding situations. Stress can be adaptive because it _____(3) the body to respond, but it can have negative effects. Selye proposed the general _____(4) syndrome to describe general physiological reactions to all stressors. In the

_____(5) phase, the sympathetic nervous system is activated, causing general arousal. In the _____(6) phase, arousal is still high, but the body maintains resources and function. Susceptibility to other stressors is high and health problems may begin to develop. In the _____(7) phase, the body starts to give up, maladaptive behavior occurs, and serious damage is possible. Criticisms of Selye's proposal involve evidence that the stress response is variable and depends on the cognitive _____(8) of the situation and coping resources. Gender differences occur, with _____(9) being less likely to show a fight or flight response. Stress also involves emotional and behavioral components. Dealing successfully with stress can lead to improved self-image and immune system strength.

The Holmes and Rahé social Readjustment Rating Scale uses significant _____(10) to predict health problems. Life events involve either positive or negative _____(11). Although criticized for some limitations, the scale is still widely used. Little irritations, _____(12), also correlate with health problems. Noise, especially if unpredictable or intermittent, and crowding are stressors that produce health problems. _____(13) psychology studies environmental influences on health and behavior.

Internal sources of stress include perceived _____(14), _____(15) style, and personality characteristics, including the _____(16) personalities. If attributions about negative events are _____(17), stable, and global, stress is more likely. Optimism and perceived control reduce stress, and cardiovascular problems are more likely with a hostile Type A personality.

Evaluating Your Progress. Select the one best response. Answers are on page 389. If you make any errors, reread the relevant material before proceeding.

1. The author of your text defines stress as
    a. a stimulus that places a demand on the person.
    b. an internal process through which external events are interpreted as threatening or demanding.
    c. the physical and psychological reaction that people have to demanding situations.
    d. demanding situations that threaten the well-being of the person.

2. The phases of Selye's general adaptation syndrome, in the correct order, are
    a. activation, exhaustion, resistance.
    b. activation, adaptation, alarm.
    c. alarm, resistance, exhaustion.
    d. resistance, exhaustion, alarm.

3. Which of the following is false concerning Selye's general adaptation syndrome?
    a. It proposes that different stressors produce the same sequence of stress reactions.
    b. It proposes that stressors cause the somatic nervous system to initiate physiological arousal.
    c. It proposes that extended stress causes health problems to develop during the resistance stage.
    d. It proposes that the body cannot maintain high stress for long periods without suffering damage.

4. The Holmes & Rahé Social Readjustment Rating Scale is based on the idea that
   a. events involving change produce stress.
   b. stress occurs only for events that have negative consequences.
   c. stress is dependent on people's perception of the situation.
   d. perceived control is critical to the impact of stress.

5. Emphasis on people's perceptions of a situation and their ability to deal with that situation is characteristic of
   a. Selye's general adaptation syndrome view of stress.
   b. the cognitive appraisal view of stress.
   c. Holmes and Rahé's life events view of stress.
   d. the tertiary prevention view of stress.

6. Noise will be most likely to create stress if it is
   a. predictable.
   b. constant.
   c. loud.
   d. new.

7. Kelly is most likely to develop stress-related problems if
   a. someone else controls what happens to her.
   b. she makes external, situational, and temporary attributions about negative events.
   c. she has a Type B personality.
   d. she has an optimistic personal style.

8. Type A personality is characterized by
   a. cool, calm, and collected behavior.
   b. an optimistic, but dependent, style.
   c. hard-driven, ambitious, and impatient behavior.
   d. external, stable, and situational attributions.

9. Some researchers suggest that the critical aspect of Type A behavior that relates to heart disease is
   a. working long hours.
   b. the need to be in control.
   c. the feeling that everything must be done quickly.
   d. the tendency to be hostile or angry.

Reacting to Prolonged Stress (pp. 569-574)

Mastering the Vocabulary. Define or explain each of the following terms. To check your answers, consult the text pages listed.

1. lymphocytes (p. 570)

2.   posttraumatic stress disorder (p. 572)

3.   burnout (p. 573)

Mastering the Concepts. Fill in the blanks to create a summary of the section. Answers are on page 389.

Stress increases susceptibility to illness because it suppresses the _____(18). People with high stress were more likely to catch the common cold in one experiment, and other studies found lower levels of _____(19), a type of white blood cell, and more rapid growth of tumors. Stress increases the risk for cardiovascular disease, possibly because stress increases _____(20) and cholesterol.

Stress influences psychological health, but is not sufficient to cause major problems for most people. One serious condition due to traumatic events is _____(21) stress disorder. Symptoms include _____(22), avoidance of stimuli linked to the trauma, and chronic _____(23) symptoms, such as sleep problems and irritability. _____(24) is a state of physical, emotional, and mental exhaustion caused by long-term involvement in emotionally demanding situations. Sufferers are usually highly motivated, but become disillusioned and perhaps feel as if life is meaningless.

Evaluating Your Progress. Select the one best response. Answers are on page 390. If you make any errors, reread the relevant material before proceeding.

1.   Teachers should expect students will get sick during the final exam period because stress inhibits
     a.   the cardiovascular system.
     b.   the immune system.
     c.   the sympathetic nervous system.
     d.   the endocrine system.

2.   One reason stress might increase the risk for developing heart disease is that stress
     a.   increases cholesterol.
     b.   increases the number of lymphocytes in the blood.
     c.   reduces autonomic nervous system activity.
     d.   reduces blood pressure.

3.   Posttraumatic stress disorder is characterized by
     a.   loss of memory for the traumatic event.
     b.   avoidance of stimuli that are associated with the traumatic event.
     c.   a tendency to become dependent on family and friends.
     d.   chronic low arousal symptoms.

4. Burnout is most likely to occur in people who
   a. are idealistic.
   b. have a Type B personality.
   c. are not very committed to their job.
   d. have had little experience on the job.

Reducing and Coping with Stress (pp. 575-580)

Mastering the Vocabulary. Define or explain each of the following terms. To check your answers, consult the text pages listed.

1. coping (p. 575)

2. biofeedback (p. 576)

3. social support (p. 576)

Mastering the Concepts. Fill in the blanks to create a summary of the section. Answers are on page 389.

Ways to cope with stress include _____(25) techniques, forming _____(26) systems, and reappraising the situation. In _____(27) muscle relaxation, specific muscle groups are relaxed, one after the other until all the body is relaxed. Autogenic relaxation focuses on directing _____(28) to a muscle group to warm and relax it. Providing information about relaxation through _____(29) is helpful, but the sense of _____(30) it produces might be critical. Misleading feedback produces equal pain relief.

Social support reduces health and mental problems, perhaps because healthy _____(31) are encouraged, or because there is opportunity to talk about problems, which reduces stress. Pets also provide positive support. Social support can have negative effects, reducing _____(32) and perceived control. Some people increase stress by _____(33) situations too negatively. Events can be made less stressful by taking attention off of the disturbing aspects, reappraising the outcome, or by planning for future situations.

Evaluating Your Progress. Select the one best response. Answers are on page 390. If you make any errors, reread the relevant material before proceeding.

1. Autogenic relaxation involves
    a. mental repetition of a word and the focusing of attention inward.
    b. relaxing one muscle group after another until the entire body is relaxed.
    c. using monitoring equipment to provide information about the state of the body.
    d. concentrating on directing blood flow to particular muscle groups to relax them.

2. Research on the effects of misleading biofeedback suggests that
    a. improvement in physical symptoms (headache) is due to greater relaxation with biofeedback.
    b. biofeedback is another form of meditation, which is known to reduce tension.
    c. biofeedback gives a sense of control that reduces stress and stress-related disorders.
    d. biofeedback provides a sort of social support that reduces the impact of stress.

3. Compared to people with little social support, people with well-established social support systems show
    a. improved physical health and psychological health.
    b. the same physical health, but better psychological health.
    c. lower death rates from cancer, but higher death rates from cardiovascular problems.
    d. the same levels of physical and psychological health.

4. When women were given a difficult math problem to solve, they showed the least stress when
    a. a good friend was in the room with them.
    b. their dog was in the room with them.
    c. either their dog or their friend was in the room with them (equal effects).
    d. they were alone in the room.

5. Changing how a situation is interpreted to make it less stressful is the stress management technique of
    a. social support.
    b. cognitive reappraisal.
    c. autogenic relaxation.
    d. tertiary prevention.

Living a Healthy Lifestyle (pp. 581-585)

Mastering the Vocabulary. Define or explain each of the following terms. To check your answers, consult the text pages listed.

1. aerobic exercise (p. 581)

2. primary prevention (p. 584)

3. secondary prevention (p. 584)

4.   tertiary prevention (p. 584)

5.   AIDS (p. 584)

Mastering the Concepts. Fill in the blanks to create a summary of the section. Answers are on page 389.

Healthy lifestyles can reduce the impact of stress. _____(34) exercise improves mental and physical health and increases resistance to stress, although a placebo effect might be involved. Smoking contributes to many deaths and increases birth _____(35), and it is _____(36). Kicking the habit is very difficult. Withdrawal is a DSM-IV diagnosis and often includes insomnia, irritability, difficulty concentrating, and weight gain or increased appetite. Most Americans have a poor diet that is too high in _____(37), calories, cholesterol, sugar, protein, and salt. Fat and cholesterol are linked to _____(38) problems.

AIDS is caused by a _____(39) and transmitted through contact with bodily fluids, most often by sharing needles or by sexual contact. Health psychologists use three types of prevention programs to combat unhealthy lifestyles and disease. Primary prevention centers on _____(40) about ways to avoid problems. Secondary prevention involves early identification of risk factors or looking for early signs of disease. Tertiary prevention handles an illness or habit once it is present.

Evaluating Your Progress. Select the one best response. Answers are on page 390. If you make any errors, reread the relevant material before proceeding.

1.   The relationship between aerobic exercise and psychological health is
     a. imaginary; no controlled studies have found any benefit other than improved physical health.
     b. questionable; research shows that people report feeling less stress, but still show the same physiological characteristics of stress.
     c. questionable; research shows that people report feeling psychologically healthy, but psychological tests show no change in psychological status, especially concerning depression.
     d. significant; people who exercise have reduced depression and react less to stressful situations.

2.   The nicotine in cigarettes
     a. stimulates the central nervous system.
     b. depresses the central nervous system.
     c. is not considered addictive by most health-sciences researchers.
     d. decreases blood pressure.

3. When health psychologists focus on identifying risk factors or early signs of disease, they are using
   a. primary prevention.
   b. secondary prevention.
   c. tertiary prevention.
   d. terminal prevention.

4. The primary problem associated with AIDS is
   a. cholesterol-related heart disease.
   b. emphysema.
   c. damage to the immune system.
   d. stroke.

MAKING FINAL PREPARATIONS

Complete these sections without consulting your book or notes. For a more accurate estimate of how well you know this material, wait at least a day or two after studying the chapter before working on the questions. Some material you "know" immediately after working with the chapter will be quickly forgotten. Immediate tests will overestimate what you know well.

Short Essay Questions. Write a brief answer to each question. Sample answers are on page 391.

1. Explain how the stress response can be considered adaptive.

2. Discuss the role of cognitive appraisal in stress and stress management.

3. Explain why stress management should be a part of the treatment given people who are HIV-positive.

4. Discuss the role of perceived control in stress.

5. Explain why social support seems to be an effective way to reduce the impact of stress.

Matching. Select the correct definition or description for each item. Answers are on page 391.

_____ 1. tertiary prevention	**a.**	serious trauma-induced psychological disorder
_____ 2. stress	**b.**	program to deal with problem once it develops
_____ 3. Holmes & Rahe	**c.**	attribution patterns that impact stress
_____ 4. explanatory style	**d.**	physical, emotional, & mental exhaustion
_____ 5. primary prevention	**e.**	study of biological, emotional, environmental, and cultural effects on health
_____ 6. health psychology		
_____ 7. Selye	**f.**	demanding or threatening situation
_____ 8. burnout	**g.**	program to educate in order to prevent a problem
_____ 9. stressor	**h.**	hard-driving behavior linked to heart disease
_____ 10. posttraumatic stress disorder	**i.**	white blood cells in the immune system
_____ 11. lymphocytes	**j.**	devised "life event" scale
_____ 12. Type A personality	**k.**	proposed general adaptation syndrome
	l.	physical & emotional reaction to demanding event

Multiple Choice Pretest 1. Select the one best response. Answers are on page 391.

1. The stage in Selye's general adaptation syndrome that corresponds to the fight-or-flight response is
   a. the activation stage.
   b. the resistance stage.
   c. the exhaustion stage.
   d. the alarm stage.

2. Which freshman should experience the most stress as he begins his first semester at State College?
   a. Ron, who expects State College to be very competitive and very difficult.
   b. Clay, who expects State College to be moderately competitive and moderately difficult.
   c. Ely, who expects State College to be no more difficult than high school.
   d. All of them should experience the same stress because they are in the same college situation.

3. The relationship between daily hassles and the chance of developing stress-related health problems is
   a. nonexistent because daily hassles do not produce significant stress.
   b. significant only if the person already has health problems that are not stress-related.
   c. strong, but negative, because people with many daily hassles have fewer health problems.
   d. at least as strong as the relationship between major life events and stress-related illness.

4. Increased risk for stress-related illness in middle age is found for people whose attributions about negative events are
   a. external, situational, and specific.
   b. internal, global, and stable.
   c. external, stable, and Type A.
   d. internal, situational, and Type B.

5. In one experiment, the people who were most likely to get sick after being exposed to the common cold virus were those who
   a. were Type B personalities.
   b. had high stress lives.
   c. had low stress lives.
   d. felt in control.

6. Carla blows little hassles out of proportion and creates stress unnecessarily. Being caught in traffic means she will never be able to fix dinner or do her homework, when it just will delay things a few minutes. Carla could avoid much of the stress she now experiences if she would try
   a. developing social support.
   b. meditation.
   c. exercise.
   d. cognitive reappraisal.

7. Ellie keeps seeing images of the World Trade Center collapse, and sometimes seems to feel the dust filling her lungs. She refuses to go back to New York City and is having trouble sleeping. Ellie's behavior is consistent with
   a. Type A personality disorder.
   b. burnout.
   c. generalized anxiety disorder.
   d. posttraumatic stress disorder.

8. Vanda is moving to a high-rise apartment from a smaller apartment building. She should expect
   a. more aggressive behavior by the tenants of the high-rise.
   b. more tolerance to daily hassles by the tenants of the high-rise.
   c. fewer health problems among the tenants of the high-rise.
   d. little or no change in the attributes of the tenants of the high-rise if everything else is the same.

9. Walter changed to a less stressful job. The next time he goes for a checkup, he is likely to find
   a. his heart rate is higher.
   b. his lymphocytes are lower.
   c. his cholesterol is lower.
   d. his blood pressure is higher.

10. Raj is an award-winning social worker, but recently he often has skipped work, and he looks exhausted both physically and emotionally. Raj's behavior is consistent with
    a. posttraumatic stress disorder.
    b. burnout.
    c. dissociative disorder.
    d. antisocial personality disorder.

11. Chuck is listening for a tone that tells him he has relaxed the muscles in his forehead. Chuck is using
    a. biofeedback.
    b. the autogenic relaxation technique.
    c. the progressive muscle relaxation technique.
    d. meditation.

12. Research on coping with traumas suggests that people cope better if
    a. they are left alone to work things out.
    b. they are given general support, but are not questioned about what happened.
    c. they are encouraged to talk or write about what happened.
    d. they are told to just forget about what happened.

13. Nicotine withdrawal can lead to
    a. insomnia.
    b. reduced appetite.
    c. vomiting.
    d. hallucinations.

14. Counseling an HIV-positive individual about how to avoid transmitting the virus to other people is
    a. ancillary prevention.
    b. primary prevention.
    c. secondary prevention.
    d. tertiary prevention.

15. Chuck is tensing and then relaxing each of the muscle groups in his body, moving from his head down. What stress-reduction technique is Chuck using?
    a. biofeedback
    b. progressive muscle relaxation
    c. autogenic relaxation
    d. the general adaptation syndrome

16. Depressed college students were asked to either engage in aerobic exercise, use relaxation techniques, or do nothing to treat their depression. After 10 weeks researchers found
    a. the relaxation group's mood was more improved than that of the other two groups.
    b. the exercise group's mood was more improved than that of the other two groups.
    c. all three groups' moods improved equally.
    d. the relaxation and exercise groups' moods didn't improve, but the control group's mood worsened.

Multiple Choice Pretest 2. Select the one best response. Answers are on page 392.

1. Gina has three big exams tomorrow. People keep disturbing her, and she has discovered her notes for one class are lost. Gina feels overwhelmed. Your text's author would identify the stress to be
   a. the three exams.
   b. finding her notes lost.
   c. being disturbed by other people.
   d. feeling overwhelmed.

2. Bart has been under high levels of stress for the past year. He is nearly bankrupt, working 100 hours per week at two jobs, and now faces criminal charges in a crime he didn't commit. He has developed stress-related illnesses and his body seems to be giving up. Bart is probably in Selye's
   a. alarm stage.
   b. adaptation stage.
   c. exhaustion stage.
   d. collapse stage.

3. If stress hormone levels are recorded for everyone taking the SAT, an achievement test used for college admissions, the hormone levels should be correlated most strongly with
   a. the student's sex.
   b. the student's IQ.
   c. the student's age.
   d. the student's income.

4. Will has a very high score on Holmes & Rahé's Social Readjustment Rating Scale. This suggests he
   a. probably has a Type A personality.
   b. has an external locus of control.
   c. usually makes internal, global, and stable attributions.
   d. is at increased risk of developing health problems.

5. Hal and Marvin are a bomb disposal team. Hal's only role is to hand Marvin tools. Marvin, who is well trained, is in control of the dangerous procedures. Based on stress research, we should expect
   a. Hal will be more likely to develop stress-related disorders than Marvin.
   b. Marvin will be more likely to develop stress-related disorders than Hal.
   c. Marvin and Hal have an equal, very low, likelihood of developing stress-related disorders.
   d. Marvin and Hall have an equal, very high, likelihood of developing stress-related disorders.

6. Russ is most likely to develop stress-related problems if he
   a. feels competent to succeed in his very difficult new job.
   b. shares a crowded apartment with four other people.
   c. lives beside a factory that makes a constant thumping noise.
   d. has an optimistic outlook.

7. Nan's life is very stressful now that she is a single parent, and she has noticed that she catches every illness that her little girl gets. If Nan had a complete physical, she would probably be found to have
   a. lower blood pressure than usual.
   b. lower lymphocyte levels than usual.
   c. lower hormone levels than usual.
   d. lower blood cholesterol than usual.

8. When their trip home was interrupted by car trouble, Sam got very upset even though they had no reason to hurry and the repairs were covered by a warranty. Trudy said, "This isn't so bad. We can relax by the pool and the car will be better than before." Trudy experienced less stress because
   a. she had good social support.
   b. she has an internal, global, and stable attributional style.
   c. she used autogenic relaxation.
   d. she used cognitive reappraisal.

9. Tallal is a straight-A student who insists all assignments be done perfectly and devotes all his attention to being the best student in every class. Tallal quickly becomes impatient with anyone who doesn't perform to his standards. Tallal's behavior is characteristic of
   a. a negative explanatory style personality.
   b. a controlling personality.
   c. a Type A personality.
   d. a Type B personality.

10. Melvin narrowly escaped death when a tornado destroyed his home. Two years later, Melvin still has flashbacks of the storm and has withdrawn from family and friends. He even moved to a milder climate to avoid the intense anxiety any storm produced. Melvin's behavior is most consistent with
    a. burnout.
    b. post-traumatic stress disorder.
    c. daily hassles.
    d. generalized anxiety disorder.

11. Mary tries to direct increased blood flow to each muscle group, one by one. Mary is using
    a. biofeedback.
    b. autogenic relaxation.
    c. meditation.
    d. progressive relaxation.

12. Without Paul's knowledge, his son changed the settings on his biofeedback equipment so that it will sound a tone when muscle tension increases, rather than decreases. We should expect Paul's headaches to
    a. immediately increase in frequency.
    b. continue to decrease in frequency.
    c. temporarily decrease, then increase in frequency.
    d. stay the same frequency.

13. After the Oklahoma City bombing disaster, counselors came in to help the survivors and rescue workers cope. Some counselors said they just let the people talk about their experiences. Based on Pennebaker's research, this procedure was probably
    a. helpful; talking about troubles leads to better coping and less stress.
    b. harmful; trauma victims always need intense psychotherapy.
    c. harmful; talking just reopens the wounds so that they are slower to heal.
    d. neutral; talking doesn't hurt, but it doesn't help, either.

14. Men interested in reducing the impact of stress by exercising should remember that research shows
    a. aerobic exercise works better than strength training.
    b. strength training works better than aerobic exercise.
    c. aerobic exercise and strength training work equally well.
    d. neither aerobic exercise nor strength training reduces stress or its impact.

15. A health psychologist is involved in "safe sex" programs in hopes of preventing sexually transmitted diseases among college students. This is an example of
    a. primary prevention.
    b. secondary prevention.
    c. tertiary prevention.
    d. quadratic prevention.

LANGUAGE DEVELOPMENT GUIDE

Core Terms

In discussing stress and health, your instructor is likely to use the term *optimal*. That means best or highest level; *optimal health* is the best level of health of which your body is capable. But stresses and injuries may add up and have a *cumulative* (added together) effect. One stressor after another may *compromise* (damage) your health. If the damage cannot be cured, you might end up with a *chronic* condition (one that lasts for a long time). As the text suggests, good diet, exercise and so on can help you avoid this unpleasant scenario -- your instructor may call these good habits *preventative maintenance*.

In relation to the section on perceived control, your instructor might use the term *locus of control*. That refers to whether you sense that control is inside you our outside you (locus is related to the word "location"). You may also hear the term *learned helplessness*. When stressed, people can learn to stop trying to control or change their situation. Naturally, that can lead to even poorer health and coping.

Idioms

p. 558	claim exclusive rights	say that we are the only ones who deserve something
p. 559	jack-knifed tractor trailer	a large truck which has gone out of control and is blocking the road
p. 560	life-threatening jams	situation that might kill you
p. 562	a black belt in the martial arts	the highest level of training in a specialized form of fighting (such as karate)
p. 563	exhaustive list	complete list; a list of all
p. 566	in the eye of the beholder	depends upon who is looking at it or experiencing it
p. 567	manned space program	project to send people into space
p. 571	compromising the function of	causing something to not work properly
p. 571	wear and tear	rough usage; damage through use
p. 572	vet	short for veteran, that is, a soldier in a past war
p. 573	syndrome	a set of symptoms of an illness
p. 575	skirts	goes very near
p. 575	a regimen of	a fixed set of
p. 578	buffer	that which protects from outside influences

Word Parts

Here are some words that are made up of word parts, and that you can find in this chapter. After you've looked at these, you can look for others in the chapter with the same word parts.

WORD	WORD PART IT USES	MEANING
autogenic	auto = self gen = birth, race, kind	self-creating; that which gives birth to itself
beneficial	bene = good	good or helpful
prevent	pre = before vent, vene = come, happen	to stop something from coming or happening
promote	pro = forward mot = to move	to move something or someone forward
require	re = again quir, ques, quis = to seek	to need, to seek out

Knowing the word parts listed above, you can also create the following words. You can get an idea of their meanings from the word parts they use.

psychogenic	_____ + _____	that which is born of the mind; coming from the mind
convene	con + vene	_____
benign	_____	good, kind, not harmful
congenital	_____ + _____	present at birth; born together with
prerequisite	pre + re + quis	_____

Pronunciation

p. 570	lymphocyte	lim´-fo-site		p. 584	tertiary	ter´-shee-air-ee
p. 581	aerobic	a-row´-bik				

388

ANSWERS AND EXPLANATIONS

To find relevant material in your textbook, consult the pages cited with each answer. Also, PN and PT citations refer to modules in *PsychNow!* and *Psyk.trek* materials, respectively.

Mastering the Concepts

1. Health (p. 558)
2. reaction (p. 559)
3. activates (p. 560)
4. adaptation (p. 560)
5. alarm (p. 560)
6. resistance (p. 560)
7. exhaustion (p. 560)
8. appraisal (p. 561)
9. females (p. 562)
10. life events (p. 563)
11. change (p. 564)
12. daily hassles (p. 564)
13. Environmental (p. 565)
14. control (p. 566)
15. explanatory (p. 567)
16. Type A and B (p. 567)
17. internal (p. 567)
18. immune system (p. 570)
19. lymphocytes (p. 570)
20. blood pressure (p. 571)
21. posttraumatic (p. 572)
22. flashbacks (p. 572)
23. arousal (p. 572)
24. Burnout (p. 573)
25. relaxation (p. 575)
26. social support (p. 576)
27. progressive (p. 575)
28. blood flow (p. 576)
29. biofeedback (p. 576)
30. control (p. 576)
31. lifestyles (p. 579)
32. self-reliance (p. 579)
33. interpreting (p. 579)
34. Aerobic (p. 581)
35. defects (p. 582)
36. addictive (p. 582)
37. fat (p. 584)
38. cardiovascular (p. 584)
39. virus (p. 585)
40. education (p. 584)

Evaluating Your Progress

Preview & Experiencing Stress

1. **c**
(p. 559)

   a, b, & d.   Wrong.   These are alternative definitions, but not your author's.

2. **c**
(p. 560)
(PT11G)

   a & b.   Wrong.   Activation and adaptation are not among Selye's phases.
   d.   Wrong.   Alarm is the first, not last, stage.

3. **b**
(p. 560)

   a, c, & d.   Wrong.   These are all true, but stressors cause autonomic arousal.

4. **a**
(p. 564)

   b.   Wrong.   Some of their "life events" are positive events (vacation, marriage).
   c & d.   Wrong.   Their scale does not consider the person's perceptions at all.

5. **b**
(p. 562)

   a & c.   Wrong.   These do not emphasize perceptions. They emphasize the stressor itself.
   d.   Wrong.   This is not an actual approach to stress.

6. **d**
(p. 565)

   a, b, & c.   Wrong.   Even loud noises don't matter unless they are unpredictable, intermittent, and new to the situation.

7. **a**
(p. 566)

   b, c, & d.   Wrong.   These are associated with reduced stress.

8. **c**
(p. 567)

   a, b, & d.   Wrong.   Type A people are ambitious, easily annoyed, impatient, and hard driving.

9. **d**
(p. 568)

   a, b, & c.   Wrong.   Hostility is the factor receiving the focus of attention currently.

Reacting to Prolonged Stress

1. **b**
    (p. 570)   a, c, & d.   Wrong.   These systems are more active during stress.

2. **a**
    (p. 571)   b, c, & d.   Wrong.   Stress has the opposite effect listed.

3. **b**
    (p. 572)
    (PN7D)   a, c, &d.   Wrong.   These are the opposite of the true symptoms.

4. **a**
    (p. 573)   b. Wrong.   Personality type is not strongly predictive.
                 c. Wrong.   Burnout occurs in highly committed people.
                 d. Wrong.   Burnout requires a long-term experience.

Reducing and Coping with Stress

1. **d**
    (p. 576)   a. Wrong.   This describes meditation.
                 b. Wrong.   This describes progressive relaxation.
                 c. Wrong.   This describes biofeedback.

2. **c**
    (p. 576)   a, b, & d.   Wrong.   Symptoms improved even with misleading biofeedback, leading researchers to propose the key is perceived control, not actual relaxation.

3. **a**
    (p. 576)   b, c, & d.   Wrong.   These are not true. Social support generally aids both physical and psychological health.

4. **b**
    (p. 578)   a & c.   Wrong.   A human companion was associated with the highest levels of stress.
                 d.   Wrong.   Being alone led to intermediate levels of stress.

5. **b**
    (p. 579)   a. Wrong.   Social support is help received from others, not reinterpreting a situation.
                 c. Wrong.   Autogenic relaxation is a way to relax muscles, not a reevaluation of a situation.
                 d. Wrong.   Tertiary prevention is treating the effects of stress, not reducing the source of stress.

Living a Healthy Lifestyle

1. **d**
    (p. 582)   a, b, & c.   Wrong.   Controlled studies support a positive relationship.

2. **a**
    (p. 583)   b & d.   Wrong.   Nicotine stimulates the central nervous system and increases blood pressure.
                 c.   Wrong.   Nicotine is considered addictive by most mainstream researchers.

3. **b**
    (p. 584)   a. Wrong.   Primary prevention educates people about how to *avoid* mental and physical problems.
                 c. Wrong.   Tertiary prevention seeks to handle an illness or habit once it has been acquired.
                 d. Wrong.   This is not a health psychology prevention program.

4. **c**
    (p. 585)   a. Wrong.   Cholesterol is associated with poor diet and little exercise, not AIDS.
                 b. Wrong.   Emphysema is associated with smoking, not AIDS.
                 d. Wrong.   Stroke is associated with poor cardiovascular fitness, not AIDS.

MAKING FINAL PREPARATIONS

Short Essay Questions

1. Stress involves arousal which can ready the organism to respond to environmental demands. This is adaptive. (p. 560)

2. One's cognitive appraisal of a situation is critical in determining whether stress results. If the situation is not perceived to be demanding, or people perceive they have the resources to deal with the situation, stress is eliminated or reduced. By reappraising a potentially stressful situation (e.g., seeing a death as a release from pain), stress is reduced. Personality factors that lead to negative appraisals increase stress. (pp. 562, 579)

3. An HIV-positive diagnosis brings with it situations involving stress---employment concerns, social stigma, and the prospects of a terminal disease. HIV itself suppresses the immune system, so stress management will reduce the additional impact that stress has on the immune system and will help to maintain other aspects of physical health. An HIV diagnosis has psychological effects which stress management can address. (pp. 570-571, 575)

4. Perception of control reduces stress. Animals able to terminate a shock by making a response showed fewer stress-related physical problems (ulcers) than animals experiencing the same amount of shock but given no control. Control relates to the evaluation of one's ability to cope with a stressor, and this is critical in determining whether stress results. (p. 566-567)

5. People with social support systems show fewer physical and psychological stress effects. This might occur because the social support system encourages the individual to maintain a healthy lifestyle and to follow medical prescriptions. Social support provides a chance to talk about problems, which has been shown to reduce stress. Social support may boost the evaluation of coping resources, which can reduce stress effects. (pp. 576-579)

Matching

1. **b** (p. 584)	3. **j** (p. 563)	5. **g** (p. 584)	7. **k** (p. 560)	9. **f** (p. 559)	11. **i** (p. 570)
2. **l** (p. 559)	4. **c** (p. 567)	6. **e** (p. 558)	8. **d** (p. 573)	10. **a** (p. 572)	12. **h** (p. 567)

Multiple Choice Pretest 1

1. **d**   a.   Wrong.   This is not one of Selye's GAS stages.
   (p. 560)   b & c.   Wrong.   Fight-or-flight is rapid physiological activation, which occurs during the alarm stage.
   (PT11G)

2. **a**   b & c.   Wrong.   Clay and Ely perceive State as less of a threat than Ron does.
   (p. 562)   d.   Wrong.   Their perceptions differ, which is very important to the stress experienced.

3. **d**   a &bc.   Wrong.   Daily hassles are at least as predictive of stress-related illnesses as life events.
   (p. 564)   c.   Wrong.   The relationship is a positive correlation.

4. **b**   a.   Wrong.   This is the opposite pattern associated with stress-related illness.
   (p. 567)   c & d.   Wrong.   Type A and Type B are not attributional styles.

5. **b**   a. Wrong.   Type A, not Type B, personality is more associated with stress-related illness.
   (p. 570   c. Wrong.   Low stress is not associated with illness.
              d. Wrong.   The perception of control reduces stress.

6. **d** a. Wrong. Social support assists coping, but doesn't necessarily eliminate the source of stress.
(p. 579) b. Wrong. Meditation won't stop the catastrophizing or eliminate the stress; it reduces its impact.
          c. Wrong. Exercise moderates the effects of stress, but doesn't stop it at the source.

7. **d** a. Wrong. Type A personality disorder involves impatient, hard-driving competitiveness.
(p. 572) b. Wrong. Burnout involves feeling emotionally drained and losing a sense of accomplishment.
(PN7D) c. Wrong. Generalized anxiety disorder is a chronic state of anxiety unrelated to any specific event.

8. **a** b, c, & d. Wrong. High-rise housing is more crowded, which is associated with greater stress.
(p. 565)

9. **c** a, b, & d. Wrong. The opposite would be expected.
(p. 571)

10. **b** a. Wrong. There is no trauma, flashbacks, avoidance, or arousal in Raj's case.
(p. 573) c. Wrong. There is no break in normal consciousness and memory in Raj's case.
          d. Wrong. There is no disregard of law or cultural norms in Raj's case.

11. **a** b. Wrong. This involves directing blood flow to a muscle group, not using feedback about tension.
(p. 576) c. Wrong. This involves relaxing one muscle group after another, without feedback.
          d. Wrong. This involves concentrating on a word or image and clearing the mind.

12. **c** a. Wrong. Social support assists coping.
(p. 579) b & d. Wrong. Talking about negative events improves coping.

13. **a** b. Wrong. Withdrawal often causes increased appetite and weight gain.
(p. 583) c & d. Wrong. These are not associated with nicotine withdrawal.

14. **d** a. Wrong. This is not a type of prevention.
(p. 584) b. Wrong. Primary prevention involves education to prevent a problem.
          c. Wrong. Secondary prevention involves identifying risk factors or early signs of the disease.

15. **b** a. Wrong. There is no external feedback concerning the state of his muscles.
(p. 575) c. Wrong. Chuck is not directing blood to his muscles, as characteristic of autogenic relaxation.
          d. Wrong. The general adaptation syndrome describes the stages of physiological changes with stress.

16. **b** a, c, & d. Wrong. Exercise was associated with the greatest improvement.
(p. 582)

Multiple Choice Pretest 2

1. **d** a, b, & c. Wrong. These are (situations), not stress (reaction to stressors).
(p. 559)

2. **c** a. Wrong. This is the first stage, before stress-related problems occur.
(p. 560) b & d. Wrong. These are not Selye's stages.

3. **b** a, c, & d. Wrong. Studies show high IQ is associated with lower stress levels prior to exams,
(p. 562)   probably because the test is not perceived as very threatening.

4. **d**   a, b, & c.   Wrong.   This scale predicts stress-related health problem, not any personality
(p. 563)   characteristics.
(PT11F)

5. **a**   b, c, & d.   Wrong.   Marvin has more control than Hal, so he will experience less stress.
(p. 566)

6. **b**   a. Wrong.   Feelings of competency reduce or eliminate stress, but crowding increases stress.
(p. 565)   c. Wrong.   Constant noises are not particularly stressful, but crowding increases stress.
              d. Wrong.   An optimistic style is associated with lower stress, but crowding increases stress.

7. **b**   a, c, & d.   Wrong.   Stress increases these, but decreases lymphocytes.
(p. 570)

8. **d**   a. Wrong.   She is receiving no help from other people.
(p. 579)   b. Wrong.   She isn't making attributions about causes.
              c. Wrong.   Autogenic relaxation involves directing blood to muscles to relax them.

9. **c**   a, b, & d.   Wrong.   Competitive, impatient, ambitious, and hard-driving describes Type A
(p. 567)   personality.

10. **b**   a. Wrong.   Burnout is associated with long term stress, not a sudden traumatic event.
(p. 572)   c. Wrong.   These are typical daily events that are stressors. Trauma is not involved.
              d. Wrong.   This involves chronic anxiety not related to any specific situation.

11. **b**   a. Wrong.   Mary wasn't getting feedback from a machine that monitored her bodily responses.
(p. 576)   c. Wrong.   Meditation doesn't typically involve directing blood flow to parts of the body.
              d. Wrong.   Progressive relaxation involves relaxing muscles, not increasing blood flow.

12. **b**   a, c, & d.   Wrong.   When misleading biofeedback is given, symptoms continue to improve, perhaps
(p. 576)   due to perceived control.

13. **a**   b, c, & d.   Wrong.   These are not true. Talking about negative experiences has been shown to help.
(p. 579)

14. **a**   b, c, & d.   Wrong.   Aerobic exercise works best.
(p. 582)

15. **a**   b. Wrong.   Screening for disease or identifying risk factors is secondary prevention.
(p. 584)   c. Wrong.   Tertiary prevention involves managing and containing an illness once it has developed.